Beyond Florence

Beyond Florence

The Contours of Medieval and Early Modern Italy

Edited by Paula Findlen, Michelle M. Fontaine,
and Duane J. Osheim

Stanford University Press
Stanford, California
2003

Stanford University Press
Stanford, California
© 2003 by the Board of Trustees of the
Leland Stanford Junior University.
All rights reserved.

Printed in the United States of America
on acid-free, archival-quality paper.

Library of Congress Cataloging-in-Publication Data

Findlen, Paula.
  Beyond Florence : the contours of medieval and early modern Italy /
edited by Paula Findlen, Michelle M. Fontaine and Duane J. Osheim.
     p. cm.
  Papers from a conference held at Stanford University in November 1998.
  Includes bibliographical references and index.
   ISBN 0-8047-3934-X (cloth : alk. paper) — ISBN 0-8047-3935-8 (pbk. : alk. paper)
   1. Italy—History—Congresses. I. Findlen, Paula. II. Fontaine, Michelle.
III. Osheim, Duane J.
DG470 .B49   2002
945—dc21   2002004726

Original Printing 2003

Designed by Eleanor Mennick
Typeset by Heather Boone in 10/12 Sabon

Contents

Maps and Figures	vii
Acknowledgments	ix
About the Contributors	xi
Preface	xv

PART ONE. FLORENCE, ITALY, AND THE RENAISSANCE   1

1 Florence Redux   5
   Gene Brucker

2 In and Out of Florence   13
   Paula Findlen

PART TWO. CITY AND COUNTRYSIDE   29

3 The Other Florence Within Florence   33
   Samuel K. Cohn, Jr.

4 A World of Its Own: Economy, Society, and Religious Life in the Tuscan Mugello at the Time of Dante   45
   George Dameron

5 The Country Parish at Late Medieval Lucca   59
   Duane J. Osheim

6 "Do Not Say That This Is a Man from Assisi"   72
   Robert Brentano

PART THREE. LAW AND SOCIETY   81

7 Concubines, Lovers, Prostitutes: Infamy and Female Identity in Medieval Bologna   85
   Carol Lansing

8 Lost Faith: A Roman Prosecutor Reflects on Notaries' Crimes   101
   Laurie Nussdorfer

Contents

PART FOUR. URBAN AND RELIGIOUS IDENTITIES — 115

9. Pilgrim-Tourism in Late Medieval Venice — 119
   Robert C. Davis

10. The Hermit Returns: Sanctity and the City in the March of Ancona — 133
    Robert L. Cooper

11. In the Shop of the Lord: Bernardino of Siena and Popular Devotion — 147
    Cynthia L. Polecritti

12. "Angels of Peace": The Social Drama of the Jesuit Mission in Early Modern Southern Italy — 160
    Jennifer D. Selwyn

PART FIVE. TOPOGRAPHIES OF POWER — 177

13. Topographies of Power in the Urban Centers of Medieval Italy: Communes, Bishops, and Public Authority — 181
    Maureen C. Miller

14. In Search of the Quiet City: Civic Identity and Papal State Building in Fourteenth-Century Orvieto — 190
    David Foote

15. Back to the Future: Remaking the Commune in Ducal Modena — 205
    Michelle M. Fontaine

16. The Spanish Foundations of Late Renaissance and Baroque Rome — 219
    Thomas Dandelet

AFTERWORD Where Is Beyond Florence? — 233
Randolph Starn

Notes — 243
Bibliography — 283
Index — 315

Maps and Figures

Florence and Beyond, Twelfth to Eighteenth Centuries   3
City and Countryside: Tuscany   31
Law and Society: Florence, Bologna, and Rome   83
Religious and Urban Identities: Florence, Venice, Ancona, Siena, Fabriano, Naples   117
Topographies of Power: Central and Northern Italy   179

MAP 5.1   The Diocese of Lucca   61
MAP 15.1   Modena circa 1633   212
FIGURE 15.1   *The Madonna of the Rosary, San Geminiano, and the City of Modena* by Ludovico Lana   215

Acknowledgments

The idea for this volume first took shape as a way of honoring William Bowsky's contributions to the field of Italian history. One former colleague and two of his former students began to conspire about how we might suitably embarrass Bill—and thank him for all the great advice, mentorship, and collegiality he has offered many of us over the years. A good Italian meal or two later, the Bowskyfest was born.

Our thanks go to three institutions—Stanford University, the University of Virginia, and the University of Arkansas at Little Rock—for providing the sponsorship that made possible the November 1998 conference out of which this volume emerged. We especially thank the Stanford History Department, the associate dean of humanities, the dean of research, and the Stanford Humanities Center for their hospitality and financial support of this event. Further funding of the project came from the Office of Research and Sponsored Programs at the University of Arkansas at Little Rock, and the Office of the Vice President for Research and Public Service and the dean of arts and sciences of the University of Virginia. Sabbatical leave for Michelle Fontaine from the University of Arkansas at Little Rock, combined with a Solmsen Fellowship at the Institute for Research in the Humanities at the University of Wisconsin, Madison, and a grant from the American Philosophical Society enabled substantial revision of this book.

This volume has benefited from the help of two anonymous readers for Stanford University Press, who read the initial version, and from the comments of John Martin, who read the revised manuscript. Randolph Starn also offered a number of suggestions while writing the Afterword. Special thanks go to Norris Pope of Stanford University Press, whose interest in this project has been most gratifying, and to Judith Hibbard for her careful work on production as well as Tom Finnegan for his copyediting. The staff at the Cartography Laboratory at the University of Wisconsin, Madison, masterfully created the maps for this book. Louisa Parker Mattozzi and Danielle Culpepper of the History Department of the University of Virginia and Christina Osheim all played an essential role in the copyediting and final preparation of the manuscript.

Our thanks also go to all the contributors to this volume, whose enthusiasm and interest in the project have made the editors' job an enjoyable one. They have all reminded us of the pleasures and rewards of collaborative scholarship. Of course, our final thank-you goes to Bill himself, without whom none of this would have happened. *Un caro saluto.*

Stanford, Charlottesville, and Little Rock, April 2002

About the Contributors

Robert Brentano is professor of history at the University of California, Berkeley. His major publications include *Two Churches: England and Italy in the Thirteenth Century* (1968), *Rome Before Avignon* (1991), and *A New World in a Small Place: Church and Religion in the Diocese of Rieti, 1188–1378* (1994).

Gene Brucker, Shepard Professor Emeritus at the University of California, Berkeley, is the author of many books on Renaissance Florence, among them *Florentine Politics and Society, 1343–1370* (1962), *The Civic World of Renaissance Florence* (1977), and *Renaissance Florence* (1983).

Samuel K. Cohn, Jr., is professor of medieval history at the University of Glasgow and the author of seven books. The most recent are *Creating the Florentine State: Peasants and Rebellion, 1348–1434* (1999) and *The Black Death Transformed: Disease and Culture in Early Renaissance Europe* (2002).

Robert L. Cooper is completing his dissertation at the University of California, Davis. Among his research interests are the religious and urban history of late medieval Italy. His chapter in this collection springs from his dissertation.

George Dameron is professor of history and coordinator of the Humanities Program at Saint Michael's College in Colchester, Vermont. The author of *Episcopal Power and Florentine Society, 1000–1320* (1991), he has also published on a variety of topics related to medieval Italy, such as rural communes and north Italian magnates.

Thomas Dandelet, assistant professor of history at the University of California, Berkeley, works on the western Mediterranean world in the early modern period with a special emphasis on Italy, the Spanish Empire, and their connections. Among his publications is *Spanish Rome, 1500–1700* (2001). He is presently at work on a history of the Colonna family.

Robert C. Davis is associate professor of history at Ohio State University, where he teaches and writes on Renaissance and early modern Italian history. His current interest in the story of tourism in Venice stems from his years of work in that city, together with his mixed sense of stunned revulsion and grudging admiration at what the mass-tourist industry has been able to do with the Most Romantic City in the World. Out of this has come *Venice, Tourist Maze: A Cultural Critique of the World's Most Touristed City.*

Paula Findlen is professor of history at Stanford University and director of the Science, Technology, and Society Program. Her publications include *Possessing Nature: Museums, Collecting, and Scientific Culture in Early Modern Italy* (1994); *Merchants and Marvels: Commerce, Science, and Art in Early Modern Europe* (2001, with Pamela H. Smith); and *The Italian Renaissance: Essential Readings* (2002).

Michelle M. Fontaine is associate professor of history at the University of Arkansas at Little Rock. Her interest in Italian urban history stems from her work for her master's degree with William M. Bowsky. Her research on the urban and religious culture of early modern Modena has resulted in a number of articles.

David Foote is assistant professor of history at Mississippi State University. Among his research interests is the Italian church in the age of communal formation. He is the author of several articles and has recently completed a book manuscript, *Lordship, Reform, and the Development of Civil Society in Medieval Italy: The Bishopric of Orvieto, 1100–1250.*

Carol Lansing is professor of history at the University of California, Santa Barbara. She is the author of *The Florentine Magnates* (1991), *Power and Purity: Cathar Heresy in Medieval Italy* (1998), and a forthcoming study of medieval ideas about politics and the expression of grief, *The Lament for the Dead: Gender and the Vita Civile in Communal Italy.*

Maureen C. Miller is associate professor of history at George Mason University. Her book *The Bishop's Palace: Architecture and Authority in Medieval Italy* (2000) won the 2001 Marraro Prize of the Society for Italian Historical Studies. Currently she is preparing a documentary history of the Gregorian Reform and writing a brief urban history of Florence.

Laurie Nussdorfer, professor of history and letters at Wesleyan University, is the author of *Civic Politics in the Rome of Urban VIII* (1992) and essays on urban space, print culture, and artisan guilds in early modern Rome. She is currently at work on a book about the history of writing practices that focuses on Roman notarial documents.

Duane J. Osheim, professor of history at the University of Virginia, is the author of *A Medieval Monastery and Its Social World* and *An Italian Lordship: The Bishopric of Lucca in the Middle Ages*. He received his Ph.D. in history from the University of California, Davis, where he studied under William M. Bowsky.

Cynthia L. Polecritti is associate professor of history at the University of California, Santa Cruz, and the author of *Preaching Peace in Renaissance Italy: Bernardino of Siena and His Audience* (2000). She is currently working on a book about street life in nineteenth- and twentieth-century Italy.

Jennifer D. Selwyn, assistant professor of history at the University of New Hampshire, is the author of several articles on the Jesuits in southern Italy. She is completing a book manuscript titled *A Paradise Inhabited by Devils: The Jesuits' Civilizing Mission in Early Modern Naples*.

Randolph Starn is professor of history and Italian studies and currently director of the Italian Studies Center and Program at the University of California, Berkeley. His most recent book is a collection of his essays, *Varieties of Cultural History* (2002).

Preface

Beyond Florence: The Contours of Medieval and Early Modern Italy emerged from a conference held at Stanford University in November 1998 to celebrate the career and accomplishments of William M. Bowsky, well known among historians of medieval and early Renaissance Italy for his work on the social, political, and economic history of the medieval commune of Siena, and more recently for his work on the religious history of Florence. This conference brought together several generations of scholars of Italian urban, religious, and social history—many of them former students and colleagues of Bill Bowsky—for a lively discussion of the current state of the field. We spent three memorable days returning to some of the classic problems of Italian history, debating the use of sources, examining each other's case studies, and discussing the reasons periodic conversation among medievalists and early modernists sharpens our perception of both fields.

We chose the theme "Beyond Florence" for several reasons that become apparent throughout this volume. In the past two decades, the study of Italy among Anglo-American historians has broadened considerably from an intense focus on the Florentine Renaissance to a much more diffuse exploration of Italy's geography. The chapters in this volume reflect the results of this research. Although acknowledging that the field, in its entirety, has never focused exclusively on Florence—nor for that matter is it ignoring Florence now, since there is currently a considerable renewal of Florentine scholarship—we are nonetheless convinced that historical research today on premodern Italy is much more reflective than it was some fifteen years ago of the complexity and variety of social and political arrangements in the Italian peninsula, much more willing to look at the small city and *contado* in conjunction with the well-known city-states.

At the same time, our conversations have made us well aware of how much our methodological approaches to those regions beyond Florence have been shaped by the powerful imprint of Florentine historiography. Florence is almost always a crucial point of reference in any study of Italy that attempts comparative analysis. We might simply say that historical scholarship on Florence reached a state of maturity before work done on virtually any other city-state, or even on other parts of Tuscany. The confluence of popular fascination with Florence as a city of living history, abundant manuscripts for virtually every imaginable kind of history, and successive generations of historians trained to cut their teeth on such materials has made Florence rather like the image of ancient Rome that Florentine historians confronted in the fourteenth and fifteenth centuries: shaping the landscape for better and for worse. Most of the participants in this volume were trained by the generation of American scholars who initiated the American encounter with the Italian archives, such as William Bowsky, Gene Brucker, David Herlihy, Marvin Becker, and Richard Goldthwaite, preceded by such German emigrés as Hans Baron, who spent a large part of his career in the United States. We are the direct progeny, in other words, of the renaissance of Florentine studies in the postwar period, even though many of us have moved in other directions in search of new historical terrain.

The direct relationship between Florentine studies and the diffusion of Italian history suggests the irony of the title. In many respects, we have hardly moved "beyond Florence" at all. Bill Bowsky is an excellent example of this trajectory. Having deliberately chosen to make Siena—a republic that resisted Florence's attempts to annex it until the early sixteenth century—the subject of his considerable research to show its differences from the better-studied Florentine model, in recent years he has returned to Florence to take advantage of its abundant archives for religious history. Florence continues to be a key point of reference for work on late medieval and early modern Italy and the centerpiece of study of the Italian Renaissance. But we are much more aware of the possibilities of sources in other Italian archives than we used to be. These essays as a whole testify to the wealth and range of materials that social historians continue to uncover in the Italian archives and the diffusion of many of the research techniques developed by Florentine scholars.

At the same time, we should remain well aware of the fundamental differences to which historians of Italy must attend. No single city or region can sum up such a variegated landscape, or stand as the model against which all others are measured. To invoke the second part of our title, this volume explores some of the *contours* of Italy from the Middle Ages through the seventeenth century. It creates a landscape against which to evaluate the current state of Florentine studies, the resurgence of Venetian studies, renewed interest in Italy under Spanish rule, and the continued development of many other regional histories that were formerly deemed the province of local history and are now of considerably greater interest to scholars who use these local histories as case studies to facilitate a broader understanding of Italy as a whole. Juxtaposing case studies, we invite readers to consider fruitfully how we might compare developments in political systems and law, urban and rural life, religion and society throughout the Italian peninsula.

Given the complexity of Italy's politics from the age of the communes to the era of hereditary principalities and foreign rule, no single volume can hope to reflect the range of work being done today on medieval and early modern Italy or encompass the myriad communes, city-states, duchies, principalities, and regions under foreign rule that defined Italy during these centuries. *Beyond Florence* offers a representative sample of current scholarship to an English-speaking audience. It reflects on what has preceded and inspired this work and suggests what might emerge from it. Implicitly, it invites the reader to consider the possibility of a more continuous history of Italy from the age of the communes to the decline of the early modern republics and principalities. What were the principal features of this world? To what extent did social, political, and religious factors create a common culture, as much as divide it into many Italies?

Nineteenth-century historians insisted on the value of distinct and all-encompassing historical epochs, but we have not done so for a long time. We have often avoided the issue entirely, since it is hard to break out of one's own specialized niche and survey the *longue durée*. Recognizing that this is rarely the task of an individual historian, we have tried to create a collective project that, in its organization, allows readers to consider some of the major themes in Italian history across the medieval and early modern periods. These themes are not new; rather, it is their enduring value to the social and urban history of Italy and their intrinsic interest to often artificially separated fields of medieval and early modern Italy that make them well worth revisiting through new case studies.

We have organized the volume into five distinct parts. The first, with chapters by Gene Brucker and Paula Findlen, offers a historiographic reflection on the relationship between Florentine Renaissance studies and the development of medieval and early modern Italian history. Part II, with chapters by Samuel Cohn, George Dameron, Duane Osheim, and Robert Brentano, examines one of the fundamental themes of Italian history—the relationship between city and countryside—looking at the Tuscan and Umbrian countryside in particular. The third part, with chapters by Carol Lansing and Laurie Nussdorfer, discusses legal and notarial culture by examining two case studies in Bologna and Rome. Part IV explores the intersection of urban and religious identity through a series of case studies by Robert Davis, Robert Cooper, Cynthia Polecritti, and Jennifer Selwyn, discussing respectively Venice, the Marches of Ancona, Siena, and the Kingdom of Naples. The final part examines what Maureen Miller, in her comparative study of the urban form of the medieval city, aptly describes as the topographies of power. Her chapter is complemented by studies of politics and urban life in the cities of Orvieto, Modena, and Rome, written by David Foote, Michelle Fontaine, and Thomas Dandelet.

In his Afterword, Randolph Starn returns to the question of whether or how historical studies can move beyond the field's concern with Florence, especially since the Renaissance and Florence remain central images for students of European History. Even contributions that offer exceptions, he observes, do so to a Florentine rule. He makes clear what is implicit in the chapters that make up the heart of the volume: as much as moving beyond Florence, the authors of these works are moving beyond simple visions of Florence and Italy.

Beyond Florence

PART I

Florence, Italy, and the Renaissance

Part I explores the relationship between Florentine history and Italian history. It presents a historiographic introduction to the volume as a whole. Gene Brucker offers a personal reflection on the somewhat accidental, even serendipitous growth of Florentine Renaissance history in the postwar era. Reflecting on the scholarly community that transformed the archival study of fifteenth-century Florence into a sophisticated laboratory for a succession of kinds of history, he underscores the contingent nature of historiography as much as of history. He also suggests some of the reasons historians are now returning to Florence, examining the city in light of a renewed appreciation for regional history that makes Florence an important part of understanding Tuscany.

Paula Findlen's chapter reminds us that the emphasis on Florence coincided with the enormous success of Italian Renaissance studies in America and Great Britain. Examining how the "demise" of the Renaissance as the crucial category of analysis was an impetus to studying other parts of Italy, she discusses developments in medieval and early modern Italian history in the past two decades and the possibilities for this field in the coming years. In particular, she emphasizes the idea of reviving the kind of scholarly experimentation that has made Renaissance Florence a well-known historiographic laboratory to encompass a more comparative history of Italy in the medieval and early modern period. New experiments might be comparisons—regional, thematic, and even chronological. They might also provide the ingredients for syntheses that give the new work on Reformation Italy its place in rewriting Italy's history in the age of the Renaissance. The Reformation, after all, is a concept much like medieval Italy, or like regions such as the Kingdom of Naples and the Republic of Venice, whose histories are more comfortably "early modern" than "Renaissance."

Florence and Beyond TWELFTH TO EIGHTEENTH CENTURIES

CHAPTER ONE

Florence Redux

Gene Brucker

When, in November 1952, I made my first tremulous entrance into the reading room of the Florentine Archivio di Stato, I joined a small coterie of researchers that, on any given day, numbered no more than a dozen.[1] The group included two distinguished historians from the United States, Felix Gilbert and Raymond De Roover, and Nicolai Rubinstein from London. The only Italian scholar in daily attendance in the archives was Elio Conti, then in the early stages of his research on fifteenth-century Florentine society. The older generation of Florentine historians had either died (Davidsohn, Caggese, Barbadoro) or were no longer actively engaged in research (Salvemini, Rodolico). Few students from the University of Florence ventured into the archives; their professors (Sestan, Garin, and Cantimori) encouraged them to work instead in the Biblioteca Nazionale. Students of the eminent economic historian Armando Sapori did work in the archives, and members of the staff (Guido Pampaloni, Francesca Morandini, Roberto Abbondanza) published the results of their research in the *Archivio storico italiano* and in other Tuscan journals. From this very modest nucleus of scholars then working on medieval and Renaissance Florence, it would have been difficult to predict the explosive growth of the field in subsequent years. But already in the 1950s, a cluster of young historians from the Anglo-Saxon world was coming to the archives to work on their research projects: Louis Marks, Philip Jones, Lauro Martines, Marvin Becker, David Herlihy, George Holmes, Peter Partner. This was the generation that revolutionized Florentine studies.

These scholars came to Florence from varied academic backgrounds. They were not linked to any historical tradition, nor any particular ideology or methodology. The influence of German refugee scholars (Baron, Kristeller, Mommsen, Gilbert) on this generation of Americans has been exaggerated.[2] Though my mentor at Princeton, Theodor Mommsen, did suggest my dissertation topic on fourteenth-century Florence, I was converted to the study of Florentine history by two Oxford scholars: William Deakin and Cecelia Ady. Lauro Martines visited Florence to study Renaissance painting, when I induced him to explore manuscript sources in the archives. Marvin Becker had planned to write a biography of Walter of Brienne, when he began his research in the commune's fiscal records and developed his thesis on the evolution of the Florentine territorial state. David Herlihy came to Florence by way of Pisa and Pistoia and then began his monumental study based on fifteenth-century tax records, the *catasto*. He found his partner in that enterprise, Christiane Klapisch-Zuber, through a chance encounter with Emmanuel LeRoy Ladurie.[3] English and Australian students migrated to Florence through their apprenticeship with Nicolai Rubinstein and Philip Jones, but their choice of research topics was often dictated by their particular interests and encounters with specific archival sources. It was these encounters, often accidental, with those records that fostered the research agendas and kindled the passions of those students. For some, fiscal records provided the raw material for their investigations; for others, it was the official sources of the commune; and for still others, private records: diaries, letters, account books.

This combination of an exceptionally rich documentary record and a group of historians endowed with tenacity and imagination has produced a body of scholarship with no equal in European urban history before the French Revolution.[4] Hans Baron's *Crisis of the Early Italian Renaissance* is the crown jewel of this corpus, its thesis still hotly debated four decades after publication.[5] Rubinstein has recently published the second edition of his classic work on the Florentine constitution under the Medici.[6] "Marvin Becker's powerful hypothesis regarding the transformation of communal government into . . . the 'territorial state' has continued to reverberate in works devoted to the history of the late medieval state."[7] Books based on the catasto records by Herlihy and Klapisch-Zuber and by Conti constitute the most thoroughly documented study of the demographic and economic foundations of a Renaissance society.[8] Martines's two books on Florentine humanists and lawyers developed a sound methodology for studying professional elites in Italian cities.[9] Richard Trexler's pioneering and controversial work on Florentine civic ritual is required reading for students of Italian urban history.[10] Richard Goldthwaite's books and articles on the Florentine economy have established him as the heir of a grand tradition that includes Alfred Doren, Armando Sapori, Raymond De Roover, and Federico Melis.[11] Of the large number of books devoted to family history, the monographs of F. W. Kent and Anthony Molho, and the collection of articles by Klapisch-Zuber, stand out as works of exceptional quality.[12]

In 1983, I published a review article on Florentine historiography in which I emphasized the domination of English-speaking scholars, the relatively modest achievement of Italians, and the absence of German historians, who had been so prominent in the field in the prewar period.[13] I noted that in the 1970s, twenty books on medieval and Renaissance Florence had been published in English; the pattern continues today. In the past decade, sixteen history books on Florence have been published by American scholars, seven by British authors, eleven by Italians, two by Australians, and one each by French and Canadian historians.[14] There has emerged, in the past two decades, a generation of Italian historians, well versed in the literature and methodologies of current scholarship, who are making a significant contribution to Florentine historiography.[15]

A remarkable feature of postwar Florentine historiography is the intense concentration on the fourteenth and fifteenth centuries, and the neglect of the period before Dante. How to explain this lack of interest in the medieval centuries, in favor of the period after the Black Death? Where, among Italian medievalists, are the successors of Gaetano Salvemini, Nicola Ottokar, Gioacchino Volpe, Cinzio Violante? Why did Rubinstein—a student in Florence of the Russian medievalist Ottokar, who wrote his first book on a thirteenth-century topic—decide instead to concentrate on the fifteenth century? Why did Herlihy, whose first book was a study of thirteenth-century Pisa and who had written articles on the economy and demography of Carolingian Europe, write his next books on late medieval Pistoia and on fifteenth-century Florence? The history of medieval Florence is essentially that constructed by Robert Davidsohn a century ago.

The concentration of Florentine research on the post-Dante period can be explained primarily by the unparalleled richness of the documentation, both public and private. A prime example is the catasto, the volumes of tax reports that have survived from 1427 to 1480. These thousand-odd tomes contain information about demographic patterns, births and deaths, marriages and dowries, economic investments; and about such topics as familial relationships; the status of women, orphans, and bastards; illness and disease; and literacy. The information contained in these tax records can be supplemented by private letters and diaries (some 150 of the latter from the fifteenth century); by notarial protocols; by court records; and by the deliberations of the civic magistracies established to confront particular problems. These include records of inventories of the property of orphans; guild records furnishing information on the lives of laborers in the cloth industry; as well as data on the identities and lives of prostitutes and on males accused of homosexual acts.[16]

But there is a downside to this massive accumulation of source material. Florentine scholars can become so absorbed in the particular niche they have carved out for themselves that they do not see the forest for the trees. In a review article published thirty years ago, Randolph Starn noted this obsession with documents, so characteristic a feature of Florentine historical scholarship.[17] This could lead to tunnel vision, to unwillingness to look beyond the immediate object of study to search for contexts and connections, or to consider comparisons with other Italian communities. I will cite an example of how deep immersion into the archival sources transformed the scholarship of a major historian.

I first met Elio Conti in 1952, when he was embarked on an ambitious enterprise to write a comprehensive history of fifteenth-century Florentine society based primarily but not exclusively on the catasto records. Conti had been encouraged to undertake this project by Salvemini, who had returned from exile in the United States to teach at the University of Florence after the war.[18] Conti's plan was to identify the "classes" in Florentine society, and to demonstrate how their relations transformed the economy, the political system, and the culture. But while exploring the documentary record, Conti realized he could not understand urban society without knowledge of the rural world that surrounded and nourished it. He then published three volumes on this agrarian milieu, but he never moved beyond preliminary studies to analyze Florentine urban society, a task later undertaken by Herlihy and Klapisch-Zuber with the aid of the computer.

Conti and his students edited and published a range of documentary sources: notarial records and deliberations of municipal councils. His last published work before his premature death in 1988 was a study of the Florentine fisc in the fifteenth century, a work of vast erudition, but one that puzzled readers for its empiricism and failure to summarize and contextualize the argument.[19] Conti's plan to write an *histoire totale* of Quattrocento Florentine society was ultimately defeated by the "many tons of paper" that he had collected in thirty-five years of research but could not organize and synthesize.

Conti's inability to integrate his material is a symptom of a serious defect in Florentine historiography: the failure to summarize and integrate recent scholarship. In his 1970 review article, Starn observed that "a serious, full-scale history of medieval and Renaissance Florence ... cannot be expected for a long time."[20] More recently, John Najemy has described Florentine historiography as being in a state of disintegration. Reviewing five books on fifteenth-century topics, he stressed the differences in their methods, their interpretations, and their "languages," concluding that their arguments were fundamentally irreconcilable.[21] Felix Gilbert made the same point in an essay describing the various interpretations of three books on Florentine topics, "so different the reader may wonder if the

Florence one scholar writes about can possibly be the same city another scholar discusses."[22]

Najemy is certainly correct in concluding that controversy, not consensus, reigns in Florentine historiography. Molho has been sharply critical of what he describes as the "anglophone" tradition of Florentine history, accusing its practitioners of idealizing the republican government and ignoring the pattern of class conflict and exploitation of the urban working class and the rural peasantry by the city's dominant elite.[23] One "anglophone" historian, Humfrey Butters, has delivered a broadside against his colleagues who (he claims) have been seduced by the lure of writing "total history" and by the claims of social science to establish historical laws.[24] Thus on the one hand are scholars who deplore the positivist character of much Florentine historiography and who urge greater attention to theory[25]; on the other hand are those who criticize any commitment to theoretical models, whether Marxist or *marxisante*, or Annaliste, or Foucaultian.

In some areas of Florentine history, a rough consensus has been achieved, most notably with respect to the city's political development "from a faction-ridden and ungovernable commune to a guild republic to an oligarchic one."[26] Also generally accepted is the tripartite structure of Florentine society: a small, wealthy elite of entrepreneurs and rentiers; a middling class of artisans and shopkeepers; and a large underclass of the poor and the destitute. Recent scholarship has focused less on class distinctions and more on the bonds (patron-client relations; neighborhood, parish, and confraternal associations) that linked together the members of this community.[27] The city's economic development after the Black Death remains a very controversial subject, with some historians emphasizing its growth and prosperity, and others its stagnation and decline.[28]

The character and evolution of the Florentine economy is linked to a more fundamental issue, formulated most dramatically 140 years ago by Jacob Burckhardt when he described Florence as being "the most important workshop of the Italian, and indeed of the modern European spirit." The "modernity" of Renaissance Florence—its politics, its economy, its social order, its culture—continues to divide Florentine historians. The most forceful and eloquent exponent of the "modernity" thesis is Goldthwaite, who described his most recent book as "an enlargement of Jacob Burckhardt's classic—and much debated—vision of Renaissance Italy as the birthplace of the modern world; to his formulation about the Italians' discovery of antiquity, nature, man and the individual is here added their discovery also of things."[29] A prominent spokesman for the opposing camp is Molho, who argues that "an immersion in the Florentine culture of the fifteenth century leads one . . . to an uncompromisingly nonmodern world.... It was not a bourgeois world but rather one whose values were closer, more akin, to those of a feudal, aristocratic society."[30]

These controversies among Florentine historians over method and interpretation can be seen as evidence of the sustained vitality and dynamism of the field. Michael Rocke's book, *Forbidden Friendships*, is an original, pathbreaking analysis of Florence's homoerotic culture in the fifteenth century. Samuel Cohn's study of Tuscan and Umbrian wills as testimonials of shifting patterns of piety should muffle if not silence those who have criticized the failure of Florentine historians to engage in comparative analysis.[31] Cohn's new book, *Creating the Florentine State*, challenges current orthodoxy on the construction of a regional state in the fifteenth century and throws new light on rebel mountaineers on Florence's northern and eastern frontiers.[32]

So long neglected, Florence's religious history has experienced a remarkable revival in recent years.[33] A work in progress that is notable for its scope and depth is the study of the pre-Reformation Florentine church by David Peterson, the most comprehensive analysis of an Italian regional church that has yet been written.[34] Equally impressive for its range and its interdisciplinary character is Dale Kent's *Cosimo de' Medici and the Florentine Renaissance*. No other book on Florence, or indeed on any Italian Renaissance city, has used so broad a range of sources or integrated so effectively the various strands of cultural activity in the Medici era: oral, literary, visual; Christian, humanist, *popolare*.[35] The occasion of the five-hundredth anniversary of the death of Lorenzo de' Medici (1992) unleashed a torrent of publications dedicated to Il Magnifico, whose career has been more fully documented and analyzed than that of any other Florentine with the possible exception of Dante. Together with the corpus of Lorenzo's correspondence and newly discovered sources, these studies will be integrated into F. W. Kent's projected two-volume biography of Lorenzo.[36]

The insularity that once characterized Florentine historiography has been replaced by a sustained effort to integrate the city's history into a broader regional (and peninsular) context, and to develop comparative perspectives. This integration has been a central theme in the series of volumes dedicated to Tuscan ruling elites, and in a collection of articles edited by William Connell and Andrea Zorzi on Florentine Tuscany.[37] The focus of these volumes is the structure of relationships that linked the capital city, provincial towns, and rural villages (and their inhabitants) together. Included in this conceptual framework are the economic relations between Florence and its territory; the political and social bonds between Florentine patrons and their clients and dependents in the dominion; as well as the ties binding members of guilds, confraternities, and neighborhoods.

Another distinctive feature of recent scholarship is the interweaving of topics (political, socioeconomic, religious, cultural) that in the past were often treated as autonomous categories. Thus the production of a work of art is perceived as a complex process "in which Church, state, individual power, intellectual endeavor, artistic propaganda and private delectation come together in the multi-faceted synthesis."[38] Even a field as conservative as diplomatic history has been transformed by the felt need to broaden horizons and perspectives. Daniela Frigo describes Renaissance diplomacy as "the arena of action with which the manifold currents of a state's political life flowed: power balances within ruling elites or at court, individual careers and fortunes, the influence of groups and factions, legal and political culture, religious and confessional motives, military force, economic expansion, the degree of consensus enjoyed by the government or dynasty."[39]

In recent years, as Edward Muir has noted, there has been a significant shift in Italian Renaissance historiography away from Florence.[40] Venetian historical writing can match both the quality and the output of its Tuscan rival, and the historians of the Adriatic republic have been more active in synthesizing their research.[41] Of the major Italian cities, only Milan has failed to attract the interest of foreign scholars, who "mostly prefer Florence, Venice and Rome, for various good reasons . . . and for various bad reasons, including snobbery and inertia."[42] Within Tuscany itself, a rich historiography has developed in recent years, focusing on the major cities (Pisa, Siena, Lucca, Arezzo) and also on the smaller provincial towns (Prato, Pescia, Poppi, Pistoia).[43] The multivolume history of Prato has been described as "an enterprise which will surely set a new standard of excellence in the field of European urban history in the early modern age."[44] Florentine historiography could benefit greatly from a comparable enterprise.

Although Florence's historiographical hegemony has been weakened in recent years, so too is its status as the primary (if not sole) creator of Renaissance culture. The city has always been fortunate in the quality and reputation of its panegyrists, from Bruni, Ficino, and Vasari to Burckhardt and Baron.[45] Burckhardt was a particularly influential promoter of the notion that the Renaissance was fundamentally a Florentine achievement. "Not only did Burckhardt frame what remains one of the grandest and clearest expositions of what the Renaissance was," writes Graham Dixon, "and why it mattered, but he also left a clear trail for those who would follow in his footsteps and decide for themselves whether his large claims were actually true. Burckhardt's advice was simple. If you want to understand the Renaissance, go to Florence."[46]

There are few, if any, scholars of Renaissance Italy who today would accept this Burckhardtian axiom. Bruni's claim for Florence's central role in the revival of antiquity has been challenged, as has the general significance of humanism in Italian (and European) cultural history.[47] Giorgio Vasari's hugely influential *Lives of the Most Excellent Painters, Sculptors and Architects* emphasized Florence's preeminence in the artistic revolution, but recent scholarship has given equal weight to the achievements of northern Italian artists, particularly those working in princely courts.[48] Nevertheless, a case can still be made for Florence's "exceptionalism," and for stressing those dimensions of its historical experience that distinguished it from other Italian urban societies. These unique features include the vital strand of republicanism in its political practices and ideology; the balance of its economic system, among its commercial, industrial, banking, craft, and agrarian components; the remarkable receptivity by its elite of classicizing influences in literature and art; the symbiotic relationship between elite and popular culture; and the strongly empirical element in that culture.[49]

Today, Florence is a museum city barely able to survive the phenomenon of mass tourism, while its inhabitants choke on its polluted air. Yet it continues to work magic on our imagination and our sensibilities. A recent issue of the *New Yorker* contained a review by literary critic George Steiner of Michael Levey's book on Florence.[50] Steiner, who notes that he "has walked and walked that city a hundred times over," still finds it "obstinately new"; "Florence exceeds its masterpieces," he writes. "There is about this city, frequently morose, even harsh, a mystery of implosion, as if singular forces of intellect and feeling had been compelled into fruitful collision by the ring of hills, by a climate susceptible of white heat and bone-jarring cold. Genius and civic ferocity were intimately meshed.... Out of catastrophes sprang energies that have, in essence, come close to defining Western civilization. As our millennium limps to a close, it does more and more appear as if the foremost poetic intelligence—the preeminent act of shaping thought and philosophy in the Western legacy—were Dante's. There are whole continents that have contributed less to mankind than this one small city."

CHAPTER TWO

In and Out of Florence

Paula Findlen

When Jacob Burckhardt wrote *The Civilization of the Renaissance in Italy* (1860), he created an enduring portrait of Italian society between the thirteenth and sixteenth centuries that spanned the length and breadth of the Italian peninsula. Foreign kings in Naples, upstart mercenaries in Milan and Urbino, ambitious nobles in Rome, feudal lords in Ferrara, Genoese seafaring merchants, and Venetian patricians deliberating in the rooms of the Great Council all played their part in constituting Burckhardt's image of a Renaissance society. Although Burckhardt personally preferred Rome as the city in which the past most came alive for him, he nonetheless harbored some affection for republican Florence, "the city of incessant movement," as the part of Italy that best embodied the virtues of the Renaissance. In a world of eloquent humanists and scheming oligarchs, the Florentines earned Burckhardt's praise for having created the first modern state and having best articulated the sort of "modern" individualism that he associated with the Renaissance.[1]

Despite Burckhardt's praise of Florence, he did not devote the majority of his classic work to this city. One of the most striking aspects of his history of the Renaissance is its broad geographical perspective, which reflected his willingness to think comparatively about the development of the major Italian states and their political and cultural expression. Burckhardt devoted many pages to the rule of the Visconti and Sforza in Milan; he praised the southern empire of Frederick II as the earliest example of the state as a "work of art" and returned frequently to Frederick's Angevin and Aragonese successors in the Kingdom of Naples. He did not neglect the smaller duchies and principalities ruled by such dynasties as the Este and Gonzaga. Burckhardt's image of Italy, in other words, was much as Machiavelli and Guicciardini had portrayed it: a peninsula in which Florence was, in the best of times, its most glorious center, but never a territory to be seen in isolation from the rest of Italy, or indeed the world. It included cities such as Verona, which, as David Herlihy once observed, had a population almost as big as that of Florence at the beginning of the sixteenth century.[2]

Since the advent of professional historical scholarship, it has been hard to write history as a grand narrative in the tradition of the nineteenth-century German scholars who made the idea of historical writing broadly appealing to subsequent generations. Burckhardt had the advantage of writing history without ever once setting foot in the archive, or worrying if he had read enough to generalize about Italy as a whole. Though many of his most vivid portraits of Renaissance individuals and events derived from recently published manuscripts in various archives and libraries, suggesting the importance of both the Italian and German historical traditions in shaping the emergence of the Renaissance in the mid-nineteenth century, this kind of work played no self-conscious role in his own presentation of the Italian Renaissance.

Despite Burckhardt's relative lack of interest in the kind of history his mentor Ranke had ably pioneered, he and other scholars who between the 1860s and 1930s wrote in praise of Florence played an important role in the further growth of archival scholarship on medieval and early modern Italy by creating a powerful synthetic portrait against which scholars might test their own findings. Careful examination of manuscript sources has become the hallmark of this field.[3] Had Burckhardt done his research buried in the documents of the Florentine State Archive rather than in the comfort of various European libraries and in contemplation of Italy's artistic masterpieces, he might have offered a very different account of Renaissance Italy, no longer the history of the entire peninsula but a detailed account of the activities of a single city. This is precisely what Nicolai Rubinstein did when he began his work in the Florentine archives in the 1930s, building upon the legacy of great Florentine historians such as Robert Davidsohn and Gaetano Salvemini.[4] Rich in notarial registers, council minutes, tax records, family and religious archives, and thousands of other scraps of paper and parchment that recorded the daily activities of Florentines, the city's archives have yielded enough material for several generations of scholars to interpret without ever worrying that we might exhaust their contents.

Since the 1950s, Florence has been the historical laboratory par excellence for study of the premodern world. Between the late 1950s and early 1980s, dozens of books appeared on late medieval and Renaissance Florence in several languages.[5] Fundamental works such as Hans Baron's *Crisis of the Early Italian Renaissance* (1955) elaborated the image of fifteenth-century Florence as a unique moment in the history of political thought and action, suggested but never fully described by Burckhardt.[6] Subsequent scholarship has greatly enhanced our understanding of the nature of Florentine civic and political culture, debating where its uniqueness lay but never fundamentally questioning this presupposition. Economic historians have used the records of Florence and its surrounding territories to examine competing theories about commercial growth, urban development, and territorial politics.[7]

Studying Florence became a vast, collaborative project that produced a series of heated debates about its role in the transition from the medieval world to the modern. Historians of other cities and regions marveled at the fact that one could discuss fifteenth-century Florence "person by person and stone by stone."[8] So great was Florence's hegemony that when Gene Brucker reviewed Edward Muir's important *Civic Ritual in Renaissance Venice* (1981), he inadvertently retitled it "Civic Ritual in Renaissance Florence."[9] At that point in time, it was hard to imagine an influential book on Italy (in English) discussing any other city —despite the equally venerable tradition of studying Venice, which Burckhardt polemically described as "the city of apparent stagnation and of political secrecy."[10]

The sheer variety of history written from the Florentine archives—most notably social, political, and economic history—suggests how well historians have responded to the challenges of analyzing this particular record of the past. Burckhardt provocatively called Florence, along with Venice, "the birthplace of statistical science"—a sign that he understood how monumental Florentine records might appear to future historians.[11] He did not say the same of Rome, since the evidence he preferred there emanated from the political and cultural record of the papacy. Examining this material has demanded every possible methodology, from paleography to the (now outdated) punch card; as a result, a great deal of innovative scholarship on the premodern world has made Florence its case study. New historical methodologies emerged from multiple encounters between modern historians and Renaissance documents. When David Herlihy and Christiane Klapisch-Zuber's monumental study of the 1427 *catasto* (tax record), *Tuscans and Their Families*, appeared in 1978, it marked the culmination of almost two decades of collaborative work and made the history of Florence a model for a new kind of marriage between history and the social sciences.[12] Quite remarkably, we still know more about the taxes of fifteenth-century Florence and its surrounding countryside than those of almost any other region in the world.

By the early 1980s, social and anthropological theory had replaced statistical sampling techniques as the primary lens through which to view the Florentine experience. Historians such as Richard Trexler and Ronald

Weissman argued persuasively that Florence offered a dazzling array of cultural material whose analysis might tell us a great deal about the nature of human relations in the premodern world. Issues such as patronage, friendship, exchange, kinship, and ritual supplanted the questions of humanist values and the transformation of communal and republican politics. Klapisch-Zuber dramatically evoked this move in a series of influential essays on women and family in Renaissance Italy, in which an exploration of marital strategies and gift-giving practices replaced the answers to a tax questionnaire as the means of generating new information about Florentine society.[13]

Florence became the site of a new kind of social and cultural history that had strong connections to historical work being done beyond Florence—for other Italian cities and for Europe as a whole. It became a well-documented centerpiece of a more comparative kind of history. When Peter Burke created a "historical anthropology" of early modern Italy in 1987, he no longer thought only of Florence. In fact, he virtually displaced it by burying the Florentine archives in a wealth of citations from archives in Milan, Venice, Genoa, Rome, Naples, and other Italian cities.[14] As foreign historians of Italy began to cast their net more broadly, exploring regional archives as well as the archives of less well-studied cities, and paying closer attention to the work of their Italian colleagues, the image of the Florentine archive necessarily changed. Even the primacy of the latter as the generator of the best material to address the most interesting historical questions was now in doubt, since this assessment depended entirely on the questions one wished to ask.

As if to punctuate this shift, the Florentine State Archive closed up shop and moved across town to Piazza Beccaria in 1988, after residing in the Palazzo degli Uffizi for over two centuries. The Florentine State Archive may go down in the annals of scholarship as the only Italian archive whose temporary closing has ever merited an article in an American historical journal, not to inform the public about its new location so much as to reflect with nostalgia on the passing of a great age of archival scholarship, camaraderie, and even rivalry that shaped the collective project of writing Florence's history since the 1950s.[15] The archive reopened —surprisingly, on schedule—and the work of researching and writing Florence's history continued. Yet no one would deny that an era had ended. Florence no longer dominates the writing of Italian history among an international group of historians in the way it once did. Although still an important location in which to study medieval and early modern Italy, it is now one of many sites in which historians choose to investigate Italy's past.

Beyond the Renaissance

The decline of Florence coincided not just with a shift in methodology but with a growing disillusionment with the Renaissance as an organizing principle for the study of late medieval and early modern Italy. The foreign fascination with the Renaissance has shaped a great deal of Italian history since the age of Burckhardt. Historians have been predicting the conceptual death of the Renaissance since the late 1970s, though it has lately enjoyed a revival.[16] The new kind of social and cultural history practiced in the 1980s no longer highlighted the uniquely "Renaissance" characteristics of the late fourteenth through early sixteenth centuries, nor did it tie the study of social behavior to a single political and cultural moment such as the flourishing of civic humanism or the rise of the Medici. The Renaissance became the context for studying other aspects of Italian history rather than the object of inquiry. Historians began to speak of the "age of the Renaissance," as a means of reminding readers that the new things they described occurred synchronically with the more familiar events of the Renaissance itself.[17]

The results of this transition are amply apparent at the end of the 1990s. Several recent trends mark the history of medieval and early modern Italy. First and foremost, the less visible project of studying Italy, in all its parts, has become a more explicit preoccupation of a current generation of scholars. Italian history now has a much broader geography than it did in the 1980s, one more in keeping with the kind of work done predominantly by Italians rather than foreign historians of Italy, who have never privileged Florence as the most important center for their work, or the Renaissance as the watershed of Italian history.

In part, this tendency reflects growing emphasis on the importance of the medieval history of Italy, which has focused on such cities as Siena, Pisa, Lucca, Genoa, Padua, Verona, and Rome and stressed the value of regional studies, as seen in the work done on Tuscany, Lombardy, Lazio, and Sicily.[18] In part, the transition is indebted to a new generation of historians who have taken up Eric Cochrane's call to revisit "the forgotten centuries," shifting the study of postmedieval Italy away from the Renaissance to the sixteenth through eighteenth centuries, emphasizing continuities rather than discontinuities in the formation of the early modern world.[19] The result is a renewed interest in the Venetian Republic, the papal states, Spanish Lombardy, and the Kingdom of Naples.[20] Both approaches have self-consciously distanced themselves from the Florentine Renaissance.

The new configuration of Italian history is the product of a greater degree of collaboration between Italian and foreign historians in the study of Italy. Few books appearing in English on Italy today would ignore the lively historical scholarship in postwar Italy.[21] Influential journals such as the *Archivio storico italiano, Rivista storica italiana, Studi storici,* and especially *Quaderni storici* have reshaped a great deal of Italian social, political, and economic history. Microhistory, one of the most important methodological innovations of the past two decades in the study of the premodern world, is a decisively Italian invention.[22] Although one or two examples of this genre have used Florentine materials, the vast majority have mined archives in less well-studied parts of Italy such as Friuli and Piedmont and preferred sixteenth- and seventeenth-century documents to fourteenth- and fifteenth-century materials. Similarly, renewed interest in the history of religious beliefs, practices, and institutions has highlighted the importance of episcopal, monastic, and inquisitorial archives, as well as lay religious writings, in creating a more complex history of Catholicism.[23] This subject, too, has emerged as curiously un-Florentine, even though Florence has a rich religious history.

The past decade of scholarship reveals a growing self-consciousness about the limits of Florence as an account of Italian society, politics, and culture. Burckhardt may have considered republican Florence the "Italy of Italies," but modern scholars are more inclined to emphasize its anomalous status in a peninsula noted for the complexity of its feudal and seigneurial agreements and for a long history of foreign rule. As Trevor Dean has suggested recently, perhaps we should see Ferrara, the first of the northern and central Italian cities to come under seigneurial rule, as typical of some of these other tendencies in a largely agrarian society.[24] Robert Lopez's wonderful comment—"Italy was never medieval, yet no medieval phenomenon left her unaffected"[25]—suggests an entirely different way of seeing Italy in the age of the Renaissance, one that emphasizes continuities between the twelfth through early sixteenth centuries rather than differences. In this account of Italy, Florence's marked territorial expansion and emphasis on the city as the focal point of political and economic development finds at best a loose parallel in Visconti Lombardy and the Venetian Republic. Perhaps we need to consider *incastellamento* and other such practices as more indicative of the process by which communities developed.[26] Even Venetian historians, best positioned to think comparatively about Florence because Venice has been second only to Florence in establishing a strong scholarly tradition, are quick to point out the limits of the Florentine analogy in understanding the Venetian Republic.[27]

Scholarship on southern Italy has been vocally critical of the hegemony of the Florentine model. Historians of Sicily such as David Abulafia, Henri Bresc, and Stephan Epstein have argued that our perception of Florence as an advanced economy is based on lack of careful analysis of the flourishing southern Italian economy prior to the seventeenth century.[28] In keeping with the strong tradition of studying the Mezzogiorno that was developed by Neapolitan scholars such as Giuseppe Galasso and Rosario Villari, they reject the simple polarization of northern and southern Italy as a division between politically autonomous and economically advanced city-states and a feudal, agrarian kingdom under foreign rule.[29] Currently, the Sicilian economy looks more successful in the century after the Black Death than the Tuscan one, even if it lacked a capital city with the ability to draw upon the resources of an entire regional economy. Sicily may not have had a Renaissance, but it certainly had a surplus of wheat to export throughout the Mediterranean.

Some of the most interesting reassessments of Florence's role in the medieval and early modern period have emerged from the work on Tuscany. Recent historians of Tuscany have emphasized the strong divergence between Florence and the rest of Tuscany, leading them to reexamine the relationship between the city and the region.[30] They point to the unevenness of Florentine relations with its various subject cities, the continued strength and relative autonomy of many rural communes, and the inability of more remote parts of Tuscany to be integrated successfully into the Florentine image of a territorial state. The continued fascination on the part of many scholars with Lucca, the one Tuscan city-republic to resist the incursions of the Florentines, further reinforces the idea that the history of Tuscany and the history of Florence are hardly one and the same. Similarly, the history of Siena, whose study was pioneered so effectively by William Bowsky, continues to flourish as a means of exploring how Florence's leading urban rival within Tuscany ended up as a subject territory by the mid-sixteenth century.[31] Studying Tuscany has not only sharpened the portrait of Florence but also cast doubt upon some of the earliest and strongest claims made for the success of the Florentine state beyond its city walls. It is a cautionary tale in further exploration of the nature of territorial states in Italy.

Florence necessarily looks different even to Florentine historians. Anthony Molho recently described it as "an atypical territorial state" because of its frequent political transitions.[32] More strongly, Carol Lansing has asked us to imagine what medieval Florence might be like: "a raw new town, the product of a flood of immigration in the twelfth and thirteenth centuries." Encouraging her readers to erase the Renaissance city from their memory, she conjures up a fragile society in which magnates established social bonds through tower societies rather than the sophisticated networks of neighborhood politics and family lineage portrayed in the work of F. W. Kent and Dale Kent on fifteenth-century Florence.[33] Architectural historian Marvin Trachtenberg further defamiliarizes Florence when he argues that many of its quintessential "Renaissance" features are actually late medieval buildings that reflected efforts to bury, quite literally, the material traces of Florence's city of towers under the cobblestones laid by a communal government.[34] We are in the midst of a significant reevaluation about the history of Florence that offers a more complex and satisfying account of the emergence of this quintessentially Renaissance city in light of a broader and more comparative appreciation of Italian urban history that eschews overly neat and often artificial boundaries of chronology.

The Comparative Project

The idea of comparative history has become a distinctive feature of recent work on medieval and early modern Italy. This point has been argued most explicitly by Samuel Cohn in *The Cult of Remembrance and the Black Death: Six Renaissance Cities in Central Italy* (1992). In the preface to his book, Cohn highlights the uniqueness of the Italian archives in facilitating comparative studies: "The city-states of Italy from the appearance of Europe's earliest communal charters in the late eleventh century until political unification in 1871 supply the historian with an ideal 'laboratory' for comparative study."[35] Edward Muir also echoes this perspective when he describes the Italian city-states as a "historical laboratory" for the study of factionalism and violence.[36]

What features facilitate the terms of comparison? Both historians highlight the wealth and relative uniformity of notarial records as being ideal material around which to ask comparative questions of the past. The symmetry of documentation within the diversity of many Italian cities—what Philip Jones aptly calls the traces of "a nation addicted to writing"[37]—suggests one of the premises by which Italian history can be considered an explicitly comparative project. Put simply, the range and degree of documentation provides an adequate level of detail in facilitating comparison.

Notarial registers formed the bedrock of scholarship on Renaissance Florence, but they are also fundamental to any work done on Italy from the twelfth century onward. Robert Brentano aptly characterized the Italian church as a "notarial church" in the thirteenth century. Similarly, Chris Wickham has highlighted the utility of notarial registers in understanding the rural commune, using them to compare communal developments in Tuscany, Lombardy, and the Veneto.[38] Despite the fundamental importance of notarial records, we still know very little about the process by which they were generated, the means by which notaries became so important in urban and rural communes, and how people interacted with them. The notary is, after all, one of the few important figures to be present in virtually every type of Italian community. Through the records of the notary, we can reconstruct the process by which medieval and early modern Italians not only documented their familial and business practices but came to understand the nature of social relations and the power of the written word.[39] Making this invisible figure and his documents visible surely goes a long way to enriching the comparative history of Italy.

Identifying institutions, practices, and beliefs that are mostly unique to Italy, or expressed distinctively in this part of the world, has been an important aspect of transcending local histories. The city-state, for example, has long been a subject of comparative analysis; historians have spilled a great deal of ink attempting to explain why Italy created and continued to modify this distinctive kind of government. As the idea of empire as a unifying force in Italian politics receded from memory, the cities became an important marker of identity. Praising Italian cities was a very old tradition, stretching back at least to the eighth century.[40] By the late Middle Ages, the Italian cities collectively shaped an image of Italy as an unusually urbanized region of the world. In 1588, Giovanni Botero commented with pride that the Italian elite preferred to dwell in cities more than their equivalent in "the cities of France or other parts of Europe."[41] He wrote these words not from the Renaissance city of Florence but from Milan, heart of an ancient *signoria* and the second city of Spanish Italy after Naples. This was the same city that Bonvesin de la Riva described as populated by some two hundred thousand inhabitants at the end of the thirteenth century—undoubtedly an exaggeration, but a good example of the idea that the city might contain the world.[42]

Cities offer an important but limited vantage point from which to view a society. Other aspects of social and political organization, such as the rural commune and the rise of the Renaissance and Baroque courts, suggest the importance of alternatives to the city-republics and oligarchies.[43] We now have a much greater appreciation of the complexities of urban and rural society. Among other things, recent research has renewed interest in the territorial state, not as an entity brought into being by the power and wealth of key cities but as a negotiated enterprise in which many players assayed the advantages and disadvantages of subject rule. The resulting image of Italy is a series of highly distinctive topographies—maps that we might superimpose, one on top of the other, without ever having the geographic contours in perfect alignment. Perhaps more clearly than some other regions of the world, Italy allows us to see how a society forms out of multiple kinds of relationship, in part because medieval and early modern Italians were so articulate about the importance of their personal and political arrangements.

Comparison need not be solely at the level of large-scale institutional structures. Some of the most interesting examples account for highly specific practices that emerged from Italy's distinctive urban culture, for example, the appearance and growth of public health boards in most regions of sixteenth- and seventeenth-century Italy that Carlo Cipolla has studied.[44] The fact that public health boards appeared throughout the Italian states, and almost nowhere else, suggests that factors other than local politics were at work in shaping the culture of the Italian peninsula. Studies of social phenomena such as violence and criminality, marriage and sumptuary laws, and sexuality also have emphasized the growth of shared concerns among the urban elite regarding the behavior of their citizens.[45] In these instances, we cannot talk about social phenomena that were necessarily unique to Italy, but it is possible to discuss the response of many Italian cities to the problem of social order as grounded in a shared set of beliefs and institutions.

If social and political comparisons allow historians to ask how Italy created a distinctive society, cultural analysis invites us to examine why this environment fostered activities that gave Italy its reputation as one of the most literate and culturally sophisticated regions of Europe—a traveler's paradise, from the days of medieval pilgrimage to the age of the Grand Tour. Paul Grendler's important work on Renaissance schooling, for example, argues that the distinctive needs of many Italian city governments, coupled with a relatively high rate of urban literacy and an interregional network of humanist schoolmasters and scholars, created a relatively uniform educational culture in many Italian cities. Intellectual and cultural historians have demonstrated quite effectively how the mobility of humanists and artists created a cultural life that linked Naples to Florence, Venice to Milan, and numerous other locations in between.[46] In a society in which networks of patronage, friendship, family, and business usually extended beyond the walls of a single city, it is hardly surprising that culture, too, should travel.[47]

Italy is indeed a comparative laboratory. Despite the pronounced localism of a great deal of research, historians have made renewed efforts in the past decade to return to the grand narrative in light of new research questions. The number and proximity of Italy's archives are a constant reminder that we study cities, towns, and villages whose inhabitants lived within less than a day's ride of each other. They frequently traveled, made agreements with each other across these distances, and did not hesitate to emigrate elsewhere when the prosperity of their own region declined. The human traces of these activities create another set of organic connections whose pattern adds yet another layer to Italy's topography.

Immigration is another phenomenon that reminds us of the limits of the city as a summation of a society. The status of the immigrant, like that of the notary, captures some of the fundamental attributes of life in the Italian cities. By the thirteenth century, immigrants played an important role in the prosperity of cities such as Bologna and Florence, and they quickly became the focal point of urban anxieties.[48] They often maintained family and business ties with their natal villages, creating complicated regional networks of kinship, profit, and politics that we are only just beginning to understand. The presence of such ordinary men and women on the move offers an interesting juxtaposition to the quintessentially Italian phenomenon of the *podestà*, a foreigner invited to rule temporarily over a city-state. Learning from one's neighbors—indeed, relying on one's neighbors for human and material resources—was as much an Italian tradition as the deep-seated suspicion of foreigners that pervaded many discussions of urban life by the fifteenth century.[49] Such behavior created an infrastructure, a delicate calculus of human relations, that linked many of the regions of Italy even as they argued for their uniqueness.

Social, legal, political, religious, and cultural borrowings pervaded the society of medieval and early modern Italy—a world in which the word *vicini* (neighbors) defined one of the most important relationships that people could have with each other.[50] We would be unwise, however, to imagine the boundaries of this dynamic society as anticipating something that approximately resembled a nation. Similarities at times masked important differences, the fascination with the idea of Italy notwithstanding. The persistence of Lombard law in certain regions of Italy, when Roman law generally predominated, is one example. The Byzantine heritage of Venice; the German and imperial allegiances of the Trentino; and the Greek, Arabic, and Spanish heritage of Sicily are but three of many instances in which politics, culture, and language reflected the connections of various regions of Italy not to each other but to the rest of the world.

These examples evoke another important aspect of studying premodern Italy: might we not see Italy as the ideal site in which to explore a variety of political and cultural relationships between foreign rulers and local citizens, and between metropols and colonies? The diversity of episodes that Italian history offers on this subject is staggering. On the one hand, republics such as Genoa and Venice are interesting case studies of nascent Italian imperialism emerging from the mercantile culture of the late Middle Ages. On the other hand, regions such as Lombardy, Naples, and Sicily are fascinating examples of Spanish imperialism within Europe, preceded variously by Arabic, Norman, Angevin, and Aragonese rule.[51] This project, yet to be fully realized, is surely one of the important subjects that will require more than the work of a single scholar to complete. Interestingly, the study of Italian rural society—a project of similar scope and ambition—is much further advanced at this stage than the study of Italy's foreign relations.[52] Cities may be Italy's best historical laboratory, but the continued strength of Italian rural history indicates that this subject will have its place in any new history of Italy that might emerge in the next decade. One can only hope that the same will be true for the study of Italy as a central part of understanding its strategic position between northern Europe and the Mediterranean.

An expanded sense of Italy's geography would surely include greater attention to Fernand Braudel's image of Italy as the centerpiece of the Mediterranean. His classic definition of the Mediterranean as "a series of regions isolated from one another, yet trying to make contact with one another" suggests a premise that is applicable to comparative research within Italy and in proximity to it. Italian history is full of many moments in which we can see truly different societies interacting with each other—French, Spanish, German, English, Turkish, Greek, and Slavic encounters, conflicts, and coexistence with the inhabitants of the Italian states. In 1480, for example, the Ottoman Turks briefly captured Otranto. For the next few decades, the Venetian Republic periodically gained control of this city on the eastern edge of the Kingdom of Naples, a strategic outpost in the struggle for control of the Adriatic.[53] Such episodes underscore the importance of Italy as a meeting point for many parts of the world.

A final layer of our imaginary topographical map might include an accounting of Italy's relationships with the rest of the world, more complex in the medieval and early modern period than in almost any period since the demise of the Roman empire. The implicit interest of this project is surely one of the reasons Venice has replaced Florence as the collective project of the current generation. Led by scholars such as Edward Muir, Guido Ruggiero, James Grubb, Dennis Romano, John Martin, and Robert Davis, many of whom write in the shadow of Frederic Lane's magisterial *Venice: A Maritime Republic* (1973), Venice has become the focal point of a great deal of late medieval and early modern Italian history.[54]

The new prominence of Venice is an obvious by-product of the fact that it has always stood next to Florence and Rome as the city that most fascinated foreign scholars; the generation that studied Florence has been replaced by the one that studies Venice. Interest in Venice has brought new kinds of historiographic concern to bear on Italian history; it is an obvious point of departure for historians who wish to reclaim Italy's Mediterranean history. A republic of many ethnicities and religions—populated by citizens, territorial subjects, foreign traders, and Eastern slaves—Venice was the epitome of a Christian society on the edge of a marginally Catholic world. The full history of Venice, as an empire rather than a city, has yet to be written, but when it appears it will certainly offer one of the best case studies for a more Mediterranean account of Italy.

Between the Middle Ages and the Reformation

Comparisons exist across time as well as space. One important question of Italian history concerns the relationship between the medieval and the early modern eras. Historians have long been of two minds on this vexed question. Needless to say, it is a remarkably convenient fact to discover that the period one studies is absolutely autonomous from anything that preceded or followed it. A classic Burckhardtian account of the Italian Renaissance demanded this sort of separation, though Burckhardt himself was somewhat ambivalent about the differences between the Middle Ages and the Renaissance, and the Renaissance and the Reformation. Each era, like the arc of a pendulum, obliterated the path of its predecessor and was compelled to do this over and over again. Benedetto Croce's influential explanation of the Baroque era as the beginning of Italy's age of decadence offered a new account of the inevitability of such movements, presenting the early modern era as an embarrassing episode of stagnation and Italian decline filling the void between the Renaissance and the Risorgimento.

As long as the idea of the Renaissance dominated the historical work of Anglo-American scholars, there seemed little reason to offer a strong retort to this overly schematic view of the past.[55] Many historians simply ignored the issue entirely. David Herlihy's *Medieval and Renaissance Pistoia: The Social History of an Italian Town, 1200–1430* (1967) and William Bowsky's *A Medieval Italian Commune: Siena Under the Nine, 1287–1355* (1981) assumed that the emergence of the late medieval commune was one of the crucial stages in the growth of the Renaissance city. Italian historians, perhaps more than historians of other parts of Europe, argued *de facto* for continuity in their research, even as they participated in debates about the status of the Renaissance. We might say that they voted with their documents.

There are new reasons to explore the problem of periodization. They emerge from the relationship between the Middle Ages and the Reformation rather than the relationship between the Middle Ages and the Renaissance. An important trend in the past decade lies in the emergence of the Italian Reformation as a subject of great interest for Anglo-American as well as Italian historians. Many of the latter have considered the Reformation to be a more important watershed in Italian history than the Renaissance.[56] Their studies of the institutional church, local religious organizations, lay spirituality, inquisitorial practices, and heresy have finally gained the attention of more than a handful of foreign scholars in the past decade.[57] By contrast, foreign scholars have devoted considerably less effort to understanding Italian Catholicism. As perhaps the only phenomenon that truly linked all the regions of Italy, at least by the late Middle Ages and certainly in the century following the Council of Trent, this oversight is all the more surprising. It is a sign of how effectively the fascination with the Renaissance, and with key questions of social, political, and cultural history, have made the problem of faith less compelling than it ought to have been.

The patterns of religiosity observed in Italy are by no means exclusively Italian, but they are generally Catholic. Yet we can observe numerous ways in which the distinctiveness of Italian life contributed to the kind of religious beliefs, practices, and institutions evident in medieval and early modern Italy. "Do not think of me as a man of Assisi," proclaimed St. Francis in the piazza of Perugia.[58] One suspects that it was impossible for people to forget that he was a citizen of this small Umbrian town, even as he preached a universal message of faith. In a world in which every city cultivated its local preachers and patron saints, the close identification between religious and urban values was very important indeed.[59]

The Italian religious landscape is a fascinating arena of research because of the wealth of evidence documenting the interrelations between social, political, and religious institutions in the urban and rural communes. Medieval bishops participated openly in the struggle for power in many Italian cities, erecting palaces to rival the buildings of the communes and the magnates, and finding other means to claim their prerogatives. The rural monastery was rarely a world apart, but often entangled in messy jurisdictional disputes about property and inheritance that illuminate the nature of the rural commune as much as convent life. Confraternities organized lay religious life and charitable giving. Mendicant preachers sought to mold social values with their words. "Living saints" enjoyed privileged status and access to authorities.[60] Madonnas did not bless every street corner in Italy, but they appeared with enough frequency in a variety of Italian cities to have us believe that the Italian sense of the sacred created a spirituality sensitive to the secular features of their world.[61]

One important example of this phenomenon returns us to definition of the Italian city. Early celebrations of Italian urban life often did not describe the brilliance of the cities as a function of an urban patriciate or a specific form of politics. The city was not a gloriously secular creation, *pace* Burckhardt, or a revival of Roman republican virtues as Leonardo Bruni emphasized in the fifteenth century, but a community of the faithful organized around its bishop. This medieval image of the city did not disappear in the early modern period. Instead, it underwent a revival. In the age of Tridentine reform, the bishop played a prominent role in restoring civil and moral order, just as he had helped to bring the idea of the city as a Christian community into being in the Middle Ages. Many cities rediscovered the virtues of their patron saints in an era of renewed religiosity.[62] Botero's Milan, in other words, was the pride of its archbishop, Carlo Borromeo, and his successors, who believed it to be a model Christian community—a legacy of the Italian reforming bishops who had attempted to return many Italian cities to their gloriously Christian past. Recent work in Italian urban and religious history has made it possible to see the relations between medieval and early modern Italian cities, making the Italian response to the Reformation more comprehensible in light of preceding religious activities.

Religious history is another arena in which historians have renewed their appreciation for the study of smaller communities. Rieti, Orvieto, and Verona have been important sites for some of the most recent studies of medieval religious life.[63] The rural communities of Naples and Friuli have proved especially rich terrain for the study of heresy.[64] Some of the most interesting episodes of faith did not occur at the centers of power, but in proximity to large cities such as Rome and Venice. Inadvertently, renewed interest in Italian religious history has done a great deal to move us beyond a familiar geography.

Religious history raises the question of continuity in a distinctive way. The Catholic Church is perhaps the most continuous institution of medieval and early modern Italy. Governments came and went, but the papacy, the bishops, and the monasteries remained—hardly a static presence, since they were not themselves immune to change, but they were nonetheless relatively stable features in a shifting landscape. Catholic beliefs and practices created a shared sense of tradition among many Italians—a cultural resource that grew only more important in the post-Reformation era. Just as Renaissance humanists claimed to find the origins of their political and cultural practices in the Graeco-Roman past, post-Tridentine reformers discovered the importance of late antiquity and the Middle Ages as a historical era offering important precedents for their definition of early modern Catholicism.

Understanding the early modern origins of medieval studies is a subject that has yet to receive adequate attention. Petrarch may have invented the idea of the Dark Ages, but it was figures such as Cesare Baronio and Federico Borromeo who made the Middle Ages a truly historical concept, out of their desire to establish a foundation for a reformed Catholicism in light of a fragmented Christian world. They wrote of the Christian past, uncovered its archeological remains, and restored its churches.[65] Without the early modern interest in late antique and medieval Christianity, it is arguable that very little of it would have survived for modern historians to ponder. This aspect of Italian religious history makes the desirability of examining medieval and early modern history together even more apparent.

What would the history of Italy look like if its medieval, Renaissance, and early modern features were considered together, not just synchronically but diachronically? Local archival research cannot answer this question. Perhaps we are in danger nowadays of becoming victims of our own industriousness in finding new case studies everywhere without asking ourselves more critically how they effect the larger themes of the period that we study. Inviting historians to step outside their archives and place their findings next to each other, as edited volumes often do, is only a first step toward exploring some of these questions. Burckhardt's insistence on the history of Italy as a history of the whole might be a good starting point for a broader discussion. The field of Italian social history is ripe for the sort of new methodological innovations that animated it in the 1970s and 1980s. It is also ready to make some of the implicit categories of scholarship in the past two decades explicit criteria for a new synthesis.

PART II

City and Countryside

Town and *countryside* imply a simple dichotomy. Yet each study in this section makes clear that the dichotomy is inaccurate. The relationship of town to country, or of the individual to either, is never simple or straightforward.

Samuel Cohn shows that the debate over exploitation of the *contado*, or countryside surrounding and controlled by a particular town, has largely been misconceived. Florence, Cohn notes, did not treat surrounding territories as cut from a single cloth. Those who lived close to the city generally were treated no more harshly than the townsmen themselves. Exploitation and oppression were issues in the mountains on the edge of the state. It was in the mountains that Cohn finds hints of an unrecorded civil war that forced the commune to lighten the burden of oppressed countrymen. Along with heightened awareness of the countryman's plight, there came a clearer sense that all of the countryside had to be integrated into a unified territorial state.

Perhaps a hundred years earlier, the isolated world of the Mugello was slowly drawn into the Florentine economic and social world. Where Cohn emphasized the role of the state, Dameron discusses the role of ecclesiastical institutions and elite families. Both expanded their influence outward from Florence by buying lands and jurisdictions. By the early fourteenth century, the Age of Dante, the isolated rural world of the Mugello had been tied firmly to Florence.

The issue of town and countryside played out otherwise as one moves away from Florence, away from this growing economic and political power. Duane Osheim shows how parish communities in parts of the Lucchese countryside could have profoundly differing relationships to the city. At a distance from the city, in strategic areas bordering on Pisan and

Florentine lands, the bishop and commune of Lucca had to tread lightly. The parishes of Lucca were never to be fully integrated into a territorial state like that being created at Florence.

It was not just rural communities that had a complex relationship to the Italian town and city. The ubiquitous Franciscans also challenge a simple view of urban identity. As Robert Brentano notes, Francis and his friars reject identification with their home towns. Their missionary activities, on the other hand, contributed to the development of strong urban identities. Even as the friars moved through Italy, Brentano concludes that they "thought in terms of cities."

All the chapters in Part II underline the importance of geographical difference and economic, political, and religious experiences in forming the connection of individual to town and countryside.

City and Countryside TUSCANY

CHAPTER THREE

The Other Florence Within Florence

Samuel K. Cohn, Jr.

Florence has been at the center of several major debates in late-medieval Italian historiography, in which historians of other Italian city-states have begun with the Florentine debate to frame their own arguments before embarking on their local evidence. One of these debates concerns the relationship between city and countryside.[1] Briefly, in the early years of the twentieth century, Romolo Caggese argued that the relationship between Florence and its contado was wholly exploitative; Florence taxed to the bone its rural dependents.[2] Fifty years later, Enrico Fiumi contested this view with more archival rigor. In place of oppression and conflict, he saw Florence's tax policy toward its contado as benign, arguing that it taxed its own citizens more severely than those from the countryside. Although Fiumi's argument extended to the fifteenth century, his evidence focused on the period before the Black Death.[3] In the 1960s through 1980s, Marvin Becker, Anthony Molho, David Herlihy, and Christiane Klapisch-Zuber[4] attacked Fiumi's picture of Florentine city-country relations, in one case calling it "little short of idyllic."[5] But their evidence focused on the post-plague period. With Judith Brown, the pendulum swung back to the other side. By viewing in detail one place within the hinterland—Pescia—she argued that the relationship between the dominant city, Florence, and its region was symbiotic, benefiting both center and periphery.[6] Her most compelling evidence came, however, from the much later period of the Florentine Grand Duchy and not from the later Trecento and early Quattrocento. More recently, historians have again stressed Florence's exploitation of its territory, such that its efforts proved counterproductive both economically[7] and politically.[8] But these works also have failed to draw conclusions about this relationship over time.

This chapter has been drawn largely from Cohn (1999); for further evidence and elaboration, the reader should turn to that book.

The one striking exception is Becker's work on the rise of the "Florentine territorial state." Although it accepted Fiumi's thesis for the period before the Black Death, it saw in the formation of the funded debt (*Monte*) in 1345 a new departure in Florence's taxes and in its relation with the contado.[9] Before this cardinal date, Florentine governance in the city and the territory was marked by a "gentle paedeia" (or cultural ideal); afterward, policy turned increasingly toward bureaucratic control and governmental severity. But for the long period from 1345 to perhaps the end of the Florentine republic, Becker marked no further changes. The Milanese wars, the Florentine catasto of 1427, the rise of the Medici, and shifts with the Laurentian oligarchy did not register a shift in the fundamental paths of political strategy set in motion and necessitated by Florence's state debt, which began its inexorable rise on the eve of the Black Death.

Does this long history from the Black Death to the end of the republic constitute a single historical period? Second, was it a question of a simple dichotomy—city versus the countryside—as historians have assumed, or did Florence treat its territory, even its traditional contado, in a differentiated manner? Finally, in assessing the exploitation of the countryside, this debate has concentrated on questions of fiscality, employing mainly fiscal records.[10] Can this debate be widened to other areas of dominance and incorporation using other archival records?

To consider whether Florence's contado constituted an "other" Florence, separate and even in opposition to the interests of the city's ruling oligarchy, this chapter begins with matters of fiscality but fans out to consider the wider spectrum of social, political, juridical, and even moral interactions between the city of Florence and its territory. It does so by tapping the rich resources of its day-to-day legislative deliberations, called the *provvisioni*.[11]

Curiously, the city-countryside debate has not concentrated on the period from the Black Death through the Medicean republic, that is, at the very moment when the fiscal records of Florence take off. From 1348 to 1495, at least twelve fiscal surveys survive more or less intact from the countryside. A quantitative study of these records shows clearly that before the reforms of the catasto of 1427 Florence did not treat its surrounding countryside as though cut from a single cloth. Instead, its fiscal policies illuminate a mosaic of fiscal communities whose connections with the city differed drastically from Florence's privileged suburbs to its mountainous extremities. Indeed, throughout the second half of the fourteenth and early fifteenth centuries, communities such as Santa Lucia Ognissanti *fuori le mura*, whose members attended churches located within the city but whose districts lay outside the city walls, experienced the symbiotic relationship with the city and the favorable fiscal treatment that Fiumi generalized for the entire contado, mostly before the Black Death. For those periods, when both the *estimo* surveys and the city's final tax or *Lira* registers survive, this suburban parish was assessed less than 0.5 percent of its villagers' estimated wealth, which meant that even in times of war before the crisis years of the 1390s, this parish rarely was forced to pay more than 1 percent per annum of its wealth in direct taxes.

Even at the end of the century, after Florence had raised rates by a multiple of more than twelve times what they had been during the previous decade,[12] the burden placed on Santa Lucia and other parishes within the surrounding plains of Quarto, Sesto, and Campi still was hardly crushing. As a consequence, unlike other villages further afield and at higher altitudes, the lowland communities surrounding Florence are not found in the *Libri fabarum* or the *Provvisioni* lamenting the hard times of the 1390s, nor do they appear in the opening years of the fifteenth century with long lists of unpaid taxes stretching back to those troubled years.

Yet the historian can hardly generalize from these lowland parishes close to the city. Further from the city, and particularly on the highland fringes of the Florentine territory, the story was woefully different. From the 1370s to the turn of the century, Florence increasingly placed an unequal burden on these communities. By the time of the Albizzi reforms in 1393, highland communes such as Mangona in the Mugello's *prope Alpes* were charged on their assessed wealth twenty-nine times more than that charged on equal values in the suburban parish of Santa Lucia next to the city walls. With the Milanese war escalating and Florence's desperate need for revenue, the parishes of Mangona were required to hand over 44 percent of their wealth annually by 1395 in direct taxes alone. Nor was this a single, extraordinary year; matters grew worse through the remaining years of the decade, reaching their pinnacle with a new *estimo* and the peak in the direct tax coefficients in 1401.

The years at the turn of the century were, however, a watershed in Florence's fiscal policies toward its hinterland. Despite increasing fiscal pressure that continued to mount through the early years of the fifteenth century, Florence began to lessen the burden it placed on the contado, particularly on the highland communes on or near its northern frontiers, then the principal theatre of warfare with Milan, Bologna, and its own peasantry. From 1402 to the catasto of 1427, the tax inequality between the mountains and the plains lessened at the same time that the coefficients and rates based on the *estimo* declined. In 1427, Florence's rulers brought to a conclusion a process that had begun a quarter of a century earlier: in place of a fiscal mosaic of different and unequal tax rates, now all communities within Florence's contado were charged direct taxes at the same rate and according to the same principles. Indeed, first discussions of such a "universal tax" come to light in the debates of Florence's highest offices, the Consulte e Pratiche in 1402.[13]

Why had Florence's oligarchy changed its mind toward fiscal policy and the well-being of its rural subjects, particularly toward those along the northern mountainous fringes? First, the tax records themselves show that the Florentine highlanders had been staging a silent tax revolt through the 1390s. As marginal comments reveal, peasant families had fled perfectly good farms in the 1390s to escape Florence's mounting taxation. Quantitatively, the sources reveal that the demographic decline of these supertaxed mountain communities was more extreme after 1348 than in the plague year itself and that the most serious decline occurred in the 1390s and early years of the fifteenth century. Politics more than pestilence was the cause of this abandonment of the countryside.

Immediately after the Black Death, the Commune of Mangona, for instance, possessed more than 220 families and perhaps as many as a thousand individuals. But by 1402, Mangona's numbers had dropped to 86 families and 278 persons, and in 1412 it was cut in half again, declining to 47 families and 138 individuals—thus now possessing only one-fifth of the numbers recorded even after the onslaught of 1348.[14] Neighboring Montecarelli's decline was even sharper, and villages further north in the Alpi Fiorentine such as S. Paolo a Castiglione appear momentarily to have ceased to exist. Moreover, these mountain peasants did not migrate downward to supposedly greener valleys close to the city but instead upward and out of the Florentine contado altogether, leaving the Florentine state with a lower tax base and their own former villagers with heavier fiscal debts. At the same time, valley communities near the city remained relatively stable in the second half of the fifteenth century.[15]

By 1402, highland peasants across the northern and eastern frontiers of the Florentine state, from the Montagna di Pistoia to the Aretine Pratomagno, united with Florence's enemies—the Milanese war captains and Florence's feudal families—and thus turned a silent revolt into armed combat. Although only obliquely recorded by contemporary chroniclers and diarists, these insurrections dredged a well-formed path through the judicial records and the city's *provvisioni*. The first of these sources lists by name and village a far greater number of insurgents from 1402 to 1404 than all those condemned a generation earlier in the more famous urban revolt of the Ciompi. These rural insurgents, mostly peasants with middle-size holdings, were sentenced not only for following their feudal lords or Milanese captains but also for planning and leading sieges such as the bombardment of Florence's northern frontier bastion, the town of Firenzuola, for capturing old feudal castles such as the Castel di Pagnano near Susinana, and for building new ones on mountain peaks above Firenzuola and in the Podere Fiorentino.

The second of these sources, the *provvisioni*, show that the insurgents were not suppressed by Florentine might, as the few chroniclers who deigned to mention these events claimed and as the long death-sentence lists might suggest. Instead, the peasant ringleaders won major concessions for themselves and their communities—license to carry weapons freely throughout the territory of Florence, sinecures as officers of the Florentine state, rights to select who would be permitted to return to their villages without government reprisals, and perpetual immunities from all forms of taxation for the leaders and tax exemptions that endured as long as fifteen years for communities as a whole.

Between 1403 and 1405, the Florentine *provvisioni* explode with acts of negotiation and special concessions granted to Florence's rural inhabitants, mostly from the contado, and mostly from villages above five hundred meters in altitude. The normal case loads that came before the city's *Tre Maggiori* (highest chambers) and its two legislative councils—mostly urban matters, such as bankruptcies, pleas for lowering citizens' taxes (*prestanze*), elections to special committees, appointments to a post in the territory, and even how much to feed the town's lions—had to be temporarily pushed aside to consider these petitions and negotiations from the countryside. In these three years alone, Florence bestowed tax exemptions and cancellations of public debts to 282 villages. But by the end of 1405, this legislative business had returned more or less to the levels witnessed before the crisis of 1402. Had these insurrections and their successful petitions been only a momentary blip on the surface of history without long-term consequences for the city's relations with its territory?

As we have seen, 1402 was a major turning point in the history of Florentine fiscal policy toward its territory. In addition, a systematic study of Florence's wider policies toward its territory (found in the laws, decrees, and petitions approved in the *provvisioni*) shows that the oligarchy's perception of its territory changed fundamentally after 1402. Before this date, the pleas that made it through Florence's bureaucratic rungs show the city acting as a tributary state, interested in its contado for the supply of produce and tax revenue and as a buffer zone, protecting Florentine citizens from foreign military incursions. From the Black Death to 1402, the major reason Florence answered rural pleas for tax relief depended on war-related issues and frontier defense. Even in these cases, Florence did not remedy the misery and weakness of its countrymen by rescheduling tax assessment, granting tax exemptions, or canceling private or public debt. Instead, its usual grant of "mercy" was only "to convert" some of the taxes of hard-hit communities toward partial payments of repairs to village defenses or for building new castles and bulwarks. In these years, Florence also initiated major castle construction within its territory at Prato, Scarperia, Firenzuola, Figline, and Castellina and devised new rural taxes for funding these projects that ran as high as 20,000 florins.

A comparison between the pleas that won governmental approval before and after 1402 shows an earlier deafening silence in Florence's willingness to relieve the misery of its rural population or to stem the tide of its territory's depopulation. First and foremost among these silences was the Black Death and the subsequent plagues of the latter half of the fourteenth century, which were stated as the cause for governmental clemency and fiscal relief. In 1348, only one community successfully gained a hearing before the councils on the basis of arguments of the plague's massive toll in population. On September 12, 1348, the Commune of Mangona sought clemency from the heavy fines Florence had charged for missing its last payments on an 1,800 florin land deal made with Florence in December 1345. Mangona's syndics pleaded that the plague had hit their commune particularly severely, that three-quarters or more of its population had been wiped out; those who remained believed that "everyone was about to die." The local syndics argued that the commune had missed its May and July payments because the plague left no one with any memory of the commune's obligations, and that because of the loss of population it would be most difficult if not impossible to pay the May and October installments for 1348, much less the penalties that had been added on to them. But despite the catastrophic consequences of 1348, the government answered Mangona's pleas only in part, absolving the fines but demanding that their Black Death installments be paid in full.[16]

Nor did the government's sympathies toward its territory change with the recurrence of plague. No petitions succeeded in conjunction with the minor plagues reported by either Matteo Villani or Marchionne di Coppo Stefani in the late 1350s or, more astoundingly, for the plague of 1363. It was not until the plague years 1374–75 that a rural petition won governmental approval by citing the plague and its destruction of a community's tax base. Even for these years, the plague alone does not arise as the crucial reason for the government to grant relief. Unlike earlier plagues, this one was the first to present all four horsemen of the apocalypse acting in concert; in particular, it was war that was stressed as the principal reason for government relief. Moreover, all those villages that won governmental subsidies were within the upper Mugello, Alpi Fiorentine, Podere Fiorentino, and Romagna Fiorentina—the regions then bearing the brunt of foreign invasions. With the plague of 1383, the provvisioni return to silence. Nor did the outbreaks of influenza in 1386 that devastated mountain communities in the Casentino[17] win concession from the Florentine State. General relief for the Florentine contado as a whole came only in the aftermath of the plague of 1400, when Florence granted a month's extension on the September salt taxes and the ordinary *estimo* to every village in the contado.[18]

Although the plagues took a far heavier toll on the population of Tuscany in both town and countryside in the latter half of the fourteenth century than they did in the early fifteenth century,[19] nearly two-thirds of the petitions that won governmental relief by citing the plague as the cause of need came in the thirty-three years after 1402. In other words, they were won after the plague of 1400—the last plague to inflict devastating mortality levels in Tuscany until at least the middle of the fifteenth century. Per annum, the results are even more surprising: after 1402, successful peasant petitions citing plague almost trebled their earlier appearance during the plague-ridden second half of the Trecento, when plague was more frequent, was more virulent, and accounted for a far higher level of mortality.[20]

To judge by contemporary chronicles and estimates made from tax records and other sources for demographic growth and decline, none of the plagues between 1402 and 1434 was comparable to the devastation wrought by plague in 1348, 1363, 1374, 1383, or 1400. Indeed, only one or two plagues stand out for special mention at all in contemporary accounts between 1402 and 1434, the plague of 1417 and perhaps 1424. Yet between 1409 and 1432, at least one petition in all but five years won government relief by claiming that plague was the source of a village's misery. Moreover, twenty-nine of thirty-three petitions that won government concession because of plague did so for reasons of plague alone and its demographic consequences, not because disease happened to have coincided with military invasion (as with almost all of the pre-1402 plague petitions). As a result, after 1402 successful plague petitions moved from the war-weary villages along Florence's northern frontier toward the more protected hills and plains of the contado's center.

Many of these so-called plagues were certainly not of epidemic proportions; many may have been localized diseases of the sort that had brought populations in check throughout the preindustrial past—food poisoning, cholera, yellow fever, smallpox, typhoid, and other illnesses.[21] Yet the significance of such minor plagues in peasant petitions should not lead us to conclude that diseases other than "true plague" were becoming more rampant in the countryside after 1402. If anything, the Black Death may have created new immunities to other bacteria or viruses; diseases such as leprosy appear to have been on the decline—perhaps, as some historians have speculated, as a result of the Black Death. The decline in the frequency and mortality due to the Black Death coupled with rising standards of living (at least by the Estimo of 1412) was making Tuscany a healthier place to live than it had been in the darker days of the late Trecento.[22] What had changed was the Florentine oligarchy's sensitivity to the well-being of its rural inhabitants and the demographic fragility of the countryside.

In the petitions after 1402, peasants often made their positions clear: if their complaints were not met with tax relief and cancellation of public debts, they would simply abandon Florence for foreign lands. For example, in 1415, the small parish of San Bartolomeo de Corbinaria complained that its salt tax was too high, given the number left in the village. Instead of referring to the usual reasons for a sharp decline in population—warfare, brigandage, destruction of crops, death, and capture for ransom—the village syndics criticized Florence directly, blaming its onerous obligations, both public and private, for the village's troubles: "it is for these reasons that so many men had been forced to leave their village." They further threatened that if their injuries were not redressed, the rest of them who remained in the village would leave."[23] Such threats can be found in sixty-eight (more than 16 percent) of the petitions that made it through the Signoria's scrutiny and were voted through from 1403 to 1434; beforehand they can be found in only 5 percent of the petitions (26 of 485).

In the same vein, if one were to use the *provvisioni* as a guide to the occurrence of natural disasters, the latter half of the fourteenth century would appear as a rare and blessed moment of climatic calm. Before 1402, petitions that managed to reach the councils show peasants complaining of crop failures and poor harvests only in conjunction with military disaster and their need to rebuild fortifications. Not a single petition won tax relief by pointing to a hailstorm or inclement weather as a cause of its misery. By contrast, after 1402, peasant communities ranging from as close to the city as the villages of Sesto and those around Monte Morello to the far-flung corners of the Romagna Fiorentina and Chianti borders with Siena reported the widespread devastation of hailstorms that ruined crops and made daily life with unrevised taxes an impossibility, according to the peasant petitioners.[24] Yet descriptions of inclement weather found in the chroniclers Matteo Villani, Stefani, and the pseudo-Minerbetti suggest that God had not been so benevolent in sparing Florentine Tuscany from the scourge of climatic disaster between 1347 and 1402, only to redouble His wrath after 1402. What had changed was not the weather but, again, the attitudes of Florence's ruling elites toward their rural subjects.

The only natural disaster reported in successful peasant and small townsmen's pleas before 1402 was flooding, perhaps because as in Signa, Settimo, Empoli, and San Giovanni Valdarno these disasters did more than simply impoverish Florence's rural subjects; on occasion, they washed away parts of town walls and caused fortifications to collapse. Nonetheless, before 1402 the councils did not heed such petitions with moratoria on tax payments, rescheduling of gabelles, or exemption from other taxes. Instead, in case after case, the government answered these desperate pleas by merely establishing special committees of "wise citizens of Florence" to study the damages, resolve property disputes caused by rivers changing course, and determine who among the villages and the surrounding zones would be taxed to pay for the damages, especially those to fortifications. After 1402, the government's response changed; such petitions demanded and received extensions on tax payments, five-year exemptions from *estimi* and gabelles, and the immediate lowering of taxes.

Even more significant than the change in the Florentine government's reasons for granting relief to its territorial subjects was a change in what its peasants could expect to win from the hands of their urban lords. Before 1402, peasants who found themselves in desperate straits, unable to pay their taxes (usually because of war), won concessions only grudgingly. As we have seen, the most common governmental act of clemency was directly connected with governmental military strategy and the defense of the realm. Rather than outright remission of debts, reduction of taxes, or immunities, the government allowed the communities to convert their taxes into maintaining or building new fortifications, provided these tasks were completed according to government guidelines and within restricted deadlines. Sixteen percent of the government's concessions to successful petitions from the hinterland before 1402 were of this sort, where a community's taxes remained the same but were shifted from one account in the Florentine treasury to another.

Next in importance came governmental absolution of communitywide condemnations (14 percent of the petitions),[25] followed by absolution of fines for not paying taxes, rents, and other fees to the government on time (9 percent). Yet in these cases, similar to conversion of taxes for fortifications, the government refused to redefine the village's tax structure or debts that had brought the stricken community into debt in the first place. Measures that actually reduced the community's public debts and taxes remained rare before 1402. Afterward, the picture changed, and these three most important remedies to peasants' pleas of the latter half of the fourteenth century sank to negligible proportions.

In their place, four categories of governmental clemency rose to the forefront after 1402 that previously had put in only a rare appearance. Unlike a makeshift response that did nothing to alter rural subjects' obligations to the Florentine treasury, all four of these new governmental remedies changed fundamentally the community's debt or tax structure. In the early years of the fifteenth century, the government answered the pleas of peasants and subject townsmen by cutting their administrative costs; these constituted 10 percent of the post-1402 acts of Florentine clemency, as opposed to only 3 percent earlier.[26] First and foremost among these costs was the expense of maintaining public order—the large salaries and expenses paid to Florentine officers of the peace, from the captains in the larger subject cities to the *vicarii* (officers) and podestà of rural regions, along with their bevy of notaries, soldiers, and horses. Second, 11 percent of the post-1402 petitions[27] won government action to recalculate and reduce gabelle or *estimo* assessments. Such reduction and realignment even touched the salt tax—a sacred cow of the Florentine commune. Although this tax was based on the number of "mouths" in a community, before 1402 the government refused to adjust this tax to reflect new demographic realities even after the devastations incurred by plagues and wars. The first petition to reduce the salt quotas a community was forced to consume came only in 1403.[28]

Third, the number of immunities from taxes, usually for five years, trebled after 1402. Moreover, before 1402 these grants were seldom renewed, and in no case was an immunity renewed more than once; afterward—for impoverished and war-torn communities such as Foiano, at the vortex of foreign invasions; and the Isle of Giglio, which was, according to its petitions, continually hammered by Barbary pirates and the Genoese navy—such immunity was renewed with almost automatic regularity from the early years of the century to the end of my survey in 1434.

The most significant change in the appeals from the territory, however, regards reduction or cancellation of public debts on past taxes, fines, and fees. Such solutions to peasant misery and their threat to leave the Florentine hinterland amounted to more than 40 percent of petitions after 1402. Moreover, these reductions show a qualitative change as well. Before 1402, when the government gave its *"misericordia et gratia,"* or mercy and concessions, to peasant communes burdened by debt, its clemency nonetheless usually treated the debts as inviolate, canceling only the heavy fines attached to them and often giving the indebted commune no more than ten days to pay them off. Afterward, such debts were reduced significantly and the remainder transferred to Florence's funded debt, or Monte.

Such a solution to the indebtedness of the hinterland strengthened the sense in which these communities were incorporated into the city of Florence's fiscal universe. Instead of being hammered for these back payments in the face of rising taxes to be divided among a shrinking population, the indebted community was now faced with paying off only the interest on the principal, at a low rate of 5 percent to the Monte—much lower than that charged by private bankers and money lenders. Such an incorporation during the early fifteenth century reversed the territory's (and primarily the contado's) place within Florentine finances since the Monte's foundation in 1345. It was the contado's direct taxes combined with payments from the gabelles that offset Florence's ever-growing mountain of debt and made possible from time to time redemption of its shares to Florence's privileged urban elites at a handsome rate of interest.[29] After 1402, peasants were no longer only on the paying side of the Monte; in their petitions, protests, and threats to abandon the Florentine state they now also swung to the receiving end as the Monte stepped in to relieve them of their debts and fiscal misery. If not in title, then in effect *contadini* had become shareholders in the Florentine State.

Once again, 1402 and the successful peasant revolts on Florence's mountainous frontiers had been the dividing line in the attempt to incorporate its hinterland into a new sense of a regional state, or "territorium," as humanist legists began to call it at the turn of the century.[30] In addition to equalizing and lowering taxes in the contado during the early fifteenth century, Florence looked on a wide range of peasant problems with greater sympathy and generosity. Such a change in governmental attitude paralleled a shift in the geographical distribution of villages that won tax remission after the first wave of peasant revolts. From the military hot spots on or near Florence's frontiers, successful petitions spread across its agricultural heartland to parishes often of little fiscal or military importance, such as the tiny parish of San Bartolomeo de Corbinaria cited earlier.

This process of territorial incorporation broke the mosaic of community inequalities, blurred the line between the contado and districtus, and standardized justice and jurisprudence through a large swath of the territory,[31] but it also had repressive consequences for Florence's subjects in the hinterland. As seen in the debates of the Consulte e Pratiche and prosecutions in the criminal acts of the new vicariates of Pisa, the Valdarno Superiore, Anghiari, and other places in the hills and mountains of Arezzo, incorporation was accompanied by a new Florentine zeal to bring these communities under its sense of law, devotion, and *buon costume*.[32] As the criminal records of the new vicariate courts of the early fifteenth century make clear, these "good customs" were often sexual. Increasingly, the Florentine police entered the bedrooms of mountain dwellers, using force, torture, and mutilation to repress practices and relationships it found *contra naturam*.³³ By 1416, local mountain statutes even required election of secret guards (*guardie segrete*) to fine those "who cursed and blasphemed the Lord or saints."³⁴ This desire to control and force Florence's subjects into behavioral conformity was intensified in 1429 with the creation of a new tribunal, the *Conservatori delle leggi*, which passed new laws prosecuting crimes of blasphemy, gambling and card games, luxury consumption, and "crimes of the night."³⁵

Thus, although Florence insisted that every new subject community make its own laws, it also approached Leonardo Bruni's dream that all people subject to Florence live under the same laws (although, it must be added, not with the same resources and advantages).³⁶ This stamp of unity can be seen symbolically as well in Florence's early fifteenth-century campaign to plaster or paint its insignia of the lion (Marzocco) in the square of every major village and town within its territory.³⁷ Although the archival records do not cite a single incident of an attack against this symbol of Florentine pride in the waves of insurrection from 1401 to 1404, with the tax revolts that spread through the Casentino mountains in 1426 such attacks had become the first stage of insurrectionary violence.³⁸

On the other hand, the change in Florentine clemency toward the peasantry, particularly within the traditional contado, shows that the waves of peasant revolt of 1402 had a lasting impact on the mentality and policy of the Florentine elites, despite their eradication of these events in public histories and private memoirs. By 1403, the territory's welfare had become intertwined with the well-being of the city in a way that was absent from the ruling elites' calculations in the mid to late Trecento. The Florentine contado of the latter half of the fourteenth century now was integrated into Florence's new sense of its state and territory as "imperium."³⁹ Its otherness was transformed. It was a transformation resulting not simply from the designs of a ruling center on a passive periphery. Instead, peasant revolts on the mountainous margins of the Florentine state were the spur of change.

CHAPTER FOUR

A World of Its Own

Economy, Society, and Religious Life in the Tuscan Mugello at the Time of Dante

George Dameron

Two related issues continue to fascinate historians of premodern Italy: the transition from the medieval commune to the early modern regional (or territorial) state, and the nature of the relationship between city and countryside.[1] Scholars now recognize that throughout Italy the political and economic physiognomies of the regional state varied tremendously. For example, urban subjugation of the countryside was more complete in the Po Valley and north central Tuscany than it was in the regions of central Italy. In the Alpine north, communities were able successfully to resist territorial integration because they were often the location of a strong ecclesiastical or secular principality. In the past, historians have tended to characterize the relations between city and countryside as either symbiotic or exploitative. Today many scholars portray those connections as organic and reciprocal, which usually benefited the former at the expense of the latter. The close ties linking city and countryside, coupled with the unbroken historical presence of the city in both the medieval and early modern periods, distinguished north and central Italy from the lands north of the Alps.[2]

In Tuscany, for some communes like Arezzo and Lucca, the subjugation of the surrounding contado (countryside) by the city was virtually complete by the early thirteenth century. At Florence, where there were relatively fewer urban landowners in the countryside before 1300, the process of subjugation took longer.[3] Nevertheless, the Florentine city-state has served as a model of a coherent, well-organized, and powerful political entity, where urban landholders dominated the immediate countryside from at least the end of the thirteenth century.[4] Today, however, the late medieval Florentine territorial state seems much less cohesive and integrated than it did a generation ago. Urban magistrates did not apply the same administrative and fiscal policies to every region of the hinterland, and smaller cities such as San Miniato al Tedesco and Colle continued to retain some independence from the Arno city. Furthermore, as Samuel K. Cohn, Jr., has argued, harsh fiscal policies in the \mountainous areas of the contado in the second half of the fourteenth century caused many mountain residents to migrate and turn to violence. Such policies, he has suggested, may have helped generate certain cultural and social traditions as well, including hostility to the state and unique religious customs.[5]

This chapter examines these two historical problems by focusing on a particular case study: a mountain valley in the Apennines in northern Tuscany, the Mugello.[6] Much of the recent research on Tuscany has focused either on the early communal period (eleventh through twelfth centuries) or on the era after the arrival of the Black Death (post-1348). Unfortunately, scholars of late have tended to neglect the thirteenth and early fourteenth centuries. Yet, as Duane Osheim shows in the next chapter, this century and a half can be a fruitful period for exploring community life in medieval Tuscany.

A study of the Mugello can therefore be instructive on a number of levels. First, the focus on these two issues in recent historiography has tended to prevent historians from exploring, recognizing, and understanding distinct traditions and cultures within specific rural localities. The city—its social, economic, and political development in relation to the countryside—has remained a primary area of interest; rural communities and their unique and distinctive traditions tend to be neglected.[7] A study such as this one (with emphasis on a particular rural zone) can suggest reasons some rural communities in Tuscany remained "worlds of their own"—economically, socially, and religiously—well into the fourteenth century. Of central importance to the preservation of local particularities, this chapter argues, though certainly not the only factors, were the presence of several rural territorial lordships, a heritage of resistance to the exercise of urban power, and distinctive ecclesiastical and religious traditions.

Second, even as historians continue to explore the factors that distinguished medieval from early modern Italy, studies such as this one can remind us that there also existed continuity that spanned both periods, such as a tradition of resistance to urban authorities stemming from the early thirteenth century.

Third, we can learn from such a study that relations between the city and the country do not always fit into the neat categories of symbiosis and exploitation. Indeed, the interaction of a city with its hinterland was not uniform or consistent for every region of the contado. The history of a valley like the Mugello demonstrates such a variety of complex relations between urban authorities and country that generalization is difficult. Where integration with Florence was strongest was precisely where urban lords (the bishopric and cathedral chapter) had had long-standing connections: in the central valley and the foothills above it. Paradoxically, however, this was precisely where there had also been a tradition of resistance to the power of those urban lords (especially the bishopric). Though a portion of the Mugello was integrated economically and politically into the urban orbit by 1300, other zones remained distinct, autonomous, and even resistant to urban influence well into the fourteenth century. It was indeed a region *beyond Florence*, in every sense of the word.

Among the principal river valleys of Tuscany, the Mugello is one of the least studied. Located within the dioceses of Florence and Fiesole, it was linked closely to the Romagna, the Casentino, and the Pistoiese. The sources for a study of the Mugello are frustratingly sporadic for the period before 1250, but, as is true for Florentine sources in general, after that date they become numerous.[8] This valley and its tributary streams, enclosed by a continuous circle of mountain ridges and oriented in a northeast to southwest direction, extend about thirty kilometers from the Monti della Calvana in the west to the junction of the Sieve with the Comano, south of Dicomano.

For the three centuries that are the subject of this chapter (1000–1330), the Mugello was economically, strategically, and politically important to the urban elites in Florence. Not only did it serve as a source of grain for the growing city, but it was also the strategic gateway that controlled the several roads linking northern Tuscany with the Romagna and northern Italy. The principal artery was the road in the valley along the Sieve itself, which intersected several north-south roads linking Florence and Tuscany with the Romagna. Florentine magistrates long recognized that the Mugello was also a potential source of revenue and manpower for the army. From the tenth century, two principal urban ecclesiastical lords (the bishopric and the cathedral chapter) drew significant income from the region. The Mugello also served as a human resource, providing emigrants for the needs of the growing city. Early estimates of the population before 1300 are unavailable, but we can surmise that the Mugello in the early fourteenth century numbered at least fifteen thousand souls.[9]

Many Mugellani immigrated to the city as artisans, apprentices, or workers, especially in the last decade of the thirteenth century. Some, like Ciecchino di Birretto from Borgo San Lorenzo, a flax dresser, and Giotto di Bondone, the painter from Vespignano, came to the city to seek greater opportunity. In the second half of the thirteenth century, 18 percent (241) of the total number of documented immigrants to the city (1,340) came from the northwestern area of the contado, which included most of the Mugello.[10]

The zones around Vespignano and Borgo San Lorenzo were closely connected to the city in the early fourteenth century. In 1307, Vespignano chose rectors to set its tax (estimo) for payment to the Florentine tax collectors. Two years later, the local patrons of its parish turned to the Florentine urban church of San Simone to choose their new rector. In 1327, a local resident gave the rector, Presbyter Ridolfo (who collected for the Florentine bishop), ten lire that represented ill-gotten gains of uncertain origin (*pro incertis et male acquisitis*).[11] Florentine money lenders were also at work at Vespignano, such as Lapo Strozzi, who loaned the commune fifty florins. Other Florentine money lenders were active there as well. In the central valley near Vespignano, the bishops held a significant amount of property. In this area Florentine officials were able to direct local communities to construct public works. The aim was to guarantee that major arteries were open for grain transport and military operations. In 1284, 1285, and 1297, for example, Florentine officials ordered several communities to conduct road and bridge repairs on the Sieve.[12]

By the end of the first third of the fourteenth century, however, the power of the Florentine magistrates and landholders from the city was tenuous and limited to the central valley, portions of the south ridge line, and the Apennine foothills above present-day Vicchio. The central valley of the Sieve itself and the roads connecting it with Florence appear to have been within urban control only by the second decade of the fourteenth century. Even where the urban presence was most apparent, there had developed early in the thirteenth century traditions of community-based resistance to the presence of the bishopric at Vespignano, Borgo San Lorenzo, and Valcava. Furthermore, even in 1300 there was still no effective urban jurisdiction in the lands of the powerful rural lords of the region (the Ubaldini and Guidi). They held sway in the mountainous regions of the north central and eastern Mugello, and in the valley of the Godenzo River. In 1328, emboldened by the campaigns of the emperor Lewis, the Ubaldini and their Ghibelline allies in the Romagna were again in rebellion in the Mugello.

In addition, as a recent local study of the communities of Uzzano and Rostolena in the Mugello has demonstrated, even as late as the third and fourth decades of the fourteenth century there was little evidence of urban investment or emigration in the direction of Florence. Although almost a fifth of late-thirteenth-century immigrants to the city came from the northwestern section of the contado (which included the Mugello), a considerable number of that figure came from settlements close to the city and not from the Mugello itself. More immigrants came from the southern and eastern sections (*sesti*) of the *contado* than from the Mugello.[13] Giotto di Bondone was the most famous immigrant to Florence from the Mugello at this time. Yet the sources are clear that many of his family members chose to remain in the Mugello at Vespignano. His son, Francesco, was serving as prior of Santa Maria di Vespignano in 1330, where he was very active in local affairs and helped manage his family's interests.[14]

Why did so much of the Mugello remain a world apart, well into the first third of the fourteenth century? The mountainous terrain, isolated settlement patterns,[15] continuous warfare in the region between Guelfs and exiled Ghibellines after 1268, lack of urban investment, and perpetual factional conflict within Florence itself all contributed to the isolation of the Mugello and to the unwillingness (or inability) of Florentine officials to subjugate it effectively. Indeed, its geographical location between Florence and Bologna made it a perfect gathering point for Ghibelline exiles from both cities.

But there are other reasons that deserve particular attention: the presence of strong rural territorial lordships, a tradition of resistance to urban lords, and a distinctive ecclesiastical culture. The Mugello was one of the few regions of Tuscany where strong rural territorial lordships (*signorie*) emerged in the twelfth and thirteenth centuries.[16] Two dominant rural lineages developed in the twelfth century to control mountain passes and roads. They were the Ubaldini and the Guidi, and their power bases were local and rural. They apparently had no urban properties or possessions; the only significant urban lords present in the Mugello at that time were the bishopric and cathedral chapter.[17] In the far west of the valley, at the end of the eleventh century—on the eastern slopes of the Monti della Calvana and in the valley of the Stura—the Cadolingi were also present. The landed possessions and proprietary rights in the Mugello of the Guidi were concentrated primarily east of the Mugello, particularly in the Casentino region in the dioceses of Fiesole and Arezzo. Nevertheless, at Campiano, controlling the main artery along the Sieve, the Guidi apparently had a fortified settlement (*castello*) and a proprietary church, at least as early as the eleventh century. Beginning in the late eleventh century, the lineage of the Ubaldini acquired extensive possessions in the central Mugello, the valley of the Santerno, and the *contado* of Bologna. In the eleventh and twelfth centuries, they were closely associated with the Tuscan marquis, the Bishop of Florence, and the Guidi.[18]

Political circumstances in the early thirteenth century led to consolidation of the power of the Ubaldini in the Mugello. In 1220, after abandoning any plans to rule a unified Germany, Frederick II went to Rome to be crowned emperor, establish control over the kingdom of Sicily, and restore imperial rights in northern Italy. In the same year, eager for allies in his quest to reassert imperial authority, he issued a privilege of protection for the possessions of the Ubaldini. This privilege confirmed their rights to collect public taxes (the former imperial *datium*), exercise public justice, and collect tolls. On the left bank of the Sieve, they possessed a variety of *castelli* situated on the roads along and east of the brook (*torrente*) of the Tavaiano: Galliano, Montepoli, Luco, and Montaccianico. These castelli were located on important roads connecting Bologna with Florence. Their control of strategically located castelli on the Ensa (Oliveta, Pulicciano, Ronta) along the road to Faenza were also crucial to the power they wielded in the valley. On the right bank of the Sieve, their possession of the castelli of Pila and their properties at Polcanto, Faltona, and on the slopes of Monte Senario allowed them to control a vital artery connecting the Mugello and Borgo San Lorenzo with Florence. Finally, north of the Mugello, in the valley of the Santerno, their possessions gave them the ability to project their power along the road to Imola and on into the Romagna.[19]

To protect their autonomy from urban authorities, the Guidi and Ubaldini tended to support whatever urban Florentine faction was out of power in order to weaken the faction that controlled the city. In 1251, the Ubaldini had first rallied behind Ghibellines exiled from Florence in 1250. They suffered an ignominious defeat at Montaccianico at the hands of the Florentines in 1251. After a brief return to the city in 1260, Florentine Ghibellines had to abandon the city again in 1267. Thereafter, the Florentine Guelfs made war on the exiled Ghibellines and their allies, the Ubaldini. After 1274, however, anxious to secure the road network and grain supplies in the Mugello from Florentine Ghibellines and their exiled allies from the Romagna and from the Mugello, Florentine magistrates created the magistracy of the *Sei della Biada*. In the same year, it required the residents of nineteen communities under Ubaldini control in the Santerno valley to swear fidelity to Florence.

There are indications in 1276, according to the principal historian of Florence, Robert Davidsohn, that the Florentines had turned to a policy of direct political rule. If so, there are few indications that this policy succeeded. Florentine ambassadors pleaded with the Council of Six Hundred in Bologna to assist the Arno city to secure the road arteries connecting the two communes from Ubaldini disruption. At the Ubaldini castelli of Montaccianico and Pulicciano, Ghibelline exiles had gathered in the late 1270s, provisioned by the Florentine Ghibelline base at Forlì.[20] After designating them a magnate lineage in 1286, the city leaned on the Ubaldini to pay the estimo, which they did from 1288. Nevertheless, they continued to interfere with delivery of grain to the city well into the fourteenth century. In

1307, thirty-one years after the mission to Bologna in 1276, the communes of Florence, Bologna, and Pistoia were still posting guards on the roads to Bologna, paid for by tolls on the goods being transported.[21]

Following the split of the Guelf Party into White and Black factions in 1300 and the expulsion of the White Guelfs in 1302, the Ubaldini and Guidi in the Mugello continued to offer a haven for urban political exiles. In March 1302, a Florentine army took the castle of Pulicciano from the Whites and Ghibellines, forcing many of them to flee into the Romagna toward Bologna. They also lay siege to vital Ubaldini holdings in the Santerno valley north of the Mugello. Four years later, a Florentine army attacked and destroyed the Ubaldini fortress of Montaccianico, for the first time since 1251. Below it in the valley the Florentines built the colony (*terra nuova*) of Scarperia in 1306. Florentine armies were not the only forces held at bay in the Mugello. In 1325, for example, Castruccio Castracane attempted to invade the Mugello through the valley of the Marina, but the Mugellesi, according to Villani, were able to stop him. In 1324, Florence created another colony below Ampinana and gave it the name of Vico (later Vicchio). As was the case with Scarperia in 1306, the absence of effective Florentine control of the region necessitated military occupation and creation of a Florentine terra nuova. In 1328, the Florentines sent an army to Ampinana to subjugate it once and for all.[22] By 1330, Florentine control of the region around Ampinana was secure.[23]

Signorial rights of the lords of the Mugello, however, continued to persist well into the fourteenth century. In the late thirteenth and early fourteenth centuries, the Guidi counts, whose signoria dominated the eastern Mugello and Casentino, continued to function as effective rulers of the Godenzo valley as well as of the eastern Mugello. They rendered both public and ecclesiastical justice on their lands, as the sources reveal, and they shared with the Bishop of the Fiesole the patronage rights to the baptismal church (*pieve*) of San Bavello.[24] In the late thirteenth or early fourteenth century, the Guidi counts had enriched themselves by usurping local ecclesiastical properties and rights, for which in the early fourteenth century they sought to make restitution in their testaments. The Guidi counts also served as judges in ecclesiastical cases, often outside the jurisdiction of the courts of the Bishops of Fiesole or Florence.[25]

The Florentine cathedral chapter and bishopric were also significant lords in the Mugello from the tenth century, and, like the Ubaldini and Guidi, were able to establish themselves in the region.[26] Imperial and episcopal privileges of protection reveal that the chapter had numerous holdings in the western Mugello from at least the tenth century.[27] Key gifts to the chapter by local aristocrats and prosperous nonnobles (such as notaries) in the second half of the eleventh century added significant holdings to their property.²⁸ We know that the cathedral chapter was still collecting the public taxes (the *datium et accattum*) at Molezzano as late as 1262, and in 1278 it was still transporting grain rents from the Mugello to the city. In fact, in that year it drew on its grain reserves in the Mugello to make bread for the feast hosted for Cardinal Latino, sent by the papacy to resolve disputes between Florentine Guelfs and Ghibellines.²⁹ In 1289 and 1290, however, the cathedral chapter decided to abandon its properties and servile tenants (*fideles*) in the Mugello to develop lucrative rental properties in the central parishes of the city. Fearful that the Ubaldini would purchase these holdings, and sensitive to the requests of the servile tenants themselves, the Florentines exchanged property worth 3,000 lire with the cathedral chapter to acquire legal rights to the property and tenants of the chapter at Molezzano, Pagliariccio, Pulicciano, Ronta, and Campiano.³⁰ This sale effectively brought an end to two hundred years of capitular holdings in the Mugello, but at the same time it ensured that control over these communities by urban authorities continued.³¹

The holdings of the Florentine bishopric were far more extensive in the central and eastern Mugello, especially in the regions around Padule and Botena. Borgo San Lorenzo was the center of episcopal holdings in the valley. The build-up of a strong episcopal presence here and in the Apennine foothills above present-day Vicchio served to establish a firm episcopal (and, indirectly, urban) presence in this part of the valley that continued into the early modern era.³² Undoubtedly the largest (and one of the few) of the urban landholders in the region, the bishopric nevertheless began to encounter significant opposition to the exercise of its lordship in the early thirteenth century.

According to Giovanni Villani, in 1218 the Florentines attempted to require all residents of the contado (especially those in regions under imperial authority) to swear allegiance to the city. In 1220, the same year that emperor Frederick II confirmed the possessions of the Ubaldini, unspecified residents of Lomena refused to make customary seigneurial payments to the bishop.³³ Lomena was situated within Ubaldini possessions on the slope of the Apennines in the baptismal church district (*plebatus*) of Sant'Agata, between the two castelli of Montaccianico and Galliano. The rebellion prompted the intervention of the Florentine civil magistrate (the podestà), perhaps because he recognized that a ruling in favor of the bishop was the only way to preserve some degree of urban jurisdiction in that region. Beginning in 1222, the rural commune of Borgo San Lorenzo, located on the road that linked Florence with the Romagna, also refused to acknowledge or accept episcopal jurisdiction. Residents challenged the episcopal magistrate (podestà) of Borgo, appointed by the bishopric to collect the datium. In 1227, the two parties compromised at Borgo San

Lorenzo, and the rural commune agreed to allow the bishopric to appoint future podestà one out of every four years. However, clashes between the two parties continued for the next twelve. The bishop responded with mass excommunication. The sources are silent, but it appears that disagreement over the degree of episcopal jurisdiction in the community continued in the following decade. In 1236, Florentine magistrates intervened again on the side of the bishop. In 1239, the Commune of Borgo San Lorenzo agreed to observe the statutes of the bishop.[34]

Borgo and Lomena were not the only places where the bishopric encountered resistance. As we have seen, in the twelfth century the bishopric acquired numerous possessions in the plebatus of Padule and Botena, specifically all or portions of the castelli of Molezzano, Pagliariccio, Rabbiacanina, Casole, Vespignano, and Ampinana.[35] Why were the acts of resistance occurring? The prosperity of this valley undoubtedly helped foster collective traditions among those who benefited from trans-Apennine trade. There were several markets in the Mugello in the early fourteenth century, each a point of exchange for goods from Emilia, Romagna, and Tuscany.[36] As population expanded in the thirteenth century, a brisk land market affecting episcopal property developed. At the same time, the bishops were commuting rents from money to grain. In 1222, Bishop Giovanni dei Velletri issued an order forbidding alienation of episcopal land. Between 1227 and 1232, local residents in the plebatus of Valcava refused to recognize the episcopally appointed podestà or to pay the customary datium. By 1243, however, the bishop was able to generate a set of statutes to govern his relation with this rural commune.[37]

The sources indicate that the bishops and other urban ecclesiastical lords continued in the fourteenth century to encounter resistance from Mugellani to payment of rent and other dues in several parishes. In mid-1299, the communities of Pagliariccio and Molezzano—located contiguously with Guidi possessions—refused to swear fidelity to the bishopric, an act for which they were excommunicated. In 1286 and 1297, the residents of the Commune of Valcava refused to accept episcopal overlordship.[38] In periods of famine, residents sought to retain control of vital grain supplies for their own needs. As we have seen, Florence depended on the Mugello for much of its grain supply. The years 1282, 1285, 1286, 1310, 1316, and 1328–30 were a time of dearth for the city and its contado, according to contemporary chroniclers, and it is probably because of this that many rural tenants of the bishop withheld or refused to pay their rents periodically.[39]

There are also examples of nonpayment to other ecclesiastical officials. For example, in 1313 the arch priest of San Gavino Adimari in the western Mugello appeared before the episcopal court and the papal collector to explain why he could not pay the papal tenth. In 1326, the church of Fabbiano in the plebatus of Corella also refused to pay a tax levied on all the Florentine clergy by the bishop; it was designed to reimburse a papal legate for expenses incurred while in Florence.[40] In August 1321, the most powerful ecclesiastical official in Florence during the episcopal vacancy at that time, Stefano de Broy, ordered a local rector to sequester the property of three men from Vespignano and Mucciano. The reason was for nonpayment of the "all rents, income, and proceeds of the church of San Martino di Vespignano." The men were ordered to appear within three days to make the payments to the arch priest (*pievano*) of Vespignano or face excommunication. Significantly, one of the men cited was the rector of the Commune of Vespignano, Pierino Guiducci. Also significantly, seven months before, the commune had paid the total bill of its estimo to the city of Florence, six hundred lire.[41]

Is it possible these men of Vespignano were unable to make payment to their parish church because they had recently paid their estimo and were short of resources? Local lay residents were themselves patrons of the parish of Vespignano. Did local parishioners use their rents as a form of credit to pay the urban tax? The sources, unfortunately, leave us no clue. However, withholding of rent to churchmen and subsequent payment of those delinquencies were widespread in the diocese.[42] It is a reasonable (but unprovable) hypothesis to conclude that Florentine fiscal pressure forced local residents to use their authority as church patrons to rely on parish income to pay the estimo.

To facilitate collecting its own rents, the episcopal administration in the early fourteenth century therefore began to lease out all its income in particular areas to a single person. Originally, those renting from the bishop were locals, but increasingly they turned to Florentine residents. The bishops initiated this policy in the principal plebatus of the Mugello where it held estates, including Borgo, Valcava, Padule, Botena, and Corella. Most of those to whom the bishopric farmed out the rents of these communities were local large landholders, not Florentines.[43] Indeed, the numerous lease books of the bishopric indicate that there were few if any urban tenants of episcopal properties in the Mugello before 1330. This was in marked contrast to other regions in the Florentine contado. In the lower Val di Sieve, for example, such Florentine families as the Pazzi, Saltarelli, and Caponsacchi begin to acquire a significant amount of property near Monte di Croce at the end of the thirteenth century. Indeed, in areas historically dominated by urban lords (the bishopric and cathedral chapter) we tend first to encounter landholding by urban laymen. In 1319, a resident of the Florentine suburban parish of Santo Stefano in Pane leased a house and parcel of land for two years, and in 1327 a resident of the urban parish of San Remigio rented out his Mugello property to a resident of Pulicciano.[44]

The presence of strong territorial lordships, a tradition of resistance to urban land lordship where it existed, and the absence of significant urban landholding were not the only reasons the Mugello remained a world apart from Florence well into the fourteenth century. Ecclesiastically and religiously, the Mugello was also a world all its own. Although relations between the residents and urban-based episcopal and papal representatives were problematic, relations were close and symbiotic with regard to the local secular clergy. The ecclesiastical organization for the care of souls in the early fourteenth century comprised seventeen plebatus (or ecclesiastical districts centered around baptismal churches), three Franciscan friaries, five monasteries, and three hospitals.[45] Most of the monasteries were located north of the Sieve, though one of the best known, the Servite monastery at Montesenario, was south of the river. In all, there were 145 parishes serving the local population, including twenty collegiate churches. The three friaries in the valley, as Charles M. de La Roncière has argued, were primarily way stations for pilgrims and travelers.[46]

Our principal sources indicate, however, that the ties between the secular clergy and their parishioners were close on a variety of levels. Parishioners exercised patronage rights in a number of churches for which we have records, allowing them local control over appointment of their rector. Two parishes in which parishioners held patronage rights were San Jacobo di Frascole and San Martino di Vespignano.[47] The fact that local lay parishioners exercised patronage rights at Vespignano in the early fourteenth century is significant, given the history of resistance by the community to the Florentine bishop. It may indicate that the parish functioned as a central focus point for the community as a whole, perhaps nurturing a tradition of solidarity well into the fourteenth century.[48] As we have seen previously, there is circumstantial evidence that local residents relied on their role as church patrons to use the income from parish property they rented as a form of credit to pay the urban estimo.

There also appears to have been some economic and political cooperation between rectors and their parishioners in the Mugello. Local rectors leased property from their endowments to local residents for moderate if not low rent. Furthermore, priests cooperated with local landowners to lease parcels that were often contiguous to their other holdings, allowing the renters to work consolidated farms.[49] Local presbyters were respected members of the community, often (as at Vespignano in 1307) acting as witness in an important local transaction such as contracting a loan or electing a magistrate.[50] We can also find some evidence that local clergy were acting in a key role as arbitrator charged with creation of a peace pact. For example, in 1312 and 1313 a clergyman presided over resolution of a local dispute at Rostolena near Botena. On April 16, 1320, the rector of San Michele di Ronta, Presbyter Buoninsegnade, served as one of the mediators. In January 1324, a canon of the pieve of San Giovanni Maggiore (Presbyter Ugolino) helped resolve a dispute involving a dowry.[51]

Regarding legacy, selection of an executor, and burial choice, the local population in the Mugello in the early fourteenth century favored the local secular clergy. Of the more than five hundred remaining testaments associated with Florence and its contado before 1330, fifty-three were from the Mugello. They all date after 1300. Forty-one testators were men; twelve were women. Few of the legacies in these testaments went to the friars. However, some prosperous residents tended to favor the mendicants, especially those who admitted they were usurers and sought to restore and make amends for their ill-gotten gain. They usually elected to be buried in the friary.[52]

The vast majority of legacies, though, went to the local church, particularly to parish churches and confraternities located in the plebatus of the testator.[53] In the mountainous community of Pulicciano on the road to Faenza, testators seem to have enjoyed exceptionally close relations with their local churches and clergy. In 1324, two women in two separate testaments made legacies to the local confraternity (at Ronta), their common confessor (Presbyter Nello), and the local hospital at Salto. Two of the presbyters who appeared as recipients of a legacy were the same two—Ugolino and Buoninsegnade—who had served as mediators in local disputes.[54] Regarding the choice of executor, members of the secular clergy were the favorites. In 1328, for example, the testator charged the prior of a church to choose the place of burial and left him explicit directions for construction of his tomb. In another typical example, in 1302 at San Bavello in the diocese of Fiesole, the testator chose the arch priest to be the executor.[55]

We have seventeen burial choices—all local. Eight testators chose their local church, two chose abbeys (San Godenzo and Razzuolo), two were unspecified, and five chose friaries. Every testator chose a local burial site in the Mugello.[56] Furthermore, the only saint whose cult a testator sought to promote was a local one, not an urban one. In 1329 Ser Jacobo del fu Ser Aldobrandino, a notary from Farneto (plebatus of Botena), left a large legacy for the divine office to be celebrated at the feast of the local patron saint, St. Bartolomeo, by five priests for twenty years.[57] The close association with the local secular clergy and saints intensified and enhanced local traditions. By 1321, however, Florentine officials were collecting money from the Commune of Vespignano for wax processional candles (*ceri*) to be used at the celebration of the feast on June 24 of the patron saint of Florence, St. John. Significantly, the urban cult of St. John symbolized the power of the city over its hinterland, and collection of these funds in the third decade of the fourteenth century testifies to the growing Florentine presence in the central valley at that time.[58]

All in all, much of the Mugello remained largely a world unto itself, at least through the first third of the fourteenth century. Its strong territorial lordships, tradition of resistance to urban land lordship in its most prosperous communities, and distinctive religious and ecclesiastical culture all help explain why the Mugello was able to retain its separateness well into the fourteenth century.

The relationship of Florentines to the Mugello was neither simply symbiotic nor exploitative. It was much more complicated than that. For some immigrants, like the flax dresser Ciecchino from Borgo San Lorenzo, the city offered new opportunities. Where there had been significant urban landholding for centuries (as in Ciecchino's home town, Vespignano), urban political and economic connections with the Mugello developed early. But these were also precisely the places where we encounter significant local resistance to the exercise of lordship by outside powers.

Rooted in strong ecclesiastical and religious communities, the population of the Mugello often demonstrated a tradition of resistance and ability to play off one urban faction against another. These legacies went back well into the early thirteenth century. Moreover, there was clearly no uniform Florentine policy toward the region. In some cases where urban landholding had been present and where disputes had arisen (Borgo San Lorenzo and Vespignano), legal remedies adjudicated by Florentine magistrates were sufficient to generate a compromise that lasted until the next flare-up. In other areas, especially where the rural lay lords still held sway, urban magistrates had to rely on military action. In both areas, urban hegemony did not come easily, if it came at all.

The most recent history of the Florentine territorial state has concluded that the fourth decade of the fourteenth century marked a major turning point in the ability of the city to impose its hegemony over its territory. However, as we have seen, many regions of the Mugello had not yet succumbed. The ability of the city to project its power in the Mugello varied from zone to zone, and in some areas it remained tenuous. Perhaps only after the defeats in 1374 of the Guidi and Ubaldini were the Florentines able to impose effective jurisdiction over the entire region.[59] Even so, it is important for historians to understand that the extension of urban jurisdiction did not necessarily expunge the local political, social, and cultural traditions of rural environments. They persisted.

Several years ago, while visiting a house in the Mugello owned by the family of a friend, I learned that my host's grandfather had run guns from the Mugello into Florence when the Germans occupied the city during World War II. A member of the Italian communist party (Partito Comunista Italiano), he was hiding Jews in his Florentine house while at the same time smuggling arms to partisans in the city. Even in the middle of the twentieth century, the Mugello valley still remained a troublesome place for urban authorities. Command of the city of Florence did not necessarily imply control of the Mugello, be it by Guelf merchants in the fourteenth century or the German *Wehrmacht* in the twentieth. It was and is primarily a rural environment, shaped by, but often independent of, the city. It has been and continues to be a world unto itself, beyond Florence.

CHAPTER FIVE

The Country Parish at Late Medieval Lucca

Duane J. Osheim

In a series of documents from the 1330s, the people of Vivinaia and the residents of the newly constructed fortress of Montecarlo on the edge of the Luccan plain petitioned for the right to place baptismal fonts in their chapels. Because of war and the continued threat of flooding, they said many were unable to bring their children to the pieve (the parish church, with the baptismal and jurisdictional rights of the other churches in the district[1]) of San Pietro in Campo. Thus many children died without the saving grace of baptism.[2]

These documents are not unusual. In fact, they support just what we would expect. First, it is a commonplace that with the growth of population during the high Middle Ages and with the rise of rural communes, pievi tended to lose control of their parishes, ceding to local churches the rights to tithes, burials, and baptisms—the three most significant indications of parish autonomy. The countryside was also being reorganized through creation of new fortified centers, such as Montecarlo, and construction of new roads and bridges throughout the Tuscan countryside.[3] Finally, the massive immigration of prosperous countrymen to the larger towns of Tuscany and northern Italy significantly changed the dynamics of country life. Local churches along the plain of Lucca, for example, were said to be in decline because of the constant movement of the local elites toward town.

In discussing the rise of rural communes at Lucca, Chris Wickham observed that after 1200 local churches and the communities that surrounded them were largely emptied of their most vigorous residents. Thereafter, he concluded, the most important chapter of the history of the rural commune was complete.[4] Rural institutions ossified; the rural population was primarily made up of peasants; and rural communes existed only to the extent that central government in Lucca found them useful. Rural parishes and local churches, by extension, were little more than minor observers in the rise of the territorial church.[5]

Certainly, when viewed from Florence the decline of rural churches and communities is part of the growth of the territorial state at the end of the Middle Ages.[6] Churches, monasteries, parishes, and ecclesiastical boundaries are all tied up in the family and government interests that dominated every region of Italy. Richard Trexler has emphasized the role of the state, while Roberto Bizzocchi has written of the role of the leading families of powerful cities such as Florence in the absorption of ecclesiastical life into the metropolitan centers of Italy.[7] But as diplomatic historians have often noted, there were limits to the authority of the regional states. Further, issues tend to look much different when viewed from the smaller towns, ones struggling to preserve their autonomy, rather than from a regional power. It is in this context that the life of the rural parish deserves a second look.[8]

The care with which jurisdictional rights were preserved as late as the third decade of the fourteenth century indicates that for parishioners and some pievani (parish rectors) at least, the matter of community life and the role of commune and parish were not entirely settled. Information is fragmentary and frustratingly incomplete, but it is worth looking again at country parishes. What were they like between 1200 (when as Wickham notes, the institutional structure of the rural community was well established) and the middle of the fourteenth century (when a succession of wars, plagues, and natural disasters reduced rural population and brought about such a massive shift of settlement that very little cohesion remained in the rural communities of the Lucchesia)?[9] Depending in part on the location, a parish church might well retain a vigorous political, social, and religious life.

Between 1200 and 1360, the diocese of Lucca was still unusually large and filled with churches, chapels, hospitals, and monasteries. It included lands south of the Arno and high in the Apennines, lands over which the Lucchese commune rarely claimed political control. Episcopal possessions south of the Arno were largely the result of the powerful political role Lucchese bishops had played before the year 1000 (Fig. 5.1). Then the Lucchese dreamed, or could have dreamt, of dominating all of Tuscany. With the defeat of Countess Matilda and the rise of Pisa and later of Florence, the Lucchese role in Tuscany was reduced, and reduced again. The diocese, however, continued to include lands controlled politically by the Pisans and Florentines. This changed only when the diocese was restructured in the sixteenth and seventeenth centuries. Most of the lands outside the Lucchese state eventually passed to the diocese of Pes-

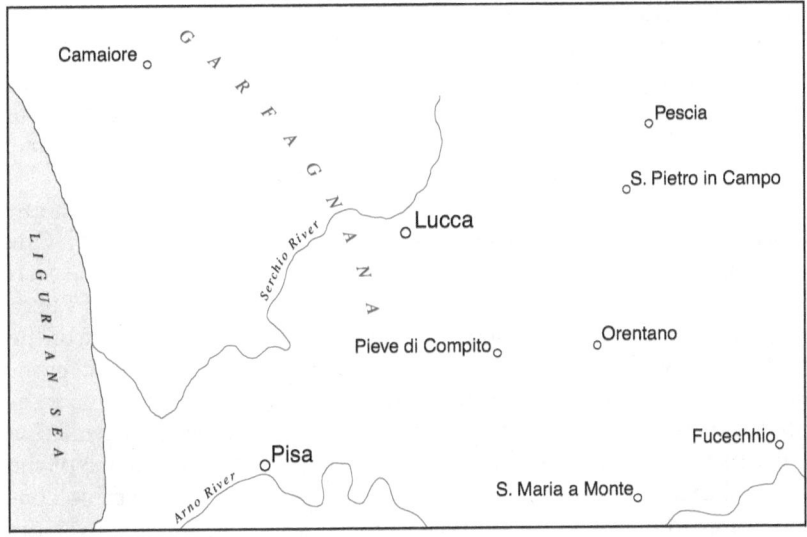

Map 5.1 The Diocese of Lucca

cia, a town clearly within Medicean Tuscany.[10] Episcopal installation of Pisans in numerous churches south of the Arno reflected that sad political reality.

The medieval diocese of Lucca can be divided administratively into three regions: land close to the city, in the so-called district of six miles; land further afield, in border areas such as Santa Maria a Monte, Pescia, and Camaiore; and finally the land south of Arno that by the fourteenth century clearly lay outside the Lucchese political sphere. The intermediate zone was on the edge of Lucca's economic network. It was also a sensitive area, where the Lucchese governors, secular and ecclesiastical, had to moderate their demands knowing that residents of these areas easily could turn to the Pisans, Pistoians, and ultimately the Florentines.[11] As we will see later, these political and economic experiences within the diocese of Lucca often led to social or even religious differences among the areas.

According to the late-thirteenth-century papal tithe receipts, the Lucchese diocese was dotted with churches.[12] Not so many as Florence, perhaps, but in the diocese of Lucca the average parish district included almost seven local churches or chapels in addition to the parish church. Florentine parish churches included more than seven other local churches and chapels within their parish districts, but most other Tuscan parishes were less populated—only three or four churches or chapels within the jurisdiction. This surely reflects reduced rural population, or at least fewer countrymen interested in building and maintaining a local church. Figures are even starker compared to north European parishes. In Germany or Poland, churches were sometimes twenty kilometers or more from each other.[13] By contrast, on parts of the Lucchese plain, in the pieve of Compito or at nearby Pieve San Paolo, for example, three or four churches often were in easy sight of each other.

Throughout the thirteenth and the early fourteenth centuries, bishops, parish rectors, and local residents continued to defend their interests. One long-running controversy concerned the parish of Fucecchio, on the eastern edge of the diocese. Here, both the Commune and Bishop of Lucca struggled to maintain jurisdiction, or at least influence. This part of the Valdinievole was in many respects independent of Lucca; it would eventually be more closely tied to Pescia and Pistoia and in the end incorporated into the Florentine state. The abbot of the ancient Benedictine house of San Salvatore at Fucecchio had long held the patronage of the parish church. Yet controversy over the parish church of Fucecchio continued into the fourteenth century. Abbot and bishop fought over the right to appoint the parish rector, over claims to burial dues, and eventually over churches and chapels subject to the parish church.

In 1122 arbiters (including the Bishop of Pistoia) were asked to adjudicate episcopal and abbatial claims. The arbitrators agreed that the abbot should select, and the bishop confirm, the rector, who along with the clerics of his local churches must promise obedience and attendance at episcopal synods, litanies, and feasts. Tithes were divided between the bishop and abbot and rents from property between the abbot and parish rector. Burial rights, however, were more complex. Those rights the abbot previously claimed and insisted on continuing to exercise them. Otherwise, parishioners had the right to choose, with the understanding that dues and gifts should be shared by the monastery and the church chosen for the burial.

The churches of the district largely remained within the jurisdiction of the monastery and its parish rector. The only exception was one chapel that belonged to the bishop, which "must remain quiet and undisturbed in the possession of the Bishop of Lucca such that the Monastery of Fucecchio may in no way involve itself there without express permission of the bishops of Lucca." This early agreement remained important to the bishops throughout the Middle Ages. It was cited in the 1220s and 1290s and figured prominently in the episcopal *Libro grande dei privilegi*, redacted in 1388.[14] At Fucecchio, parish rights remained an important issue throughout the Middle Ages—even after Fucecchio was incorporated into the Florentine state.

The relationship of parish church and subject local churches figured even more prominently in an agreement between the parish church of Compito and the nearby monastery of San Michele of Guamo in 1213. The monastery was located within Lucca's suburban district, a short walk from the city. It was a reformed Benedictine house that grew rapidly in the late-twelfth and thirteenth centuries as it benefited from the support of Lucca's rural and urban residents. Its prominent position in Lucchese society ended only in the political, religious, and social turmoil of the first half of the fourteenth century.[15]

The monastery's popularity and its rapid expansion created a locus of religious life that could easily have swamped the nearby parish. It quickly added a chapel and residence in Lucca, where the monks and their guests could stay when in town. San Michele also owned numerous properties near the monastery, where guests could stay for a short period, and houses to which they could retire if they wished a more permanent relationship with the monks. Early in the thirteenth century, the monastery added a small hermitage and chapel high in the Monti Pisani called variously Santa Maria di Fontanelle or di Valle Eremita. It was initially a cell for a single monk, but we have later records of two or three monks, or *conversi*, living there. Surviving documents give little indication of how the chapel was integrated into the life of the monks. It may well be that one or two monks lived there permanently—one Augustino seems to have spent most of his career there. On the other hand, most hermitages were a place monks might visit for a short stay during some part of the year. However the monks chose to integrate Santa Maria into their religious life, it was a potential source of problems for the parish church of San Giovanni di Compito. Thus in 1213 the rector of Compito and Augustino, the monk resident at the hermitage, came to a rather detailed agreement over the status of the chapel of Santa Maria and its relationship to the surrounding parish.[16]

The rector was primarily concerned to protect parish rights and jurisdiction. In effect, he wanted to bring an otherwise independent local church within his parish structure. Part of the idea was simply practical. The monks were not to hear the confession of any individual, healthy or sick, unless the person was actually resident in the hermitage. Further, local residents were not to be accepted as monks or conversi of the hermitage without the permission of the rector. Nor could anyone elect burial at the hermitage "without permission of the chaplain of their local church." Finally, any excommunication pronounced by the rector must be honored by the monks at Santa Maria.

The jurisdictional issues were, of course, critical to administration, but the rector went on to enumerate requirements that would have been much more evident to local parishioners. On the Feast of Saint John the

Baptist in June, the monks resident at Santa Maria were required to bring a half pound of incense to the parish of San Giovanni di Compito, "not in patronage or because of right of patronage or any right the parish church holds in the church of Santa Maria di Valle Eremita, but because the Monastery of San Michele built the church within the parish district and within the parish." Further, feasts at the hermitage were restricted. The rector of the hermitage was to celebrate only the Feast of the Virgin in September. Additionally, the parish rector required that if any clerics other than the monastery's monks and hermits were to be invited, the parish rector had to be invited first. If anyone but a monk were to officiate, the parish rector must first be offered the honor. The rector of the hermitage also was not to have the right to place any other church under his jurisdiction without the permission of the parish rector. Lastly, if any cleric other than a monk or hermit was appointed rector of the hermitage, the parish rector was to have all rights over the church that a parish rector customarily could claim.

At Compito, at least, the parish rector seems to have been in firm control. In addition to local communal officials, the agreement was witnessed and approved by a subdeacon of the parish church and the five rectors of local churches within the parish district. Further, the consuls of the Commune of Pieve di Compito were present at the agreement, and again when it was presented to the abbot at Guamo. The rector does not seem to have been concerned to integrate the hermitage fully into the parish structure. Had he wanted to do so, he could have added a number of further requirements of the type a rector regularly required of a local church.

An elaborate judgment of 1233[17] makes clear the wider interests of parish rectors. The rector of the parish of Elici complained that appointees to vacant local churches must be required to receive confirmation and installation from the parish rector. They must promise to attend any chapter meeting called by the rector or called in his name. Local rectors also must attend any feasts celebrated at the parish church and participate in common meals and rogation ceremonies. They must take care not to ring out the canonical hours fraudulently in anticipation of the bells at the parish church—the church of Massarossa seems to have been particularly flagrant in this respect. Like the rector of Compito, the parish rector at Elici demanded precedence in all local feasts. Local churches were required to send children to the parish church for the traditional baptism service on Holy Saturday. Finally, indicating the extent to which local burial rights were still at least partially parish rights, the rector required that he be invited to any funeral in a local chapel and that any testament must include a bequest to the parish.

Parish rectors did not easily concede rights even in cases where it seems patronage and control of the local church had long since been lost. In the first decade of the fourteenth century, there was an odd controversy within Lucca's suburban district, along the edge of the Luccan plain at Marlia, an area where the bishops had a palace and a rather significant estate.[18] When the rectorship of the local church of San Terenzo came vacant, those who claimed a voice in the selection process came together. The men of San Terenzo, alternately called parishioners and consuls of the commune,[19] claimed two of five votes, and the vicar general of the bishop held the other three votes. They agreed to appoint Bonaiuto del fu Guglielmo, a canon from Camaiore, as the new rector.

Matters proceeded as normal until the time came to present Bonaiuto for installation. As was customary, Bonaiuto went to the parish church and "many times and loudly" requested that his selection be confirmed by the rector or his representative. There was no response; the parish rector apparently was not resident. Bonaiuto later made the same request in Lucca to a canon of San Pietro Maggiore who represented the absent rector. After much prodding, the canon finally replied that he could not install Bonaiuto since to do so would be against custom. The issue was not explained more fully, but when Bonaiuto again returned to the curia, an episcopal nunzio was sent to the canon and to the residents of San Terenzo itself asking them to appear at the curia the next day by vespers to explain what they wished to be done. Further, the residents of San Terenzo were asked to say what they wished to be done concerning the selection and about the character of Bonaiuto himself.

Perhaps not surprisingly, no one appeared. The episcopal vicar then found Bonaiuto to be "worthy" and ordered that he be installed and given the door key, the bell cord, and the altar paraments as a sign of his appointment. The parish rector of Marlia may have wished, like the rector of Compito or Elici, to establish his preeminence within the district, but he had clearly lost out to the bishop and to the parishioners. But most interestingly, the vicar general's inquest made clear that he at least expected that the parishioners, whether or not they were in fact a commune, would have observed the election process and have expectations concerning the person of their new rector.[20] Like the nunzio, we too might ask what parishioners expect of their rector, or their local church.

When we look at the local churches, we find significant geographical distinctions. Those parts of the diocese most distant from Lucca or lying outside the Lucchese state were significantly less well served than other areas. In the diocese south of the Arno, in areas that by 1300 were firmly under Pisan control, episcopal supervision and perhaps even local influence are hard to document. Political and familial influences of the type described by Bizzocchi for Florence seem more common.[21] Clerical appointments largely seem to have conformed to Pisan interests. In the case of episcopal temporal rights in the area, bishops often found it most efficient merely to lease rights and jurisdictions for a fixed rent. In some cases, the bishop made arrangements with residents of the locality, but often the arrangement was with a Pisan.[22] Whether Pisans or local residents, episcopal representatives were often little more than tax farmers.[23]

The situation was often the same in appointing clergy. On the fringes of the diocese, local clerics often came from outside the diocese. In some cases, it was clear that the cleric was not really expected to be in residence. The clearest example may be the selection of a rector for the parish church of SS Giovanni e Martino di Tripallo. The episcopal vicar chose one Telo del fu Amico Petri of Pisa. The appointment was with and without cure of souls and recognized that he was not in holy orders.[24] A few years later, the vicar made a similar appointment at the nearby parish church at Padule. The new rector was not present, and the notary added that the appointment was made notwithstanding that the candidate was not in holy orders and did not know Latin.[25]

The intermediate zone, within the Lucchese state but in regions considered socially and politically sensitive, seems to have been handled more carefully. Commune and bishop seem to have been aware of the need to avoid problems in this area. The village of Santa Maria a Monte, just above the Arno and part of the bishop's estate, was one such area. After 1250, the village was often garrisoned by Lucchese troops as the bishops and commune continued their ultimately futile effort to keep Pisans and Florentines out of that part of the Arno Valley. In the wake of a homicide, when local passions, episcopal concern, and Lucchese policy were potentially on a collision course, Lucchese officials took no action against the murderer until they had consulted with the Lucchese city council. Similarly, in matters of taxation, the commune and bishop trod lightly in these areas.[26] Where parishioners and local clergy seem to have been largely absent from documents recording appointments at most distant churches, they were much more active in this intermediate zone. In 1293, for example, the consuls and podestà of the Commune of Montopoli appointed proctors to go to Lucca for the appointment of a new rector for their church.[27] The local communes were and remained concerned about their local churches.

As late as the middle of the fourteenth century, many rural communes maintained control of tithes collected in their districts. This was truest of the parishes on the edge of the diocese, in the mountainous Garfagnana or south of the Arno. The bishops of Lucca had transferred rights to most of the tithes collected on the Lucchese plain to the famous Hospital of San Jacopo of Altopascio in 1180. The Martilogio of 1364, an accounting of revenues owed to the bishop, showed virtually no payments owed for tithes within the district, but tithe payments and virtually no others from more distant portions of the diocese.[28] Throughout the fourteenth century, episcopal officials continued to lease these rights back to the commune. The terms varied, but usually they were for five years or less.[29] In a few cases, the lease was given to the chaplain of a local church. Yet even in those cases, local parishioners may have controlled the revenue. A marginal note in the Martilogio records a payment from the church of Aquilea in the parish of Moriano made "for the church and for the Commune of Aquilea."[30]

The local community did retain (and worked to retain) rights to local tithes. Curiously, episcopal sources say less about local burial rights. There was, of course, the famous case of a stranger who died in an area contested by two parishes. The body was literally stolen by one parish to enforce the right. Once it was determined that the parish had acted unjustly, officials ordered that the body be dug up and turned over to the neighboring parish rector for a second, legitimate burial!

The issue was, of course, the burial dues.[31] Yet controversy was rare. It was widely accepted that parishioners could choose burial in a local church or even a religious house, so long as traditional payments were made to those who held burial rights in the neighborhood. I know of only one case where a parishioner was refused the right to choose the place of burial. It was part of a complex political struggle between the Abbey of Sesto and the village of Orentano, which was under the abbey's jurisdiction. The abbot specifically claimed that persons of the village must be buried at the abbey unless bad weather or war prevented them from traveling.[32] It is telling that the abbot litigated over what were really parish rights with the individuals and Commune of Orentano and not with the "parishioners of the church of San Giovanni of Orentano." This was no doubt in part because burial dues were only one of a host of issues between abbot and villagers. But it is equally likely that for the residents of Orentano and other villages in the Lucchesia, local churches and rural communes were almost indistinguishable in their own mind. Statutes of these rural communes were as specific about the relations to the local church as they were about grazing and harvesting rights.[33]

The rural commune was in many respects like a confraternity. Members of the commune, like members of a confraternity, were often expected to share a common concern for a dead or dying neighbor. As with a larger commune, the feast of the local patron was the occasion for a *luminaria*, a candlelight festival celebrated in and around a local church. The heads of all families or representatives for them were required to attend on the patron's vigil and the mass on the following day. Similarly at

Anchiano, and probably in most other villages, everyone over fourteen had to be present for the blessing of the baptismal font on Holy Saturday. At Montopoli, heads of families were all required to bring water for the baptismal font at the beginning of Holy Week. Statutes of the village of Mutigliano required that all adult males and one female from each household should go to the house of the deceased and remain with the body until burial. The statutes further stipulated that if anyone of the village requested help because of some infirmity, the consuls should appoint men or women to aid the individual for so long as necessary.[34]

To some extent, the rights of the commune over the local church can be separated from those of the local chaplain. A communal tax register of 1311 lists some ninety brotherhoods, *luminarie*, and *opere* associated with local churches.[35] On occasion, it was the opera of a local church that leased property in the name of the church. As with the larger urban opera, they were responsible for the fabric of the local church. At Anchiano, statutes specified that two men of the commune should be appointed, with the understanding that they would only "spend what was allowed." In addition to keeping up the church, they were required to collect sprigs of myrtle for the feast of San Pietro. At Montopoli, the officials of the opera were further charged to go out each Sunday and collect donations in the name of the opera, with the understanding that these moneys were be used for embellishment of the parish church. Not surprisingly, the commune itself retained the right to audit the accounts of the opera. The statutes further showed at least partial distrust of local churchmen. The Commune of Montopoli was specifically forbidden to alienate or transfer any of its rights or properties to the local churchmen.

Many local priests no doubt were petty tyrants. One parishioner later in the fourteenth century responded to an episcopal visitor that his priest was "*una bestia*." Some priests took liberties with local women or sold the church's possessions—books, paraments, and even the mattresses belonging to their local hospice. These and other complaints are most common in the late fourteenth century and after, but they can be found throughout the thirteenth and fourteenth century.[36] But it would be wrong to assume that either these "beasts" or the absent and mysterious parish rector of Marlia were the most common sort of local clergy.

There are no firm figures, but it seems that before the middle of the fourteenth century parishioners could expect that the local clergy would in fact be in residence. The important agreements at Compito, Elici, and elsewhere were witnessed by parish and local clergy.[37] Local clergy regularly witnessed documents at the Monastery of Guamo and in the surrounding parishes. The numerous documents surviving from the modest local church of Vivinaia show that the local clergy and the canons at the parish church of San Pietro in Campo witnessed even relatively unimportant documents redacted in the locality. In 1235, for example, the rector of the parish of San Pietro in Campo disposed of a small pious bequest in the presence of his five local clerics.[38] Franca Leverotti's study of the impact of war and plague on rural Lucca in the fourteenth century comes to much the same conclusion. It was only late in the century that multiple benefices and absentee clergy became common, since it was only then that churches and church property were transferred to new jurisdictions,[39] breaking the correspondence between rural commune and local church precinct in the Lucchesia. Thus, until late in the fourteenth century, parish clergy played a significant role in their local community.

In many cases, local clergy were active in the life of the parish. In many parts of the diocese, it was the local church rector and the local commune that leased rights to tithes.[40] At San Pietro in Campo, for example, the parish rector invested in a flock of sheep. Later, local clerics in the same area entered a partnership to care for a flock of sixty-five sheep and goats. As was common in such arrangements, the clerics provided funds for which they received wool, cheese, and meat. Local transactions rarely survive, but we do find other indications of lease of fields, woods, and fishing rights. In some cases, they bought and sold for their churches, but at other times they specified that they were acting in their own name alone.[41] Further, clerics as well as laymen speculated in land rents by buying what was perpetual rent on land in the countryside. The process was simple. Hard-pressed peasants sold land, or more often improvements they claimed to have made on the land they held from other landlords.[42] The buyer then let the property back to the seller, creating a sort of perpetual loan.

In the thirteenth and fourteenth century, profits on these loans were a safe and significant source of income. This speculation was a key to one of the most important characteristics of the Lucchese countryside: tenants rarely held land from a single landlord. Thus the centralization and control typical of the classic *mezzadria* (sharecropping contract) was largely absent in the district of Lucca. Clerical involvement in this speculation can be seen on the episcopal lands on the Luccan plain, especially at Marlia and Moriano. A Lucchese tax volume of 1284–87 contains a listing of those lands owing rents to the bishop within the district of Lucca, primarily lands along the Serchio or on the plain a few miles from the city.[43] Tax officials, however, also included the rents these same tenants owed to others along with the episcopal rents. In most cases, these other rents were owed to individuals who had loaned money to tenants and in return were granted a rent *pro melioramento*, or for the rights the tenant had acquired in the land. More than half the tenants of the bishop also owed one or more other rents on the property—21 percent owed rent to another ecclesiastical institution. More interesting, however, 13 percent of all perpetual rents for improvement were owed to the parish or local church. They represent both pious bequests made to local churches and investments by churchmen themselves. As local landlords and speculators, these churchmen had a socially and economically important position in the village. In any event, the rents indicate that local churchmen had interests and connections within their villages. They were rarely if ever the most important land speculator in the district, but they did have resources.[44]

Like other landowners or speculators, local churchmen were involved with villagers in numerous ways. They seem to have bought and sold, extended credit, and held materials for others.[45] It was not unknown for notaries, money changers, grain buyers, or clerics to keep grain, wine, oil, or other property for neighbors who may have lacked space or storage vessels. Like other important villagers, clerics occasionally appeared in the Curia dei Foretani, a small claims court designed to quickly adjudicate claims made by and against residents of the Lucchese district. The majority of cases were brought by urban speculators, and then only when other means of settling matters had failed. Thus so long as there was hope of settling without a suit, creditors seem to have preferred to avoid litigation. The clerics who appear in the records of the court fit the same pattern. The church of San Giusto of Massa Macinaia brought suit in 1356, but only after rents had remained unpaid for five years.[46]

Clerics, however, were much more likely to appear in the volume in support of defendants. In 1337, the court's nunzio reported that the consul of Borgo Sant'Agostino refused to attach a countryman's possessions because the rector of the parish church of Compito claimed that the property belonged to him. In the same year, another cleric in the parish district of Compito asked to be made a defendant in a suit since, he said, the lands at the heart of the suit owed rent to his church. In several other cases, churchmen appeared in court on behalf of a defendant, confirming claims for which the countryman lacked documentation.[47] Clerics also stood between the Commune of Lucca and their parishioners in more serious matters. When a resident of Ruota, on the edge of the Monte Pisani, got in trouble with communal authorities for threatening the life of a neighbor, it was the chaplain of the local church who appeared in Lucca on his behalf and paid his fine.[48] One would like more information, of course, but in some villages at least the local clergy were an important ally of the countrymen.

Chris Wickham is certainly correct when he notes that local elites in the villages not too far from Lucca had emigrated to take advantage of opportunities in Lucca, but in many parts of the diocese the country parish retained its form, and its rector his power. If the wealthiest were leaving for Lucca, it may be that their place was quickly filled by influential parish clergy. Where parish and community suffered, the issue may be more than a matter of economics or demography. In sensitive areas such as Lucca, political geography may be highly important. In many parts of the countryside, the parish rector, his parishioners, and the Commune of Lucca all wanted to preserve the viability of the parish. In these areas especially, villager and parish church did continue to function—to manage issues of importance to the modest residents of the countryside.

CHAPTER SIX

"Do Not Say That This Is a Man from Assisi"

Robert Brentano

When Francis (the Francis of the Companions) says to the disorderly knights of Perugia, "And do not say that this is a man from Assisi," he seems clearly to be saying, and his recording followers seem to be saying it with him, that they are citizens, or denizens, of Christ, not of geographical localities, of cities.[1] They are declaring themselves free of old urban, campanilistic, local boundaries. They, merchants of the Gospel, will not have been born, grown up, entered a religious group or house, and died tied to a specific contado. They have broken these shells as they have taken off their clothes. They suggest, too, that the period between the saying and the writing, the decades ending in the mid-1240s, may have marked a crucial point, at least for some people in some places, in a changing conceptualization of man's identification of himself by place and of the city's dominance in the perception of the organization of society.

But Francis's statement bears in its specific way the ambiguity with which early Franciscan statement is often freighted and enriched. Francis and the Companions are saying that they are free, but they are also saying that it is cities that hold, control, and divide people, that it is from the cities' walled boxes, to use another image, that they must fight to be free (and even in concentrating on the geography of city one cannot avoid remembering the similar role for these Franciscans that the contiguity of family held). The city is the world (as perhaps the family is the devil). The statement "And do not say . . ." thus offers its rememberer, at the very least, a little mental game, a puzzle: Are these Franciscans minimizing or maximizing the role of the city in the organization and categorization of human beings?

The puzzle is, however, given substance by the social realities it touches, and by the Franciscans' own role in shaping those realities. Those realities in their Franciscan connection are best described in a single long narrative by the chronicler Salimbene de Adam, a man from Parma, who gathered his memories, rich from the 1240s but also significant from the 1230s, into script in the 1280s.² In different kinds of sources we can see that placement of Franciscans and other friars, groups collected in towns that were not their own various place of origin, led them to establish their own identification, and, one must assume, led their hosts to consider theirs.

In a list of sixteen Dominicans at San Domenico, Rieti, in 1310, for example, although in fact three of the friars are identified as from Rieti and four more from other towns in the Sabina, four friars are from Spoleto, and one each from Orvieto, Cortona, Arezzo, Gubbio, and Rome. The same friars were present in the house in 1315 and had been in 1305; but in 1319, although the number of (listed) friars would remain essentially the same (seventeen instead of sixteen) and the distribution of identifying places of origin would be very similar—with a map of those places extended slightly farther south, to Veroli—only four of the earlier sixteen friars would remain, to suggest a pattern, in itself not quite intelligible, of stability and mobility.³ Of thirty-two or thirty-three Augustinian Hermits gathered at the site of San Trifone in (admittedly magnetic) Rome in 1287, two are called Roman and several are identified as being from specific Roman districts, but two are from Gubbio and two from Orvieto, one each from Siena, Ascoli, Lucca, Narni, Viterbo, Anagni, Genazzano, Florence, and England.⁴

It should be noted, of course, that these identifications assume, it may seem naïvely, that identifying friars by place means by place of origin. Certainly we know, and most helpfully from Salimbene (as in the case of "Jacopino of Reggio, who was born at Parma"), that the names of the cities with which friars identified themselves and each other were not invariably the places of their actual birth; some other connection with a city could sometimes replace birth or early formation.⁵ But using these identifying names in houses of friars at this time only makes sense if they are normally understood to designate places of origin. A sense of this identification of friars by place, by city, can be gotten from Giordano of Giano's vivid description of the Franciscan missions to Germany, as the names of Italian cities, attached to friars, appear in German lands—although the place names attached to two of the most prominent actors in Giordano's narrative, John of Piano de Carpine (Magione) and Giordano of Giano himself ("who writes this to you") are not names of what could be rightly called, even informally, cities.⁶

The significance of the broad distribution of the places of origin of male friars in a place like the Sabina is not clear unless it is placed against the distribution of places of origin in other contemporary religious houses. At Farfa, the once-great and still-famous old Benedictine house in the Sabina, in 1279 the ten listed monks (besides the abbot, who is identified by office) are identified by again what surely must be places of origin. All whose place is itself identifiable come from the immediate area, from places like Fara, Toffia, Scandriglia, Cerchiara, and one, a monk named Francesco, from Rieti. The prior is from Fara.[7]

In the later thirteenth century, to the east in the Marche, in the large, very well-documented Cistercian house of Fiastra, with its relatively extended business affairs and daughter houses, there seem generally to have been thirty to forty monks. The filiation of Cistercian houses like this one in some sense obviously connected them with the world; but again, in the later thirteenth century the Fiastra monks were for the most part identified as coming from Fiastra's part of the Marche: Recanati, Macerata, San Ginesio, Tolentino, Ripe, Urbisaglia, Monte Santa Maria, Montolmo, Morrovalle, Montemilone, Camerino, Fermo, Offida.[8]

In a 1342 list from the small Cistercian house of San Pastore, situated on a hill above Rieti and only a long stone's throw from the Franciscan hermitage of Greccio—a hermitage famous because of the presence there of Francis (as in the presepio story) and later because of the residence of the Companions and the exile of John of Parma there—one finds the names of nine monks and eleven conversi, most of them identified by place names. Of the monks, three were from the village of Greccio; one each from Narni, Rieti, and Monte San Giovanni in Sabina; and one, named Pastore, from Terni. Of the conversi, five were from Rieti; three from Contigliano (a very closely neighboring town); one from nearby Rocca Alatri; and two, one of whom was named Francis, from Greccio. The map of these men's origins is very little extended, very small, even with the inclusion of Terni and Narni. Understandably, the map of the origins of the (perhaps simpler) conversi is even more restricted. There is a slight suggestion of complexity in the San Pastore names: someone named Pastore comes from as far away as Terni; three monks and two conversi are from Franciscan Greccio, and one of the conversi is even named Francis. In spite, however, of Pastore's suggestion of cult, the Greccio names underline the geographical localness ("intensely local") of this Cistercian house.[9]

Female Franciscan convents in central Italy, for obvious reasons, do not seem to have enclosed women as transient as their male brothers. Santa Filippa Mareri in Borgo San Pietro in the Cicolano and San Silvestro in Capite in Rome held very local women.[10] Some Franciscan male houses too, even in central Italy, seem very early to have become enclosed within their towns, as does San Francesco at Fabriano.[11] Nothing at all general can be said about the inhabitants of friars' houses until local historians can be induced to record electronically in an extended database the place names that identify their thirteenth- and early-fourteenth-century friars (and then perhaps neighborhoods or provinces of normal dispersal can be seen). But the visible evidence is striking.

Francis's saying, in Perugia, that he should not be dismissed as a man from Assisi and the assembly of foreign Dominicans at their house in Rieti fit together. They both talk of the importance of identification and categorization of and by city or town, and also of an invasion into that importance. The friars, and particularly the Franciscans, were, from the beginning, travelers and invaders, missionaries, beggars, and martyrs. They moved in elaborate patterns from Portugal to Padua, from Piano de Carpine to inner Mongolia.[12] They planted miscellaneous groups of themselves in Italian cities. To thirteenth-century Rieti, three orders of friars—Franciscans, Dominicans, and Augustinian Hermits—brought, at the corners and edges of the small city, three colonies. The friars were, of course, even in a provincial place like Rieti, not the first or only group of foreigners, or even settled foreigners. The international papal curia was an intermittent visitor, a royal court or a chapter general of friars themselves an occasional one. Merchants came, and podestà, a painter from Rome, a resident French medical doctor; pilgrims passed through.[13] Bishops, themselves not always from the city, brought strangers in their households.

But a house of friars was different. The friars themselves may have been transient, but their places remained. The friars preached, presumably, in their native accents; more interestingly, they heard confessions. The historian must imagine the reality of a Reatine, for example a nun from San Benedetto, listening to the foreign accents of her confessor—say, a friar from Sant'Agostino[14]; and in some places those must have been the accents that the penitent had known from youth as the accents of the enemy.

I mean to say that the existence of friars and their presence in houses in the towns and small cities of central Italy must have altered the cultural geography of the place and must have altered the self-identification and self-categorization of that geography's inhabitants. The effect of the friars' presence in the great, crushingly urban cities of Tuscany, Florence, and Siena, may have been, and presumably was, quite different. It is perhaps only a convenient coincidence, but it is at least suggestive, that the great necrological roll call of the Florentine Dominicans of Santa Maria Novella, which the friar Pietro Galigai de' Macci began in 1280, was essentially a list of the friars who came from, not to, Florence.[15]

There is necessarily a flimsiness about these conjectures. For more, one needs to look inside an observing mind. Although there are certainly observing minds from the valley of Spoleto and its environs, none, I think, has the flamboyant explicitness of Salimbene of Parma; and none reveals nearly so much about the nature of the city's importance in the friar's perception of himself and his society as does Salimbene's.

Salimbene's mouth is full of Scripture and the cities of Italy: "Once in Ferrara when Brother Bonaventure of Iseo was preaching . . ."; "On another occasion, when I was living at Ravenna, the lector, Bartholomew Calaroso of Mantua—who had once been a Minister in Milan and in Rome, but at that time was living in the convent of Ravenna without any office whatsoever—said to me, 'I tell you, Brother Salimbene, that Brother John of Parma . . .'" The city names spill out and mark the folios. They tell us where Salimbene lived: "I went to live in Tuscany where I stayed for eight years—two in Lucca, two in Siena, and four in Pisa. It was during the first year of my stay in Pisa . . ."[16] No reader of Mary Carruthers can doubt the help that these places and Salimbene's living in them gave his memory as he restated a history of his times seen with his own eyes and built around the movement of his own body.[17] But it is hard to believe that Salimbene's use of cities, his placing himself and other people, whose origin he states, within them, is only or even principally a mnemonic device. His history can almost be made to seem to be about his and their placement in specific cities. That can seem its substance; that, he can seem to be saying, is what life is—but, of course, not only that.

No other thirteenth-century writer, I believe, makes so clear the place and quality of his origin as does Salimbene. We know more of his family's genealogy, of their beauty, of the streets they lived on, of their attitude toward children, of their kinds of affection, than of any other writer's. Who else tells us anything about his crib? All those early beginnings are clearly marked, folio after folio, as Parmesan.[18] Continually through his discursive chronicle Salimbene points back to Parma, makes us aware of Parmesan connections that we might miss if he did not point them out to us.

But Salimbene is interested in (and, in different ways, cares about) other cities. He relishes the quality of Florentine wit and how it is enhanced by being spoken in Florentine dialect.[19] He, in Ravenna, is learned enough about Ravenna to guide eminent tourists through the city.[20] From the friars' house in Faenza, he observes the horrors of war there, and he joins in the kind of diverting frolic that war makes possible (or necessary).[21] He is repeatedly interesting about Pisa: "I lived in the convent of the Friars Minor at Pisa for four years, some forty years ago, and so God knows, I have sympathy and compassion for Pisa and the Pisans."

One should note the causal connection: because this Parmesan friar lived (for four years, some forty years earlier—that is, in the 1240s, as the Companions were composing at Greccio their memories of Francis) in Pisa, Ghibelline Pisa, in the friars' house there, he had compassion for them. But even with the compassion that he feels, he can observe: "And take note that just as there is a natural enmity between men and snakes, dogs and wolves, and horses and griffins, so is it between Pisa and Genoa, Pisa and Lucca, and Pisa and Florence"—and not just because of common boundaries, competition at sea, or other pragmatic reasons.[22] Even in his sympathy for Pisa, Salimbene can observe that city with this quite harsh, generic detachment, although he also laments the fact that the broad sea does not seem big enough for both the Pisans and the Genoese, and that the concepts of mine and yours exist. He is a historian who pays attention to carrocci and battles. Even if sometimes as dog or wolf, each city has its own substance and nature.

Salimbene's forty-year-old memories of Pisa are particularly helpful in recovering a thirteenth-century friar's (or at least this thirteenth-century friar's) way of viewing a city, not his own, in which he was living as a stranger in a local house of friars. Something must be said about the quality of Salimbene's memories. First of all, they have a particular texture: whether or not Salimbene was a man of profound intelligence or virtue, he was a man of acute sensory perception with the ability to convey effectively some kinds of perception, particularly auditory, in his written prose. Further, when Salimbene was in Pisa for his four-year stay, he was a young man and a relatively new Franciscan. He had been born in 1221 and joined the order in 1238. He was in Pisa in the 1240s and he was writing his chronicle's manuscript, as we have it, in the 1280s, when he was a man in his sixties. The physically small Vatican manuscript was quite surely written with his own hand, as were notes in the manuscript. Whether or not Salimbene had written earlier notes or drafts is unsure—although, I think, from the nature of the remembering and the look of the manuscript, that he probably had. This context of Salimbene's written memories is as important to the historian's way of looking at them as is the context of the Companions' memories of Francis, written almost twenty years after his death in 1226. That said, it remains unclear how the historian should, in interpretation, specifically use that context, except by constantly keeping it in mind.

Salimbene tells us of a particular day and night in Pisa. He has just spoken of a "lightheaded lay brother from Pisa" with whom as his assigned companion he had been making his rounds with his basket, begging for bread, and with whom he had had a dreamlike experience in a shaded, green courtyard in which there were exotic animals and beautiful boys and girls who played musical instruments and sang while the friars watched and listened in silence until they finally, with difficulty, pulled themselves away. When the friars left the courtyard, they met a man from Parma whom Salimbene did not know, who attacked and condemned him for having left his parents' house, where food was plentiful even for its servants, and for coming to beg bread from people who did not have enough for themselves. Salimbene, the attacker said, should be riding through the streets of Parma on his fine horse.

Salimbene confounded his attacker with scriptural quotations, but that night he lay unable to go to sleep and thought about the events of the day, and wondered if it would be possible for him, for the fifty years that might lie ahead, to bear the burden and shame of his mendicant perambulations. Finally he slept, and he dreamed that he was going door to door, begging, through the *contrada* of St. Michael of Pisa in the section of the Visconti, across from which was a hostel of the merchants of Parma (which the Pisans called their *fundicum*). In the dream, Salimbene avoided the fundicum because he was afraid the people from Parma would talk to him about his father and his desire to get Salimbene out of the order; so Salimbene walked along the Arno: "Suddenly I looked up and saw the Son of God coming out of one of the houses, carrying bread and putting it in the basket. The Holy Virgin was doing the same and so was Joseph, the foster-father. . . . And they kept doing this until the circuit was completed and the basket full. For it was the custom for the basket to be left below covered with a cloth while the friar went up to the houses to ask for bread, which he would then carry back down and place in the basket."[23]

There is clear contrast, in the dream, between the merchants of Parma enclosed in their fondaco within Pisa and the friar from Parma moving from house to house and door to door—one getting rich, the other getting poor; and behind the Pisan doors in the Parmesan dream are the members of Christ's earthly family. Salimbene does not stress the fact that Christ seems as at home in Pisa as Parma, the Franciscan and evangelical nature of the great Christian family; his Christ talks of being poor and a beggar. But the anticampanilistic, assumed message of the story is as clear as cliché. The message, though, is given a slight edge, an appreciation of the foreignness of the pilgrim, when the speaking dream-Christ quotes "your father Francis, my friend and beloved" as he wrote in the Rule (and note that Christ is quoting Francis): "Let the brothers go . . . like pilgrims and strangers."[24] A crucial aspect of the presence of the Franciscans' dwelling in foreign places is their being strangers.

Salimbene's Pisa dream returns him to one of the central themes of the early chronicle, and of Franciscan vocation: the rejection by the friar of earthly family and the reaction of that family to rejection. Harshly melodramatic scenes, in which Salimbene's father is allowed to speak pungently forceful language, and Salimbene himself hides from Adriatic pirates, are set around the city of Fano, and they lead to later scenes in

Jesi.²⁵ The Pisa scenes themselves also sign another element in the chronicle, one of movement. Salimbene shows himself not only an itinerant moving from city to city but also a walker within cities: "When I was living in Faenza (before that city was betrayed into the hands of the men of Forli), I was walking one day along the way, thinking of the Lord, when suddenly I was accosted by a man in secular life named Matulino, a man of Ferrara."²⁶

Both the Alleluia ("as it was later called") of 1233 and the movement of the Flagellants in 1260 are observed in Salimbene's chronicle.²⁷ Demonstrations of their sort that could suggest the beginning of a new age were of obvious interest to anyone who thought as much about Joachim as Salimbene did, but their urban and interurban movement dedicated to peace and salvation and to the Psalm's "ends of the earth" tied them to Salimbene's text in a further way. In the Alleluia he is given an opportunity forcefully to tie observation in Parma to the momentary history of his broader world. Again in 1260, the flagellation existed throughout the world, in Salimbene's text, but also the men from Modena came to Reggio and to Parma; and in Reggio the podestà, a citizen of Milan, joined, whipping, the procession. (Salimbene himself was in the friars' house at Modena.)

Salimbene's chronicle presents an appreciative description of the Alleluia and the Flagellants. It also presents an appreciative description of the carroccio wars. They both exist in the Italy of Salimbene's mind. He sees them both. He presents them both. Although either one might dull the other in the chronicle (and it certainly could be argued that the point of the Flagellants is to make pointless the wars), I think that they survive independently. Christ walks out of every door in Pisa; Pisa goes to war with other cities out of the doors of which Christ could walk. Christ who makes all cities one is present in the chronicle, but (along with Salimbene's laments about war) so is the diversity of cities.

Going through the cities of Italy, Salimbene can remind us of his northern contemporary, William of Rubruck, going to the Mongols.²⁸ He sees. He listens. He describes. Only sometimes does he condemn or praise. The observed phenomena have their own value. But much more than William, Salimbene can stop and be almost at home (insofar as a Franciscan is allowed to be at home) in his visited cities. He has not, like William, entered another world. But both William and Salimbene find this possible because of a visible security of background; William's is, perhaps, Paris. Salimbene abroad is always from Parma. As Italo Calvino's Marco Polo says to Kublai Khan, "Every time I describe a city I am saying something about Venice," Salimbene could say to his reader, "Every time I describe a city I am saying something about Parma."²⁹ That helps explain perhaps the intensity of his involvement, his understanding, and his reticences. It allows complexity. Salimbene is both Parmesan and not Parmesan.

Salimbene opens the mind of the transient friar. But of course, we cannot expect every friar to have been Salimbene. Talking of his stay in Ravenna, Salimbene wrote, "I myself with my companion went outside the city of Ravenna and stood on the bridge over the river, hoping to discover what the commotion was all about. While I was waiting a boy ran up to me and said to me why have not all the friars come out here?"[30] Not every friar walked out to the bridge, but Salimbene's chronicle gives the impression of conversational vivacity in friars' houses and of thought, sometimes in fact at university level, but generally at least at the level of interested local gossip.

The friar strangers in to-them-strange cities, the Parmesan mind in Pisa, and Francis's disclaimer to the knights of Perugia fit together. They emphasize the importance of the city identifier in thirteenth-century minds and the position of the mobile friars in the development and complication of that identification. It could certainly be argued that a Portuguese friar helped form the city of Padua.[31] It could certainly be argued that the traveling Italian friar thought in terms of cities, a point made unusually pictorially clear in the drawing of the Holy Family's flight into Egypt in a fourteenth-century Italian version of the Meditations on the Life of Christ.[32]

The Franciscan order was made in, or out of, cities. The Italian city was the world in which or against which the Franciscans were formed. Their deliberate movement, with that of their Dominican and Augustinian compatriots, away from their cities of origin, their connection to which they retained in their identifying names, encouraged consciousness of individual city and of rejection of individual city in them and in their hosts. This consciousness was naturally stimulated by two central and accented elements of the friars' mission, their offering sermons and personal confession. The friars both broke and made crisp the contemporary concept of city, all different, all alike, as Salimbene saw even in his dreams. The Franciscans were men with an eye for the physically particular; from it their purpose was to flee to the generality of Christ.

PART III

Law and Society

Law once seemed to reveal unambiguous universal truths about society, but most scholars now recognize that the connection of law and society is much more complex. The variety and ambiguity of legal practice, however, opens fruitful avenues for social and cultural history. Medieval and early modern Italy has an especially rich tradition of legal study centered on local legal traditions and practices.

Italy never lost touch with the complex Roman legal tradition. It was enriched, however, with German, and especially Lombard, influences with countless local variations. Although commentators had great faith in the power of law, it was not without its limits. The two chapters in Part III raise interesting and fruitful questions. Do legal documents describe reality in the towns and cities of Italy? If they do, how is it that contemporaries, or inquisitive historians, can know the difference between social life, as perceived in the courts of law, and law as a reflection of society?

Carol Lansing describes a situation in thirteenth-century Bologna in which law seems to lack categories to describe completely the world in which men and women live—especially those outside the wealthy elite who dominated public life. Honorable marriage or dishonorable prostitution were the categories understood in the law, but they do not come close to describing the experiences of women from in and around Bologna. As Lansing shows, though, if we attend carefully to the attempts of legists to shoehorn difficult social situations into a clean-cut legal reality, we can discover a great deal about female identity at a time when women are largely absent from other public records. Although Lansing gives us an excellent case study of how to read trial documents, Laurie Nussdorfer demonstrates the importance of Italian legal treatises as a resource for examining the behavior of notaries and jurists when confronted with the ambiguities of legal practice.

By reading legal treatises from the end of the sixteenth century, Nussdorfer shows how judges and lawyers tried to deal with a different problem: identifying and dealing with individuals who used legal documents in a deliberate attempt to mislead and defraud. Like modern litigants, Italians who went to court habitually salted their arguments with the numerous written documents that characterized public and private life in medieval and early modern Italy. Writing was a form of power that had become a highly sophisticated mechanism of truth and persuasion by the early modern period. The Roman jurist Prospero Farinaci's manual, based on medieval as well as early modern cases, gave judges and lawyers a method for interpreting and evaluating the waves of evidence brought to court. Farinaci's manual, and Nussdorfer's explication of it, present us with a clear picture of an essential, but little-noticed, aspect of life in Italian towns. Good order and social relations in Italy often depended on clear evaluation of legal agreements. These two examinations of legal culture suggest how law and society mutually shaped each other in medieval and early modern Italy; they remind us that we have much to learn from the records of the courts and the jurists who interpreted them.

Law and Society FLORENCE, BOLOGNA, AND ROME

CHAPTER SEVEN

Concubines, Lovers, Prostitutes
Infamy and Female Identity in Medieval Bologna

Carol Lansing

In 1289, the night watch in Bologna grabbed a couple named Cambino and Zoana. They were being chased by an Englishman named William, who was yelling, "You are carrying off my wife!" Cambino replied, "I am not going to let you kill her!" The case was adjudicated by the distinguished jurist Albertus Gandinus, author of a procedural manual that in 1289 was at the cutting edge of legal practice.[1]

An inquest was held: Zoana, William, Cambino, and their neighbors were asked a set of questions to determine whether Cambino was guilty of taking another man's wife to his house to have carnal relations. Their answers introduce the two intersecting themes of this chapter. The first is the picture of the culture and practice of the urban poor, sketched by people who were questioned in court—in particular, forms of concubinage and informal marriage practiced by women whose families were too poor to afford a dowry that would enable them to enter into a legal marriage. The second theme is the gulf between that picture and elite and juridical definitions of female identity and status.

In Cambino's case, the court's questions implied a dichotomous understanding based on sexual morality: Zoana was either an honest woman or a prostitute. The people questioned measured her status and identity rather differently, with less interest in sexual morality and more awareness of a variety of possible arrangements between men and women. The vignette they sketched offers a glimpse of the opportunities and self-understanding of a woman who lived outside of marriage and patrilineal family.

Zoana and the Culture of the Urban Poor

All of the people questioned in the inquest told roughly the same story. In response to the court's questions, Cambino, who was a Florentine, stated that he often ate and drank with Zoana and William because he had an English acquaintance who lived with them. Cambino called Zoana his *amica*, friend or lover: he felt love for her (*diligit eam amore*) and had loved her for six months. He had not had sex with her. She did sometimes have sex with men other than William. When he found her in the street weeping because William beat her, he asked her to come with him and she agreed.

When William was questioned, he agreed that Cambino had asked Zoana to come with him to escape a further beating, and even quoted Cambino: "If you don't come with me, he will kill you." William repeatedly called Zoana his *uxor*, his wife, and when asked whether she was a woman of evil connections (*mulier male conversationis*), swore that she was chaste. Was she in fact his wife? Four years before, when he brought her from England, he did not marry her (*desponsavit eam*) but promised that he would not take any wife.

Zoana agreed. She was not in fact William's wife but had chosen to live with him four years before. Asked whether Cambino was carrying her off to have relations with her, she said no. Asked by the court whether he had ever had relations with her, she contradicted Cambino and said, "Yes, four months before," memorably adding that she "did not sin with others, and with him sinned not for money but for love." A few days later, Cambino produced witnesses in his defense: two men who stated that they had paid Zoana for sex and she was a common prostitute (*publica meretrix*). Cambino was absolved.

The record of the inquest does not state the court's reasoning, but the case clearly hinged on Zoana's status. From the court's perspective, she was either an honest married woman or a common prostitute. If she was an honest wife, then Cambino would be guilty of carrying her away against her husband's will. If she was a common prostitute, she was available to all men, William had no authority, and she could leave with Cambino as she chose. In fact, almost everyone questioned called her neither a wife nor a common prostitute, but rather someone who lived in an impermanent but defined union with William and also occasionally sold sex. The evidence that she sold sex apparently led the jurist Albertus to consider her a prostitute, which is surely why Cambino was absolved: if Zoana was a common woman she was available to all men, including Cambino. Ironically, then, Zoana's categorization as a dishonest woman saved her lover from a hefty judicial fine.

This chapter draws on evidence from court inquests in Bologna to examine a little-studied aspect of medieval Italian towns: the lives of the urban poor, in particular women who lived outside of marriage, as concubines, prostitutes, lovers. Lively studies of urban marginals exist for the sixteenth century, often based on the rich court records of the Catholic Reformation period.[2] For the thirteenth, fourteenth, and often the fifteenth centuries, most sources and most studies emphasize elites, particularly the wealthy and powerful merchant families of Florence. We have clear and convincing pictures of late medieval elite culture, including honor and identity, marriage and family; but we know startlingly little about the social groups medieval Florentines termed the *popolo minuto*: petty artisans, laborers, the working poor. Elite practices were shaped by the need to transmit property and power. People with meager resources, living in transitory households, understood identity and social relationships differently.

Questions about the culture of the working poor are especially pressing for the thirteenth century, the period of the real formation of medieval Italian urban society. Massive immigration into the towns transformed urban politics and social forms. Population numbers are speculative because the evidence is patchy at best. For Bologna, Antonio Pini used member lists of guilds and armed societies to estimate the population, at its thirteenth-century peak, at about fifty thousand.[3] It may have been larger; many of the popolo minuto were excluded from the societies and guilds, and Pini's estimate of their number is conservative. Other towns grew even larger; Florence quadrupled in size in the century, reaching a population of ninety thousand to one hundred thousand.

People in the countryside were drawn to the town. A Bolognese estimo, or tax survey, of 1235 reveals that petty proprietors suffered a heavy burden of debt, largely for grain.[4] In 1256–57, Bologna freed 5,855 serfs and recorded their names in the *Liber Paradisus*. The civic government recompensed the landlords but gave the former serfs no resources to sustain them in the countryside. Many must have continued with old landlords, but we also know indirectly that they tended to seek opportunity in town. The civic government constantly struggled with the problem of rural depopulation and the need to keep a workforce in Bologna's small, and in part mountainous and unproductive, contado (rural district). Thirteenth-century legislators repeatedly attempted forcible repatriation of rural workers to increase the taxable and productive population in the countryside, while simultaneously recruiting skilled artisans—particularly textile workers—for the town.[5] Many of the people who poured in from the countryside, then, were landless laborers who worked outside of elite households and could not join a guild. Men became porters, laborers in the textile industry or in construction. Women worked in the textile trades, as spinners, seamstresses, weavers; in the trades associated with provisioning, as bakers, resellers of fruits and vegetables; as well as in domestic service, as laundresses, nurses.[6]

Rapid immigration sparked dynamic social improvisation as people coped with the changing urban environment. The result for a time was a real gulf between the culture and values of the urban elite and clergy and those of their poorer neighbors. Immigrants carried with them an older understanding of marriage, household, and even identity, views that might be little influenced by Roman law or Christian teaching. One aspect of creation of a shared urban culture was Christianization.[7] The Fourth Lateran Council in 1215 launched a serious effort to Christianize through preaching campaigns and a new emphasis on confession of sin. Another aspect was the growing reliance in the late twelfth and thirteenth centuries on notaries, professionals who drew up and recorded contracts according to specific legal formulas based in Roman and civic law.[8] These included marriages, testaments, and emancipation of children, as well as property sales and loans. The slow diffusion down the social scale of notarial record keeping redefined social relationships within the categories of Roman law. Bologna in the thirteenth century was the great center of legal and notarial culture; its university had the foremost legal faculty in Europe and produced superbly trained jurists and notaries, whose powerful guild wielded great influence in the town. Nevertheless, in Bologna too the legal and normative culture represented by the notarial instrument was not fully entrenched, even in 1280.

This chapter addresses one part of that cultural difference: understandings of marriage and female identity. There are superb studies of late-fourteenth- and fifteenth-century elite women, especially Florentines and Venetians. Their findings do not always apply to poor women in Bologna more than a century earlier. One set of questions concern how women were socialized. Christiane Klapisch-Zuber has shown for Florence that elite women were taught to be docile and to serve the interests of the patrilineal family. Stanley Chojnacki has shown that Venetian women enjoyed more initiative and control of resources within the family.[9] The circumstances of the poor were radically different from those of the daughters of the elite, especially poor women who worked outside of an elite household. In many cases, they could not marry. This was particularly evident during the mid-thirteenth to the mid-fourteenth centuries, when demographic and economic pressures limited women's access to marriage.[10] Women who did not have the social and economic protection of family and dowry were more aggressive, quick to develop survival strategies. The women visible in court records defend their interests with potent insults, at times with threats and blows, even with efforts to manipulate the courts.[11]

A related difference between elites and the poor concerns female identity. Clerics and the courts urged a strict dichotomy between honest married women and prostitutes—"common women" who were sexually available to all men.[12] These categories were more complicated in practice. Legal marriage based on exchange of dowry and counterdowry was normative.[13] But informal and temporary unions also existed; when William called Zoana his wife, he meant this kind of relationship. At the same time, prostitution was not clearly defined in practice. Most studies of medieval prostitution treat of the richly documented late-fourteenth and fifteenth centuries. By that time prostitutes were defined and marginalized, required to wear special dress, and live in identifiable brothels or a special district, with most trapped by forms of debt peonage.[14] In Bologna, prostitution was illegal inside the city walls from 1250, though women could ply the trade outside the town. A public bordello was established in the town only in the 1330s.[15] In the thirteenth century, people were not altogether convinced of this dichotomy. Again, Zoana is a good example: witnesses said that she sometimes sold sex but not that she was a common prostitute.

One strategy of lawmakers was to use clothing to establish a firm visual separation between honest women and prostitutes. The first extant sumptuary law, dating from 1250, allowed only a prostitute to wear a dress that touched the ground or had a long train.[16] Even nobles were not convinced. In July 1290, for example, the notary charged with enforcing the statute chased a noblewoman named Maxina down the street because the train on her dress looked to be longer than the law allowed. She outran him and slipped inside the door of her father's house to escape. Her husband was summoned by the court, then required to provide the dress to the court to be measured. It proved to be legal.[17] Apparently, Maxina and her servants had hemmed it in the interval. She and her husband evidently were not convinced that a long train made her look like a prostitute.

Sources

One reason for the lack of studies of the poor is the available evidence. Research on late medieval Italian women and marriage is largely based on tax records, account books, family memoirs, and notarial instruments. Those sources, with the exception of some tax records, leave out people without property unless they lived as a domestic in an elite household.[18] This chapter draws on another kind of source, testimony in civic court.

Inquests were a tool used by the court in a variety of cases, including state-initiated inquiries and cases sparked when an individual made an accusation to the court.[19] Both could lead to an investigation of the *fama*, or public reputation, of an accused person. Persons deemed "infamous" could be expelled from the town.[20] In prostitution cases, the court held an inquest into the fama of the accused women, questioning neighbors, landlords, servants, family members, the person thought to be the pimp, and even suspected customers. The accused could also produce witnesses in defense of their reputation. This chapter draws on testimony discussing approximately sixty-five women, dating between 1284 and 1299. Most derive from investigation of a woman's fama, often in response to a charge of prostitution, but they also include depositions from portions of cases concerning marriage, rape, assault, and homicide.

A deposition in a judicial inquest is a complex source. Witnesses spoke not freely but in response to specific questions. Notaries redacted their answers, translating spoken Italian into the formulaic Latin of the law. This was difficult: occasionally the notary gave up translating and shifted to Italian in the middle of a deposition. At the same time, witnesses surely calculated what could be safely said to the court. People manipulated the court to pressure each other—or even exact revenge, then as now. One example is a 1298 inquest held because a woman named Blonda notified the court that her neighbor, Meglior, was a sorceress, prostitute, and pimp who snatched young girls from their families so that she could sell their virginity. One of her victims was Blonda's own young daughter, Dulze. Meglior's defense against this lurid charge included a series of witnesses who pointed out that Blonda's son had recently been banned for an assault on Meglior. It was notorious in the neighborhood that Blonda in response had threatened Meglior with the courts. If she did not relax the young man's ban, Blonda had said, then she would lodge notifications and accusations that would get Meglior burned.[21]

For all these reasons, the testimony is hardly a direct look at the views of the people questioned, though it is by far the closest access we have. Many of the statements are best read as plausible stories. People did not always tell the absolute truth, but they were under considerable pressure to say things that were credible. Meglior's defenders argued convincingly that Blonda's daughter, Dulze, was not a kidnapped girl held against her and her mother's will, but that she was a man's amica, his lover or concubine. To give another example, a neighborhood woman testified that a young woman named Beatrixa had been given by her father to Tuccio, the priest, for a price of thirty pounds. Perhaps Beatrixa had not actually been sold, but she might have been. The story was credible. References to money exchanged for a daughter are fairly common. Thus despite the fact that some statements were surely fiction, they can be read with caution as a contemporary representation of social practice.[22]

These inquiries were at times a dialogue between elite culture and the culture of the witnesses, often Bologna's street culture. The questions posed in the inquest were based on a set of legal and clerical understandings of identity and behavior, understandings that often conflicted with the views of the people who were expected to answer. The witnesses did not all share a clear dichotomy between women of good repute and prostitutes. Instead, they mentioned several kinds of relation outside marriage. They also did not measure women strictly in terms of sexual continence but spoke in terms of economic necessity. The tales told by these witnesses do describe a culture not encompassed in studies of the elite, in Florence or elsewhere. There are vivid glimpses of ideas about female identity and about what it meant to be married, to be a concubine, an *amaxia*, or a prostitute.

Concubines and Informal Marriage

Some depositions describe a long-term co-residential union, best understood as informal marriage or concubinage. The legalities of concubinage were complex. Specialists in church law, who are termed canonists, were ambivalent. They viewed lay concubinage as quasi-marriage, which meant a union between a man and a woman who could have married but did not. This meant no property rights or rights of succession were involved, though canonists generally agreed that the children could be legitimated. They were much more concerned about clergymen who had wives or concubines. Despite all the efforts of reformers, priests with concubines probably remained common in the countryside and in most cities, as Daniel Bornstein has shown in a study of Cortona in the fourteenth century.[23] Clerical children posed awkward legal problems: they could not easily be legitimated because of the father's status.[24]

Lay concubinage was less worrisome. To the Church, a monogamous relationship with a concubine was a sort of second-class marriage. There was a risk that married men would take concubines, a practice considered bigamy and subject to severe penalty. To my knowledge, concubinage was not condemned in medieval Bolognese civic law. The only statute is a text in the 1288 compilation not on concubines but on amaxios and amaxias. The meaning of these terms, which appear commonly in depositions, is vague; perhaps they are best translated as "lovers." They were not always concubines, since this implies shared residence: an amaxia and amaxio could demonstrably be lovers who did not live together. The law does not ban the practice but simply insists on monogamy: people who are married are barred from having amaxios as well.[25] This recalls William's explicit arrangement with Zoana: if she lived with him he would not take a wife.

Why would a woman engage in an informal marriage? It may be that she did not have a dowry, which was the property a woman's family provided on her behalf at the time of her marriage. Poor households struggled to put together the dowry that made legal marriage possible for a daughter. Again, sources for women without dowries are elusive. In 1329, the Bolognese were invited to lament their poverty on their tax returns. One common complaint was the high cost of a dowry and marriage for a daughter. This was particularly hard for widows whose husbands had not provided for their daughters. A widow who was the head of a household with a declared patrimony of thirty-six lire somehow hoped to give each of her three daughters a fifty lire dowry. Another widow with a forty-three lire patrimony lamented that her twenty-year-old daughter "could not marry because of her lack of dowry."[26] These women had some modest resources. What proportion of households had virtually no ability to pay dowry? In a sample of two parishes, 23 and 32 percent of households declared themselves to be indigent.[27] Some daughters from these households might find the opportunity to earn a dowry, perhaps by working as a domestic.[28] Others would enter into an informal union. The actual numbers of women who did not marry are elusive. Isabelle Chabot's study of a fiscal survey from Florence in 1352 reveals that of 812 female heads of household, 43 percent were not widows. Only a small proportion of these women had ever married.

Informal marriage may have been the continuation of forms of peasant marriage for which we have no direct evidence. It resembled and perhaps originated in the Germanic *friedlehe*.[29] Marriage between peasants without property could be looser and more informal than the union based on exchange of dowry and counterdowry recorded by contemporary notaries. The *Liber Paradisus*, the list of serfs freed in 1257, is suggestive. It identifies 1,499 adult women, and in only 149 cases is there any indication of a husband, living or dead.[30] This evidence must be read with caution. Servile marriage was complicated by the fact that a free man who married an unfree woman shared in her status. Ironically, because serfs were exempt from some forms of civic exaction, marriage to a woman who was a serf became a tax dodge, which is one reason the town decided to eliminate serfdom.[31] Still, the scarcity of women with names indicating a husband or married parents suggests that informal arrangements were common.

Some women are described as given to a man by their family for a price, like Beatrixa, whose father was said by neighbors to have given her to Tuccio the priest as a concubine for a price ("pater . . . dedit dictam Beatrixam in concubina dicti Tucci ut teneret eam pro suam amicham et hec pro pretio et nomine pretii libras. . . .").[32] Perhaps this represents the persistence of early medieval forms of brideprice, recompense to a woman's family for the loss of her labor and reproductive capacity.[33] However, it was not considered honorable; witnesses stating that a woman had been exchanged for money were used to characterize her as *inhonesta*.

Occasionally, a woman left what was apparently a legal marriage to become a concubine. A husband would charge a runaway wife or his lover with adultery in court, probably often as a prelude to claiming the wife's dowry. In a number of cases, a man charged that his wife had left his house and was living with another man as his amaxia and bearing that man's children.[34] For example, Giovanni in 1287 charged Bartolomeo, who was a scribe, with adultery with his wife, Thomaxina. Soon after, he charged her with adultery, stating that she had become Bartolomeo's amaxia, lived in his house, and had borne him a son. Bartolomeo and Thomaxina did not respond to the summons and were banned in absentia. In another case, the husband charged that his wife had already borne her lover a daughter and now people were saying that she was pregnant again. A third adultery case was clearly driven by passion. In 1286, a Florentine named Tegna was charged with committing adultery "many times and many times" with Floriana. When her husband reclaimed her, Tegna went to their house and threatened to blind the husband with a lance if he did not give her back. Tegna's sentence of death by decapitation was probably carried out.[35] Thomaxina and Floriana apparently chose to leave whatever economic stability and status they had as wives. The choice reflects back on their marriages. Perhaps marriage was not so different from concubinage for a woman who had little dowry to lose, where there was little property to be passed to legitimate children. Surely some women fled husbands who, like William, were violently abusive.

A 1285 rape inquest suggests that in some circumstances concubinage—despite the lack of economic protections—might seem a reasonably good choice for a woman without a dowry. A youth named Zannos, accused of rape, responded with a long tale. He met Divitia, who is called a *puella*, a girl, in a man's house in Bologna. She was without resources and, as he pointed out to her, at risk of becoming a prostitute. Zannos asked her to come with him to his village. The two differed on the terms of the deal: she stated that Zannos promised marriage. Then, when he insisted on sex with her in an inn on the way to the village, it was against her will because he had not married her. Zannos claimed that he had made a different commitment to her: "I do not have a wife, and if you will come with me I will keep you as an amica until I have children from you. When I have children from you I will have just cause to ask my father's permission to take you as my wife without a dowry and then I'll take you as my wife."[36] This was a pretty good story and apparently did get him absolved of rape. He distinguished neatly between marriage and concubinage, with the line ultimately determined by paternal permission.

In canon law, of course, the couple needed only to exchange words of present consent to marry. But in practice, parental consent was crucial because marriage concerned family identity and transmission of property across generations.[37] It may be that Zannos and Divitia had varying understandings shaped by urban and rural customary differences. Zannos's promise could reflect practice in his village, where a concubine who produced heirs might become a wife. The inquests that mention urban concubines suggest that this would be implausible in town. A concubine like Zoana or Beatrixa tended not to rise in status but to lose it, ending up not legally married but rather providing sex to other men. It may be that when Divitia heard Zannos speak of possible marriage, her expectations were genuinely different from his intentions.

It cannot always have been obvious whether a woman was a wife or a concubine, as William's references to Zoana as his wife suggest. Testimony in a 1286 inquest into the fama of a woman called Margarita of Prato underscores this. A witness, asked how he knew that Margarita was married to Francisco, replied, "Because he saw Francisco and Margarita living together for the past ten years, and saw them many times at the same table and believed that they treated each other as a husband treats a wife and a wife a husband." He knew that there were three offspring, whom Francisco and Margarita receive and hold as their own children. Further, the husband "would not treat Margarita in this way if she were not a woman of good fame."[38] He judged on the basis of intangible patterns of behavior, how they sat together at table and how they treated the children.

What of the men who engaged in a temporary union? The common pattern was a man with property but for some reason unmarried, and a woman who lived in the household and surely provided domestic work as well as sex. One witness explained that he believed a woman to be a man's concubine because she lived in his house and very often prepared dinners and suppers for him.[39] As Zannos's story suggests, young men might be unable to marry. For economic reasons, families often postponed marriage for a son. There also were young men who could not marry because they had no property. Men did abduct women and sometimes claimed that they sought them as wives. Zannos and Divitia may be an example. Again, when Izo raped Umelta and tried to take her away from her father's house in a village in the Bolognese contado, he explained to her that he did not have a wife and "now accepted her as his wife."[40] Perhaps he hoped to force her father to acknowledge a fait accompli and pay him her dowry, assuming she had one. Perhaps he sought her as a concubine, or informal wife. Maybe he just hoped to coax her out the door, with no intention of marriage. His plan at any rate was ill-judged, since she went to the Bolognese court to accuse him of rape and attempted abduction.

Some men, like Tuccio the priest, took a concubine because they were barred from marriage. For the well-to-do urban layman, concubinage could be a temporary stage. A young man who for familial and financial reasons postponed marriage might look instead for a temporary relationship until he could marry and gain a wife's dowry, especially if he lived on his own. A merchant like Cambino, temporarily resident in a town, might well seek an equally temporary housekeeper and concubine. There was a double standard, since a man could move from concubinage to marriage, but a woman who had been a concubine was inhonesta.

There was a clash of interests, then, at the heart of the relations between a propertied man and a concubine without resources. Women were best served by a permanent union. Propertied men by contrast benefited from a temporary union without permanent obligation. It is for these reasons that Florentine merchants like Gregorio Dati in the late fourteenth century turned to female slaves to play the concubine's role.[41] The relationship was better defined and controlled, since a slave was not a second-class wife but rather chattel and could remain useful in a married household.

I have not seen evidence that prior relations with a concubine and illegitimate children could jeopardize a man's marriage. One fragmentary dispute from 1285 suggests the tension that could arise when a man replaced a concubine with a dowered wife. Neighbors said that the husband, Henricho, had had an amaxia named Adelasia and in fact had had a child with her. When he was married, Adelasia left his household. There is no suggestion that he contributed to her support. The section of the case that survives is the accusation against Adelasia by the wife's family: she had expelled the wife, had moved back in with Henricho, and was guilty of adultery. A witness told the story rather differently, however: it was when the wife's dowry was not paid in full that Henricho refused to allow her in the house and spoke with Adelasia in the street, and then Adelasia moved back in. The implication is that whether or not the husband felt any obligation to his amaxia, he did prefer her to his wife. Perhaps like William he had made a verbal commitment, giving Adelasia grounds for expecting monogamy.[42] Ironically, Adelasia was convenient for the wife's family as well. It would have been awkward to accuse Henricho, since they sought to restore his wife to her rights; instead, they could blame Adelasia.

There are a few incidental references to amaxios who did not have property. In 1290, a man produced three witnesses to prove that his sister Bendonia had built her "little house" with her own money, earned by doing washing for students and through a loan of six libras, which was carefully documented. Her amaxio, Stefano, was a tailor but did not exercise his profession and gambled, and ultimately murdered her. The witnesses were produced in an effort to argue that the little house belonged not to Stefano but rather to Bendonia and therefore should be inherited by her young son, Paul.[43] Their picture of a hard-working laundress victimized by her shiftless amaxio must at least have been credible.

Amaxias and Prostitutes

Many women had amaxios who did not live with them. In practice, they ranged from women who were monogamous to those who had an amaxio but lived in a brothel and sold sex to many men. Women who did not live under male authority were particularly apt to be suspected of prostitution. One example is a group of women who were denounced in 1287 by the ministrales of their neighborhood as prostitutes. Two of them, Bellotina and her sister, were the daughters of a late notary from Bologna (an example of downward social mobility). The people summoned to testify included the women themselves, the landlady, and some neighbors. Their landlady, a widow named Gasdia, stated that they had lived in her house in the parish for months. She was at risk of a charge of brothel keeping, which would mean a large fine. Asked whether the women were prostitutes, she said no. But, she said, "They certainly have their lords whom they serve when the lords want."[44] In Gasdia's version, they were not prostitutes. However, they did give services to men with whom they had a defined relationship: the men were their lords.

What did Gasdia mean? The relations she described recall a form of prostitution in colonial Nairobi studied by Luise White: women had defined clienteles of migrant workers, to whom they gave what were called the comforts of home, services that included hospitality and meals as well as sex.[45] In Bologna, a town with about two thousand male students, it seems entirely credible that these three women played a similar role, offering services that included sex and other comforts as well. Students, after all, have needs like those of migrant workers, and also probably meager resources. The use of the term *dominus*, or lord, is revealing; like the vassal of a feudal lord, a woman traded service for some support.

A witness in a 1288 inquest into the condition of four women made a similar comment. He did not call them prostitutes. Instead, he said, "They are women of a band and give themselves to serve men for a price and wash their heads and do other various services."[46] Similarly, Flordelixia, a woman from Padua whom a neighbor accused of prostitution, responded that she and her mother lived in rental housing, for which they paid fifty *soldi* a year. She was not a prostitute but did have an amaxio, named Nutus of Castro Plebis, who paid her expenses.[47]

Another inquest is similar. Two sisters, Nuta and Santa, were suspected of prostitution. Their mother came from Imola; it is not known how long they had lived in Bologna. Their landlord admitted that he rented the house (on behalf of the owner) to the mother of Nuta. "He denied that they were prostitutes and kept a brothel there but said that each of them had her amaxium whom she served with her person, as he Tebaldus believed."[48] When Santa was questioned, she said the same thing but mentioned payment: "She certainly had her lover who paid her expenses." Nuta said the same thing. In effect, they were not common women but had lovers who did not live with them though they paid expenses for them. This was, if not true, at least a credible defense. It was to no avail; they were fined and banned from the city under threat of a beating. In other words, the court defined them not as concubines but as prostitutes.

The defense of a woman named Guicciardina, who was accused of prostitution, is revealing. She earned her living selling candles, oils, and herbs from her home. A witness stated that she was considered a woman of good reputation and good condition, and the people of her neighborhood treated her as a good woman and freely associated with her; the witness had never heard that she did any evil. She was the amaxia of a student, but in all other things she was held to be a good woman."[49] Clearly, the witness did not accept the dichotomous view of female identity urged by the courts.

In sum, a poor woman who had no prospect of marriage might establish a relationship with a man (or men) who visited her for services in exchange for "expenses," which meant a supplement to income. In one case, a man is described as bringing bread and wine when he visited his amica.[50] The economic opportunities available to independent women in a medieval town were quite restricted. They tended to be very poor.[51] It is entirely credible that despite the obvious drawbacks—including pregnancy as well as the question of fama—a woman might choose to supplement a desperately meager income in this way without becoming a prostitute in the sense of being a woman sexually available to all men. This was perhaps a more straightforward economic exchange than concubinage. It was surely preferable to prostitution, among other things because no pimp or procurer shared their earnings. Some women admitted to prostitution but stated that they wanted no pimp but themselves. Other prostitutes described paying half of their revenues to a pimp.[52]

In some cases, a woman's amaxio was also her pimp. In a 1286 prostitution case, a man named Corsino responded to questions by stating that a young woman named Lucia was his servant and amaxia and that he kept her in a house in San Lorenzo. Prostitutes did frequent the house and associate with her, so the neighbors might well consider her to be one of them. But even though university students and other men came to her for services, this meant that she washed their hair and rendered other care.[53] Was this creditable? A 1293 addition to the town's statute on prostitution made reference to an association between head washing and prostitution: no prostitutes, no keepers of prostitutes, and no woman who washes hair was allowed to remain in a particular parish.[54] Lucia may have been a common prostitute and Corsino her pimp. Or perhaps she served as Corsino's servant and lover and made money by washing students' hair.

What happened to these women as they aged? The frequency of references to young women who were amaxie or prostitutes and lived with their mothers suggests that their status tended to be passed on to their daughters, who were illegitimate and would have little chance at legal marriage but might help to support an aging mother. Mothers often were charged with prostituting their daughters. One example is a woman named Maria who, a witness testified, had formerly been a priest's concubine and now was her daughter's pimp.[55]

The court tended to subsume amaxie under the category of common prostitutes. The result is a fascinating example of the interplay of gender and state formation: the city government was eliminating ambiguous categories of women (defined by sexual availability) to draw a clear line, creating a single and easily identifiable marginal class of common prostitutes. In theory, the line separated the monogamous from those who were sexually available. But in practice, residence in a household under male authority was crucial. A concubine lived in a monogamous household headed by a man and was tolerated as a second-class wife; a woman who had a single lover and thus was monogamous but did not live with him was defined a prostitute.

Conclusions

Historians tend to think of the late medieval town as a society governed by customary practices and a code of honor that had little flexibility.[56] The people described here, at times despite material constraint, enjoyed a startling liberty. To return to Cambino and Zoana, the pair was able to view their relations as freely chosen.

Unlike a contemporary elite, whose union depended on money, politics, and family connection, they could talk in terms of love. Cambino repeatedly explained his relations with Zoana in these terms, although it did not help him with the court. A neighbor stated that when Cambino was carrying her off and William yelled, "You are doing an evil thing because you are carrying off my wife," Cambino answered, "Thief, you beat her for my love and I will do you an injury if I can." It is true that according to another witness he was more vivid and specific. A modern translation might be "You filthy piece of excrement, I'm going to rip you up good."

Zoana's circumstances are fascinating. Her apparent categorization by the court as inhonesta saved Cambino from a legal fine. It also probably saved her, since it placed her outside patriarchal controls. William had no authority over her. Had she been his wife, she could not easily have left him and might perhaps, as the neighbors pointed out, have been beaten to death. In fact, her circumstances were more ambivalent. Living as a concubine and occasional prostitute, unprotected by dowry or patrilineal family, she was in many ways at risk but also at liberty. She could choose to leave with Cambino. This does not mean, either, that Zoana had an easy life. She and her children were not protected by law or even by custom. Cambino had no obligation, and the court could have had her beaten and expelled from the city as a common prostitute, though there is no evidence in the register that they did so. Still, like Cambino, she was at liberty to understand their relations in terms of love. By contrast, a love match was literally unthinkable for a dowered bride of the elite, who lived and married within a patrilineal system of values.

This was a period of rapid change and social improvisation, much of it not visible to us because it was not recorded in notarial instrumenta. There was no single, shared understanding of the various kinds of female role discussed here. The inquests at times reveal a collision of values. A woman who gave a man she called her dominus services in exchange for expenses considered herself an amaxia; court officials genuinely thought her a prostitute. The thirteenth century was a period of Christianization, a time in which mendicant preaching campaigns and the new emphasis on confession of sin taught the town population shared moral categories. Infamy, after all, was an administrative category shaped by Roman law and by Christian ideas about moral behavior and reputation. The inquest testimony suggests that campaigns to teach these ideas enjoyed limited success, even in sophisticated Bologna.

Nevertheless, the court inquiries were very much a part of those campaigns. They can be viewed as an effort to inculcate a set of normative understandings of identity. This is the process Foucault termed "normalization": definition of certain practices as normal and exclusion of alternatives as deviant. Inquests into suspected prostitution surely fit this approach. As Maria Serena Mazzi has pointed out, a court inquiry into a woman's *fama* reinforced behavioral norms that defined a woman as "honest."[57] Such cues as dress, demeanor, network of sociability, and neighborhoods frequented were recited publicly as a way to determine whether a woman was *inhonesta*. Of course, penalties could be severe. Zoana is exceptional in that she may have benefited from being categorized as *inhonesta* because she was able to escape a violently abusive lover. Nuta and Santa, who were probably driven into common prostitution, were more typical. In effect, poor women were pressured to live within a set of restrictive behavioral norms. The inquests thus contributed to gradual narrowing of the range of social possibilities that characterized the late medieval town.

CHAPTER EIGHT

Lost Faith

A Roman Prosecutor Reflects on Notaries' Crimes

Laurie Nussdorfer

Although the high literacy of the Florentine merchants made them fertile ground for the cultural movements of the Renaissance, Italy's other urban communities were equally committed to the written word. In Europe's first commercial society, even those who could not read understood the force of the documentary record. In the Middle Ages, the cities of Italy invented a powerful new way of certifying the truth. Instead of relying on divine intervention, through sworn oath or trial by ordeal, Italian urban dwellers created a profession endowed by organs of government with the status of official truthteller: the notary.

It took several hundred years for all the elements to come together, but by the thirteenth century they were in place. Rulers of cities, professors of law, and judges on the bench all agreed that a designated set of writers were public persons; their words were thus suffused with the power of public authority and must be believed. They expressed the special quality of these scribes as their possession of *publica fides* ("public trustworthiness"). The words of notaries, they said, were proof.[1] Armed with this knowledge, Italians became the first Europeans routinely to seek a legal guarantee in writing when they bought or sold, rented or hired, married or died.

Although the statutes of the Italian cities were most responsible for establishing the notary's peculiar character as a writer, medieval jurists were the ones who thought about it most thoroughly. Teachers, in the recently founded universities, of the exciting new curriculum of ancient Roman legal texts, the jurists were forced to think hard and inventively about public notaries because the Romans, who did not have them, were silent on the subject. So from the twelfth to fourteenth centuries such Italian law professors as Ruggerius, Tancredus, Azo, Bartolus of Sassoferrato, and Ubaldi Baldus fleshed out the implications of the ingenious concept that private individuals could be transformed into creators of "public writing" (*scriptura publica*), in their commentaries on the great sixth-century compilation of Roman laws, the *Corpus Iuris Civilis* ("Book of the Civil Law") of Justinian. The power of their interpretations cannot be underestimated because only those passages in Justinian's text that they had glossed were recognized by the courts.[2]

The significance of the notary's words for these scholars requires attention to their conception of truth and its relation to proof. Truth was divine and needed no proof; thus crimes that were obvious (*notorium*) did not have to be proved.[3] For those misdeeds and disputes that were more obscure, however, the scholarly commentators fell back on reasoned judgment on the basis of evidence. They developed a hierarchy of proof to indicate how evidence should be evaluated in a courtroom, and they located notarial documents, also known as instruments, in the highest place.[4] The truth might elude them, but the law professors, who were also judges, could at least hope to serve the cause of justice by creating powerful juridical conceptions and buttressing the legal institutions that put them into effect. Proof was arguably one of the most potent conventions at their disposal. Their decision that the notary's word proved in court had immense consequences for the history of the written word in medieval and early modern Italian society.

The teachings of the medieval jurists were extraordinarily durable. In the late sixteenth century, they were still so authoritative that their commentaries on Justinian's "Book of the Civil Law" were published in repeated editions. This was in the face of challenge from a humanistically inspired legal scholarship that sought in the same century to read Justinian's text in a more historically sensitive manner than theirs. This movement toward a renaissance in law, though influential elsewhere, made no headway in early modern Italy.[5] Instead, what happened there was that the printing press gave a new burst of energy to the tradition of commentary. As the sixteenth century progressed, new legal lights, such as Philip Decius and Giulio Claro, contributed their glosses on Justinian's text to those of their forebears, and publishers began to cater to the lucrative market for law books not only by promoting single authors but by launching ambitious compilations. In 1584, for instance, a group of Venetian printers brought out a complete set of all the medieval and modern legal texts ever published, in twenty-four grand folio volumes.[6] This was the intellectual and economic context for the work that concerns us here, a vastly successful manual on crime written for legal professionals by the famous Roman lawyer Prospero Farinacci (1544–1618) over a thirty-five-year period of 1581 through 1614.

When Farinacci began his labors, he was a bright attorney in his late thirties in desperate need of a way to improve his reputation. Having lost his left eye in a fight, he was arrested for carrying an unlicensed weapon and even deprived, temporarily, of the right to practice law.[7] Between one scrape and another, he launched into a treatment of how to initiate legal proceedings, as discussed in the commentaries of medieval and early modern jurists, which eventually grew into an eighteen-part compendium on criminal law and procedure. Farinacci had seen an opportunity for profit in what others might have viewed as a problem. The commentators set out their arguments in the scholastic form of debate, in which opinions for and against a particular proposition were each elaborated as convincingly as possible. Early modern judges reading these treatises might well find them putting forth contradictory positions. If what the jurists meant to say was not clear, how were judges and attorneys to apply their teachings correctly?

The need for a guide, especially in the field of criminal law, was evident; what was called for was a handbook that would sum up everything written on a given topic by these learned predecessors and by those who had subsequently commented on them. Thus, in eighteen sections (*titoli*) published between 1589 and 1616, Farinacci tried to provide this helpful manual to the trade, remaining as faithful as possible to the jurists' statements on crime and procedure but organizing them in a manner that he hoped would make them accessible to a readership of legal professionals.[8] In the process, this brilliant and unscrupulous attorney overcame the liability of a deservedly bad reputation and progressed almost to the pinnacle of the Roman judicial hierarchy, becoming chief state prosecutor under Pope Paul V (1605–1621) before his eventual fall from grace.

Farinacci made no attempt to treat the crimes most commonly committed in his era, focusing instead on those that were most serious. He had already covered treason, homicide, and "carnal crimes" in the fifteen preceding titles when he took up the subject of forgery, more precisely the crime of *falsum*, which in Roman law covered any form of counterfeiting, in the tome first published by the Giunti's prestigious firm in Venice in 1612.[9] Falsifying documents of any sort, from personal letters to notarial acts, fell into this category since all forms of writing had some, though not equal, probative value in the hierarchy of proof. Since a text could be criminally manipulated, a judge needed to know what to look for or whom to listen to when the authenticity of a written artifact was challenged in court. It turned out that the jurists who had done so much to build up trust in the notary's words had not neglected the problem of what would undo that trust. Although they did not agree on all the details, they had a great deal to say about how notarial writing might lose its power to prove.

Farinacci's much reprinted handbook offers a fresh way to look at early modern attitudes and assumptions about documents, especially the notarial record. We follow this Roman prosecutor as he guides his seventeenth-century readers through the thicket of contradictory advice from the medieval jurists on when to believe and when not to believe the notary's public words. But first we have to ask why it mattered to Farinacci. Why single out the notary for such scrutiny? The son of a Roman notary himself and an active criminal magistrate and student of penal law, Farinacci, we might suppose, would often have had occasion to ponder the deeds and misdeeds of a profession so caught up in the operation of the law courts.[10] Though chary of speaking for himself in his treatise, he does seem to think that use of notarial instruments had grown more frequent since the days of Bartolus and Baldus.[11] Given that belief, Farinacci must have thought that contemporary judges needed to be all the more alert to untruth in notarial text.

But in some ways, his concern about notaries seems perverse. Medieval Italian citizens may have been taught by their magistrates that notarial writing was the best and safest mode of inscribing their desires, but they had never confined their record keeping to the notary alone. Their business account books, letters, and family diaries all attest to their understanding that the important point was to document a transaction. Notarial writing had always competed with what the jurists called *scriptura privata* ("private writing"), the records penned by ordinary persons; use of private documentation was the real growth area in sixteenth- and seventeenth-century Italy.[12] If Farinacci thought his contemporaries paid too many visits to notaries, he did not notice that they were bringing them their own texts to certify and transform into public writing.

To appreciate why Farinacci lingered on the falseness of notaries, therefore, we need to include in our view both of the worlds he inhabited, the law courts and the study. As an author, he desired that his treatise on crime be comprehensive and complete; he wished, to the point of obsession, not to miss a single topic raised by his sources. If the jurists he read had their sights fixed on the notary, Farinacci would make sure his readers did too. Farinacci wanted his manual to be the last word—perhaps the last book any judge or lawyer needed to buy. Because it was based on the best theory available, it was meant to stand as an encyclopedic statement for all time, not to reflect the fleeting idiosyncrasies of a particular moment.

Farinacci's ambition reminds us how powerfully medieval legal discourse maintained its capacity to shape early modern understanding in

Italy. This was certainly the case with the idea of proof and the concept of public writing. The success of Farinacci's discussion of mostly medieval texts presented in the traditional genre of scholastic commentary underscores the roles of both the conservative Italian legal profession and the entrepreneurs of the new technology of print in preserving this potent intellectual heritage.

Conforming to the conventions of scholastic argumentation, Farinacci's eighteen-part treatise was structured as a series of questions, each followed by a general answer or rule gleaned from the largest number of authorities, followed by elaboration and limitation on each rule, with supporting and opposing citations from the jurists. The sixteenth part, "On false and fictitious acts" (*De falsitate et simulatione*), consisted of questions 150 to 164, of which 153 to 158 were most directly relevant to the notary.[13]

Let us begin with the jurists' positive assessment of notaries' words, and then consider how these words could be weakened or lose their force. The special strength of writing from the pen of a notary was its credibility; it had *magna fides* ("great trustworthiness"). "The doctors of law," wrote Farinacci, "say that the notarial instrument is 'evident truth,' 'real proof,' and is called '*noli me tangere*' ['touch me not']." Within a juridical context, three assumptions underpin the notarial document: "that it is true, that it is correct, [and] that everything described in it has occurred." Summing up the medieval commentators, Farinacci stressed the invincible character of the instrument as a graphic marker: "It has definitive force, it has ready execution, it is said to be 'proof proven,' to make a manifest matter very manifest, an evident one very evident, transparent and publicly known (*notorium*)."[14] Because of the notary's trustworthiness, he goes on to argue, when we find something suspicious in a notarial document we should assume that the notary had simply made a mistake rather than deliberately falsified his text.

Nevertheless, with feigned reluctance Farinacci directed his readers to the problem of the notary's misdeeds. "Let us pass now to the subject of falsehoods that are committed by notaries in many ways, would that it were not so."[15] From his detailed exposition in questions 153 to 158, we learn that the credibility of a notarial document could be undermined essentially in two ways: by questions about its physical appearance and by the testimony of witnesses who denied that what it said was true. Let us begin with the material defects that could make the instrument suspect and unable to prove. The notary was supposed to produce a meticulously crafted artifact and to preserve it in a carefully ritualized way. Its credibility depended on graphic and physical integrity, and on how it was archived.

Let us follow Farinacci's typical scholastic mode of presentation in the example of additions to a text. He began with the statement of the general rule gleaned from his sources: any addition, especially in the margin, to an instrument or other piece of writing automatically rendered it suspect (Q. 153, no. 2). The nine subsequent limitations to this general rule characteristically both sharpened and obscured its clarity. Additions found in a suspicious place in the text (no. 4) or in a "substantial part" (no. 5), in a different hand or in a different ink than that used in the body of the text (nos. 7, 15), were warning signs of forgery. Some authorities added that totally irrelevant marginalia were also suspect (no. 22), and others limited the general rule by local custom, which might permit the notary to make a marginal addition to an instrument (no. 23). The rule was almost completely undercut by the seventh limitation, which said that in doubtful cases the addition should be assumed to have been made at the same time as the original agreement and with the consent of the parties (no. 24).

Farinacci's eighth limitation recognized, more fully than the general rule, the actual ways the notary worked. Additions to the finished and authenticated instrument or testament were stigmatized, but not those found in the earliest stage, the *matrix*, prior to its acceptance by the testator or parties.[16] As he pointed out, the notary had to make additions, interlineations, and erasures in the process of writing down the unstable desires of the client, especially in the case of a will (Q. 153, no. 26). Not only was it perfectly justifiable for these documents to betray the marks of revision; Farinacci thought it impossible for them not to, affirming that making changes to the *matrix* was the custom among notaries that he observed (presumably in Rome).

The final limitation to the general rule against additions to a text enabled formulation of a significant theme. Additions in the same hand might arouse suspicion of forgery, but they were insufficient to prosecute. Instead, they took away the credibility (*fides*) that the instrument had acquired as a result of being drawn up by a notary (Q. 153, no. 29). The notion that the probative worth of writing was not absolute, that it needed to be evaluated on a spectrum ranging from total proof to complete forgery, was pervasive in Farinacci's discussion.[17] The power of the public instrument was in the end relative. A notarial document might begin by being completely believable but then lose trust as a result of disfiguring marks—yet not so completely that it carried no claim whatsoever to truth. It was not false, but it did not prove.

Crossing out words, adding words between the lines, and erasures were additional suspicious signs that created doubt about the veracity of an instrument; each of these material defects was discussed at length by

Farinacci. Into an omnibus category he grouped all the other physical markers that carried a presumption of forgery. These included bad grammar or poor phrasing (Q. 153, nos. 151, 153); stained and dirty paper or paper with holes (no. 185); cut pages (no. 184); watered ink that might seem older than it really was (no. 173); and crowded lines of text, especially where they might have been added in the blank spaces at the top or bottom of a page (no. 178).

Up to this point, the disfiguring marks emphasized by Farinacci's authorities were those of which any forger was capable. But the jurists knew that clients chose notaries over other scribes because of their official status as public writers and their expertise in the legal language of contracts and testaments. If notaries did not live up to specific expectations, their documents would be worthless and they might even be prosecuted. What were the most vulnerable points in their writing practices?

One was the business reality of scribal labor. The notary's signature and seal on a document identified it not merely as his production but as public writing, with the full power to prove that that quality entailed. Yet the notary who put his signature and seal to a writing had not necessarily written it out himself. If he had a large clientele or ran a government bureau, he had a staff of clerks working for him. The jurists seemed reluctant to accept the possibility that the name and hand of the notary might diverge, and despite the fact that this was customary in his own day, Farinacci duly reported their hesitations (Q. 153, no. 120). What was the status of an instrument that the notary claimed he had written but that was not in his script? When could a notary without an impediment have an instrument written by someone other than himself? What if two different hands were present in the same document (Q. 153, no. 112)? Early modern judges who routinely reviewed instruments produced by the employees of busy notarial offices may well have found Farinacci an unsettling guide when he raised such questions.

A second vulnerable point was the language of the instrument itself. Although neither jurists nor Farinacci remarked on it, clients showed a remarkable degree of trust in the notary's translation of their wishes. They summoned the notary or went to his office, told him what they wanted in the vernacular, and paid him. He quickly jotted down a few abbreviated phrases in Latin, recorded the place and date of the encounter in the presence of witnesses, and took their money. Later, he took this original or *matrix* and made a full Latin version (*protocollum*) complete with what the jurists called the "customary formulas" (*consuetae clausulae*).[18] The jurists never specified what the customary formulas were; that depended on local formularies. But they did debate the consequences of omitting or manipulating any of them.[19] A judge should also be wary of a notary who put unconventional clauses or articles into an instrument (Q. 153, no. 162).

Beyond the question of the legal phrases included or left out, however, was the more fundamental issue of whether the notary had accurately rendered what the testator or parties to a contract intended. Was the notary's full Latin version (protocollum), which could not have been in the same words as the one registered in the presence of the client and witnesses, faithful to it? Moreover, there was an additional optional phase of documentary reproduction. Italian clients did not routinely receive their own copy of an instrument or will; if they wanted a signed and sealed copy of the protocollum, normally kept on file in a bound volume in the notary's office, they had to pay an extra fee. So textual discrepancies at three distinct points—the hastily scribbled matrix, the full file version, and the customer's eventual copy—gave the jurists a great deal to think about. If contradictions appeared, which document should be believed? This question inevitably foregrounded the notary's legal responsibilities as the client's archivist.

Indeed, their archival practices distinguished notaries most thoroughly from all other scribes. As we have seen, the notary made two and possibly three kinds of record of each transaction and was legally responsible for keeping some, if not all, material traces of this process.[20] A judge could expect a dispute about missing documents to bring the notary and client into court. Some jurists reasoned that since it was the duty of the notary, not his client, to keep the original and the full file version, if these could not be found the notary was guilty of forgery.[21] At the very least, a copy lacking its master was worthless. As Farinacci put it, "instruments without their protocolla are suspected of forgery and prove nothing."[22]

If a missing matrix or protocollum cast doubt upon an instrument supposedly copied from it, the jurists were also suspicious when a copy of an instrument differed from either of them (Q. 153, no. 126). The protocollum had greater credibility than any copy subsequently taken from it (no. 127), but if there were a conflict between them the jurists advised going back one more step to examine the matrix, the very first notes that the notary had written down (no. 128). The jurists insisted on the value of these rough and hasty scrawls, so long as the original was legible, even if it was crossed out or missing the notary's signature and seal (nos. 130, 131). Farinacci cited no less an authority than Baldus for the view that the substance of an agreement lay in the *prima scriptura* ("the earliest writing"; no. 142). He quoted another jurist who advised, "when the trustworthiness of an instrument is in doubt, go to the notary's notebook (*bastardellum*) or sheet of paper on which the first writing of the instrument is made, as long as it is not so completely crossed out that it cannot be read."[23] The jurists had higher archival standards than the notaries of Farinacci's own time. Although their discussion assumed that these notebooks and loose sheets of paper, as well as volumes of bound instruments, were in the notary's possession, Farinacci had to acknowledge that it was not a universal custom for notaries in his day to keep their original jottings.[24]

In his catch-all category "various other presumptions of forgery," Farinacci included a number of suspicious archival practices. Among these were bound volumes composed of nonmatching paper booklets (*quinterni*) on which notaries had written out the full version of instruments (no. 168), as well as extra holes visible on the cover of a bound volume—implying that pages might have been removed (no. 169). The judge should also be wary of a notary who delayed making the full file version and binding it in chronological order with the others (no. 181); who mixed up the order of pages in the bound volume (no. 189); or who failed to list an instrument in the volume's table of contents, if it was customary to have a table of contents (*rubricella*; no. 162).[25]

Material defects in the written artifact and suspicious preservation practices challenged and sometimes took away the power of the notary's words. There was no question that a prosecutor had to take seriously the physical and graphic integrity of notarial records. But the document could look perfect and still be false. Why not? A notary who knew how to draw up a legitimate act could certainly draft one that looked legitimate. There was no necessary sign to give away the fact—for example, that the notary had written down a different heir than the one named by the dying testator. In a legal system without notaries, Roman law had placed high evidentiary value on the witness. It was easy for medieval Italian jurisprudence to combine tradition and innovation by insisting that there be witnesses to any notarial act; at least two witnesses for an instrument; and, following the ancients, seven for a last will and testament. But this opened up a conundrum. What if the notary's record was disputed by its witnesses? Farinacci admitted that the jurists "torture this topic amazingly," and he tried to guide his readers through the bewildering variety of opinions on the problem.[26]

In a contest between a notary and witnesses, whose word proved? The general rule was plain: witnesses could disprove a notarial instrument. But how many witnesses, what kind, and under what circumstances (Q. 158, no. 2)? Most authorities agreed that if two witnesses who were actually present at the transaction and whose names were recorded at the end of the instrument or will, the so-called instrumentary and testamentary witnesses, denied that the parties had made an agreement or had said what the notary had written down, the document was false (no. 4). Furthermore, it was false if two such witnesses denied that they had really been there, even if a hundred other witnesses testified that what was written in the instrument was true (nos. 7, 10). However, if only one witness disputed the record, it merely lost credibility (no. 13), unless it was a will or a codicil, which would be invalidated if it lacked the minimum number of seven witnesses (no. 20).

We can get a clear sense of what the notary's presence meant in a text by comparing the fate of a piece of private writing (*scriptura privata*, what the law called a document by an ordinary person). "Such writing gets its strength from witnesses," one authority commented, so "it is naked and proves nothing" if they are not available to defend it.[27] Scriptura privata could be undone by a single witness, or by the unhappy circumstance that all its witnesses were dead. The force that the notary added to words was the power to endure beyond the grave.

Should a witness who had not been present at the transaction, but who might have pertinent information, be treated in the same manner as an instrumentary witness? The jurists agreed that "extraneous" witnesses could also undermine a notarial document, but they disagreed about how many it would take.[28] Some supported the opinion of Innocent III that two or at most three were sufficient (Q. 158, no. 32), but the much respected *Glossa ordinaria* ("Ordinary Gloss") demanded a higher test—as many as five witnesses—declaring that "the authority of the notary was the equivalent of two witnesses" (no. 37). As he often did in an intractable dispute between his sources, Farinacci ultimately settled for the most commonly held opinion and for giving a broad role to the judge actually hearing the case to decide on the exact number required to prove an instrument false (no. 48).[29]

In the event that the judge felt he needed more information, the jurists offered assistance. In doubtful cases where repudiation of the instrument by two witnesses was insufficient to prove it false, a deeper investigation was justified and the notary should be tortured (Q. 158, no. 69). If the notary had a bad reputation, some authorities even argued that one witness might be sufficient to invoke torture (nos. 72, 73). On the other hand, witnesses of low social status (*viles personae*) who disputed a notary in good repute might find themselves heading for the torture chamber instead (no. 103).

Of course, witnesses to a will or instrument might not agree with each other. Faced with contradictory testimony, the judge needed to weigh those supporting the document against those saying it was false. At first glance, the jurists seemed to prefer witnesses speaking in favor of an instrument; Farinacci cited six authorities for the statement that "two witnesses supporting the instrument and affirming that what is contained in the instrument is true are more to be believed than a thousand denying it."[30] He himself advanced the view that if two sets of witnesses both offered detailed narration of the facts, those supporting the document were more trustworthy (Q. 158, no. 151). However, this preference was more apparent than real because numbers in the end did count, and if there were more naysayers than supporters the instrument would lose credibility.[31] For all intents and purposes, therefore, the notary did not seem to have much advantage over the minimum two witnesses. But the jurists would not permit public writing to be dismissed quite so lightly. Before putting faith in witnesses, they insisted on checking who they were, and they set high standards for their testimony.

The judge had to make sure that he had the right witnesses and that they were credible. Many people had the same name, and it was easy for a witness to change his name (Q. 158, no. 137). A witness objecting to an instrument had to prove that he was the same person named in it, and he had to prove who he was if the adversary in a case showed that there were others in that community with the same name and surname.[32] Some jurists thought that it was only necessary to prove the identity of a witness who was a foreigner or unknown person; in other cases, it was enough that the information about each witness given in the notarial document had not been contradicted (no. 140). The judge also needed to consider the trustworthiness of the witness. The jurists agreed that women and dishonorable (*infamis*) men were not believable (nos. 92, 94), but Farinacci could not squeeze anything more specific out of them, at least in this volume, despite a lengthy discussion.[33]

The jurists had more to say about the quality of the oral evidence required to disprove a notarial document (Q. 158, no. 116). It was poor testimony if witnesses to an instrument or will said they could not remember being there (no. 118); not remembering was weak evidence against a notary. A witness who said he could not recall a written agreement drawn up by someone who was not a notary automatically disproved it, but a witness who forgot whether he was present when a notary drew up an instrument did not even raise doubt about it (nos. 124, 118). More credible was a witness who stated under oath, "The notary made a mistake; we did not hear those words, but some other words that we do not remember," for this constituted stronger testimony against the document.[34]

Similarly, it was not enough for witnesses to say that they believed or judged the instrument to be false (Q. 158, no. 117); they must offer hard sensory data, the evidence of what they had actually seen and heard. The instrument should not be rejected because a witness said that he had not heard the words the notary had written down, unless he added that if they had been said he would have heard them; nor could they have been said without his hearing them (no. 125). However, some jurists thought this degree of explicitness was not necessary for a witness to an instrument or will because those witnesses were asked to be particularly attentive listeners; it was enough for them to say simply that they had not heard the words (no. 128). Witnesses attempting to disprove an instrument or will had to give reasons for what they were saying, without being prompted (no. 136). They also had to testify that the writing they witnessed took place at a particular moment and location because identical instruments could have been drawn up at another time or place (nos. 131, 132).

Notaries working for the courts often recorded the deposition of a witness in a criminal investigation or civil suit, sometimes on their own and sometimes before a judge. Although Farinacci had much more to say about the writing a notary did for a private client than for the magistrate, he did not neglect judicial labors entirely. What should a judge do if a witness whose interrogation had been recorded by a court notary claimed that his deposition was false? On the whole, the jurists seemed to give more faith to the notary in a judicial context than outside it. Their general rule in such cases was to trust the notary (Q. 158, no. 187), especially if a judge had also been present at the examination or the notary had asked the questions while another scribe recorded the witness's answers (nos. 189, 191). According to one jurist, the notary's word should also be preferred if the witness had signed the deposition, as long as the signature was properly rendered and the notary had read the deposition aloud to him. To this, Farinacci added the telling comment that "among us" the witness needed to ask the notary to read his testimony back to him, implying that this was not automatic in Rome (no. 192). Nevertheless, these judicial marks of esteem for the notary were tempered by some contrary indications. If the notary had a bad reputation or was a suspicious and base (*vilis*) person while the deponent was a noble, trustworthy, or notable person, such as one with a university degree (*doctor*) or a magistrate, then the judge should decide whom to believe (no. 193).

As we might expect, the jurists debated whether the fact that more than one witness disputed the notary's courtroom record of their words upset the rule favoring the notary. Some said the number had to be taken into account, while others said that it was not credible that a writer (*scriniarum*) would write something different from what the witnesses said, and therefore the deponents should not be trusted (Q. 158, nos. 197, 198). One jurist argued even more decisively in the notary's favor, saying that such a naysayer should be tortured "because the authority of the notary prevails and has the force of two witnesses."[35] Farinacci saw a way to resolve the contradiction between his authorities by emphasizing again the respective reputations of witness and notary (no. 199), and by distinguishing civil and criminal cases. In civil cases, he said, trust the notary; in criminal cases, believe neither one (nos. 202, 204). Then he moved on to other forms of falsehood.

Farinacci's handbook on crime had tremendous success not only in Italy but elsewhere in Europe in the seventeenth century and even until the eighteenth century, when the first complaints about its prolixity, confusion, and repetitiveness began to be heard.[36] It was not until the scholastics' hold on Italian legal thinking began to waver with the reform movements of the Age of Enlightenment that it fell out of fashion. Until that time, Farinacci's desire to bring to his professional colleagues the sophisticated and complex arguments of the great medieval and early modern commentators on penal law seems to have borne fruit. We confront in his text, therefore, the authoritative theoretical statement, or statements, on the character of notarial writing in early modern Italy. What are the implications of these teachings for seventeenth-century notaries, clients, and judges?

A notary could no doubt take some comfort in the knowledge that it was not easy to prove his writing was false. Notarial words took longer to fall from their quasi-sacral status as "evident truth" to the abyss of forgery than the words of other writers. But the early modern notary knew that his clients had learned over the centuries how to imitate the forms and rituals of a notarial agreement, and that the judges would have to lend some credence to these rival words. The notary must have been uneasy therefore about the jurists' willingness to give weight to private writing, about their reluctance to define the correct customary formulas, and about their demanding standards for conserving documents.

Clients who had recourse to notaries confidently hoping to certify their exchanges of property and dying wishes might well have wondered whether it was worth the price, after reading Farinacci. Knowing the myriad ways that instruments and testaments could lose their credibility was not likely to have been reassuring. It certainly might have made them more curious about how their favorite notary stored and indexed their papers. But protected from these professional secrets by the fact that they were in Latin and by the intricacies of scholastic argument, a client was the least likely reader of Farinacci's handbook. Clients showed their unshakable faith in notaries not only by continuing to patronize them but by imitating the formalities, legal clauses, and use of witnesses in documents by their own hand. No doubt they were encouraged in such faith, at least in Farinacci's Rome, when the state itself began to demand that notaries bind, paginate, and index their clients' legal business.[37]

We come finally to the judge, Farinacci's intended audience. What help could this text give a magistrate confronted by a conflict over a dowry agreement in which one family contested the notary's record, or by a will challenged by a disappointed heir who said the notary had added the name of a false beneficiary? Actually, it offered a good deal of help. Farinacci's authorities gave the judge many lessons in scrutinizing the physical and graphic features of a contested notarial act and in seeking texts with which to compare it. They instructed him in how to evaluate the testimony of the witnesses called to answer questions about what they had seen and heard. Farinacci's sources also taught him how to read efficiently for juridical purposes; beneath all the variety of local custom and the details of a specific contract, the valid notarial agreement had only four essential pieces of information: a place, a date, witnesses, and the name of a notary. Most valuable of all, perhaps, were two elements: the manifest truth of Farinacci's own text that the learned doctors did not agree, and the author's recurrent advice to leave thorny matters to the judge. The medieval hierarchy of proof was designed to restrict tightly the judge's latitude in interpreting evidence; Farinacci was one of the writers on penal law who contributed to widening the ambit of judicial discretion.[38] The judge would have to make up his own mind on whose were the true words, and just how true they were.

PART IV

Urban and Religious Identities

Since the late 1970s, historical studies on Italian cities, aided by the insights of sociology and anthropology, have highlighted the imprint of religious sensibilities on identity formation. Catholic religious culture in individual towns, as seen particularly in the development and practice of "local" religion—that marked by particular saints, relics, and rituals—distinguished each city from its neighbors. Through an interactive dynamism, both the secular and the sacred shaped urban identity in medieval and early modern Italy.

In Part IV, both Robert Davis and Robert Cooper examine how city and clergy alike fashioned an urban and religious identity through possession of holy objects and the stories surrounding them. Davis studies an early form of tourism in Venice and finds that lay and clerical Venetians knew how to craft the identity of their unique city to entice (and sometimes fleece) their pilgrim guests who were awaiting transportation to the Holy Land. From the famous city of Venice, Cooper's essay takes us to the little known city of Fabriano in the March of Ancona in central Italy; he studies the collaboration of secular and clerical leaders and the impact of holy men on the sanctification of urban space and the evolution of both the city and the Silvestrine order.

Traveling northwest into central and northern Italy, Cynthia Polecritti examines the sermons of the famous Franciscan preacher Bernardino of Siena. Polecritti demonstrates how Bernardino adapted his own identity to that of the individual townspeople to whom he spoke, how he modified his message to make his listeners identify their own experiences in the Italian cities with the fate of Christ, and how his audience responded to his style of preaching. Similarly, Jennifer Selwyn discusses how Jesuit preachers adapted their own identity to that of their audiences by turning to the Italian *mezzogiorno* (the South) of the late sixteenth and seventeenth centuries. Selwyn explains that through theatrical display, the Jesuits styled themselves as "angels of peace," to encourage peacemaking and reconciliation among warring factions in society. Each of these chapters demonstrates that the interaction of city and religion altered the identity of both.

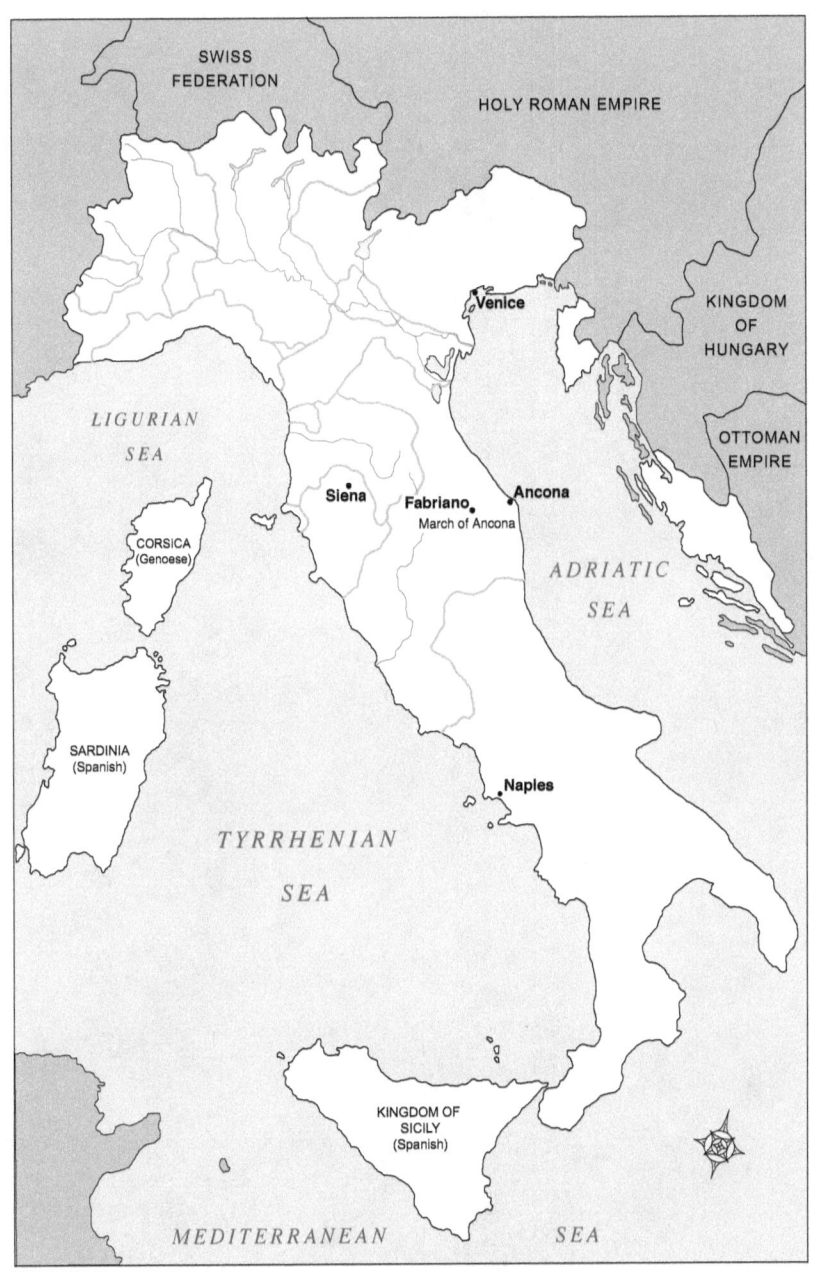

Religious and Urban Identities FLORENCE, VENICE, ANCONA, SIENA, FABRIANO, NAPLES

CHAPTER NINE

Pilgrim-Tourism in Late Medieval Venice

Robert C. Davis

One of the most scenic and one of the most touristed places in the world, Venice has, perhaps inevitably, inspired a number of scholarly and general studies on its place in the history of tourism. These have been alive to the city's impact on the imagination and fantasies of foreigners, aware of the many levels on which it has captivated its admirers. Yet such works have for the most part also been limited in two significant ways. First, they have been overwhelmingly about one relatively circumscribed aspect of tourism to Venice: the so-called Grand Tour, carried on by those fairly few, young, mostly British patrician males who journeyed there as part of what was considered an appropriate education for the wealthy elite from the early 1600s to the 1850s. Second, as a result, this history has for the most part been told not as part of the social and economic story of Venice itself, but rather as an element of British (and occasionally French or German) cultural history—specifically, the story of how a cosmopolitan consciousness developed among the ruling elites of these rising states, one that paralleled and abetted the rise of western European expansion and colonialism during the early modern era.[1]

Such a focus has, in the end, only told half the story and perhaps not the more interesting half. From it we learn little or nothing about the tourist experience of the city before 1600, nor if indeed there was any such thing as tourism in Venice at all, during those earlier centuries. Moreover, the traditionally xenocentric approach to Venetian tourism, by focusing on the visitors rather than the visited, has left the Venetians themselves as oddly passive background figures in what remains fundamentally a northwestern European story of self-discovery. As such, despite their otherwise well-established fame—already a thousand years old by 1600—of being among Europe's shrewdest traders, entrepreneurs, and hustlers, Venetians have received scant acknowledgment from modern scholars of having any ability at all when it came to promoting their own city, or even any awareness that theirs was a city that could be promoted.

This neglect hardly seems justified—doubly so when one considers how famously the Venetians have proved themselves in this regard since at least the fall of the Republic in 1797. It must also be kept in mind that in the two centuries before 1600, the European cultural shoe was still very much on the Venetian foot: this was one the continent's great metropolises—indeed, one of the world-cities of the late Middle Ages—sophisticated and alluring to those gaping visitors from such feudal and rural backwaters as the British Isles or even Germany. It is simply hard to imagine that those who lived in Venice, brought up in the city's millennial mercantile traditions, would either ignore the steadily increasing tide of visitors that was coming at them from over the Alps or fail to find some way to turn it to their own (and their city's) financial advantage.

Of course, most of the foreigners to be found in Venice before 1600 (or, indeed, before 1800) were not there just to see the sights. This commercial hub was filled with whole colonies of foreign artisans and merchants pursuing their trades, some in constant rotation back and forth to their home country, and some in a state of almost permanent residency in Venice.[2] It would be difficult to call them—any more than Venice's flocks of political and religious refugees, or its occasional visiting ambassadors and princes—"tourists" in any meaningful sense of the word. Such outsiders, who came to the city for business or politics, were by definition interested in aspects of Venice far removed from the sort of aesthetic, cultural, or recreational attractions that we now accept as being fundamental in turning a traveler into a tourist.

On the other hand, pilgrims on their way to the Levant, even though their true destinations were the shrines and sacred sites of the Holy Land fifteen hundred miles to the east, did have both the free time and the apparent inclination while there to go about "visiting the sights of Venice," as one of them put it, as early as 1494.[3] In the process, they exhibited a number of the characteristics associated with present-day notions of what it means to be a tourist. Having detached themselves—like most successful vacationers—from the claims and duties of their regular lives, pilgrims usually came to Venice as the first major stop on their sacred itinerary, the jumping-off point into an unknown filled with rumored fantasies, real dangers, and hoped-for spiritual attainment.[4] Like present-day visitors to the city, these pilgrim-tourists found Venice posed between the familiar and the exotic. They prepared themselves for their visit by reading whatever sort of guidebook was available; if nothing was at hand, they made do with gossip and tales about the place, passed on by others like themselves who had already seen it. Once arrived, they were struck by the otherness of the topography and the local mores, to which they struggled to relate, with greater or lesser success, through their own cultural optic. They developed, for themselves and for those who came after, a hierarchy of sites to visit, a circuit that could be lengthened or shortened as appropriate to the duration of their stay. While in the city, they also found one of the tourist essentials common throughout history and the world: an already developed infrastructure of support services ready to aid (or exploit) them during their stay in this unique city.

Only late in the fourteenth century, after decades of contention with other Mediterranean cities, did Venice manage to capture the overseas pilgrim transport business, emerging victorious with near-monopoly control over the entire transit trade between Europe and the Levant. It was a monopoly that the city enjoyed for the next century and a half, from the 1380s until at least the 1530s, during which time the Venetians ran regular, annual galleys (and more sporadic merchant cogs) to the Holy Land, attracting a minimum of two to three hundred German, British, French, Spanish, and Italian pilgrims yearly—and some years several times that many.[5] Those holy travelers who wrote about their experience (or who, being the literate ones, wrote on behalf of others) tended to be clerics. By the end of the fifteenth century, the gossip and written accounts that they had generated about the Pilgrims' Trail in general and Venice in particular was so extensive that it moved one of them, the Milanese canon Pietro Casola, to become perhaps the first tourist to the city (but hardly the last) to complain that Venice was a place "about which so much has been said and written . . . that it appears to me there is nothing left to say."[6]

By Casola's time, Venice had clearly become an attraction in its own right, meriting more pages in most pilgrims' journals than just a few devoted to the practical necessities of outfitting and booking one's passage to the East from this jumping-off point.[7] These pilgrim-tourists often wrote of it rhapsodically: "*Splendidissimo*," "*grandissima*," and "*ornatissima*," Santo Brasca raved about the Ducal Palace, which Arnold van Harff agreed, "is very fine and is daily being made more beautiful." Casola himself exclaimed that "I declare that it is impossible to tell or write fully of the beauty, the magnificence or the wealth of the city of Venice," although he then went on for some pages trying to do so. As they approached Venice by boat from the mainland, the very sight of "[this] famous, great, wealthy and noble city . . . standing in wondrous fashion in the midst of the waters, with lofty towers, great churches, splendid houses and palaces," left Friar Felix Fabri and his companions "astonished."⁸ These pilgrim-tourists marveled about Venice's cleanliness, its cosmopolitan nature, the power and efficiency of its Arsenal, and above all its wealth; even the most widely traveled among them had never seen so many sorts of goods, treasures, and edibles from such a variety of countries, so many "large and beautiful palaces splendidly furnished and decorated," and—especially attractive for pilgrims—so many imposing churches and monasteries. As Casola put it,

> I have been to Rome, the chief city of the world, and I have travelled in Italy, and also very much outside of Italy, and I must say—though I do not say it to disparage anyone, but only to tell the truth—that I have not found in any city so many beautiful and ornate churches as there are in Venice. It would take too long to name them all.⁹

Despite such praise, often bordering on adulation, many pilgrims also expressed their great eagerness to leave Venice and get moving toward the Holy Land, which was, after all, the whole point of their journey. As it happened, however, many found themselves stranded in the city far longer than they had planned. Although the *galee de Zafo* (that is, "galleys of Jaffa") that specialized in trafficking pilgrims to the Holy Land left only twice a year, in late spring and early fall (and, after the 1450s, mostly just in the spring), many pilgrims seem to have been completely unaware of this rather restricted schedule and could say, like Casola, that "I found that I had been in too great a hurry to leave home, and that I must wait several days before the departure of the said galley" (in fact, he was stuck there for nearly three weeks). The Castilian pilgrim Pero Tafur came to Venice so much ahead of time in 1435 that he decided "in the meantime I should travel in Italy, which was well worth while." Even so, on getting back to Venice two months later, Tafur found that he would still have to wait another four weeks.¹⁰

"We were beginning to be exceeding weary of Venice," groused Felix Fabri, and "we were eagerly looking forward to our departure." Indeed, for many pilgrims, Venice on the outbound leg of their voyage turns out to have been the city they ended up staying in by far the longest—much longer even than Jerusalem. In drawing up their contract of passage with their galley owner, these travelers insisted that, barring storms, they were not to be kept in any port of call for more than three days; but Venice was their jumping-off point, and few pilgrims managed to get moving in less than three or four weeks. Ship captains, grumbled Friar Felix, often "promised that they would begin their voyages directly, which I knew to be a lie." The vagaries of the sea had much to do with this, as these captain-owners waited, sometimes for weeks, for the right weather, for necessary outfitting, or simply for a few more paying passengers. Despite "the tediousness of waiting," many pilgrims would not even risk a side trip to Padua if they, like Casola, were "anxiously waiting for the time of departure, which was put off from day to day."[11]

One might well suspect a certain complicity among Venetians, if not actively to delay pilgrims in their city then at least not to hurry them away too quickly. There were, in fact, many who had an interest in keeping these foreigners around. What Frederic C. Lane has called "the very profitable tourist trade to Palestine" was not just a money spinner for those who ran the ships, after all; Ugo Tucci has estimated that in the boom years of pilgrim trafficking these travelers could bring twenty-five thousand or more ducats a year into Venice's economy in what they spent on their tourist needs while in the city—for lodging, food, supplies, entertainment, and gratuities.[12]

Although not well documented, there are indications that Venetians of every class tried their best to take advantage of this potential market and in the process helped lay the social mechanisms that would later put Venice in the forefront of the secular tourism that came to prominence in Italy in the seventeenth and eighteenth centuries. Indeed, it could be said that the unique relationship Venice enjoyed with its captive clientele of pilgrim-tourists went a good way toward explaining the city's precocity in the tourist industry, making it in this regard far more like Rome—the undisputed queen of tourism in Italy since classical times—than its fellow republic of Florence, despite that city's increasing attraction as the peninsula's center of artistic production.[13]

Fortunately, Venice had a good deal to offer the stranded pilgrim-tourist, beyond its renowned wealth and beauty. In particular the city boasted a collection not so much of holy sites (these were the prerogative of Rome and Jerusalem) but of holy objects that may have been without equal in the western Christian world. Having assiduously collected relics in the Levant for centuries and helped themselves generously to Constantinople's sacred treasures when they looted that city in 1204, Venice's patrician merchants had over the years brought back home an incomparable hoard of saints' relics and other holy objects.[14] The Irish friar Simon Fitz-Simon, who journeyed to the Holy Land in 1323 and who was probably one of the earliest pilgrim-tourists to write of Venice, noted that "in the city lie the bodies of saints, which are whole and uncorrupted," and he went on to list, besides St. Mark himself, Saints Zacharias, Gregory of Nazarenus, Theodore the Martyr, Lucy, Marina, "and many more martyrs, confessors, and holy virgins." By the end of the fifteenth century, in the heyday of pilgrim-tourism, when a visitor could exclaim "the Relyques at Venyce can not be noumbred," virtually every one of Venice's seventy-six parish and four-score monastic churches could boast at least something holy that had been bequeathed to it by a neighborhood patron and that was suitable as an attraction for pilgrims.[15]

Pilgrim-tourists, especially those who were priests, canons, or friars, inevitably made pursuit of relics a top priority of their time in Venice. Some shared the motives of Piero Casola, who had made a vow to visit certain shrines in the city when, earlier in his journey, he had found himself threatened by a storm at sea.[16] Others, like Fabri, were on something of the opposite tack, seeking in the day before departure to pray before the relics or images of those "saints [who] are of peculiar service to those who are about to go on a pilgrimage."[17] But cleric or lay, most of these pilgrim-tourists had a driving impulse simply to see and (if possible) touch as many of these sacred objects as possible. Although every relic was meritorious to seek out, many carried the extra benefit of conferring an indulgence if visited on a particular day or situation; Lionardo Frescobaldi put the resulting blend of sacred and secular tourism rather bluntly, in describing how he passed his three weeks in the city in 1384: "I searched for indulgences and notable places."[18] Many narrators turned the list of the relics they had visited into a prominent feature of their description of the city: the English pilgrim William Wey and the Milanese Santo Brasca, for example, enumerated (with surprisingly little overlap) fifty-two and forty relics respectively, which they had managed to see in visiting only a relative handful of the city's many churches. Finding himself stuck for an entire month in Venice, Friar Felix, by contrast, persuaded the four German nobles and seven retainers for whom he was the spiritual guide to join him in a series of minipilgrimages to see the relics in no fewer than thirty-four churches, located all over the city.[19]

When possible, the pilgrims sought to kiss the actual saints' bodies, often "many times," as Fabri noted. They also attempted to collect some of the power implicit in the relics, both for their own sake and for friends and relations, by touching the saintly bodies with objects—especially jewelry—that those back home had entrusted to them for the purpose: "Whenever they [pilgrims] meet with any relics, or come to any holy place, they take those jewels and touch the relics of the holy place with them, that they may perchance derive some sanctity from the touch; and thus they are returned to the friends of the pilgrims dearer and more valuable than before." Friar Felix, though "the poorest of our company," seems by his own account to have been the best furnished in this regard—indeed, he was virtually loaded down with "precious jewels which had been lent me by my friends, patrons and patronesses." He also took the time to touch these saints with all sorts of "easily carried trinkets" that he knew from past experience he could give as "presents to those who are dear" while at the same time "receiving a reward for doing so." Pilgrim-tourists who were not as well furnished with such trinkets as he was, Fabri noted, could still buy all the glass beads, paternosters, and little crosses of gold or silver that they might need for the purpose from obliging Venetian craftsmen and vendors who were evidently hovering nearby.[20]

Eager to make contact with saints' relics that were spread all over the city, many of these late medieval pilgrims braved this tangled city and sought out these tourist draws wherever they lurked in Venice. Still, for visitors the town's main attraction in this regard remained the central church of San Marco, which boasted not only the intact body of the Evangelist Mark himself but also a host of other treasures. These included both secular objects—crowns, gems, the four bronze horses from Constantinople, "a large and long unicorn's horn, most highly chased"—and sacred marvels, ranging from standard saints' relics to holy trophies that approached the bizarre. Indeed, fifteenth-century San Marco was something of a medieval Madame Tussaud's of Biblical curiosities, offering an elaborate range of sacred objects. A visitor in the 1600s enumerated just a few of the more unusual relics still to be found within the treasury:

> diverse heads of Saints, enchased in gold; a small ampulla, or glass, with our Saviour's blood; a great morsel of the real cross; one of the nails; a thorn; a fragment of the column to which our Lord was bound, when scourged; the standard, or ensign, of Constantine; a piece of St. Luke's arm; a rib of St. Stephen; a finger of Mary Magdalene; numerous other things, which I cannot remember.[21]

These were only the more "official" relics, however. San Marco also vaunted a range of still-rarer and more bizarre objects, including (among many others) the rock from which Jesus had preached at Tyre; "an image of Our Lady made from the stone which Moses struck with his rod when the Children of Israel were asking him for [water] to drink, and out of it issued a fountain"; two spiral alabaster pillars from King Solomon's temple; images of Saints Francis and Dominic (painted before either of them had lived) by the fabled Abbot Joachim; "one of the large teeth of a giant named Goliath, whom David killed," and "a wooden crucifix which was struck by a disappointed gambler and which has performed many miracles," in particular, that of shedding blood.[22]

Besides these holy curiosities, San Marco also attracted these pilgrims as the ceremonial and architectural focus of the city. Visitors more accustomed to the gothic styles of the north might find the church "beautiful but low," "a small thing," or "not at all in the fashion of those in France," but most of them still waxed enthusiastic about the building's decorations and those of the adjoining Ducal Palace, even if, like van Harff, they had happened to come by in the middle of the palace's extensive renovations.[23] Pilgrims also came to San Marco when they wanted to pay their respects (or make complaints) to the Venetian authorities.

Those of high rank could expect an audience with the *doge*, for a formal welcome (with an embrace and kiss "in the Italian fashion"), or a ducal intervention (to free personal possessions impounded by overzealous customs, for example). Even those of more modest standing could arrange a guided tour of the palace with one of the ducal pages.[24] Piazza San Marco also drew pilgrims because it was there that those seeking to book passage on the Jaffa galleys had to sign up; they were notified as to how many galleys were accepting passengers by the number of white flags with red crosses that were run up on the poles in front of the church. The competition between galley owners could be fierce, according to Friar Felix: although pilgrims might be treated to a free snack of "Cretan wine and comfits from Alexandria" while touring each galley, first they had to weather the assaults of the touts in the Piazza, who "each invited the pilgrims to sail with their master, and they endevoured to each lead the pilgrims [to their own galley] . . . [and] each abused the other and defamed him to their worships the pilgrims, and each tried to make the other odious to the pilgrims, and suborned men to do so."[25]

Piazza San Marco was also the center of Venetian festive and ceremonial life, home of splendid processions that were world-famous well before 1500. Those who came to Venice in the spring could expect as many as three major festivals while they waited for their galley to depart: Saint Mark's day on April 25, the Ascension in mid-May, and Corpus Christi in early June. Although all three days had a significant place in the Christian calendar, for Venetians they were also (and perhaps fundamentally) civic festivals, patriotic occasions that brought together in a showy procession the entire active citizenry. By the fifteenth century, the three holidays had to some extent flowed into one: "a vast spring festival complete with public entertainments," including a fifteen-day fair, held in the piazza and along the adjoining merchants' streets, the *Mercerie*.[26]

Although the procession celebrating the festival of St. Mark was a strictly Venetian affair, with foreign visitors relegated to watching from the wings, both the Ascension (or *Sensa*, to the Venetians) and Corpus Christi paid particular attention and respect to outsiders, and to pilgrims in particular. "They make a great festival for the day of the Ascension," wrote Philippe de Voisons about his visit in 1490, "and all the pilgrims who are [in town] willingly go there."[27] They did so primarily to witness the doge's Marriage to the Sea, where, together with attendant dignitaries, Venice's ruler was rowed in the enormous and ornate *Bucintoro* from Piazza San Marco out through the Bocca del Lido to the open Adriatic, throwing a wedding ring into the water, to the accompaniment of fireworks, music, and general aquatic splendor. Pilgrims of the highest rank, like Roberto da Sanseverino, nephew of Francesco Sforza, duke of Milan, got to sail in the

Bucintoro itself, as a companion to the doge; as Pero Tafur put it, "[i]f strangers or honorable men are present they take them also, carrying crosses and pennons, very richly worked in drawn gold." Those somewhat further down the social ladder, such as Santo Brasca or Friar Felix and his four German lords, had to make do with a hired boat of their own, but they may have had even more pleasure, rowing in the thick of "so many boats of citizens and most finely dressed ladies."[28]

For the feast of Corpus Christi, pilgrims of every sort were brought even more directly into the festivities, especially the procession of confraternities, religious orders, and the seigniory, which began with an early mass in the church of San Marco, wound through the piazza, and then returned to the church five hours later. By the end of the fifteenth century, if not earlier, pilgrims were "expected to assemble in the Church of St. Mark to join the procession." In Casola's day, this meant their marching toward the end of the ensemble, each paired off with a Venetian noble who accompanied him or her around the piazza and then up the grand staircase within the Ducal Palace to be personally greeted by the doge.[29] Twelve years later, during the visit of Richard Guylforde, the stature of the pilgrims seems to have increased, since "there was greate honoure done to the Pylgrymes for we all moste and leste wente all there nexte the Duke in the sayd processyon, byfore all the Lordes and other Estat."[30]

This central role of foreign pilgrims in one of Venice's key religious and political manifestations is not altogether unexpected. Over the course of the 1400s, the departure date for the spring galleys to Jaffa was with increasing regularity set at just after Corpus Christi. Although the city's formal celebration of the holiday dated back to the late thirteenth century, it was only in 1407, about a quarter century after the beginning of Venice's pilgrim boom, that the senate moved to make the event a grand civic spectacle that would include among the marchers the doge and his councilors, the city's aristocracy, and all the priests and canons attached to the church of San Marco. In 1454, the procession was broadened still further, to include virtually every major corporate body in the city: the *Scuole Grandi* and all the regular clergy, as well as the local bishops and abbots.

Although the Venetian procession of Corpus Christi, like all such civic-religious celebrations, was multivalent, one of its salient aims was clearly to recognize, honor, and welcome pilgrims and stress their importance to the city—no other body of so many foreigners, after all, was invited to join in the event on any such footing. Achieving their recognized primacy among Italian cities in the trafficking of pilgrims was an honor for Venetians. It was a rare type of commerce that could bring a city both profit and sanctity; treating these men and women with respect and fairness also meant (it was hoped) that they would spread the word about Venetian integrity once they returned to their homelands.³¹ Integrating and weaving such special travelers into the center of this sacro-civic manifestation meant not only that "there was greate honoure done to the Pylgrymes" but also that, in the process, Venice could make manifest to the world its own centrality to this entire holy business of pilgrimage.

To accomplish this, the rulers of Venice were willing to alter and adapt Corpus Christi—indeed, the holidays of St. Mark's and the *Sensa* as well—to fit the presence and interests of this, their first major tourist group. The resulting block of May festivities would in fact become a draw in its own right, a series of grand spectacles designed to impress, entertain, enthrall, and loosen the wallets of pilgrims great and small before they set off for their encounter with the East. It was not only the state that was willing to accommodate itself and its rituals to the interests of pilgrim-tourists. Ordinary citizens also recognized the opportunity presented by these foreign visitors, to the extent that as far back as 1229 swarms of would-be guides, touts, agents, and pimps, both Venetian and foreign, seem to have already begun preying on travelers to the city and fighting with each other over the right to do so.³² On arriving at Piazza San Marco, pilgrims might be set upon by contending packs of *tolomazi* (as such guides were called) offering to escort them about the city, assist in changing money, act as translators, arrange lodgings, and book their passage to the Holy Land. In the process, however, they also might demand extortionate tips from their clients, as well as kickbacks from the money changers, innkeepers, and ship captains whose businesses they fed; they were also reputed to talk their way into foreign hospices normally off limits to Venetians, quarrel among themselves over who would get the better class of pilgrim, and book their clients on galleys that were not only not proper pilgrim ships but that were not bound for the Holy Land at all.³³

Interested in maintaining a transport service that could be both economically and diplomatically profitable to the state, the Venetian Senate sought to ensure that while in the city pilgrims, in their naïveté and confusion, were not too easily plucked by these enterprising locals. Placing the tolomazi under control of the magistrate of the *Cattaveri*, the senate tried to organize the guides into a loosely formed guild, or *universitas*, which would oversee collection and division of individual booking commissions and (most important) tips. Guides were to be limited in number and officially licensed; so that they might actually help and not merely exploit visitors, pairs of them were ordered to wait every morning and afternoon by the Ducal Palace, the church of Saint Mark's, and the Rialto. Each pair would be composed of men who knew the city's sights and facilities and who were able to speak, between them, at least two foreign languages.³⁴

One of the tolomazi's principal functions was to arrange rooms for their charges, and from the beginning of Venice's pilgrim boom in the 1380s these two activities of guiding and lodging were closely intertwined. The city's inns and taverns were brought under the jurisdiction of the *Giustizia nuova*, which attempted to establish an "official" hotel list of the dozen to twenty or so *osterie pubbliche* clustered around San Marco or the Rialto, each offering lodging and board under supposedly state-supervised conditions to around forty guests. As with the tolomazi, the Venetian state was pursuing multiple interests here, seeing that guests were issued sheets and blankets on the one hand, while making sure on the other—at least as assiduously—that it both knew exactly who these guests were and how much of the lucrative wine tax (the *dazio del vino a spina*) it was owed by the osterie.[35] Even with state oversight, competition between osterie for the pilgrim trade was ferocious, with the more enterprising innkeepers sending "garrulous and importuning agents" inland, along the mainland routes as far as Mestre and Padua, to waylay and hustle any travelers who had not yet fixed their place to stay. According to Friar Felix, their technique was none too subtle:

[We] were passing the tower which is called the Torre de Malghera [marking the beginning of the Venetian Lagoon], when . . . [a]fter a while there met us another boat with people on board, one of whom asked us what inn we meant to put up in at Venice. When we told him St. George's . . . he began to abuse that inn and its landlord, and stood on the prow of his boat, trying to prevent our going there, and pointing out some other inn to us. As he stood there and noisily tried to persuade us, he suddenly . . . fell from the prow of his boat into the sea. . . . He was dressed in new silk clothes, which received baptism together with him, which caused great laughter on board of our boat.[36]

Although Friar Felix's St. George was a public inn, it catered almost exclusively to German pilgrims, and "[t]he entire household spoke German . . . which was a very great comfort to us; for it is very distressing to live with people without being able to converse with them."[37] Many pilgrims managed to lodge with members of their own "nation": Casola put up at "the house of the Master Courier of the Milanese merchants," Santo Brasca stayed at the house of the Archinti family of Florence, and van Harff was "taken in by the merchants to the German House, . . . the Fondigo Tudisco."[38] Many others, however—even some of quite high status—had to settle for osterie, like the White Lion or the Savage Man, even though they may have agreed with Friar Felix's opinion (which he thought the Venetian state shared) that it was "unbecoming that pilgrims bound on so holy a pilgrimage should be lodged in public inns . . . [which] are not well famed."[39] In fact, many pilgrims were lucky to get a room at all; the demand for lodgings grew steadily in Venice, and by the mid-1500s it appears to have far outstripped the capacity of the state's licensed osterie. To meet the shortfall, more than a few private citizens came forward, eager to get into the act; fifty or sixty years after Fabri's time the Venetian authorities were complaining that "in 1500 one found only thirteen houses that ran hotels and lodged foreigners. Now it is common knowledge that there are between five and six *thousand* houses that put up foreigners, something that is almost incredible, but in truth they are in number very great and infinite, and every day multiply more."[40]

Such a figure may well seem incredible—it meant that something like a fifth of all the dwellings in the city were involved—but it may not have been an altogether wild exaggeration. The state's real worry was the massive invasion of the lodging industry by hard-to-monitor amateur *albergatori*—the thousands of ordinary home owners and even humbler renters who rushed to join the licensed osterie pubbliche in riding the rising tide of foreigners by letting or subletting one or more of their rooms. Indications are that by the last years of the Republic this semiprivate lodging sector had become a regular if not exactly stable feature of Venice's social landscape, still offering necessary accommodations for a growing stream of secular tourists, long after the flow of pilgrims to the city had dried up.[41]

Even more freewheeling was Venice's public transport sector. Although a terrestrial network of alleyways and bridges existed in the city for pedestrian traffic, late medieval Venice was far more a boat city than it is today, especially for local elites, who had themselves rowed in their own gondolas on even the shortest trips around town. The result is well captured in Carpaccio's *Miracle of the Reliquary of the True Cross*, painted the same year as Casola's visit to the city and showing the Grand Canal crowded with the private gondolas of such elites, each piloted by a liveried gondolier serving his master in very much the same role as a coachman elsewhere. Casola observed that "almost every citizen keeps at least one gondola," which would, by the most tenable census figures of the time, mean that there were something like four thousand of these private craft in the city at the end of the 1400s.[42]

Yet the fifteenth century also saw the emergence in Venice of independent gondoliers for hire, usually by the day. These enterprising individuals were available for any Venetian who did not have his own gondola at hand, but unquestionably they were most needed by foreigners such as pilgrims who, as brief visitors, tended to know the city less than anyone and were as likely to get lost as any modern tourist in its maze of alleyways. That pilgrims were timid in confronting the city on foot is confirmed in Fabri's account of the minipilgrimages he organized for his group. As he put it, for twenty-nine of the thirty-four churches that the Germans visited, "we rowed," "we went in a boat," or "we went by water"; his group appears to have been willing to walk only to those churches that were no more than three hundred meters from their inn.[43]

As with the city's tolomazi and albergatori, Venetian gondoliers seem to have been more than willing to meet the needs of foreigners like Fabri's Germans. Over the course of the sixteenth century, private boatmen would blossom much in the manner of the renters of private rooms, and by 1608 Thomas Coryat could say that "of these Gondolas they say there are around ten thousand about the citie, whereof six thousand are private, serving for the Gentlemen and others, and foure thousand for mercenary men, which get their living by the trade of rowing."[44] If there were indeed four thousand gondoliers hacking for hire in Venice (there are barely a tenth that many today), it is no surprise that another seventeenth-century visitor could report that "there are always a World of them standing together at several publick Wharfs; so that you need but cry out, *Gondola*, and you have them launch out presently to you."[45] By the mid-1600s, the trade was becoming so popular among working-class Venetians that some in the ruling elite were worried it was luring away too many of Venice's shipwrights and house carpenters. No wonder: an average gondolier could earn half again as much as a master craftsman at the state arsenal, mostly for just standing around all day.[46]

By the mid-1500s, Venice's pilgrim trade to the East had largely collapsed. What had for a century and a half been one of the city's great engines of income and prestige was killed off in fairly short order, with the epochal changes marking the beginnings of the early modern era. The Ottoman conquest of both Palestine and all the eastern Mediterranean produced a state of nearly constant warfare between the Turks and Venice, making travel to the Holy Land on Venetian ships too risky for even the doughtiest of knights and the most pious of friars. At the same time, the English and the Germans—once among the most enthusiastic of pilgrims—largely abandoned the practice of such holy journeys as they embraced Protestantism and its new modes of religious expression. Rome itself, with its jubilee years and baroque boom, began to replace the Holy Land as an appropriate destination for those who continued in the pilgrimage tradition. Marginalized by the shift in global trade routes set off by the voyages of Columbus and Da Gama, the Venetians eventually called a halt to their regular galley runs to Jaffa. Their commercial traffic shifted over to less tightly regulated sailing ships, and those few who still aspired to play the role of pilgrim had to book on as regular passengers on such vessels; the last properly organized pilgrim voyage from Venice to the Holy Land appears to have taken place some time around 1580.[47]

Yet even as it withered, it is clear that Venice's pilgrim trafficking had put its mark on the city, leaving behind an infrastructure of support services and a wealth of practical experience that would prove vital to the Venetians in handling coming waves of tourism. When, right around 1600, Fynes Moryson and Thomas Coryat visited the city, they could avail themselves of directions and advice about Venice from a succession of published and manuscript travelers' accounts that stretched back before William Wey and went right up to their near-contemporary (some would say inspiration), Michel Montaigne.[48] Moreover, when they arrived in town, they found Venice already well stocked with hotels, guides, eating establishments, transport-for-hire, and (something most pilgrims had avoided mentioning) prostitutes.[49] Brought into life by the confused needs of generations of pilgrims and nurtured by the expanding demands of an increasingly wealthy local aristocracy, the service sector of Venice was by the 1600s more than ready to meet the requirements of even the most fastidious and demanding of Grand Tourists.

Proud of their city and eager to sell it to visitors, Venetians were talented at converting the city's existing attractions to suit changing tastes. The great cycle of spring festivals lost much of its traditional air of patriotism and civic piety, even as it lost the participation of pilgrims. Venetians found it a simple matter, however, with the addition of masques, burlesque performers, gaming parlors (the *ridotti*), legions of prostitutes, and fireworks to turn these festivals into a second, springtime carnival: a good-weather bacchanal that was perfectly timed to the opening of the Alpine passes and the arrival of the season's first Grand Tourists from Germany and eastern Europe.

Likewise, churches whose relics had once attracted the attention (and the donations) of the likes of Friar Felix and William Wey had by the late seventeenth century been reborn as sites of aesthetic pilgrimage. Flocks of connoisseurs were drawn to the architecture, the sculpture, and the paintings of such artists as Titian, Tintoretto, and Veronese; many expressed all the reverence before such works that the pilgrim-tourists had once shown to the saintly bodies they touched or kissed and that now often lay, largely forgotten and neglected, only a few feet away. Like the late medieval pilgrims, whether they came to worship at these cultural shrines or plunge themselves into an endless whirl of pomp and revelry, these Grand Tourists would find their way guided and made easier by a host of Venetians, waiting (usually with their hand out for a tip) for a chance to advise, explain, and lead them through this most complex, charming, and seemingly changeless of all of Europe's great cities.

CHAPTER TEN

The Hermit Returns

Sanctity and the City in the March of Ancona

Robert L. Cooper

Several scholars of late medieval and early modern Italy have drawn attention to the role of "civic religion" in the ascendance of the communes in northern and central Italy.[1] These scholars have pointed to communal government participation in the cults of patron saints, acquisition of relics, and assimilation of sacred ritual into the rhythms of civic life as evidence that sacralization of the cities was part of a conscious design on the part of municipal authorities to augment the legitimacy of the communes. In his seminal study of public ritual in early modern Florence, Richard Trexler notes that this sacralization of urban space was accompanied by a thorough and aggressive desacralization of the countryside.[2] Trexler suggests that this "geography of ritual"—in which cities filled themselves with shrines competing for the attention of the prayerful while the countryside was stripped of such sites—grew out of a perception that the commune's political order was illegitimate and needed to be buttressed by a monopoly of the sources of ritual legitimization.[3] Religious communities intervened in this process as well, trying to shape communal patronage to their own advantage.[4] The resulting convergence of interests between communal elites and religious communities frequently favored the new mendicant orders, whose emphasis upon popular preaching changed the shape of urban sacred space.[5]

Both the struggle of communal government to establish and defend its political and social order and the increasing association of cult observance with urban and commercial centers are themes common throughout northern and central Italy. Looking beyond Florence and the great communes of Renaissance Tuscany, this chapter examines the connection of sanctity and the city in the more modest communes of the late medieval March of Ancona. In particular, using as a case study the evolution of the Silvestrine Congregation of Benedictines from mendicant hermits to urban priests, I argue that the sacralization of the city was inherent in the very process of urbanization itself and was less a product of design than a confluence of forces little appreciated by the participants.

In 1227, Silvestro Guzzolini of Osimo, who had earlier abandoned the study of law in Bologna, wore out his welcome as a canon in the cathedral chapter of his native city. According to his hagiographer, Silvestro had incurred episcopal displeasure because he "did not cease to correct his bishop who had ordered his life less than well."[6] Inspired by a vision that reinforced his own mortality, and by dreams of "solitary and deserted places," Silvestro abandoned Osimo and "worldly glory" in the dead of night to seek such a lonely place: a dank cave about thirty miles from Osimo on the land of an important aristocrat, Corrado di Rovellone.[7] Gathering disciples, Silvestro began constructing a series of monasteries, always preferring, in the words of the *Vita Silvestri*, "lonely and deserted places to towns."[8] This construction project brought him in 1231 to Montefano, a mountain outside of the commune of Fabriano in the March of Ancona. His hagiographer describes Montefano as "a high and wild mountain . . . so solitary and wild that no one, even though his age made him very strong, would go to this hermitage without a companion."[9] Reinforcing Montefano's isolation, and the holy man's asceticism, the vita relates that when three citizens of Fabriano climbed the mountain to speak with the holy hermit, they found him sitting by a pool of water, eating a crust of bread, with a wolf lying at his feet.[10]

Seventy years later, the most illustrious of Silvestro's disciples, Giovanni dal Bastone, fell ill in the Silvestrine monastery of Montefano, now mother house of an order with seventeen monasteries. Giovanni had also been an academic washout at Bologna,[11] but his particular virtue was to have lived as a recluse at Montefano for the last decades of his life, in the process acquiring a reputation for great sanctity. As Giovanni's condition deteriorated, prior general Bartolo had a vision of "a beam of sunlight stretching down the slope of the mountain from the cell of the holy man to the [Silvestrine] monastery in Fabriano, and on it walked one in the habit and cowl of the order."[12] Shortly after, the monks of Montefano carried Giovanni dal Bastone down to their sister house, where he died and was buried in the crypt of the Silvestrine church of San Benedetto in Fabriano. San Benedetto became the focal point of Giovanni's cult; the greater part of his vita consists of accounts of some forty-two miracles authenticated by a tribunal sitting in Fabriano.[13]

The contrasting hagiographic images of Silvestro fleeing the iniquitous city by night in search of the purifying solitude of the mountaintop and of Giovanni dal Bastone returning down the mountain to the city center bathed in sanctifying light draw attention to an important shift in the spiritual topography of the thirteenth-century March of Ancona. It was a shift born of two closely related historical developments of the thirteenth century affecting both the reality and the perception of space. The first was the process by which the growing communes established and consolidated control over the physical space of the contado, the territory immediately surrounding a town, contesting authority with aristocratic families and feudatories of the great monastic houses of the Ottonian age. The second was the sanctification of urban space, as the growing cities established themselves as centers of cult observance and the focal point of late medieval religious activity. The convergence of these trends is clearly revealed in the archival records of the order founded by Silvestro Guzzolini of Osimo, and in the long relationship of that order with the commune of Fabriano in the March of Ancona.[14] As the young order expanded along with the commune, a confluence of interests between the two helped forge the urban and religious identity of Fabriano, and shape the local, civic religious cult.

The political landscape in which Silvestro sought refuge in the early part of the thirteenth century was one in which the castelli of the rural nobility—men such as Corrado di Rovellone—still played an important, although diminished, role as they submitted, one by one, to the communes. In the Esino Valley, and its tributaries—the Sentino and Giano— the great monastic houses of the late Ottonian age still dominated the political and religious landscape.[15] Analysis of the network of roads and tracks that characterized communications in the Upper Esino in the late eleventh and early twelfth centuries reveals no hub. Instead, the somewhat trapezoidal patchwork of minor roads derived much of its appearance from the economic and political dominance of two monasteries founded in the tenth century: the Benedictine houses of San Vittore delle Chiuse and Santa Maria d'Appennino.[16]

The more important of these, San Vittore delle Chiuse, had been founded as a proprietary monastery in the last years of the tenth century by the counts of Genga, lords of the gastaldate of Castel Petroso. Within a generation, San Vittore had proved highly successful at acquiring lands and jurisdictions, and by the middle of the eleventh century a great number of the castelli in the Upper Esino Valley, including those of the counts of Genga, had been deeded over to the abbot of the monastery in perpetuity.[17] In general, these were granted back to the nobles in emphyteusis, that is, on the basis of a long-term lease at nominal rent.[18] In perhaps the apogee of the monastery's temporal power, the lords of Civitella,

Sassa, Precicchie, Ceresola, Serrasecca, and Valle all ceded the castelli they held in fief to the abbots of San Vittore delle Chiuse in 1104 and renounced their rights of patronage over San Vittore and the nearby convent of San Salvatore di Valle.[19] In addition to lands and castelli, by the end of the twelfth century the abbots of San Vittore had acquired rights to forty-two churches in the region—generally as a component of aristocratic bequests.[20]

It is among the documents of San Vittore delle Chiuse that one finds first mention of the "*castellum*" of Fabriano, a fortified outpost of the gastaldate of Castel Petroso.[21] A little over a century later, an act of emphyteusis makes note of "*ambo castra Fabriani*," which will sort themselves out in later documents as the *Castrum vetus* and *Castrum novum* or *Podium*, which still lend their names to the Castelvecchio and Poggio quarters of modern Fabriano.[22] These twin castelli were the nuclei around which the town of Fabriano developed.[23] Fabriano first emerges as a commune in a document of 1165, in which counts Rainaldo and Alberto di Rodolfo of Attiggio submit to the consuls, as well as the *maiores* and *minores* of the commune.[24]

Increasingly, the rural aristocracy submitted to the authority of the rising commune, and by 1200 Fabriano and San Vittore delle Chiuse were running up against each other in a variety of unpleasant ways.[25] In 1212, the abbot of San Vittore signed a deed in which the castello, inhabitants, and lands of Castel Petroso were placed under the jurisdiction of consul Todino of Fabriano. The commune was allowed to build fortifications in the territory of Castel Petroso but was prohibited from either fortifying or destroying the castello itself. In return, the consul agreed to respect the rights and privileges of the monastery and its vassals, and to grant a parcel of buildable land in Fabriano to each family subject to San Vittore that agreed to live in Fabriano.[26] Similarly, Abbot Damiano of Santa Maria d'Apennino submitted his monastery and a number of aristocrats subject to his monastery to the jurisdiction of the consuls of Fabriano in 1224.[27]

By the time, therefore, that Silvestro began his search for a suitable refuge from the glories of the world, Fabriano had already established its hegemony as temporal authority in the Upper Esino Valley. The monasteries, however, with their numerous dependent churches, retained their effective dominance of institutionalized religion. Even as the monks of San Vittore delle Chiuse recognized the jurisdiction of Fabriano, they constructed the church of San Biagio in the newly inhabited part of the town. San Biagio was granted rights to burial in 1218, and established as a parish by the Bishop of Camerino in 1232.[28] The abbots of San Vittore proceeded to acquire properties in Fabriano, installed a small community of monks under command of a prior in San Biagio, and retained a significant presence in the political and economic life of the region.[29] The great monastic houses of the March of Ancona continued to exert a real presence in thirteenth-century religious topography even as their political importance faded. With their strategically placed fortress-abbeys and their numerous dependent churches, the old monastic houses remained an important visual and psychological backdrop, against which the vital spiritual life of the Marches took place.

The most dynamic participants in the thirteenth-century religious life of the Marches were the new religious movements, steeped in the language and practice of religious poverty and the eremitic life.[30] The flowering of such groups in the March of Ancona, and their popularity, helped transform the spiritual topography of the region while causing consternation in conciliar circles. Francis of Assisi is said to have preached in Fabriano as early as 1209, and to have made at least six journeys in the region during his lifetime.[31] By the end of the thirteenth century, the March of Ancona had more Franciscan houses, a total of eighty-eight, than any other Franciscan province.[32] The lasting image of the Franciscans is in the role of urban preachers, reshaping the religious space of the city with their vast churches and piazzas. However, Franciscans came to the Marches first as hermits and only gravitated to the cities as the thirteenth century progressed.[33]

Along with Franciscans, the region was fertile ground for many houses of the newly organized Augustinian friars. Of the five hermit congregations joined together in 1256 by Pope Alexander IV into the Order of Augustinian Hermits, two were native to the Marches. The Hermits of Brettino, an austere congregation originating in the northern Marches in the early thirteenth century, supported themselves entirely from collecting alms and stressed strict poverty. They were given the Augustinian Rule by a papal bull of Gregory IX in 1228, and they may have had as many as forty-five houses in the Marches at the time of the Great Union of 1256.[34] The Williamite Hermits of Montefavale, whose mother house was near Pesaro in the southern Marches, were included by Alexander IV in the Great Union even though they had formally adopted the Rule of St. Benedict. Although they were not mendicants and supported themselves from their own property, the Williamites did practice a rigorous life of prayer and mortification.[35] Additionally, the Giamboniti—a third congregation from the Great Union, although centered in Romagna—had several houses in the March of Ancona.[36]

Besides Williamites, there were other hermits in the Marches living an austere life but formally adhering to the Benedictine Rule. The best known of these are the Hermits of S. Angelo in Volterino, in the rugged territory of the southern Marches, who began the thirteenth century under the protection of a Benedictine monastery in Rieti. Granted independent status by a papal bull of Gregory IX in 1235, S. Angelo was mother house to a collection of nine small hermitages by midcentury.[37] There was, as well, a long tradition in the Marches of miscellaneous hermits, recluses, and anchorites of all description. Romualdo Sassi has identified some seventy-four anchorites living in the Fabriano area, mentioned in documents between 1261 and 1428.[38] Several anchoresses appear in the Silvestrine records of Montefano, in some cases passing into the protection of the abbey.[39]

The March of Ancona was clearly fertile ground for the new religious movements of the thirteenth century, and a defining characteristic of these movements was their proud and occasionally defiant embrace of religious poverty and mendicancy. This was the home of Angelo of Clareno and the radical wing of the Franciscans who became known as the Spirituals. When rumors reached the Marches from the ecumenical council in Lyons in 1274 that, falsely, all Franciscans would be required to possess property, the Spirituals responded with open defiance. Ecclesiastical authorities met this defiance with repression, severe in its own right, and a precursor of more gruesome measures taken against the Spirituals in the next century.[40] Among Augustinians joined in the Great Union, differences of practice regarding religious poverty led to contention as well. The Brettini, who practiced mendicancy and very rigorous poverty, chafed at their union with the more prosperous and comfortable Tuscan hermits, but they stayed within the fold.[41] On the other hand, despite their practice of religious poverty, the Williamites of Montefavale opposed alms begging and strongly resented their treatment in Alexander IV's Great Union. Accordingly, they bolted the newly formed order and sought the protection of the Cistercians.[42]

The active religious movements of the thirteenth-century Marches, therefore, offered a range of solutions to the divisive questions of religious poverty and mendicancy. There were poor Benedictines and prosperous Augustinians. Among those dedicated to poverty, begging for alms was regarded as abhorrent by some and essential by others. Situating the early Silvestrines within this constellation of religious ideals is not easy, as the actual practices of Silvestro and the first generation of Silvestrines with regard to mendicancy are obscure. For the most part, Silvestrine hagiography was written after (and, one might argue, in direct response to) the Second Council of Lyons in 1274.[43] The order's first extant constitutions date from the early fourteenth century; they offer no guidance about practices two generations earlier.[44] Despite the difficulty of reading behind these documents, doing so is essential to understand the order's journey from the mountaintop to the city.

The Ecumenical Councils of the thirteenth century aimed to inhibit precisely the sort of freewheeling practices that characterized religious life in the Marches. In 1215, the Fourth Lateran Council had inveighed against "too great a variety of religious orders lead[ing] to grave confusion in God's church."[45] It was in response to Fourth Lateran that the Williamites adopted the Benedictine Rule and the Brettini adopted the Rule of St. Augustine. Silvestro's own opportune embrace of the Benedictine Rule seems to reflect similar concerns.[46] The Second Council of Lyons (1274) affirmed the warnings from Fourth Lateran and, in Canon 23, identified proliferation of mendicant orders as particularly obnoxious. Orders founded since 1215 without papal confirmation were to be suppressed. Even those orders confirmed by the apostolic see, if founded after 1215, "whose profession, rule or constitutions forbid them to have revenues or possessions for their fitting support but whose insecure mendicancy usually provides a living through public begging," were suffered to continue only on terms that they admit no new members and acquire no new houses or land, forgoing preaching, hearing confessions, or granting burial to the laity.[47]

The Silvestrines clearly perceived themselves at risk of falling within the scope of Canon 23, although very little concerning mendicancy survives in the documentary record. The *Life of Silvester* does recount two miracles involving Brother Simone, an early disciple of Silvestro, begging for alms on the road to Roccacontrada.[48] The *Life of Blessed Ugo*, a later hagiographic work of dubious provenance, presents Ugo degli Atti begging for alms on the road to Venatura.[49] But the mendicant roots of the order would be largely invisible to us were it not for a bitter controversy that erupted in 1268 between Silvestro's successor as prior general of the order, Giuseppe, and Bishop Guido of Camerino.[50] In the course of this conflict, which ultimately engulfed Montefano along with the other three Silvestrine monasteries in the diocese of Camerino, Bishop Guido prohibited the order from begging, asserting that the Silvestrines inappropriately called themselves paupers and had no need to beg, being perfectly able to support themselves by their own property and their own hands.[51] Prior Benedetto of the Silvestrine monastery of San Bartolo in Serra San Quirico appealed the order, arguing that the monks of San Bartolo were so poor that without the help of others in the form of alms they could not live, let alone serve God.[52] On the issue of mendicancy, therefore, Silvestro, despite his profession of the Benedictine Rule, was aligned with the more radical of the new religious movements.[53]

Another common feature of the new religious movements in the thirteenth-century Marches was their almost universal embrace of the eremitic life. When he set off for the "solitary and deserted places," Silvestro was following a well-beaten path for thirteenth-century holy men, both literally and figuratively. Practice of the holy life required renouncing the temptations and cares of the world, which was symbolically enacted through physical separation from those temptations. As the *Life of Giovanni dal Bastone* expressed it, as long as Giovanni remained in Bologna "he greatly feared the danger to his purity and more to his soul."[54] The true solitude of the hermit is internal, however, and its expression in physical space is frequently metaphorical rather than real. This metaphorical use of the language of solitude has been common to the literature of Christian ascetics since the time of the Desert Fathers.[55] In the case of Silvestro, neither his first refuge along the Gola della Rossa nor the mountain of Montefano are by any means as remote as they are presented in the vitae. The vitae, including the *Life of St. Bonfils* by Silvestro himself, employ eremitic images and language that serve to reinforce the virtues and austerity of the first members of the order.[56]

The picture that emerges is one of mendicant hermits drawn to the towns solely (and reluctantly) in performance of their apostolic duty to preach; in some ways, it is literally a picture. In one of Silvestro's miracles, a woman suffering from chronic headaches receives a vision that she might be cured by hairs from Silvestro's beard. She conspires with Silvestro's barber to acquire the hairs and is subsequently cured.[57] The vitae reinforce eremitic principles not only through their narrative structure and vocabulary but iconographically as well. With Silvestro's beard and Giovanni's staff, we have the classic features of the hermit recognizable to all.

Despite the eremitic focus of their hagiography, by the early fourteenth century the Silvestrines had carved out a more urban mission, pursuing and acquiring rights to parishes in several Italian cities. The principal architect—although not the originator—of this shift was the fourth prior general of the order, Andrea di Giacomo, prior general from 1298 to 1325. He was also the author of the two most important vitae—those of Silvestro and Giovanni dal Bastone—and no one knew better than he the literary rather than literal use of such eremitic language. Under his stewardship, new Silvestrine houses were founded almost exclusively in urban locations such as Florence and Siena, and by the end of his tenure the order was established in urban parishes in Perugia, Florence, and Fabriano as well.[58]

Enrico Guidoni suggests that the dynamics that produced the distinctive urban religious landscape of late medieval Europe should be understood as the product of a general convergence of interests between the new mendicant orders and the urban elites, rather than the result of explicit mendicant or municipal strategies.[59] In the March of Ancona, the documentary record preserved in the Silvestrine archives clearly testifies to such an identification of interests between the young Silvestrine order and the elites of Fabriano, as their fortunes rose together during the course of the thirteenth century.[60] Active patronage of the Silvestrines clearly assisted the commune in its effort to develop the physical space of the city inside the walls as well as establish effective and friendly control of territory outside the walls. Within the walls, the monastery and church of San Benedetto was a nucleus of development in the new Borgo Nuovo quarter, and in 1323 the Church of San Benedetto would acquire parish rights. In the contado, communal authorities facilitated Silvestrine acquisition of mills and estates, extending a friendly presence into formerly suspect areas and, as well, blunting the influence still exerted by the older monastic establishments.

In the hagiographic rendition of the founding of Montefano—Silvestro's second monastery—Silvestro arrived at the site unbidden, attracted by its very solitude, and it was curious pilgrims from below who initiated contact with the commune. As Andrea puts it: "Thus far Silvestro was alone in the hermitage of Montefano, when three men, one of whom still survives although used up by old age, came to him for the sake of a visit from the castle of Fabriano, which is situated almost at the foot of the mountain."[61]

The archival record suggests a much more active role on the part of agents of the commune in attracting Silvestro to Fabriano and encouraging him to build the monastery of Montefano. Three canons of the collegiate church of San Venanzo appear as witnesses to the first donations of land around the Fonte Vembrici—where Silvestro had been reposing with his wolf and was now expected to construct a monastery—and sale of a third parcel took place in the cloister of San Venanzo.[62] The first parcels of land at Fonte Vembrici were obtained easily, but it took the active cooperation of the commune to acquire the rest. In a series of transactions in the summer of 1235, the podestà of Fabriano, Uguccione, exchanged land presumably held by the commune in a variety of locations around Fabriano with fifteen individuals representing ten families asserting rights to Fonte Vembrici—a circumstance hardly likely if Montefano were as remote as suggested in the vita.[63] All of the land so acquired by the commune was donated by the podestà to Silvestro and "his brothers and successors in the church of Montefano."[64] In 1237, Atto di Mede enacted a will that, among numerous ecclesiastical bequests, included five soldi each to the Franciscan *"ecclesie"* at Cantiro and to the *heremite* of Montefano—the first extant testament in Fabriano that renders a bequest to the new monastery.[65]

At the same time the Silvestrines were consolidating their holdings on the mountain of Montefano, they were also encouraged to begin development in the new quarter of Fabriano proper. In 1244, the podestà of

Fabriano, Tommaso da Spello, with the consent of the general and special councils of the commune and meeting in the church of San Venanzo, ordered that whatever piece of buildable property the Silvestrines found most suitable be handed over to the order in the Borgo Nuovo quarter, outside the gate.[66]

A document from 1270 presents further evidence of the symbiotic relationship developing between commune and monastery. On August 5, Maestro Giacomo di Bonora, *syndicus*, or rector, of the commune, reported to the podestà that a panel of notable citizens charged with examining the conduct of two brothers of Montefano, Giacomo and Benincasa, in the handling of public funds for the purpose of building new city walls, had found that they had spent the roughly fifteen hundred *libbrae* in proper fashion.[67] By 1270, the Silvestrines had constructed thirteen monasteries in a generation, ten of them in the March of Ancona; it stands to reason that they would have acquired some organizational and engineering skills of use to the expanding cities. Undoubtedly the most famous of thirteenth-century Silvestrines, Fra Bevignate of Cingoli, appears first as a monk of San Giovanni di Sassoferrato in the general chapter held at Montefano in 1268 to find a successor to Silvestro.[68] By the late 1270s, he was in Perugia, where he designed and supervised construction of the aqueduct and the Fontana Maggiore, whose sculptural program was undertaken by Nicola and Giovanni Pisano and includes a scene of Silvestro receiving the Rule from St. Benedict. In the 1280s, Fra Bevignate was appointed first architect of the new cathedral in Orvieto.[69] The Silvestrines were not just in the cities at the end of the thirteenth century, but active participants in shaping the urban landscape.

Andrea's painstaking presentation of the Silvestrines as fully in compliance with the conciliar decrees of the Second Council of Lyons allows us to place the composition of the *Life of Silvester* after 1274, and it is also an opportunity for the hagiographer to explain the origins of the cozy business relationship between the order and commune. In a chapter cataloguing miracles and apparitions associated with relics of Silvestro, Andrea recounts the founder's intercession in the ensuing dispute:

> The General Council had now been conducted at Lyons during the time of Gregory X. Brother Bartolo, third prior general, and the brothers, fervently desiring to stop begging for alms, decreed that they would receive everything necessary for their sustenance only from their properties, in accordance with the Rule of St. Benedict and the privilege of their order. But, what they had was not sufficient for their needs, and so they asked the commune of Fabriano to provide for them.[70]

As it turned out, the general council of Fabriano was unimpressed by this presentation, but an apparition of an outraged Silvestro was able to stampede them toward a vote authorizing the expense. The more prosaic documents in the archives are mute as to apparitions, but they do tend to support the idea that the mid-1270s marked a new level of communal support for the Silvestrines. On June 10, 1275, Bonagrazia di Bartolo sold to Venimbene di Guido, syndicus of the commune of Fabriano, an assortment of properties and mills (*molendina*) in the contrada of Ponte del Gualdo for the price of fifteen hundred libbrae.[71] Three days later, *im palacio comunis*, Venimbene granted to prior general Bartolo, "for the love of God and his mother Blessed Mary always Virgin," all use and proceeds from the lands, mills, buildings, homes, and irrigation channels, in perpetuity.[72] The entire proceeding had been refereed by eight "wise and good men," two from each quarter, elected by the special council of the commune.[73] Among these eight wise and good men was a certain "Iacob[us] Tabelii de quarterio Podii." The Podii, or Poggio, is also known as the Borgo Nuovo and was the new district in which the Silvestrines were constructing their monastery and church of San Benedetto. Iacobus Tabelii was the father of Andrea di Giacomo, who may already have been engaged in writing the *Life of Silvester*.

In 1278, an identical arrangement was employed for additional mills and lands, this time in Fossatelli. Egidio di Giovanni di Gentile sold mills, millstones, lands, homes, canals, weirs, and so forth, to Venimbene di Guido di Ognibene, on behalf of the commune, for 400 libbrae.[74] Only seven of the eight wise and good men were on hand that day to witness the transaction; Iacobus Tabelii was among them.[75] Once again, the commune turned around and granted "fructus et usufructus" to the Silvestrines in perpetuity.[76]

The relationship between the monasteries of Montefano, on the hill, and San Benedetto, in the newly developing quarter of Fabriano, merits attention. In 1244, the monks of Montefano first obtained a parcel of land suitable for building in the Borgo Nuovo quarter of Fabriano. Originally designed for overnight stays by monks with business in town, through a series of purchases and bequests the new development became a fully operational and self-supporting monastery. In the testaments of late thirteenth and early fourteenth-century Fabriano, burial in the church of San Benedetto, along with construction and maintenance of altars, stands out as an important expectation for those leaving bequests to the Silvestrine congregation.[77]

Documents in the archives of Montefano are organized by monastery of origin. That is the way they were organized when Abbot Stefano Moronti first inventoried them in the sixteenth century, and it appears to have been the method of storage from the beginning.[78] During the last decades of the thirteenth century, there was considerable blurring of the lines between the fondo Montefano and fondo San Benedetto. In 1282, for example, San Benedetto was referred to as a dependency of Montefano operating under direction of a subprior.[79]

Although an episcopal grant of indulgences in 1286 presumed an independent community at San Benedetto, with its own prior, it is difficult to find any document distinguishing monks of San Benedetto di Fabriano from those of Montefano.[80] In the 1290s, the only extant records of chapter meetings of the monks of Montefano are for meetings that physically occurred in the church of San Benedetto in town.[81] Convocation letters for the general chapter that elected Andrea prior general in 1298 listed attending monks from each of the monasteries, but other than the prior no monks are listed for San Benedetto di Fabriano.[82] It seems that the sheer volume of business between monastery and town had blurred the lines between the two monasteries and that no effort was made to disentangle them. By 1298, therefore, Montefano itself was essentially an urban monastery; when the substantial new contingents from Orvieto and Viterbo are counted alongside those of Rome, Perugia, and Montefano, monks from the sleepy little backwaters favored early in Silvestro's career were heavily outnumbered.[83] Indeed, as prior general, Andrea maintained a permanent room in the monastery in town, and by the 1340s the Silvestrine prior generals officially called San Benedetto di Fabriano their residence and administrative center.[84]

Urbanization of the order became complete with the election of Andrea di Giacomo as prior general. Few biographical details concerning Andrea can be teased from the archives beyond his deeds as prior general, but those all point to a thoroughly urban man. We know that his father was a citizen of Fabriano, occasionally serving on communal councils.[85] It is not clear when Andrea joined the Silvestrines. No Andrea appears among the 119 monks who met in general chapter in 1268 to select a successor to Silvestro.[86] The first unambiguous record of Andrea is in a communal document of 1277, naming him as one of two monks assigned by the commune of Fabriano to carry a formal offer letter to Orso degli Orsini as prospective podestà.[87] We know, as well, that in the years just before and after his election as prior general of the order, Andrea served as vicar for the Bishop of Florence.[88] In this capacity, he was very much involved in the land rush that took place as episcopal properties were leased and traded in the new Cafaggio district, around San Marco. It was surely this proximity to episcopal authority that facilitated Silvestrine acquisition of the parish rights at San Marco, the second Silvestrine parish. The accompanying monastery immediately became one of the largest and most important Silvestrine houses until it was wrested from them and transferred to the Dominicans in the early fifteenth century.[89]

In counterpoint to Andrea the urban administrator, there is Andrea the literary creator of an eremitic past. The eremitic life by the end of the thirteenth century, however, was defined by interior space rather than by physical solitude. As an example, the Augustinian from the Marches with the greatest reputation for sanctity was Nicola da Tolentino, who died in 1305. San Nicola was considered by his contemporaries to be a hermit, and the designation stuck; André Vauchez categorizes him among the "hermit saints."[90] Yet, although Nicola was a friar of the Hermits of Brettini, he spent almost his entire career as a religious in an urban monastery in the center of Tolentino. He was said to live apart from his brethren—in a cell, like Giovanni dal Bastone—but he was known to the community as a fiery preacher, a counselor, and a healer.[91] His cell may have been private, but both he and his order were very much active in the communal life of Tolentino. The 365 witnesses who testified at the canonization process for Nicola in 1325 were drawn from the towns of the central Marches. The witnesses, the miracles and hopes they related, and their journeys to Tolentino grant us a glimpse into the social history of urban life in the March of Ancona. They also show that the cult of the hermit of Brettino was rather thoroughly based in the cities and towns.[92]

In like manner, when Giovanni dal Bastone came down from the mountain and took up his final residence in San Benedetto, his sanctity and reputation as a hermit were indelible. The city no longer threatened his purity; now it offered a sacred resting place. In contrast to the scattered tracks of the beginning of the century, the network of roads in the Upper Esino Valley now had a definite hub—and the roads led to Fabriano.[93] Along those roads—from Gubbio, Matelica, Pergola, Bergamo, and other points—came the sixteen men and twenty-seven women with vows to fulfill before the altar of that church, and whose cures were recorded and authenticated by the notables of Fabriano.

We know when the Augustinian friars turned their attention to the cities, as they have left us explicit discussion of their strategy. In the bull announcing the Great Union, Alexander IV had stressed the need for a new apostolate to combat the preachers of heresy in the cities.[94] In his fourteenth-century history of the order, Jordan of Saxony explains this shift to his fellow Augustinians:

The Supreme Pontiff, Pope Alexander IV, decreed that they ought to move into the cities and acquire houses there. By their preaching and teaching, as well as by the example of their holy lives and the hearing of confessions, they were to bring forth fruit among the people of God. Some of these brothers found this difficult, and preferred to remain on their own in the wilderness and be with God in their accustomed way, than to expose themselves to the bad influence of the world among worldly people.[95]

Despite his exaltation of the eremitic life, Jordan regarded this action of Alexander IV as praiseworthy. The friars "are not to be thought of as having thereby fallen off from their original state of perfection, but rather as having acquired a state of greater perfection, since now they do not live for themselves alone but are of service to the Church of God."[96]

Franciscans and Silvestrines in the Marches during the thirteenth century shifted their operations to the city center more subtly. The movement of saints, living and dead, from remote locale to urban cell and crypt is apparent, but there is no suggestion within the literature of the religious communities themselves that the change was recognized. Silvestrine hagiography evoked the strongest commitment to eremitic principles even as the order pursued most avidly its urban ambitions.

The migrations of Silvestrine holy men are a good indicator of the shifting relationship of sanctity and the city in the late medieval Marches. Silvestro's flight from the city became a magnet for young men seeking the purifying isolation of the ascetic life. The return of his disciple, Giovanni dal Bastone, sixty years later served as a magnet as well, this time drawing pious visitors to his shrine in Fabriano. Seen in concert with the relocation of Augustinian and Franciscan holy sites into the towns and cities, it is clear that the return of the hermit in Fabriano was but part of a broader pattern of the sacralization of urban space in late medieval Italy. Trexler and others have looked at this process from the focal point of the commune and seen most explicitly how it served the strategies of the municipal elite. This is undoubtedly true, and the composition of the tribunal authenticating Giovanni's miracles, with its representatives from the canons of San Venanzo and the powerful Chiavalli clan, reinforces the claim that ambitious townsmen were actively creating an urban ceremonial center.

Viewed from the perspective of a religious community like the Silvestrines, however, the lure of the city seems more an inexorable tide. The abbot of San Vittore delle Chiuse was farsighted when he secured a place in the rising commune for families formerly subject to his authority. If the first patrons of Silvestro and his followers were rural aristocrats like Corrado di Rovellone, by the middle of the thirteenth century they were members of the urban elite, and their bequests were likely to include urban properties. Not only were the patrons and the pilgrims urban, so too were the new leaders of the order. Men like Andrea di Giacomo might write of the holiness of the lonely places, but their feet were firmly planted in the sacred space of the city.

CHAPTER ELEVEN

In the Shop of the Lord

Bernardino of Siena and Popular Devotion

Cynthia L. Polecritti

In the spring of 1425, the Franciscan Bernardino of Siena (1380–1444) told his audience a story about another preacher who was having trouble attracting people to his sermons. One Sunday, with only six persons present—all of them women—the friar announced that the next time he would show the devil himself to anyone who came. The women spread the exciting news and the following week the church was filled with eager listeners, men and women alike. The wily preacher then gleefully pointed to a devil painted on the wall and, having thus fulfilled his promise, proceeded to berate the crowd for being more excited about viewing Satan than the true Body and Blood of the Lord. We can assume that he went on to preach a useful sermon to his chastened—and now captive—audience.[1]

Unlike the hapless friar in his exemplum, Bernardino seldom had to worry about a low turnout. As the most famous preacher of the Quattrocento, he was a traveling celebrity whose visits were associated with both instruction and pleasure. Popular because of his wit and his storytelling, his preaching, which was often held outdoors in piazze, also inspired exorcisms, peacemakings, and bonfires of vanities. Although he might be dissatisfied with attendance at a particular sermon, he usually faced a large and enthusiastic audience. When this itinerant holy man paid a visit, he could be confident that many people would eventually attend, some for reasons of genuine piety, others drawn by curiosity, and many more from an easy conflation of the two.

Bernardino occasionally preached in the countryside, but he primarily spoke to urban listeners, like other great reformers who swept through Italian towns during the fifteenth century, in campaigns that combined preaching and mass ritual. In metropolises like Milan or Florence, there were reportedly gatherings in the tens of thousands; in a smaller place like Prato an eyewitness noted that as many as eight thousand people would turn up, depending upon the scheduled topic.[2]

Women formed the majority of Bernardino's regular audience, but many men, from humble artisans to rich and powerful merchants, were also drawn to the piazze. The heterogeneity of these urban audiences explains his wide range of subject matter, from the smallest domestic dilemma to the deepest longings of the soul. The sermons describe personal encounters with perplexed usurers, demoniacs in need of exorcism, and defiant participants in vendetta. Aristocrat and learned cleric though he was, Bernardino's contact with a variety of human types and his ability to empathize with his listeners also gave him excellent credentials for understanding lay piety, even if his observations were filtered through his own persona of highly educated priest and preacher.

The historiography of late medieval and early modern religion is no longer framed in terms of the subordination of an unruly world by intellectuals and reforming clerics. During the last two decades, scholars have developed a more nuanced understanding of the relationship between so-called elite and popular religious culture; Natalie Zemon Davis, for example, has suggested that popular devotion is best seen as "relational" or "interactive." More recently, Katherine Ludwig Jansen has characterized sermons as "the crossroads . . . the point at which the transmission of ideas and their reception often intersected." The interpretative shift has thus been from a model of indoctrination to one of interaction and cultural exchange, with greater emphasis given to the laity's role in both belief and practice.[3] How we study preaching has accordingly changed, with greater attention now paid to the audience and the reception of the spoken word. Bernardino is a key figure because he served as an exemplar for contemporary preachers and for those who followed. His vernacular sermons are especially instructive since they are repositories, however incomplete, of a complex interaction between preacher and listener. Preaching was not merely an instrument of social control but a manifestation of a social process.

Bernardino's sermons were a place where learned theology and popular culture met. Since many were recorded verbatim, they give an opportunity to listen to the process of cultural transmission as it actually took place. We will never be able to trace this process in its full complexity, but the sermons show that Bernardino was versatile enough to modulate the preacher-listener relationship whenever it served his purpose and the needs of a highly demanding audience. This versatility was particularly striking when he instructed his listeners in what he considered basic

Christian etiquette, trying to mold them into outwardly respectable and internally sincere worshippers. Even when he was laying down rules for "proper" devotional behavior, the respective roles of preacher and listener were never fixed, but elastic: Bernardino saw the people before him not just as his children and pupils, but also as partners—or, in a startling image, even as customers. He tacitly conceded that urban audiences had a rich repertoire of devotional behaviors, not all of them controllable by clerics. While fully exploiting his own charisma and its powerful hold over his listeners, he was also open enough to acknowledge the participatory nature of late medieval religion.

Bernardino had a multifaceted idea of his vocation as preacher, and this inevitably affected how he viewed his audience and its spiritual capacity. He could be both gentle and aggressive: sometimes he saw himself as a loving parent or as a doctor who healed ailing souls, while at other times he bragged that he was a swordsman dueling with obstinate sinners.[4] But his contemporaries described him as a second St. Paul, and the preacher in fact usually presented himself in these heroic terms, as a mighty evangelizer who had come to instruct an incompletely Christian laity. He possessed firm and seemingly straightforward ideas about his mission of Christianization. When he preached to the Florentines during the 1425 Lenten season, for example, he stated at the outset that his goal was to make them "all wise and full of knowledge and the learning of God, in order to acquire holy Paradise; illuminated by virtue and science, having cast out ignorance, that evil beast."[5] At least a few of his listeners needed the most elementary lessons before they became "wise and full of knowledge." Despite numerous opportunities to hear preaching in the urban centers of Italy, there were apparently laypeople who had never even attended a sermon. Early in his visit to Siena in 1427, Bernardino welcomed them: "O you who have never heard a sermon, are you here today?" Surprisingly, there were some novice sermon-goers present, since the recorder put down the answer, "Yes."[6]

Like other preaching friars, Bernardino worked primarily as a teacher and missionary. Most of his visits were structured in order to provide a general religious education, for both adepts and the ignorant, during a long bout of vigorous preaching; during the Lenten season, for instance, he would stay in a given city for many weeks, preaching daily for up to several hours at a time. The recorded sermons give us the chance to examine the range of his preaching and his most pressing concerns. In his visit to Siena in 1425, for example, several sermons in the preacher's repertoire indicate that some people lacked knowledge of the most basic Christian behaviors. His complaint is familiar to those who study late medieval religion, and in part it supports the scenario of learned preacher talking down to a confused laity—or as Bernardino would put it, of a father instructing his children. The first step in socializing the "ignorant" was to teach them decorum. Bernardino assumed that many listeners had no idea of the most elemental etiquette in the face of the divine, even when they were in the church itself. A modern historian, of course, would characterize their casual behavior not as "ignorance" but as a fluid sense of the boundary between sacred and secular space.

Like other clerics in the late middle ages, Bernardino struggled to make the boundary between sacred and secular more distinct, sometimes in terms implying that the laity were as unschooled as toddlers. In a sermon on sacrilege, he gave a long and windy list of reasons for restrained behavior, most of them completely obvious: God dwells within the church, it holds the consecrated body of Christ, many angels are present, the Church offers many benefits, God and his saints are a good example, and the divine office is celebrated there. Nevertheless, many people were still oblivious to the sanctity of the holy place, according to Bernardino. He taunted his listeners with the good behavior of the Saracens, who acted in a respectful fashion in *their* worship of the devil, the men entering and exiting before the women, the former with bare feet, the latter with faces modestly covered: "And they pray to the demon with such faith that sometimes they rise above the ground in contemplation, and when they hear about our ways they make jokes about them."[7]

"Our ways," the preacher believed, consisted of an easy and gawking familiarity with the holy. Two years later, he would still complain to the Sienese that some people came to the sermon when it was already half over, while others would rush into church just at the moment in which the Host was elevated—and then immediately rush back out.[8] We might read the latter as a sign that people consciously chose to invest their energy in what they recognized as the highlight of the mass; Bernardino, instead, reproved what he thought of as childish misbehavior. Once inside the church, his laypeople were unsure of how to manage their bodies; he warned each to stay in his or her place (he did not want them wandering in the priests' area) and he ordered those who became weary not to rest their heads upon the altar. Many others forgot to genuflect in front of the host, so Bernardino reminded them that if someone failed to take his hat off in the presence of a pope or emperor, any request would not be granted and he would be ridiculed. In the case of slighting the Body of Christ, both humans and angels would make jokes (*beffe*) at the offender.[9]

Predictably, the preacher complained that the Renaissance church was a noisy one: "Alas! what can we say of those who carry hawks on their arms or bring the dog to church, and of the women with babies? The baby wails, and the hawk beats his wings, and the bells ring, and so think about the scandal you cause that priest!"[10]

Aside from the squalls of animals and infants, there was a constant stream of conversation to disturb the holy silence. People bought, sold, and made contracts, while women chattered incessantly, cheerily greeting their relatives and neighbors: "This one embraces that one there, or this one here; one gossips, the other laughs. 'How are you doing? And your children?' and other such nonsense."[11]

When he preached again in Siena in 1427, some of his fellow citizens still had not improved their manners in the presence of the holy. His irritation came from personal experience. "O *donna*," he chided his female listener, "How shameful it is that in the morning when I say mass, you make such a noise with your calling out that I seem to hear a pile of bones!"[12] He also repeated familiar criticism of women who led a daughter to church or sermon in order to lure a potential husband. The 1427 sermons, the liveliest and most complete of any recorded preaching from the medieval and early modern periods, show us that he sometimes abandoned calm instruction for a rougher tone. Bernardino tried to shock his audience into good manners with blunt, and certainly offensive, language. Women who attracted men in the cathedral were not ladies but whores, their evil mothers were go-betweens, and they made the Virgin their procuress (*ruffiana*). Better to act out their desires behind the communal palace, in public, on the street of the prostitutes rather than in the holy church! He was equally gruff when he insulted predatory sodomites who used the cathedral as their hunting ground.[13] Even the respectably married could receive a tongue lashing. In a sermon on marriage, he forbade his listeners to engage in sexual intercourse on holy days. The preacher made a sarcastic comparison: Was it permissible for spouses to have sex on the altar or in the presence of others? He apparently wanted to leave his audience with this shocking image since he abruptly ended the sermon with "that's enough for this morning."[14]

Along with his campaign to teach proper decorum, Bernardino also needed to deliver sermons that taught basic techniques of worship. One talk, given in Florence on May 2, 1424, is an extremely simple outline of prayer methods, clearly aimed at the unproficient. Patience, rather than sarcasm, was required in this instance. The preacher began by telling his listeners how to enunciate their words. Your voice should be clear so that others could understand if you spoke loudly enough, and each word should be clearly delineated from the other. Clear words would expedite the message to God: "If you don't understand them, God won't, either." It was necessary to chew over all the words carefully to get the most from the experience, just as a drinker savors his wine. Stance was as important as speech; truly reverent prayer demanded that you not lay down or sit "like a pig." But Bernardino also cautioned the more fervent to restrain their enthusiasm when praying in public, reminding them that husbands and wives behave differently in their private apartments than they do, say, in church. For instance, in private you might choose to pray kneeling and with your head touching the ground.[15] In a sermon to the Sienese in 1427, he had to tell his listeners to pray only for things that were good for the soul. Don't be like the mercenaries, he warned them, who ask God to give them booty![16]

Yet even these simple instructions confused listeners, according to Bernardino. Some people did not feel capable of mastering all of this advice, protesting, "I'm not able to do so many things!" The preacher's answer was that they at least try to raise their minds toward God. If you can do nothing else, do this, he encouraged them, following up the advice with a brief exemplum. A person traveling to Rome would like good company, a good inn, a good road. But if he was already at Rome, the rest hardly mattered. In other words, if you prayed with sincerity, the accompanying actions were secondary. Typically, Bernardino was careful to recognize the limitations of his listeners, and in his guise as father-teacher he encouraged them to do no more than was possible; he never berated them for not managing to achieve a clerical ideal and accepted the difference between decent lay piety and the more stringent behavior required of the religious professional.[17] His frustration more often centered on their inability to meet what he defined as a bare minimum, whether behaving modestly in church or saying one's basic prayers. For some members of the laity, a respectful and simplified piety sufficed.

It is difficult to know whom Bernardino was really targeting with this elementary advice, which implies that many listeners were both clumsy and unschooled. Ironically, the examples given above come from Florence and Siena, two of the most sophisticated cities of late medieval Europe. Far from being novices in terms of religious practice, many Tuscan men were active participants in a highly developed confraternity system, where they practiced complex ritual, prayer, and organized charity.[18] And Bernardino's criticisms were almost certainly *not* aimed at untutored women. In terms of absolute numbers, his regular audience was dominated by female sermon-goers who had often heard similar advice, given the many opportunities in a large city to hear preaching by both local priests and famous friars. In fact, despite his impatience with their chattering, Bernardino assumed that women had far less to learn than their men, and he praised the women for their steadfastness. They were far from novices and possessed a rich devotional life. Perhaps when he talked down to a supposedly untutored laity, he was aiming not at these regular listeners but at the slow, the cynical, and the youngest children. Like the Apostles, a preacher, according to Bernardino, was a fisherman casting for souls—sometimes it was necessary to cast the net as widely as possible.[19]

Even though one stance of the preacher was that he was enlightening the ignorant, it never became the primary relationship between himself and his listeners. Most of his sermons on lay piety were meant for more experienced devotees. Sometimes his reprimand was actually an attempt to redirect even praiseworthy belief and practice, including joining a confraternity, civic deployment of a local saint, or a visit to a shrine. Bernardino approved of these activities, but more than a century before the reforms of Trent he tried to instill a stricter and streamlined version of worship, one that was firmly directed by the Church. For example, when the devout layperson's idea of piety contradicted clerical, Christocentric priorities, he tried to rechannel that devotion. He was displeased that many worshippers, when they first entered a church, hurried to a saint rather than to Christ himself: "They leave the Lord in order to visit the servant."[20] His complaints even included the cult of Mary, despite his intense personal devotion to the Mother of Christ and her status as patron and protector of Siena. Prayer to the city's other patrons was of course efficacious, he told the Sienese, and Mary's personal appeal to Christ was worth more than the pleas of all the martyrs, angels, and saints.[21] Bernardino did not want devotees to abandon the cult of the saints or of the Madonna, but he tried to instill a proper sense of its place in the totality of Christian worship. If you fasted every Saturday in Mary's honor, he pointed out to his fellow citizens, you would still sin if you missed even one fast day commanded by the Church; in fact, the Madonna herself would prefer that Christ be honored instead.[22]

Most important, the preacher wanted the religiously diligent to understand that outward behavior—the cult of the saints, pilgrimage, building chapels—was secondary to what happened within the soul. Bernardino, a renowned peacemaker, told his listeners that it was "a greater merit to pardon than to visit the Holy Sepulchre a hundred times." God does not promise that you will be saved by pilgrimage, but many parts of the Gospel say that you will be saved if you forgive your enemy.[23] He punctured the pride that some took in their supposedly good behavior. In Florence, for example, he imagined that listeners asked him: "How can anything bad happen to the Florentines, who do so many good things, give so many alms, have so many hospitals?"[24] Bernardino's sharp reply was that external acts, especially those financed by usurious profits, were worthless without an inner marrow of charity.

This did not mean that the externals of popular devotion were unimportant, only that they should hold a supplemental place within a deeper spirituality.[25] If someone had a relic of St. Francis in the household, the preacher agreed that it was holy. But the most beautiful relic, he explained, was Christ's heart, His own Word.[26] For Bernardino, the Word of God, and its resonance in the soul, was the central aspect of faith. The mass, he flamboyantly claimed, was less important than the sermon.[27] The sermon was the place where the diligent could go a step beyond even an appropriate external act; it was the setting where preacher could help listener develop a finely tuned self-consciousness, and a more interior religion.

In this formulation, the listener became the preacher's partner. Bernardino emphasized their intimate connection in the opening moments of a sermon delivered early in the Siena 1427 course. He confided that he had been so ill the day before that he could barely stand upright; now, however, he had revived to such an extent that "I'd fight with Orlando." The prayers of his listeners had restored his strength, so that he was able to preach.[28] Their participation could extend to the apostolic mission itself. At several points, Bernardino explicitly told his listeners that he wanted them all to become *predicatori e predicatrici* (male and female preachers).[29] In a metaphor designed to appeal to male listeners (participants in Siena's republican government), he urged them to rush to the sermon when they heard the morning bell, in the same way that they would hurry to a council meeting.[30]

Bernardino saw women as his special helpmates, asking them to bring children to the sermons and to transmit the message to husbands and invalid mothers at home. They should even persuade lazy men to come to the sermon: "Don't let your husband stay in bed, nor your brother or son; but wake them and make them come with you to hear that which will make them live again, if they are dead."[31]

But listening to sermons was only the first step in one's spiritual revival and the word of the preacher only the initial trigger in a deeper conversion, which depended on the listener herself. The sermon was far more than a list of rules for good behavior offered by an all-knowing preacher. It was, rather, a means of persuading the individual will to change. Bernardino wanted to ensure development of good habits through exertion of the will, or, as he often put it, inner strength or *fortezza*. Sound doctrine and good preaching eliminated the sinner's pathetic excuse of I-didn't-know ("Io non lo sapevo"). The end result for the listener was a sturdy combination of knowledge, will, and vigilant self-awareness. For instance, when Bernardino preached on business practice, he wanted the lesson to have this effect: "And when you make a contract you'll think about it first, asking yourself: 'What did Frate Bernardino say? He said to me such-and-such: This is wrong, I mustn't do it this way; this is good, this I want to do.'"[32]

The sermon, then, should expand outward into every moment of the day, with listeners actively applying its lessons as they went about their normal routine. Self-reflection needed to become a daily habit, for it was simple acts of everyday fortitude that would bring the devout closer to salvation. When a woman burned her finger, for instance, she should use the discomfort to remind her of the pain of hell.[33] When you get up in the morning, the preacher advised, you should think about all the benefits God has given you, while at night you should mull over your sins and cry about them (but Bernardino was careful to warn his listeners not to linger over their carnal sins).[34] This careful reckoning of behavior was compared to that of the good merchant who regularly checked his accounts in order not to end up bankrupt when he died. A sermon should spark an accelerated process of intensive schooling that would continue even after the preacher left town.

Confession was naturally a major part of Bernardino's campaign of spiritual discipline and self-awareness. Along with attentive sermon-going, it forced the devotee to concentrate on the internal state. Because his most important assignments were during the Lenten season, this was his main arena for preparing people to partake of their Easter communion duty. When he preached in Florence in the spring of 1424, confession was the subject of his first four sermons; the visit would later culminate in the Easter sermon and mass confession. One of Bernardino's greatest boasts was that he was a kind of miracle worker whose preaching inspired people to confess for the first time; in one city, supposedly thirty thousand souls confessed at a single Easter.[35]

His approach to confession was the usual mix of homely metaphor and simple instruction. The conscience needed to be swept clean just as a good housewife sweeps her home; and just as she needed to wash frequently for "beautiful, white cloths," so it was with confession.[36] He gave painstaking directions to his audience about systematically writing sins down to remember them. But what if it has been twenty years since you last cleared your conscience?

Now take a book with twenty pages and begin to write on it, the first year, "when I was a child." And divide it into four parts, spring, summer, autumn, and winter. And remember: What sins did I commit in those times? Write them down one by one. And afterwards, write on the next page the second year, and thus the third and the fourth. And think about it slowly: "In such a year I went into such a country and did such a sin with such a person in such a way." And write it on that page. And if one page isn't enough for the year take as many as you need.[37]

This paper should be hidden in a secret place, but it was helpful to take it along to confession. If you followed these directions, Bernardino promised his listener, your soul would become "white and beautiful, like a ray of sun." Of course, Bernardino did not forget the illiterate, encouraging them to do the same thing using their memory.

None of this intense self-examination was meant to burden the soul. Underlying all of Bernardino's preaching is his firm belief that the listener had the capacity to change, thanks to his words and her own willpower. Early failure did not mean devastation. He encouraged the listener with the metaphor of a sailor who made a greater effort to reach the harbor when he met with contrary winds: "Thus does such a one who wants to do good, who says to himself: 'What did I already do this year? I did this good thing, and now I want to add another, and thus I will improve.' And in this way always go forward and not backwards."[38]

Perseverance was a positive good, and with the preacher's aid it would cleanse the inner self. The lessons of the sermon thus helped everyone, novice and adept alike, to march, step by step, to salvation.

Both of the roles discussed—fatherly preacher admonishing his children, teacher-partner guiding the faithful to self-awareness—assume that Bernardino saw himself as the dominant figure in his relationship with his audience. His normal self-image was as a master dispensing knowledge, either basic or more advanced, to a receptive and obedient pupil. The dynamics of persuasion, however, tell a rather different story. Analysis of preaching messages is not enough; equally important is how the sermon is heard, received, experienced. In a busy piazza, the listener's attention span could ebb and flow, and often Bernardino had to discipline his audience within the course of the sermon itself. Real listeners behaved in the same lively fashion as they did at mass; the Siena 1427 sermons are rich with interruption whenever Bernardino stopped to reprimand a jokester or the drowsy.

Far from being passive recipients of the word, people could actively resist the preacher's message at the very moment of delivery. Some of the most revealing passages in the sermons trace the underlying tension that arose between preacher and listeners when his words did not meet with their approval. Within a few seconds, whatever bond he had established with the audience could abruptly fracture, forcing him to shift into a different mode than stern father or all-knowing teacher. Once when he was discussing the duties of the priesthood, something must have upset his listeners. Bernardino's angry reaction: "I'm not inclined to remain quiet! I'll say what seems right to me!" It is not entirely clear from this passage, or the one immediately preceding it, what angered people. A few moments before, however, the preacher had been talking about abuses, especially the Sienese custom of using priests in certain offices.[39]

Bernardino prided himself on condemning political, as well as moral, corruption. Other topics forced him to become even more defensive and truculent in the face of disapproving listeners. When he talked about sexuality, for example, he needed to construct an elaborate defense of his right to speak openly, even if he claimed that he was being discreet: "I've heard such execrable things, that by my soul, I would not say them either in the sermon or in a discussion."[40] Nevertheless, he inevitably said them. Listeners could disagree over his frankness: "This one tells me, 'Be silent!' Another says, 'Shout it out!'"[41]

Distracted, skeptical, or selective listeners meant that the preacher needed to assume yet another persona, one very different from his role as confident parent, teacher, or senior partner. Like the friar who advertised the "devil on the wall" to build an audience, real preachers sometimes relied on a certain sleight-of-hand, when necessary. In fact, according to one of his biographers, Bernardino employed a similar ruse when he preached in the town of Bergamo, early in his career. Faced with a scanty audience, he announced that an angel had sent a message expressly to this town, which he would read at an upcoming sermon. His next audience was predictably large, whereupon he began a discourse on Revelation 2:12–16, the message to Pergamum. Presumably, the Bergamaschi were not upset by this play on words, since Bernardino's preaching there was ultimately successful.[42] A device such as this one, with its false advertising, reminds us that even a great preacher and holy man could adapt himself to the whims of the crowd to save souls. Like Boccaccio's Friar Cipolla, who claimed that he had a feather of the Angel Gabriel, Bernardino was willing to become a trickster in relationship to his audience.[43] Both the *novella*, or short-story, literature and accounts of real sermons indicate that preachers often functioned as the "coyote" figure in their society: cunning, exploitative, and flexible.

Yet a subtle danger lay in this kind of manipulation of the crowd. Ironically, Bernardino's attempt to guide his listeners to a disciplined, more interior religion was in part subverted by what they experienced during his own sermons. For some people, the medium was more important than the message. The preacher was fully aware of this and joked that the dimwitted might miss the message entirely: a person who has not comprehended the sermon is asked to summarize it and foggily replies: "He said some good and beautiful things." Bernardino then told the famous exemplum of the thick friar who, after hearing a colleague preach, praised him by saying, "He spoke in such an elevated way that I didn't understand a thing."[44] Hence Bernardino's injunction to himself to speak so that all could understand (*chiarozzo, chiarozzo*). Eyewitness accounts in fact suggest that people remembered certain aspects of the sermon far more than its content, and that the focus of lay piety was on externals. Chroniclers were impressed by spectacular collective rituals—such as bonfires and peacemakings—and had little to say about the actual words of the preacher.[45] For many, the slow process of internal discipline was superseded by moments of public, and sudden, conversion. Unfortunately, there are no surviving accounts written by women, who might have had another perspective since they came to every sermon, not just the flashy ones.

Bernardino's greatest celebrity, at least among men, was thus based on a small and select group of sermons that attracted the most listeners to the piazza. He deliberately announced them in advance and often scheduled them for Sundays, when he would have the largest crowd. The bonfire, in particular, was a popular event, both visually impressive and socially useful. In addition to cleansing a town of the apparatus of sin, such as magical writings, sumptuous clothing, and gambling instruments, the bonfire ignited an internal fire within the memory. The preacher believed that it was especially helpful in teaching children, who would remember the blaze for decades to come, saying "Thus it was done because of damnable gaming, in the time of Fra Bernardino."[46]

His willingness to employ these tactics made him vulnerable to criticism: "Some people want Fra Bernardino to preach about something other than dice and gaming-tables."[47] Although he proudly thought of himself as occupying the center in terms of orthodox doctrine, other learned clerics, upset by his appeal to the crowd, tried to push him to the periphery. They especially disliked the dramatic use of his signature emblem, the YHS, a *tavoletta* that symbolized the "Holy Name of Jesus." Bernardino would display the YHS at the end of a designated talk, inspiring tears, shouts of "Misericordia," and exorcism. Although his preaching on the Holy Name was not meant to incite idolatry—he stressed its value as symbol, rather than tangible presence—his statements left room for an extremist devotion. Shockingly, he even claimed that Church doctrine, the Commandments, and the sacraments themselves were worthless without the "Name of Jesus."[48] On two occasions, in 1426 and 1431, Bernardino was charged with heresy.

The sermons thus encouraged a fervent response, which alarmed intellectuals suspicious of "popular" devotion. But far from being uneasy about the disjunction between these displays and his message of inner change, Bernardino tried to reconcile the two. He believed that watching another's conversion could trigger one's own, thanks to the public and competitive nature of urban life. In an exceedingly odd metaphor, he noted a chain reaction of piety, set off by "economic" competition: "Many people go to the fair, buying merchandise in competition with one another. And so do you during Lent, seeing one another go to confess, so much more willingly you do good, competing all the more."[49]

Bernardino used a related image that blatantly acknowledged his ambivalent stance in relation to urban listeners who were anything but passive. To appeal to his audience, the preacher needed to assume a quasi-secular guise, becoming an "economic" agent within the brisk world of the cities. He set himself up as a seller of goods in the "shop" of Christ: "I tell you to bring full purses; I want to show you the treasure there is to buy." Christ's body on the cross is compared to a *bottega*, or shop; his wounds are the shop's windows; the shop sign is the cross itself. "Now, come on, to the cross, to the cross where love is sold! Come to the cross, women, bring *molti denari*."[50] His mighty voice mimicked that of a shopkeeper in his doorway, trying to attract customers: "Come on, put your hands to your purses! I'm the broker, or middleman!"[51] We need to picture Bernardino shouting out these words in the piazza of San Francesco where he preached, hoping to attract passers-by to his goods. In the same passage, he even acknowledged that the laity might regard his merchandise as only one among several alternatives. God does not want you to buy goods other than his own, he said, and then he warned them not to seek the help of a local witch.[52] By presenting himself as a hawker of (legitimate) goods, the preacher tried to make his wares as enticing as possible.

Fifteenth-century preachers were confronted with many challenges within the urban setting. The depth and complexity of popular belief, as well as multiple outlets for its expression, required a successful preacher to constantly adjust the relationship with each audience. Swift and sometimes jarring role changes, from patient teacher to aggressive hawkster, helped reach a range of listeners. By staging a bonfire or exorcism, Bernardino and other great preachers gathered in the casual passer-by, as well as the spiritual novice, who might eventually stay for another sermon. There they would learn the less dramatic lessons that would anchor a lasting conversion. Outward acts could stimulate inner change. Advanced devotees could then inscribe themselves with the indelible marks of Christian identity (such as frequent confession). Although most of his preaching emphasized inner faith and slow and steady attainment of self-knowledge, Bernardino recognized a heterogeneous laity and a variety of ways to approach God. As middleman between God and listener, he was willing to be flexible and pragmatic, adjusting both his role and his message to bring customers to the shop of the Lord.

CHAPTER TWELVE

"Angels of Peace"
The Social Drama of the Jesuit Mission in Early Modern Southern Italy

Jennifer D. Selwyn

Perhaps no other part of early modern Europe was the subject of as much fascination and concern as Naples and its hinterlands. Even though the southern Italian capital was celebrated for its natural and archaeological wonders, numerous authors—Neapolitan and foreign—expressed an almost visceral fear and loathing for the Neapolitan popular classes, castigated for their supposed propensity toward violent behavior, vice, and stupidity. For observers, Naples came to represent the most extreme case of the increasingly disordered state of early modern Italy, as it became eclipsed economically and culturally by the shift toward the Atlantic world. From the perspective of the religious reformer, Naples represented an opportunity and a challenge: a city and region well known for its enthusiastic, even ecstatic, religious rituals, yet also seen as a moral cesspool and an area racked by violence.

The Society of Jesus viewed southern Italy as an important site within its ambitious, global mission. The Jesuits sought to conduct a broad, civilizing mission that might reshape the religious identity and practice of the individual as well as the community and change behavior profoundly. Peacemaking was a critical ingredient in this missionary vision.[1] Like earlier, medieval peacemaking movements, the Jesuits saw an inextricable link between interfamilial and communal violence and a weakened Chris-

---

I would like to thank the participants in the Stanford University History Workshop, 1997–98, and the *Beyond Florence: Rethinking Medieval and Early Modern Italy* Conference (November 1998) for helpful comments and suggestions for improving earlier drafts of this chapter.

tian community. But the specific political and social context of early modern Europe, with its dramatic economic and political upheaval, and of southern Italy in particular, gave their activity a particular valence. Events like the Revolt of Naples (1647–48) demonstrated the perils of inactivity and made Naples an especially important site for the Jesuits because it offered a dramatic and oft-noted example of the dangers of incivility and barbarity and the need for effective Christianization to combat them.

Well before the Revolt of Naples gripped the attention of many European observers in 1647, the Jesuits had begun to craft their peacemaking mission to address episodes of strife across the Viceroyalty of Naples. In 1621, for example, the newly appointed Neapolitan viceroy, Cardinal Borgia, ordered a mission be conducted in the diocese of Aversa, just outside Naples. According to Jesuit sources, the area had long been the site of vicious factionalism, discord, and apparent decline in attention to religious devotion. Just a few years earlier, the Jesuit missionary Carlo D'Orta had written an impassioned letter from Colombia to members of his congregation back home in Aversa, imploring them to "escape the dangers of sinning, embrace positive occasions, easily pardon those who offend you, and do not pay too much attention to that which will soon pass and be over."[2]

In his *Istoria della Compagnia di Gesù Appartenente al Regno di Napoli* (1756–57), the eighteenth-century Jesuit historian Saverio Santagata gives a vivid description of the motives behind the mission to Aversa, the significance of ecclesiastical support, the missionaries' "heroic" efforts to overcome initial resistance, and their use of theatrical methods to ensure the mission's success. Santagata tells us that

> the motive for doing [the mission] was this: for various reasons an implacable discord had been stirred up in the City. Acts of violence very soon degenerated into cruel factions, and the Plebe and the Nobility divided into parties, eager for mutual destruction. The blood of the many murder victims had obliged the Courts of Justice to make rigorous executions, [but] all that did not put an end to the raging of the citizens toward one another.[3]

In response to this dire situation, Cardinal Borgia called upon the Jesuits to conduct a mission, which might placate the warring factions and restore order to the chaotic situation. As was so often the case in the Jesuit missions (or at least in the representation that filled histories like Santagata's), missionary fathers faced initial disinterest among the faithful, thus adding to the dramatic flavor of the missionary endeavor. In this instance, local ecclesiastical officials also provided much-needed assistance at the outset: "Our fathers went [to Aversa], and at the beginning had no listeners of any kind. After the action of the Bishop, and of some zealous priests, a suitable audience was assembled, but [the people] were so full of . . . suspicions, that . . . they came to the Church as if armed for battle." This suspicious atmosphere was so strong that the member of the missionary team whose job it was to preach found that "as much as he toiled, no one gave a sign of wanting to cast off the bitterness of the contest."[4]

All of the normal channels of persuasion appear to have failed to move this decidedly unyielding community, so after several days the Jesuits turned to using props and exercised their theatrical training to effect the desired reconciliation. Once the missionary preacher had assembled the parishioners, he carried two skulls into the Church, asking the people assembled to imagine that these two skulls represented the heads of the two factions. He then proceeded to have the two skulls carry on a discussion of the "bitter fruit brought forth by the obstinacy of their hatreds."[5] This ritual enactment was no doubt intended to shock the community into recognizing the horrifying effects their continuous feuding engendered. The theatrical use of the two skulls engaged in animated dialogue eschewed subtlety, aiming instead to awaken an appropriate fear of death and damnation in the assembled parishioners and to open their hearts to the message of reconciliation that the Jesuit preacher offered them.

This "funereal demonstration" appeared to have had the desired effect, at least in the short run. The congregants were greatly moved by the missionary's example to renounce past rivalries and insisted that they no longer had any enemies. Crucially, the reconciliation drama ended with former enemies embracing one another, promising to do penance, and forswearing future acts of violence and dissension.

Santagata's narration of the Jesuit mission to Aversa tells us a great deal about both the order's self-perception and its view of challenges specific to the Neapolitan mission field. It demonstrates that the Jesuits took their peacemaking function very seriously. Although the mission was not successful at the outset, and indeed reconciliation appeared quite unlikely, the missionaries demonstrated perseverance and flexibility in finding effective means to win over their subjects. But the mission to Aversa has a broader lesson. In its vivid description of a community torn apart by unnamed but acutely felt divisions among its populace, we see a glimpse of the larger violence and social conflict that characterized seventeenth-century Southern Italy. As Rosario Villari has shown in his incisive, richly documented study, *The Revolt of Naples* (1993), the viceroyalty was plagued by socioeconomic conflict in the cities and countryside, exacerbated by depopulation of many rural areas and consequent overpopulation of metropolitan Naples. Neapolitans also faced burdensome taxes from the Spanish Crown, and a rising tide of banditry across the region.[6]

Moments of profound upheaval, such as the Revolt of Naples (1647–48), had an enormous impact on contemporaries' views of the city, its people, and (for elites in particular) the dangers posed by the unmastered urban poor. The event also presented the Jesuits with special challenges, which contributed in large part to the increasing emphasis the order placed upon a peacemaking agenda.[7]

The Revolt of Naples was just one of several early modern popular uprisings that posed a direct challenge to the prerogatives of regional nobility, abuse of monarchical power, and the wealth and influence of the Catholic Church. But just as something distinctive about Neapolitan life seemed compelling to chroniclers, the Neapolitan revolt captured the popular imagination of European readers and the politically minded of various stripes for its dramatic and incendiary quality.[8]

Although historians have vigorously debated the long-term significance of the revolt, its impact on the clergy and on their relationship with the laity has not been considered adequately. By any account, the Revolt of Naples posed serious problems and possibilities for the Church, which had long been the principal agent for peacemaking in this tumultuous society. Cardinal Filomarino and the panoply of religious orders sought to use their influence among the people to quell the violence and restore order, yet these goals proved elusive, at least initially.

One anonymous account of the revolt stresses the futile attempt of the secular authorities to use religious ritual to quell resistance and suggests that anger at secular authority could spill over onto the clergy. The chronicler reports that the viceroy, the Duke of Arcos, "thought to avail himself of the Religious," when other options failed to produce the desired results. Dispatching Cardinal Filomarino throughout the city's churches, displaying the standard of the "Most Holy Sacrament" in all the major churches, the viceroy also encouraged members of the clergy to "go on many processions, praying for calm and [for] the peace of the People . . . preach in the same Piazza del Mercato and exhort the People to live quietly, and to leave behind the rebellions." But such tactics apparently proved ineffectual, causing the author to lament that "this remedy was worth nothing, because the People were so inflamed with indignation from the betrayal of the Duke that they also directed some of the credit for this to the Religious." In the event, the clergy were forced back to their residences and prevented from continuing their sermons for peace.[9]

Like members of the other religious orders, the Jesuits had to confront hostility because of their close ties to elites. On the one hand, insofar as they came to be closely identified with the despised nobility and the mistrusted viceroy, the Jesuits lost any credibility they might have won from many commoners. The apparent animus toward the order is made evident in a document recently brought to light by Rosario Villari, who cites a report received by the Dutch consul in Venice (probably during the late summer or early fall of 1647) and sent to the States General in Amsterdam, in which we see that the Jesuits had been an early target of the rebels' anger: "Having discovered that the Jesuit fathers were conspiring with the nobility, citizens and merchants with the aim of oppressing the people, the latter went to the Very Eminent Archbishop Filomarino to remonstrate that if His Eminence did not put a stop to the affair, the people would expel all the Jesuit fathers from the Kingdom leaving them only their shirts and drawers."[10]

This comment points to a very real credibility problem the Jesuits faced. Although we should be cautious in accepting such conspiracy theories, given the widespread hostility toward the Jesuits already finding its way into official discourse (especially Protestant) in this period, the perception of the Jesuits' close ties to local elites is not hard to document.[11] Not only did the religious orders face hostility from the populace but they saw many of their clerical privileges threatened by the short-lived republican government and their very right to practice in the city challenged. Among their demands, rebels opposed clerical exemptions from taxation; demanded that all non-Neapolitan clergy leave the city; and sought popular, secular control over key religious rituals, such as the Corpus Christi procession.

Despite the legacy of at least fifty years of popular missionary activity in the city of Naples and across the viceroyalty, then, the Jesuits remained very much linked in the public mind to their elite patrons and supporters. Perhaps more important, although they had advocated religious and cultural reform within the context of an increasingly articulated civilizing mission, this did not mean that the Society of Jesus had any solutions for alleviating the very real social inequity and abuse of power that plagued the Mezzogiorno. What they could do, however, was strengthen their resolve to delegitimize social revolt in the wake of the upheavals of 1647–48 and redouble their labor to effect lasting social peace and rebuild a unified Christian community. In the aftermath of the revolt, the Jesuits seemed to draw an important lesson about the centrality of peacemaking and reconciliation to their apostolic work and institutional identity.

We can see this new approach in the mission to Aversa, where the "social drama" was enhanced by the Jesuits' employment of theatrical techniques to aid them in winning over the most recalcitrant sinners and combatants. Use of props, special effects, dramatic dialogue, and audience participation played a crucial role in the order's peacemaking activities, and in the rituals of penitence that inevitably accompanied the reconciling of warring parties.

The Jesuits styled themselves as "angels of peace," self-consciously articulating an important part for members in combating a whole range of disagreement among individual parishioners, religious men and women, and entire communities riven by dissension.[12] Examination of the significance of peacemaking to the Jesuits' institutional identity and its growing relevance in the face of rising social tensions in the Italian South (especially by the mid-seventeenth century) further highlights the order's complex relationship to the broader events convulsing European society in the early modern period and illuminates the special place of southern Italy in that landscape.

"Blessed Are the Peacemakers"

The practices of reconciliation and peacemaking had deep roots in the Roman Catholic Church. At the broadest level of definition, *reconciliation* was inextricably bound up with the sacrament of penance and confessional practice. Although the Church had historically varied its emphasis on confession as an individual and collective activity, the notion that it was essential for all sinners to "reconcile" themselves with their God, and with their neighbors, was intrinsic to Catholic doctrine, particularly by the late Middle Ages.[13] *Peacemaking* refers to the specifically social aspect of reconciliation, with the implication of addressing social or collective conflict. This, too, was a long-standing political function of the Church amid the ubiquitous violence of faction-ridden urban communes, as well as warring feudal entities. As one historian has recently suggested, medieval urban dwellers often viewed peacemaking efforts as a mere disguise for an attempt at political pacification and domination.[14]

Late medieval popular preachers such as San Bernardino di Siena were the apostolic forebears of seventeenth-century missionary peacemakers like the Jesuits.[15] They understood the very notion of "discord" in terms of individual, or collective, sin, believing that they could effect widespread moral reform of society while remaining careful not to challenge existing social relations to any extent. Carrying on this tradition, the Jesuits employed a highly theatrical preaching style, freely and self-consciously blending somber religious ritual with raucous entertainment. Missionary preachers sought to establish a one-to-one connection with audience members, who represented an array of the population of late medieval and early modern Italian towns and cities, and visitors as well. In addition to this freewheeling theatricality, the Jesuits also sought to formalize their work. They carefully recorded the specific kinds of reconciliation effected through their mission, sometimes even enumerating them, as part of their effort to represent the heroic qualities of Jesuit missionaries who might triumph against even the most recalcitrant sinners and overcome all obstacles.

By the early sixteenth century, the Catholic Church began to face a series of challenges that would encourage just such an institutional response to conflict, whether lay or clerical. Well before the Protestant Reformation forced the questions of reconciliation and penitence center stage, key Church reformers pointed to the serious problems within the Roman Church that would preoccupy Luther and others: alienation of the laity from Scripture, rampant corruption, clerical ignorance, and greed. The new religious orders that emerged in the early part of the sixteenth century, such as the Theatines, Capuchins, and Barnabites, emphasized popular preaching and strove to present an image of piety and moral seriousness.[16] Emerging into this new religious landscape, the Jesuits' apostolic activity forged a direct linkage between reconciliation (at both the individual and the collective levels) and acts of penance. As an important force in the Catholic Reformation Church, they promoted frequent confession among the laity, as well as encouraging training of secular clergy in promoting "good confessions."[17]

The Council of Trent (1545–63) took up the question of penance in 1547 but did not issue a refined definition of the sacrament until four years later. Broadly speaking, the Tridentine bishops focused on (1) defending the sacramental nature of penance against Protestant dissent; (2) distinguishing this sacrament from that of baptism; (3) clarifying that remission of sins involved "acts of the penitent" (contrition, confession, and satisfaction); (4) asserting the centrality of the priest's sacramental role in absolving sin, and in so doing (5) confirming Church authority in this as in other matters of faith and practice.[18] That is, post-Tridentine Catholicism paid greater attention to regulating the inner life of the faithful, as an individual and in the community, and to insisting upon ritual acts of penance as evidence of sanctity and insurance against religious and social dissension.

In other words, reconciling enemies was an intrinsic feature of post-Tridentine Catholicism and one taken quite seriously by missionary orders such as the Society of Jesus. As Adriano Prosperi has suggested in a compelling recent study of early modern Italian religious culture, the very health of the community depended upon successful resolution of all disputes among its members and their participation in all the sacraments. Jesuit missionaries did not simply report upon reconciliation; they presented them as exemplary "instruments to multiply the effects" of the mission.[19]

For their part, the Jesuits explicitly noted reconciliation (both individual and community-based) as a distinctive component of their apostolic vocation in both their foundational documents and missionary relations. In the *Formula of the Institute of the Society of Jesus* (1550), for example, Ignatius comments, "Moreover, this Society should show itself no less useful in reconciling the estranged, in piously assisting and serving those who are found in prisons and hospitals, and indeed in performing any other works of charity, according to what will seem expedient for the glory of God and the common good."[20] In his instructions on "The Ways in Which the Houses and Colleges Can Help Their Fellow Men," the Jesuit founder reiterates this theme of helping the needy, stressing that members can and should "reconcile the disaffected," along with the poor and prisoners "both by their personal work and by getting others to do it."[21]

All of this remained generally vague, however, throughout the latter half of the sixteenth century. In the early instructional manuals produced by the society, peacemaking is mentioned as one important area of focus. Positive examples of social reconciliation brought about by peacemakers were balanced, however, by a cautionary note that missionaries should remain neutral in matters of conflict, particularly among the religious. Jesuits were counseled emphatically to avoid involvement in secular matters.[22] This greater caution reflects a number of concerns within the order, among them wariness of alienating potential allies (whether lay or clerical) before they could get the lay of the land; emphasis on training novices in the basic mechanics of conducting a popular mission, rather than focusing on potentially controversial areas of pastoral work; and the fact that leading members of the order disagreed over how vigorously to pursue a peacemaking role, given all of the other responsibilities the Society faced and the grave suspicion with which many other clergy viewed the Jesuits.[23]

Despite this apparent caution, the Jesuits did become involved quite prominently in some of the most contentious social conflicts of late sixteenth-century Naples. One prime example is the case of the 1585 Revolt of Naples, one of a series of Neapolitan social revolts spurred on by hunger, price inflation, and the omnipresent suspicion in which commoners held the urban nobility. In this conflagration, Jesuit missionaries such as Carlo Mastrilli advocated an important role for the order in restoring peace to a strife-torn community, stressing the illegitimacy of revolt as an act displeasing to God, but also upholding the prerogatives of social elites.[24] Francesco Schinosi's *Historia* cites "antagonisms eradicated" as among those successful endeavors of the Jesuits in the aftermath of the 1585 revolt, alongside "extirpated superstitions ... [and] conversions from the relaxed life to penitence," though in the absence of corroborating evidence from non-Jesuit sources, this claim may be another case of triumphalist institutional rhetoric.²⁵

Similarly, non-Jesuit documents from the South are replete with examples of disputes both religious and secular that hint at the importance of peacemaking. As the papal visitor Tommaso Orfini noted in his reconnoiters throughout the Viceroyalty of Naples (1568), there was an urgent need to reconcile warring members of the clergy and the episcopacy, as well as to resolve conflict between the religious and the lay community.²⁶ In one ironic example from Bari, Orfini found a dispute raging between an archdeacon and an archpriest over which one held precedence in peacemaking activities and in preparing incense. In Ostuni, the archbishop was accused by his clergy of forcing them to give him their tithes and benefices for ten years, and falsely imprisoning them if they refused. One especially unpopular archbishop in Giovenazzo appeared to have been universally despised, most notably for his dishonesty, incompetence, and unwillingness to pay his agricultural laborers their due, and for his habit of placing 319 debtor-priests in jail!²⁷

Such division, whether among clergy or laity, often led to dire results. Violence was endemic to southern Italy in this period, beyond the hyperbolic discourse of an animalistic people and a decadent noble class found in chronicles by visitors and locals alike. An array of authors commented on the high number of homicides in the city, the prevalence of knife fights in the viceroyalty as a whole, the substantial prison population (not all of them debtors), and the notorious presence of bandits, especially across the rural landscape.²⁸ If we can trace discussion of Naples' blood-stained landscape to at least the early sixteenth century, the image of southern brutality and anarchy became much more pronounced in the wake of the anti-Spanish revolt of the mid-seventeenth century.

The Social Drama of Peacemaking

The past turbulence in the Viceroyalty has also offered frequent occasions to practice Christian acts. Many lords amply mistreated, and offended by that violent power of their vassals, who had never been accustomed to rule . . . will pardon with generosity that which they suffered with constancy. . . . Elsewhere, the multitude has been reunited in ancient affection and reverence toward the nobility and one can affirm [that] in many locales, a great number of the Plebe who had been stirred up, and in whose hearts still live the sparks of the past anger, and the ambition from the power they enjoyed, [were] grieved by the missions, and let go of any violent design; revealed [it] to confessors, and showed distaste toward any sign of carrying it out by throwing away already prepared munitions and gunpowder.²⁹

Despite their difficulties during the Revolt of Naples, to which I have alluded, the Jesuits appear to have emerged from the crisis with renewed commitment to conducting the popular mission and publicizing the order's success. Alongside the general maturation of the order's missionary agenda and the continued need to intervene in many troubled locales, the Revolt of Naples made peacemaking an ever more urgent task. The preceding passage—from Paolucci's chronicle of the Neapolitan missions, published just three years after the end of the revolt—is one of the few that explicitly mention the signal event. In its idealized view of social harmony restored, it makes a fitting introduction to a section on the "social drama" of reconciliation in the Jesuit missions.

Paolucci's description of the many examples of forgiving nobles and contrite vassals evokes an idealized image of a Southern Italian society restored to its previous equilibrium. The lords represent "nobility" in the truest meaning of the word, gladly "pardoning" the anarchic Plebe for their illegitimate (and apparently inept) experiment with social power. It is the Plebe, according to Paolucci, who need to be subdued, to become quiescent. With the help of the Jesuit fathers, however, they not only abandon further plans for violent resistance but also "throw away" the very weapons of destruction. But if Paolucci's example suggests a long-term renewal of social peace, Jesuit missionary reports tell a very different story. In the aftermath of the revolt of 1647–48, the fabric of society did not easily mend. Economic woes continued to plague the viceroyalty; the region was hit with wave after wave of famine, a major outbreak of the plague in 1656, and the range of natural disasters to which the region was all too tragically accustomed.³⁰

In response to this apparent vacuum, the Jesuits were only too ready to assume the mantle. Jesuit accounts of peacemaking had always highlighted the dramatic flavor of reconciliation, part and parcel of the intrepid image of the Jesuit missionary they were publicizing. These later chronicles bespeak a more consciously theatrical approach to missionizing. The social drama of reconciliation represented the missionary as but one actor (albeit the most important) in a complex enactment of social conflict and resolution; it formed part of a standard means of chronicling Jesuit missionary efforts.

Initially, missionary efforts to effect reconciliation were often met with skepticism, or downright ridicule. In a discussion of a mission made in Capua in 1649, an anonymous missionary reports that a primary goal of the mission had been to reconcile two rival noble families who had been locked in a vicious blood feud that had engulfed the entire community: "At the beginning, these [men] had made fun of the work of penitence, and of mortifications," but gradually, according to the author, the noblemen were moved by the example of others to support the mission.[31]

Far from merely overcoming the resistance of a few key players, however, the drama of reconciliation in this mission involved spectacular ritual acts. Such was the zealous attitude of the community that the missionary describes young noblemen, "with ropes around their necks and without collar[s]," pleading with those assembled in church to pardon them for their scandalous behavior and "bad example." He presents vivid images of esteemed men in the community leaping onto the pulpit and spontaneously confessing their sins to the Jesuit father.[32]

Nor were such ritual acts limited to the laity. Earlier chronicles had illuminated Jesuit efforts to reconcile female religious, but these later seventeenth-century accounts include the clergy as well. One missionary relation from 1666 offers the unusual sight of five clerics making a public apology to the bishop whom they had slandered. According to the author, these five troublemakers wrote a "defamatory missive" about their own bishop and then "threw it into his room." Yet apparently, the general atmosphere of penitence was too much for the restive priests, and they "offered to do everything for the Prelate—penitence and giving him every satisfaction in order to obtain the pardon."[33]

Francesco De Geronimo, also known as Francesco di Girolamo (1642–1716), was apparently an able practitioner at reconciling conflict among the religious. When it came time for the nuns of "one of the most celebrated and noble" convents to receive the *Spiritual Exercises* from their Jesuit confessor, he became suddenly ill and was replaced by De Geronimo. But De Geronimo found the nuns bitterly divided into factions, although he does not detail the reasons for this rancor. As in other cases of factional conflict, De Geronimo at first faced suspicion, then mere indifference, and finally "they passed over into devotion, and such was the concourse that it was commonly said in the convent that they did not remember a gathering so numerous [in the past]."[34]

For De Geronimo, the real benefit of the mission was in the peacemaking ritual he organized. Having gathered all the nuns and the *convertite* (lay sisters, probably servants) together one evening, De Geronimo directed each one of them who "had been offended with words or with uncomplimentary acts" to throw herself at the feet of her offender and reconcile herself with this person, soon leading every one of the seventy members of the convent to approach her adversary in a peaceful embrace.[35] Such dramatic reconciliations were especially striking given the initial resistance to the missionary's labors, yet they became an ever more common staple of missionary reports during the late seventeenth century. We may be skeptical of De Geronimo's claims that the peace was "maintained until now" in that convent, rightly suspicious of the Jesuits' triumphal rhetoric. Still, there is no reason to believe that these reconciliation rituals did not effect at least temporary peace in strife-torn communities. After all, early modern society was at home with ritualized, often theatrical, gestures, particularly in the realm of religious practice.[36]

If factional dispute divided the monasteries and convents, there was also frequent enmity between clergy and the laity. Some parish priests were considered immoral, or driven more by financial incentive than pastoral concern for a community. In one small community on the outskirts of Naples called Casollo, De Geronimo celebrated this particular brand of social reconciliation ritual by describing the conflict between a clergyman who was "not very esteemed in this place" and the laity. After community members had made many "tearful confessions and general communion," they were ready to reconcile with their parish priest. De Geronimo led the peacemaking ritual from the pulpit with a rope around his neck and a chain in his hand, imploring the faithful to prostrate themselves before their "pastor," and apparently moving them to tears.[37]

In this example, the prescribed elements of the peacemaking ritual are all in place: the dynamic, divinely inspired missionary orator; a contrite cleric; and finally, an inflamed community, eager to perform the necessary symbolic gestures of forgiveness (the "kiss of peace," prostration). Though the incident may strike some modern readers as too dramatic, or disturbing in its intensity, bespeaking an overly emotional religious devotion, such a description would not have shocked an early modern audience. Similar examples are offered for reconciliation between feuding siblings, fathers and sons, and whole families torn apart, frequently by dispute over property.[38]

If reconciliation was a symbolically vital enactment for a strife-torn community, permitting a cathartic release of grief and anger, it also served a very real function in promoting social order. In a society where the criminal justice system remained relatively underdeveloped, and where violent feuding was rampant, restoring social peace was an essential component of the religious vocation, particularly in an order committed to an active ministry, such as the Jesuits. De Geronimo cites cases where a series of homicides had left two communities in turmoil. Although in one case the two accused assassins were in the *Vicaria* (royal prison), De Geronimo arranged for a member of one of the afflicted families to pardon the accused murderers in order to restore peace within the community. This action was most effective, De Geronimo notes. After having "settled the civil controversies," he met with the ministers of the tribunal of criminals and convinced them to pardon the incarcerated men, thus permitting full reconciliation of the parties involved.[39]

Promoting social order, however, was not simply a question of reconciling criminals with their victims' families. Ongoing blights on the social landscape such as prostitution reminded the faithful that a unified Christian community had not been achieved and threatened the well-being of all. Efforts to reconcile prostitutes continued to occupy the energies of missionaries like De Geronimo, raising fascinating questions about the limitation of moral reform to address the complex and troubling realities of a highly unequal and increasingly desperate Southern Italian society.

In De Geronimo's third-person accounts of his travels through the popular quarters of Naples, the missionary presents a familiar picture of bustling urban life, the people's indulgence in profane pleasures, and the wondrous effects of vigorous missionary intervention in combating a range of social ills. His narrative highlights how Jesuit missionaries competed for public space as part of their effort to civilize Neapolitans and provide regular religious instruction. De Geronimo's custom was to preach each Sunday of the year in a large piazza, typically frequented by "innumerable [crowds of] people gathered out of curiosity to hear little farces put on there by companies of acrobats." The spectators at such a festive event tended to be composed of "the laziest people—as much [natives] of this city, as of the many peoples and nations who gather[ed] there."[40] Although people may have come together to enjoy some free entertainment, De Geronimo's intention was to use the occasion to effect reconciliation of many inveterate sinners: "That which one can say, generally, is that many sinners in that piazza, due to the confusion and compunction of their sins, were given to [shedding] bitter tears and at times came to the foot of the holy crucifix and publicly asked pardon, beating themselves with a chain on their shoulders." Where the acrobats merely offered mindless diversion from the daily toils people faced, De Geronimo's vigorous preaching "caused great contrition and edification in the listener[s] and a great many of them, at the end of the sermon, attached themselves beside the Father, crying and saying: 'Father, help me, I am damned.'" In other words, De Geronimo's public reconciliation rituals permitted the Jesuits to sacralize the piazza. Following these outbursts of renewed faith, the remorseful sinners would be taken to an oratory where they would practice penitential discipline and then make a good confession.[41]

In this instance, the Jesuits appropriated the theatricality of a profane company to captivate the "audience" and turn them toward a more pious way of life. F. M. D'Aria, one of De Geronimo's modern biographers, also evokes the Neapolitan Jesuit's highly ritualized, theatrical travels through the popular quarters of the city, seeking willing converts and souls to reconcile. Citing several of De Geronimo's contemporary biographers, D'Aria vividly describes the missionary's impact upon his would-be subjects, "women of the profession":

> Upon the arrival of the missionary in that zone ... the great majority of those unhappy [women] disappeared from the streets, and closed themselves inside their homes, "in order not to hear ... the voice of the celestial charmer." Father Francesco continued to roar, threatening the punishments of God to the obstinate and promising heavenly mercy to those who would submit. Whether out of feminine curiosity, or through supernatural influence, most [of the prostitutes] ended up standing at their windows listening to him.[42]

In this story, as in a conventional Jesuit narrative, the sinners are initially wary of the missionary reformer but cannot resist his overwhelming persuasiveness. Whether they are drawn in by mere "curiosity" or "supernatural influence" does not really matter; the end result is what is crucial. In De Geronimo's able hands, female sinners whose very livelihood had been shaped by their pursuit of illicit "pleasures" (in this case, sexual commerce, most likely a means of economic survival) are made humble, "transported as if by an irresistible force, all humble." In a symbolic gesture of their true conversion, D'Aria tells us, the *convertite* would cut off their long, flowing hair and place it at the foot of a large crucifix like a "trophy of victory."[43]

This theatrical element of Jesuit reconciliation was not always so public, however. It could also involve extraordinary examples of individuals confronting sinful, or inappropriate behaviors, and vowing to change their lives. In these cases, the drama was heightened by the degree of sin and the power of the missionary to intervene effectively to reverse its effects. For De Geronimo, the prostitute was a favorite subject for such miraculous reconciliation. He relates one story of a "very famous" and formerly wealthy and well-connected prostitute who finds herself suffering from a "horrendous" affliction (perhaps syphilis).

This woman, whose customers had included "the first names of that city," had become impoverished due to her ever-worsening condition and, in desperation, was moved to call upon De Geronimo's aid after hearing him conduct one of his sermons. When he arrives at her bedside, the woman pleads with the Jesuit to advise her on how to proceed; De Geronimo encourages her to leave her quarters and go to the "Hospital of the Incurables," where she might receive "help for the soul and for the body." At this advice, the prostitute is visibly disturbed, replying: "Father, one such as me at the Incurables? I was almost the patroness of half the nobility of Naples and of Rome; and now to the Incurables?" But De Geronimo's purpose is to force the woman to give up any residual pride and accept her fate: "Daughter, don't look at who you have been, but who you are now. It is better to go from the Incurables to paradise, than from this house to Hell."[44]

In this example, which ends predictably with the former prostitute languishing in a hospital bed for several weeks, examining her past sins, confessing, and finally dying a "good death," thanks to De Geronimo's timely intervention, we see a vivid example of how the Jesuit narratives represent moral reform as the best solution to pressing social concerns such as the widespread presence of prostitution in early modern Naples. Here, unlike the previous example of poor street prostitutes, we have the example of a formerly successful prostitute (perhaps more accurately called a courtesan, given her apparently high-level connections in Neapolitan and Roman society) facing divine punishment for her many years of illicit behavior. Given the poor state of her health, placing her in a monastery for *convertite* or finding her a suitable marriage would not have been an option; yet at least reconciliation could ensure a good death for the woman.

Moral reform made for powerful anecdotes about extraordinary conversion and reconciliation, but as the Neapolitan economy worsened and conditions for the urban Plebe remained desperate at best, such examples begin to sound formulaic and self-serving. Rather than challenging the veracity of De Geronimo's and his contemporaries' representations of miraculous reconciliation (impossible to prove, in any event), perhaps we should instead ask what purpose such edifying tales held for members of the Society of Jesus, or a lay audience interested in their activities.

There is no way to gauge whether reconciliations such as those effected by De Geronimo and others had any long-term impact on promoting social peace in Southern Italy, but images of social and economic disorder in the Italian South persist down to our times. The Jesuits, in no small part, contributed to the image of backwardness, even as they championed a civilizing mission to promote religious and moral reform in the Mezzogiorno, as elsewhere.

The Jesuits placed renewed attention on peacemaking as a central feature of their apostolic vocation in the period following the Revolt of Naples, suggesting that the society acknowledged its relevance. The hostilities the order faced from popular forces no doubt served a cautionary note, encouraging greater attention to promoting peace at all levels of society; but the more theatrical, orchestrated missions of the latter seventeenth and early eighteenth centuries were not simply a defensive reaction to outside events. Instead, the Society's increasing commitment to pursuing its peacemaking role attests to the order's overwhelming concern with civilizing the people. Civility, after all, demanded an orderly society where individuals could learn to subdue their passions, or at least channel them in appropriate directions. Violence and factionalism were clear obstacles to the Jesuits' achievement of this goal.

Further, the social drama of reconciliation, coupled with the penitential exercises that came to bring dramatic closure to the missionary encounter, epitomized the mature, highly articulated Jesuit popular mission of the period. More than a century after its founding, the order had constructed a well-defined and vibrant identity for its missionary practitioners. A novice could call upon a range of heroic forefathers from whom to gain inspiration, accessing the words and deeds of these innovators through their letters, sermons, missionary relations, and instructional manuals, all of which the order kept as part of a repository to collective memory. Through the striking examples of skillful "angels of peace" such as Francesco De Geronimo, the Jesuits publicized the order's efficacy in promoting social reconciliation and combating the so-called vices that continued to plague early modern southern Italy.

PART V

Topographies of Power

Any understanding of the diversity of the "many Italies" within medieval and early modern Italy must take into consideration use and display of power. Since the publication of Lauro Martines's *Power and Imagination: City States in Renaissance Italy* in 1979, the study of power and its focus as a category of analysis has become increasingly complicated. Rather than thinking of power in terms of a strict hierarchy between elites and non-elites, scholars now often speak in terms of "power relations," of "centers and margins," of "insiders and outsiders," and of power being "negotiated." Power is now viewed as a dynamic outcome of the relations between those in central authority and those in lesser authority, rather than emanating solely from one source or direction.

This final part examines the mapping of power in late medieval and early modern Italy. Maureen Miller compares the display of power in a number of medieval cities by examining the placement of episcopal and communal palaces throughout central and northern Italy, offering an excellent example of the virtues of comparative analysis. Orvieto, a little town in the expanding Papal State, comes alive in David Foote's account of the uneasy dynamic among the commune, the popolo, and local lords until the arrival of their new governor, an outsider appointed by the Avignon papacy. Michelle Fontaine builds on Miller's discussion of the display of power through architecture and Foote's analysis of the continuation of civic traditions in the face of state building by discussing the art and ritual of seventeenth-century Modena and the continuing importance of the image of the medieval commune for this early modern city. The final chapter in Part V, by Thomas Dandelet, further complicates the notion of power within the city by examining how the economic strength of the Spanish Empire shaped Rome, a city it did not directly rule.

These chapters remind us that Italy's variety made power a complex and multilayered experience, from city to city and from century to century. It is little wonder that some of the earliest and most articulate Italian political theorists, from Marsilius of Padua to Machiavelli, came from this region of the world. They had much to reflect on as they looked at the Italian city-states and their constant transformation over several hundred years.

Topographies of Power CENTRAL AND NORTHERN ITALY

CHAPTER THIRTEEN

Topographies of Power in the Urban Centers of Medieval Italy

Communes, Bishops, and Public Authority

Maureen C. Miller

Our understanding of the development of urban centers, like most topics in the history of medieval and early modern Italy, has been dominated by the example of Florence. Here, emergence of two distinct poles within the city's topography—a political center, dominated by the commune's Palazzo Vecchio; and a religious center, with the cathedral, baptistery, canonry, and bishop's palace—has been taken as a "norm." The commune's building of its representative edifices at a site separate and distinct from the old religious center has been interpreted as an expression of its independence, and this separation tends to be treated as natural or normal in narratives of the urban development of this era.[1] This reading of urban development acknowledges that buildings and space can make an important statement about power, but it views power narrowly as a secular phenomenon; in this model, the commune and the noble families compete for prominence in the city, building and rebuilding the urban center.

Indeed, we know from abundant work on Florence and other northern Italian cities that the arrangement of urban space was not accidental. From 1285, several Florentine councils, for example, discussed and debated the location for building a new palace for the priors; many "available" locations were rejected in favor of a site that required the commune to purchase substantial property and demolish existing structures. In other cities too (Siena, Piacenza, Milan), land was acquired and cleared of private edifices to build new communal palaces and plazas. These governmental choices often precipitated litigation, especially if a church was demolished to make way for a new communal building.² The intentional and highly self-conscious arrangement of urban space within these cities extended even to creating specific vistas: streets were opened and altered to position the viewer, and façades were refurbished to afford visual unity and a pleasing aspect. An excellent example of this is the series of changes undertaken in Florence from 1289 to showcase the new cathedral. The main street entering the piazza (Corso degli Adamari, now Via dei Calzaiuoli) was lowered so that the baptistery would not appear to "sink" as one approached it, and a uniform treatment for the façades opening on the piazza was dictated by the Signoria.³

It is, therefore, wholly warranted to see development of monumental centers as a conscious choice, the result of governmental decisions and often rather sophisticated urban planning. But not all northern Italian cities made the same choices, and it was not always a strong, independent commune that was the sole arbiter of urban space. If one moves beyond Florence, this "two poles" pattern of urban development and the meanings assigned to it appear in no way dominant. The analysis in this chapter is based upon a comparative examination of development of urban centers in thirty-three cities in northern and central Italy.⁴ Indeed, the cities actually following the Florentine model account for less than half of this sample. The patterns that emerge when many cities are considered suggest the need for a more capacious understanding of power and greater acknowledgment of the commune's relations with both religion and religious institutions in the medieval city. Particularly important in shaping urban development was the commune's relationship with the bishop.

Before the emergence of the communes, the bishop was a powerful and important lord in the Italian urban center. During the eleventh and early twelfth centuries, before the building of communal palaces, the bishop usually occupied the only palace in the Italian city. This coincided with the great age of episcopal power in northern Italy. Bishops in this era exercised significant temporal power; many of them controlled all public authority in their city (rights of justice; building of fortifications; collection of dues, tolls, and taxes), and others wielded partial rights. All of them were significant local lords by virtue of the landed holdings of their see. This heyday of episcopal lordship coincided with the period of the Gregorian reform, but it came to an end in the late twelfth and early thirteenth centuries. After a series of wars with Emperor Frederick Barbarossa in the mid-twelfth century, the newly formed citizen governments of these urban centers (the "communes") wrested public authority from their bishops.⁵

But even after the emergence of the communes, the bishop remained an important local potentate. He still held significant landed wealth and, more important, controlled the sacraments that medieval and Renaissance people believed were essential to their salvation. In conflict with the communal government, the bishop increasingly resorted to ecclesiastical censure—interdict (withholding sacraments) and excommunication—to exert authority. Bishops were not always successful, but many communes learned the cost of challenging ecclesiastical rights, and the papacy often intervened on behalf of Italian prelates with its considerable diplomatic and military resources.[6] In sum, the communes were neither the first nor ultimately the only powers to have a hand in disposing of and organizing urban space. Patterns of urban development in the medieval and Renaissance city reveal the impact of episcopal authority.

In more than a third of these cities, not two poles but a single unified center developed with the representative structures of both civil and ecclesiastical authority clustered around a central piazza. A good example is Modena. Dominating the city's central piazza is the beautiful Romanesque cathedral of San Geminiano with its sculpted portals. On one side of it is the commune's palace, on the other the bishop's. The church serves both to connect and separate the two palaces, seats of temporal and ecclesiastical power in the city. These buildings and the powers they represent cluster around one open public space at the heart of the city. They form a compact, potent center of power.[7] Such unified expression of public authority is still found today at Bergamo, Brescia, Como, Cremona, Faenza, Novara, Pavia, Perugia, Pistoia, Reggio-Emilia, and Spoleto.[8]

Other cities, moreover, originally had a unified center and only developed a two-poles pattern later. In Milan, for example, the earliest *domus consulatus* ("house of the consulate") was in the vicinity of the open space next to the cathedral and archiepiscopal palace. This field, or *brolo*, was the archbishop's, and it was here that the early commune met and assemblies of the people gathered in the twelfth century. In 1228, however, a new communal palace was built northwest of Piazza Duomo.[9] This new site of communal power was not far enough from the ecclesiastical center to create a highly distinct and separate pole of civic authority, but it did place the commune's seat more at the exact center of the medieval city. More successful in reorganizing urban space was the new communal palace of Ravenna. The commune's first building was opposite the archiepiscopal palace, just behind the cathedral. By the time the commune built its towered seat here in the late twelfth century or the opening decade of the thirteenth, this had been the archbishop of Ravenna's piazza for centuries.[10] At the end of the thirteenth century, however, the commune did establish a separate and distinct urban center on its own piazza. This new site was at the intersection of two important canals that ran through the city and closer to its major thoroughfare, the *platea maior*.[11] This piazza remains today the center of the *centro storico*.

One might note in both these examples that the commune emerged in the shadow of a powerful prelate. Although neither archbishop held full public authority in his city, both were extremely powerful through their vast landed estates and their elevated position as metropolitans in the ecclesiastical hierarchy. These archbishops were venerable and important leaders within their cities, and their power certainly influenced early siting of the commune's headquarters. Another example is Piacenza. Here the bishop did exercise all public authority within the city by virtue of an imperial diploma of Otto III.[12] The commune emerged through an alliance with the bishop, and its first seat was the bishop's old palace. As the cathedral was being rebuilt in the twelfth century, the bishop built himself a new palace.[13] From about 1171 until the early thirteenth century, the commune's documents were redacted in the "old palace of the bishop."[14] What we today recognize as the commune's palace, the stately "Il Gotico," was only begun in 1281.[15] It was built on a site northwest of the cathedral, believed by many to be that of the old Roman forum. This achieved a topographical configuration very similar to that at Florence, with the ecclesiastical center around Piazza Duomo and the civil center at the other end of today's Via XX Settembre at Piazza Cavalli.

Note that in the cases of Piacenza and Ravenna, an independent communal seat was not achieved until late in the thirteenth century, when in fact these communes were coming under the dominion of signori (lords). Exhausted by a half century of conflict with the bishop, the commune and people of Piacenza in 1254 elected Oberto Pallavicino, already lord of nearby Cremona, their *dominus perpetuus* (perpetual lord). The late 1260s and early 1270s were spent under the lordship of Charles of Anjou, but in 1281 it was a local strongman who supported the building of Il Gotico. Alberto Scotti, head of the Mercanzia, made this new, more stately seat for the commune one of his principal projects; he ruled Piacenza as captain and signore of the city through the late thirteenth and early fourteenth centuries.[16]

Ravenna's "independent" communal seat even more strikingly registers the neutralization of the commune as an independent political force. The commune here had always been weak. While other communes were subjugating the countryside around them to create a territory of dominion, Ravenna's commune spent its military force defending the patrimony of its powerful metropolitan and other ecclesiastical institutions. Even after a grant of powers from Emperor Frederick II, "the commune of Ravenna continued to find itself under the more or less heavy tutelage of its archbishop."[17] In the late thirteenth century, when the new communal palace was built, the commune had come under the lordship of Guido "Minore" Da Polenta, beginning this family's long domination of the city. The Da Polenta achieved power as servants of the see; their avid Guelph politics made them close allies of the archbishops. The new palace was built in the neighborhood (or "guayta") of San Michele in Africisco, where the Da Polenta had already established their family palazzi.[18] Thus development of a communal center physically separate from that of the archbishop was, in this case, hardly a measure of the commune's independence.

Locating a communal palace at a site separate from the cathedral is therefore not always a sign of strong, independent civic government. A two-poles topography cannot be read, following an assumed Florentine norm, as a direct index of the commune's strength and independence. But this arrangement of urban space was about power. Two interpretive shifts are necessary to understand the power it represented. First, one has to abandon the one-sided approach of trying to understand the commune and its buildings in isolation; as we have seen, the commune's own power doesn't always explain the site of its palace. Patterns in urban organization were the result of power relations, not just power. Second, the most crucial relationship influencing the commune's palace was the one between the city's bishop and the civic government. Ecclesiastical power is crucial in explaining why some cities end up with one unified center and others with the two-poles pattern.

A unified center emerged in cities where the bishop and commune collaborated and shared power for a long period of time. This often happened because the bishop was far more powerful than the commune. In cities where a bishop exercised comital authority within the walls—as in Bergamo, Brescia, Cremona, Modena, and Reggio—one center of both ecclesiastical and civil authority formed. But sometimes other forces combined to yield a long period of power sharing and cooperation between bishop and commune. At Pistoia, for example, the comital Cadolingi family abandoned the city in the eleventh century to build a territorial lordship, and the bishop then cooperated with local elites in forming the commune. Since neither the bishop nor the consuls had any legal claim to be exercising authority in the city, they needed to present a common front. Basically, weakness on both sides forced cooperation. At Faenza, it was the overbearing external threat of the archbishop of Ravenna, who had claim to comital authority in the town, that kept bishop and commune allied.[19] Whether the product of episcopal weakness or strength, it was the alliance and cooperation of bishop and commune that yielded a unified center of public authority around one piazza.

Two separate centers of civil and ecclesiastical authority emerged in cities where episcopal-communal cooperation was not crucial to the city's independence. This certainly happened where the bishop's power was limited by the presence of strong counts, and a substantial merchant class gave important support to the commune. In these circumstances (Verona and Treviso are good examples), the commune's ascendancy was established early and an independent civic center emerged.

But I must emphasize again that it is the relative power and relationship of bishop and commune that was most significant in producing these various organizations of urban space. A city could have a very powerful bishop—as at Asti and Parma—and still end up with separate centers of civil and ecclesiastical authority. In Asti, although the bishop exercised comital authority within the city and held the *castrum* once occupied by its counts, the commune gained the backing of Emperor Frederick Barbarossa and decisively superseded the authority of the bishop.[20] Outside support in this case relieved the commune of the necessity of sharing power (and a piazza) with the bishop. Parma's bishops were also extremely powerful, exercising comital authority within the city from the tenth century and acquiring such power in the contado (the territory surrounding the city) in 1036, but their close association with the emperor proved their undoing. Bishop Ugo (1027–1044) was imperial archchancellor, and Cadalus of Parma (1045–1072) became an imperial antipope (taking the name Honorius II), so when the reform party took the city in the early twelfth century it was with the backing and to the advantage of the nascent commune. Backlash against powerful episcopal lordship left the commune the heir of the immense civil authority previously acquired by the see.[21]

Why should the relative power of bishop and commune explain patterns in developing urban centers? Urban historians have not previously looked to power relations to explain the configuration of space in a medieval city. They have tended, instead, to favor functional or economic explanations. Enrico Guidoni, for example, has emphasized centrality in location and the lure of the old Roman forum in explaining development of a municipal center separate from the cathedral: "when the cathedral seemed too peripherally located to fulfill the representative and functional needs of the commune, [communal leaders] did not hesitate to detach themselves from the episcopal complex, often re-structuring the ancient forum."[22] This may have influenced the citizens of Verona, Pisa, and Parma, whose cathedrals were on the margins of the old city, but the cathedrals of Bologna, Treviso, Mantua, Padua, and other cities were quite centrally located.

In his classic *The City in History*, Lewis Mumford saw the market as determining the location of the town hall.²³ Indeed, many communal palaces within northern and central Italian cities are adjacent to the spaces used to hold the markets during the Middle Ages. But many cases also argue against the determinative role of the market in locating a communal palace. Piacenza's major markets were at the cathedral (the *mercatus boum*, or "cow market," located in the piazza in front and the cloth market, or *cantone della stoppa*, behind the church); still, the commune built Il Gotico at a new site where no market had been held.²⁴ At Asti, there was a market from the early twelfth century at San Secondo where the commune built its palace, but there was also a market at the cathedral.²⁵ The Florentine priors explicitly rejected the idea of locating their new palace at the Mercato Vecchio, also the site of the Roman Forum.²⁶

These explanatory tendencies are somewhat baffling in the face of the meaning commonly assigned to the communal palace. Contemporaries understood the building to be about power, and historians writing about them ever since have seen the construction of a communal palace as the architectural affirmation of the commune's authority. Florence's earlier communal seat, the Bargello, had a foundation inscription across its façade proclaiming of the city, "She owns the sea, the land, the entire world; like Rome, she will always be triumphant."²⁷ With contemporary interpretation as fulsome as this, historians are hardly being bombastic when they portray the building of a communal palace as an indicator of the consolidation of the urban government's powers.²⁸ Earlier secular palaces were also seen as an indicator of power; movement of the imperial palace outside the city walls, from the early eleventh century, has been seen as royal acknowledgment of urban autonomy. Frederick Barbarossa's campaign of rebuilding palaces in cities has been interpreted as part of his royal policy of reimposing imperial rule in northern Italy.²⁹

To find the missing link here in understanding how palaces and the powers residing in them shaped the urban landscape, we need to look at the late eleventh and twelfth centuries. As Carlrichard Brühl and others have noted, in most Italian towns imperial and comital palaces had moved outside the city walls by the mid-eleventh century. Communal palaces were not built until the very late twelfth and early thirteenth centuries. The urban center was not a vacuum of power in this period, and it was also not devoid of palaces. During this era, bishops began calling their residence a "palace"; indeed, by virtue of imperially granted rights and a long tradition of urban leadership, most did exercise a lordship in their city that was more than just charismatic.³⁰ The bishop held court, heard pleas, invested vassals, resolved disputes, and received dues in the large open hall of the palace. The commune knew these places well: in several cities (Lucca, Como, Verona) the first time we see consuls is in a document redacted in the bishop's palace.[31] Communal officials often met there; they understood it as a center of power. Indeed, only when one takes into consideration the bishop's palace as a center of power do patterns of development in urban topography become more legible. Building communal palaces must be read against the preexisting topography of power, and this means acknowledging the power of bishops and the palaces within which they exercised their lordship.

It is also obvious from incorporating churches into distinct civic centers that although many communal leaders wanted to part company with their bishop, they did not reject much that he stood for. Power was bound up with the holy. Mauro Ronzani has already illustrated in compelling detail how communes built their own churches and incorporated chapels into their palaces. In several cases, these communal or civic churches challenged episcopal dominance of the city's patron saint or created a new, alternative patron for the city.[32] What I would like to call attention to here is the urban "look" of some of these reconfigurations of religious and temporal power. Not only did some communes create a new center separate and distinct from their bishop's center of power and—through their choice of site, redirection of roads, creation of plazas—work to raise the prominence of their center and occlude the bishop's; in several quite striking instances, they recreated the look of the bishop's old center in their own. Thus, the communal leaders of Mantua sited their new center next to the church and monastery of Sant'Andrea; the appearance is of a piazza with a palace and a huge church.[33] The consuls of Piacenza located their new Il Gotico across from the huge new church the Franciscans had just built (the fact that the Franciscans too were not on good terms with the bishop probably made them the perfect companions for the new communal site).[34] Similarly, at Asti the commune located its seat across the piazza from the church of San Secondo.

Several well-known cases dramatically illustrate this phenomenon of the civic palace–"new cathedral" pairing effectively displacing the bishop and his church in the urban landscape. The average visitor (and even many knowledgeable ones) would be hard pressed to locate the real medieval cathedrals of Venice and Bologna. Today, there is not even a *vaporetto* line that goes anywhere near San Pietro in Castello, while San Marco is one of the most visited churches in the world. Venice may be regarded as extraordinary to the point of being grossly atypical, but Bologna's political and urban development is well within the norms of the Po Valley communes. The church of San Pietro there juridically remained the cathedral and the seat of the city's bishops. But visually it was eclipsed in the urban center by the commune's new church of San Petronio. The commune had officially proclaimed Saint Petronius the city's new patron in 1284, but it was not until a century later that they began building the immense church that now dominates Piazza Maggiore. San Petronio was more than twice as large as the Romanesque San Pietro.[35] The great expanse of Piazza Maggiore also gave more prominence to San Petronio in the urban fabric; even in the Middle Ages, San Pietro's piazza was small, and the total loss of open space before it in the modern city makes the cathedral nearly invisible.

Incorporating a large church into the communal center, creating a palace-cathedral look, well demonstrates that bishops and their buildings are crucial to understanding the urban development of Italian cities in the Middle Ages. The fact that some communes cultivated an episcopal look by pairing their new palace with a large church shows how strongly episcopal lordship influenced visual expression of power in the Italian city. Moreover, consideration of the episcopal palace as a center of lordship allows us to understand the politics of urban development, a politics already recognized in the later history of the communes.[36] An even more generalized application of a political reading of urban space, as I have tried to show here, offers a more cohesive and compelling explanation of patterns in urban development than either functionality or economics.

Looking beyond Florence in the history of urban development in medieval Italy is really, in the end, mainly a matter of looking beyond Florentine historiography and its continuing enmeshment in a Burckhardtian vision of a secular city-republic. The actual case of Florence's urban development is, in fact, well explained by the causal nexus—the relationship between bishop and commune—defined here. It is underevaluation of ecclesiastical power (common in Florentine historiography) and the historiography's silent assumption that Florence's experience can be paradigmatic that are misguided.

CHAPTER FOURTEEN

In Search of the Quiet City
*Civic Identity and Papal State Building in
Fourteenth-Century Orvieto*

David Foote

The collection of articles on state building in medieval and early modern Italy recently published in the *Journal of Modern History* began with an introductory essay titled "The State Is 'Back In.'"[1] As the title suggests, there was a time when studies of state formation were not in. The state belonged to the realm of high politics, which social historians transformed into a pejorative term. The actions of kings and princes were "surface disturbances," mere epiphenomena of the more fundamental history of social groups and groupings.[2]

Although social history was largely responsible for pushing the state to the margins of historical research, it also breathed new life into studies of state building by calling closer attention to the political activity of the local community. Previously, studies of state building in Western Europe focused on development of central administration in England and France to explain development of constitutional and absolute monarchies. During the last decade, studies of state formation have emerged with a different focus. Without denying the value of England and France as models, or the importance of royal and princely endeavors to expand and consolidate central authority, historians are paying closer attention to the political and social dynamics of the local community as a critical element in the process of state formation.[3]

The historiography of state building in medieval and early modern Italy anticipated this trend toward analysis of state formation at the periphery, that is, at the level of the local community. A number of studies during the 1970s and 1980s examined how the emergence of territorial states changed the relation between formerly autonomous city-states, or communes, and their surrounding countryside.[4] Nevertheless, there has been a marked geographic and thematic concentration of research on state building in Italy as well. Much of the work has focused on Florence, concentrating on the city's fiscal needs as the driving force of Florentine expansion. This model has dominated how historians have looked at the periphery. If territorial expansion was driven by the fiscal needs of the center, to what extent did incorporation into the Florentine territorial state impoverish the urban and rural communities that Florence absorbed?[5]

In the last decade, Italianists have begun to move beyond Florence both geographically and thematically. Among the inspirations for this trend was the translation of Otto Brunner's *Land und Herrschaft* into Italian in 1983.[6] In his study of late-medieval Austria, Brunner reacted against the nineteenth-century liberal conception of sovereignty as authority parceled out from the top (or from the center). This understanding of sovereignty was based on a theoretical distinction between state and society. The state was the bureaucratic apparatus, with its monopoly over justice, taxation, and use of force. The purpose of the state was to protect society, or the private sphere, understood largely in economic terms. Brunner rejected this theoretical distinction between state and society by expanding the concept of the state to include all of the social interests working through it. The state did not stand over against the private sphere. It was an expression or crystallization of private interests.[7]

For Italianists, Brunner's innovative model meant greater awareness of state formation as a mutual process. The relation between center and periphery was not necessarily a zero-sum game in which the expansion of one came at the expense of the other. Rather, the political and economic interests of the local community found expression in the territorial state. This emphasis on state building as a mutual process finds expression in the recurring image of the state as a network or web. Giorgio Chittolini described the state as a web of institutions that connected various forces and interests in mutual interdependence. Elena Fasano Guarini portrayed the state as a network of peripheries organized around economic and administrative centers.[8] These images suggest that forming territorial states involved spinning an increasingly dense web of institutions, an activity occurring both at the center and the periphery. So Italianists have begun to reconceptualize the distinction between center and periphery in much the same way that Brunner reconceptualized state and society. The local community was not necessarily the hapless victim of state building. It was often an active participant, looking to the emerging territorial state in conjunction with its own institutions as an instrument for pursuing and regulating local political, economic, and religious interests.

Fourteenth-century Orvietan chronicles and city-council minutes afford an especially interesting perspective on the nature and significance of state building at the periphery. In the summer of 1354, Orvieto submitted to Cardinal Albornoz, naming him and Pope Innocent VI lords of the city. The submission of Orvieto was a significant event both for the Orvietans and for the papacy. It brought peace to the city after nearly twenty years of factional violence and set the stage for Orvieto's final submission to the Papal State in 1367. From the papal perspective, the conquest of Orvieto was the first success in a long and violent struggle to reestablish the papacy's territorial authority over central Italy.

Cardinal Albornoz's Italian *reconquista* belongs to the early stages of a fundamental transition in the political and social landscape of late medieval Italy that saw the emergence of the papacy, Florence, Milan, and Venice as territorial states. Given the traditional view of state formation as a zero-sum game, many historians assumed that formation of territorial states and the decline of the communes were two sides of the same coin. Fourteenth-century Orvieto has typically been portrayed as one of these tired and decrepit communes crawling toward its death. Elisabeth Carpentier argued that by 1354 Orvieto was so overwhelmed by economic difficulties, factional violence, and demographic decline that the Orvietans were ready to flee their political responsibilities and search for peace at any cost, which for Orvieto meant absorption into the Papal State. Daniel Waley placed the demise of Orvieto's status as a free commune twenty years earlier, when the Orvietans named Ermanno Monaldeschi, one of the city's most powerful nobles, as its lord.[9]

There is no question that the first half of the fourteenth century was a period of crisis for Orvieto. At the end of the thirteenth century, the city was at the height of its glory. Between 1266 and 1303, Orvieto was one of the favored residences of the papal and Angevin courts. More important, the papal-Angevin alliance lent a degree of stability to the city's internal politics. The decline of Angevin influence and the papacy's move to Avignon in the early fourteenth century left the city with no stable center of gravity. As a result, Orvieto slowly lost control of its contado. By the late 1330s, the peace and prosperity that the commune enjoyed throughout most of the thirteenth century unraveled into a nightmare of factional violence, punctuated by a series of ineffectual tyrants. In 1348, the Black Death decimated a population that was already weakened by war and famine.

Despite these crises, Orvieto's submission in 1354 was not the last gasp of a dying commune. Sources point to a lively debate among Orvietans concerning the institutions and ideals that would govern their city during the difficult decades that culminated in the city's submission to Albornoz.

It is clear from this debate that Orvieto did not simply collapse into the waiting arms of the papacy. Papal state building was successful in Orvieto because it converged with these local debates and offered a resolution that allowed Orvietans to reconstruct a civic identity on their own terms. Thus Orvieto's submission to Albornoz in 1354 marks the commune's resuscitation, not its death.

What were fourteenth-century Orvietans debating? All Orvietans shared the ideals of civic peace and liberty, but they disagreed about the appropriate institutional framework in which these ideals should operate. Episcopal, noble, and popolani, or nonnoble, perspectives defined the terms of the debate. Bishops, nobles, and popolani did not deny the legitimacy of the others' institutions in principle, but they fought vigorously over the issue of priority. When the priority of institutions became contested, the desire for peace metamorphosed into a struggle for liberty.

The Orvietan bishops looked to the papacy as the most effective guarantor of civic peace and ecclesiastical liberty. In the special case of central Italy, this meant acknowledgment of Orvieto's subjection to the Papal State. Papal claims to Orvieto date back to eighth- and ninth-century Carolingian donations. Orvieto recognized these claims in 1157 when it swore fidelity to the papacy.[10] Thereafter, this agreement planted a tension at the heart of Orvietan politics. Orvietans sought to remain faithful subjects, while at the same time resisting any papal interference that compromised their territorial jurisdiction or the commune's right to govern itself according to its own institutions. As the administrative apparatus of the Papal Patrimony grew more sophisticated during the thirteenth century, the tension between papal jurisdiction and local autonomy increased.[11]

Although the bishops were faithful and patriotic Orvietans (practically all Orvietan bishops before the mid-fourteenth century were locals), they represented a pro-papal voice in Orvietan politics throughout most of the thirteenth and fourteenth centuries. During the fourteenth century, the bishopric represented an increasingly strong institutional link between Orvieto and the Papal State. Bishop Guido (1302–28) was papal vicar in spiritualities in Rome under Pope Clement VII.[12] Pope John XXII appointed Guido as Rector of the Patrimony.[13] Bishop Ponzio (1348–61) was papal vicar in spiritualities in Rome. He was also the first of several Orvietan bishops from France.[14] Prior to Ponzio, virtually all Orvietan bishops were from Orvieto or its surrounding region.

Nobles had a more restricted sense of community. They looked to the family as the most effective institutional framework within which to pursue their interests. For most noble families, the institutions and resources of the commune represented a store of wealth and tools to be appropriated for their private use. The factional violence that plagued the Italian city-states during the first half of the fourteenth century was little more than a violent competition to transform public resources into family property.[15]

While the bishops looked above the commune to the Papal State and nobles looked beneath the commune to the family, the popolo envisioned the commune, defined by its legal and administrative structure, as the most effective guarantor of their interests. Civic institutions and statutes in large part were an expression of popolani interests, having been crafted by notaries and lawyers, who belonged to the popolo. From the popolani perspective, the episcopal vision threatened to dissolve civic institutions into the administrative apparatus of the Papal State, thus leaving the popolo with no institutional expression of their interests. Noble families threatened to tear asunder these same institutions, as they struggled to appropriate them as family property.

Of these three competing perspectives, that of the popolo, or more precisely, that portion of the popolo constituting the legal-administrative class of the commune, is the most visible in the Orvietan sources. At first glance, the prominence of popolani voices seems out of proportion to their political influence. For most of the thirteenth and the first half of the fourteenth centuries, internal division prevented the popolo from establishing and maintaining a popular regime for any extended period of time. Instead of exploiting factional and party division among the nobility, the popolo became its victim.[16] Nevertheless, it was the political ideals and institutions of the popolani technocrats, that is, the legal and administrative class, that emerged from the factional violence and political disintegration of the 1330s and 1340s to form the core of a new civic identity. The configuration of political and economic interests underlying this civic identity laid the foundation for Orvieto's submission to Albornoz. By the time Albornoz arrived, the most difficult and violent phase of state building was largely complete—hence the irony that much of papal state building in Orvieto took place before the papacy itself was in a position to become significantly involved in the task.

An anonymous fourteenth-century Orvietan chronicle entitled "*Discorso historico con molti accidenti occorsi in Orvieto et in altri parti*" illustrates in a remarkable way the formation of a civic identity during the period leading up to and including Orvieto's submission to the papal state.[17] The chronicle contains a detailed account of Orvietan history from 1342 to 1368. The author was almost certainly a member of the popolo; at one point in the narrative he referred to "our statutes, ordinances, and Carta del Popolo."[18] Moreover, the author's familiarity with Orvietan politics and institutions, as reflected in city-council minutes, indicates that he probably belonged to the class of popolani technocrats.

The *Discorso* offers a fascinating view of papal state building from the periphery. The narrative traces the crystallization of private interests—in this case, predominantly popolani interests—into local public institutions and the convergence of this process with the papacy's own efforts to build a territorial state. In short, it offers a wonderful example of the territorial state as an expression of local interests. The *Discorso* accomplishes this by developing two themes. Emergence of the author's sympathies and interests in the course of the narrative marks the development of a popolani civic identity. The second theme traces the formation and stabilization of public institutions out of the chaos of factional violence. These themes culminate and converge with Orvieto's submission to Albornoz. Before examining the narrative in more detail, it is worth taking a look at these two themes that determine its structure.

Emergence of the author's sympathies and interests is an interesting problem, because the *Discorso* traditionally has been considered a remarkably objective narrative. Although it contains a dense description of the factional violence that plagued Orvieto from 1342 to 1354, its author, who most likely lived through the events that he narrated, remains almost completely invisible. Elisabeth Carpentier, who relied heavily on the *Discorso* in her study of the Black Death in Orvieto, described the author as informed and objective.[19] Luigi Fumi, in the introduction to his edition of the *Discorso*, writes that the chronicle is objective and dense with facts but lacks any clues that would reveal the personal dispositions of the author.[20]

It is possible to attribute the depersonalized character of the chronicle to the author's desire to remain unscathed by the frequent changes in regime from one hostile faction to another, as seems to be the case in other fourteenth-century chronicles that display the same disposition toward objectivity.[21] This, however, does not seem to be the case in the *Discorso*. In the course of the narrative, there is an important change in the author's objectivity. Throughout his account of the factional violence prior to Orvieto's submission to Albornoz in 1354, he dispassionately refers to the rival factions as "the one party and the other." After 1354, the author uses for the first time in the narrative the first-person pronouns *us* and *our* in reference to his fellow Orvietans. The narrative journey from "the one party and the other" to *us* suggests that the author's objectivity in the pre-Albornoz narrative was attributable to the absence of a civic identity capable of providing a home for his sympathies. The emergence of *us* in the narrative corresponds to the triumph of popolani institutions as one of the defining features of Orvieto's submission to Albornoz; thus it represents popolani participation in and subjective appropriation of papal state building in Orvieto.

The second theme—development of institutions from the chaos of civic disorder—is sometimes difficult to discern in the midst of the factional violence that dominates the narrative up to 1354. The narrative begins in 1342, amid a series of events that began in 1334, when Ermanno Monaldeschi, a member of one of Orvieto's most powerful families, became the city's first signor, or lord. Ermanno ruled successfully, ushering in a brief period of stability that lasted until his death in 1337.[22] After Ermanno's death, Orvietan politics rapidly disintegrated into a nightmare of factional violence between two rival branches of the Monaldeschi: the sons of Ermanno, also known as the Muffati faction; and the Bonconte, or Melcorini faction. The *Discorso* begins with Benedetto di Bonconte and his brother-in-law, Matteo Orsini, in power and with the sons of Ermanno and their faction in exile. "In the year 1342 Matteo and Benedetto di Bonconte plotted against Count Pietro [Petruccio Montemarte] and Guido di Simone. And Guido di Simone fled back to his palace near San Giovanni. And the sons of Bonconte passed the night until the next morning. Finally Guido was chased out of Orvieto by Ceccho di Ranuccio, with the consent of Matteo. Moreover, some of Count Pietro's relatives were seized and held under the guard of Matteo in the Palace of the Popolo."[23] This passage, densely packed with people and their animosities, is representative of the entire narrative.

The seemingly endless tale of conflict would become so much white noise were it not for three subplots that lend structure and rhythm to the narrative. It is through these three subplots that the theme of institutional development emerges.

First, there is the rhythm of regimes, as the Orvietans brought in one outsider after another to resolve the factional violence. Benedetto di Bonconte and Matteo Orsini ruled with the help of the Captain of the Patrimony until 1345. During the subsequent decade they were succeeded by a long list of short-lived regimes, including those of a Sienese Captain of the Popolo, Benedetto di Bonconte, Count Guido of Sovana (another Orsini), a Perugian overlordship, Benedetto di Bonconte, a Perugian overlordship once again, Benedetto di Bonconte, the Archbishop of Milan, Giovanni di Vico, and finally Cardinal Albornoz.

Beneath the rhythm of regimes is the rhythm of vendetta. The opening passage of the *Discorso* recounted the expulsion of Guido di Simone, a member of one of the most powerful Ghibelline families in Orvieto. In 1343, Nicola Orsini, Matteo Orsini's nephew, murdered Guido.[24] In 1345, Leonardo di Simone avenged Guido's death by killing Matteo.[25] Finally, in 1346, Benedetto di Bonconte handed over Leonardo to Matteo's kinsmen, who took Leonardo to the Orsini castle of Mugnano and then to Rome for the final act of the vendetta: "And on holy Monday, which was April 10, the son of Matteo had a wooden cart made and had Leonardo placed in it, naked and bound to a pole, and had him tortured with hot pincers [carrying him] throughout a section of Rome. And then he [Matteo's son] had him cut to pieces in front of the Castel Sant'Angelo and then had the pieces gathered and thrown piece by piece into the Tiber. . . . And thus went the vendetta of Matteo Orsini."[26] And thus the Orsini began their celebration of Holy Week.

A second vendetta dominates the narrative from 1351, when Benedetto di Bonconte arranged an ambush of Monaldo di Ermanno, whose murder marked the end of the first Perugian signoria and the return of Benedetto as signor.[27] Thereafter a series of reprisals punctuate the narrative.[28] The vendetta culminated in the murder of Benedetto himself and the brief signoria of the Archbishop of Milan.[29]

The alternation of regimes and the tit-for-tat of vendetta are only surface rhythms following the more fundamental contrapuntal beat of constitutional and extraconstitutional responses to factional violence. As one faction gained the upper hand, it typically set aside the city's statutes and attempted to establish its leader as an extraconstitutional lord. This only exacerbated civic discord. Eventually the Orvietans, exhausted from conflict, would call upon an outsider (the short-lived regimes mentioned just above) to impose peace and reestablish the city's institutions and statutes. Almost inevitably, these external lords were drawn into the vortex of factional violence, siding with one group or the other. Thus would begin a new cycle of extraconstitutional lordship and constitutional reaction. In certain respects, the *Discorso* is a romance, that is, a search for a stable and constitutional solution compatible with popolani political interests. The quest found its fulfillment in Albornoz, the guarantor of civic institutions and statutes, who, in certain respects, affected a Brunnerian synthesis of the territorial state and local private interests.

It is worth looking in more detail at the narrative along with city-council minutes to understand how this romantic quest unfolds. The quest begins with Benedetto di Bonconte and Matteo Orsini, who in 1343 brought in Bernardo di Lago, the Captain of the Patrimony, to serve as the Orvietan Captain of the Popolo.[30] When Bernardo took the position, he pledged to uphold the city's statutes, ordinances, and Carta del Popolo.[31] There were, however, some among the popolo, including the author of the *Discorso*, who were wary of the Captain of the Patrimony exercising authority in the city. The author of the *Discorso* writes: "In 1343 on the first of December the Captain of the Patrimony, that is Bernardo del Lago . . . entered Orvieto with that office, salary, and staff which other Captains [of the Popolo] customarily have. And he was called according to [his name] Bernardo del Lago, and not according to [his office] Captain of the Patrimony."[32] The author's insistence that

Bernardo held the position of Captain of the Popolo as a private person and not as the Captain of the Patrimony indicates his desire to protect Orvietan autonomy against the jurisdictional claims of papal provincial officials. In April 1345, in intense fighting between Orvieto and the Muffati exiles, Bernardo del Lago, still acting as Captain of the Popolo, named Benedetto as signor of the city, explicitly setting aside the city's statutes and Carta del Popolo, which made no provisions for such extraordinary powers.[33]

In August a popular revolution overthrew Matteo and Benedetto. During the uprising, the Orvietans expressed their dissatisfaction with Bernardo del Lago, the Captain of the Patrimony, by sacking his office in the Palace of the Popolo and destroying many of his possessions, including financial and judicial records.[34] With the expulsion of Matteo, Benedetto, and the Captain of the Patrimony, the popolo set about restoring their institutions. The author of the *Discorso* writes: "Monday, August 8, the Council of Consuls and of the Forty and of the others who were summoned ordered that the Seven[35] [executive ruling body] have the office and authority that they had in the past, which Matteo took from them. And [the Council] ordered that all authority and lordship that had been granted was null and void from this day. And they ordered that a Captain of the Popolo be called from Siena. And Angelino Bottone of Siena was called."[36] The tenure of Angelino Bottone as Captain of the Popolo thus represented a restoration of popolani institutions. City council minutes indicate that when Angelino took office he pledged to maintain the jurisdiction of the commune; to protect widows, orphans, churches, and hospitals; to uphold the office of the Seven; and to rule in accordance with popolani institutions, making no allowance for any tyrant or signoria.[37]

As was the case with every popolani restoration, peace was made between the warring factions and exiles returned to the city.[38] The popolo then pushed legislation through the city council forbidding the bearing of arms in the city, "both offensive and defensive, which are born in an uncivil manner by nobles and magnates and their *familiares* and followers." This was necessary to prevent Orvieto from returning "to the evils and customary tyrannical depravities" that threatened to destroy the city.[39] On the following day, the council issued more legislation that offers a telling comment on the popolo's lack of confidence in their ability to withstand the siren of factional animosities. The legislation prohibited popolani from gathering at the house of a noble, "because iniquitous and evil popolani are accustomed to live by tyranny" and because "nobles and magnates always venture to destroy and utterly desolate the city of Orvieto by seducing [popolani] with alliances, flattery, and gatherings, and oaths and conspiracies."[40] This fear that there was no center of gravity capable of holding the popolo together becomes increasingly evident in the narrative of the *Discorso*.

Within a month, Angelino Bottone was drawn into the vortex of factional strife. Benedetto di Bonconte drove him from office and in turn was driven out of Orvieto by the sons of Ermanno. Benedetto called on Bernardo del Lago for assistance. Orvieto thus found itself in a war against Benedetto and the Captain of the Patrimony. After a short but destructive war, the Orvietans called in Count Guido of Sovana (another Orsini) as lord.[41] He entered office in January 1347 and apparently fell victim to the plague in 1348.

In April 1348, the Orvietans decided to give overlordship of the city to Perugia for ten years.[42] City council minutes indicate that the Perugian overlordship was accompanied by significant constitutional reform to strengthen popolo institutions and restrain factional violence.[43] The author of the *Discorso* was careful to emphasize these reforms as well. He writes:

> Friday, September 19, there was a General Council of all the people in the palace of the Popolo. In that Council it was decided that the city of Orvieto be ruled by the popolo, and that no noble hold office, and that the name of the office of the Seven be changed to "Priors" and that it contain eight *boni homini*. . . . And it was ordered that no noble enter the palace of the popolo or the house of the Priors without permission, and that they were not allowed to attend the Council unless invited by the Priors, with the permission of the Priors and popolo.[44]

The following year the new popolo regime passed more anti-magnate legislation and instituted procedural reforms to strengthen the administration of justice on behalf of the popolo.[45]

During the two years (1348–50) of the Perugian/popolo regime, the Perugian captain maintained peace and began to reassert Orvietan control over the contado. The author of the *Discorso* writes: "And thus each of the parties worked together to strengthen the commune of Orvieto, and reason and justice was administered to each person. In this way the statutes of the popolo of the commune were strengthened and every person prospered and lived in peace."[46] This portion of the narrative stands in sharp relief to that of the preceding years, when factional violence was destroying the political, economic, and social life of the commune. The narrative becomes less crowded with names and less distracted by the difficult task of keeping track of the violence, reprisals, and shifting alliances. With the exception of a few brief moments when factional conflict threatened to return, there is, for the first time in the narrative, a sense of rest and relief. The Perugian signoria was the last successful revival of popolo rule until 1354.

The sense of rest and relief came to an end in March 1351, when Benedetto di Bonconte arranged the murder of his principal rival, Monaldo di Ermanno.[47] Between March 1351 and June 1354, Orvietan politics became the instrument of a bloody vendetta between the Bonconte, who maintained control of Orvieto throughout most of this period, and the sons of Ermanno, who waged war against Orvieto as exiles. In the *Discorso* the popolani looked on with horror as their city plunged into chaos and as many of their fellow popolani became targets of reprisal. Even when the popolani themselves were not the victims, the unspeakable atrocities committed by the warring factions still horrified them. Indeed, a new rhythm of atrocities punctuated by expressions of popolani horror emerges in the narrative. The city gradually came to resemble a ghost town, as many Orvietans fled the city for safety.

Seeing the destruction of the city, the warring factions made one last attempt to establish peace by offering the signoria to Perugia once again. The first act of the new regime was to recall the exiles and repopulate the empty city. The council minutes recording the recall of exiles echoes the same sense of desolation found in the *Discorso*, lamenting that "the city of Orvieto and its contado and area of influence is empty of people and men, because of wars and scandals and dissensions."[48] Factional violence broke out soon after the return of the exiles, and the city's political and economic crisis deepened.[49] The subsequent regimes of the Archbishop of Milan and Giovanni di Vico established equally ephemeral truces, and Orvieto remained a desolate city trapped in a political and economic nightmare.

At this point, the *Discorso* begins to intersect with papal politics. In December 1352, Pope Innocent VI succeeded Clement VI. Innocent was more determined than his predecessor to restore papal control in central Italy and more willing to commit significant papal resources to do so. He called upon Gil Albornoz, formerly Archbishop of Toledo and participant in the Castilian Reconquista, to lead an expedition of reconquest in central Italy. Albornoz arrived in Milan in 1353, where he secured military and financial support from Archbishop Giovanni Visconti. He then moved south to regain control of the Tuscan Patrimony.[50]

When Albornoz arrived in central Italy in 1353, Giovanni di Vico, the lord of Viterbo, had extended his rule over much of the Tuscan Patrimony by exploiting the complicated network of animosities that united factions of various towns in the region. By allying with the Muffati exiles of Orvieto, he conquered several strategic towns and fortresses in the Orvietan countryside. After the murder of Benedetto Bonconte, he succeeded in establishing himself as the lord of Orvieto itself. Given the alliance between Benedetto Bonconte and Bernardo del Lago, the Captain of the Tuscan Patrimony, the murder of Benedetto at the hands of the Muffati faction cleared the way for Giovanni to extend his lordship over much of the region.

In the spring of 1354, Albornoz began a military campaign that culminated in his victory over Giovanni and a treaty whereby the Orvietans gave him and Pope Innocent VI the signoria of the city. It would be a mistake to understand this treaty in terms of papal conquest, for it represents the culmination of intense negotiation. Many Orvietans, including the author of the *Discorso*, feared that papal rule would place the city under the political, economic, and judicial apparatus of the Captain of the Patrimony. This fear that Orvieto might lose its autonomy was the central issue in negotiations between Orvieto and Albornoz. In November 1353, seven months before Orvieto's final submission, the Orvietan Council sent nine ambassadors to discuss peace with the cardinal. One month later, the ambassadors reported back to the city council that Albornoz's demands would require Orvieto to surrender its customary liberties.[51] Albornoz and the Orvietans spent six months fighting and negotiating before they moved beyond this obstacle.

As indicated by these intense negotiations, the Orvietans realized that Albornoz was not simply another outsider. As the representative of a territorial state, he offered a greater pool of resources to be used against factional violence, but he also posed a significantly greater threat to the city's autonomy. The author describes the eventual compromise: "Tuesday, June 24, the feast of San Giovanni, the General Council . . . met in the palace of the Popolo, and in that Council it was decided to give lordship of the city and contado of Orvieto to Pope Innocent and Cardinal Gilio [Albornoz] for their lifetime, and as Pope Innocent and Cardinal Gilio [i.e., as private persons]. And with these pacts, the city of Orvieto would remain free after their death and . . . the Church could not claim any signoria or redemption."[52] The insistence that Cardinal Albornoz and Pope Innocent VI rule Orvieto as private persons echoes the author's earlier description of Bernardo del Lago's tenure as Captain of the Popolo. In both cases, the Orvietans wanted to clarify that the rule of these ecclesiastical officials did not mean their city would be grafted into the provincial administration of the Tuscan Patrimony. This trial marriage of sorts established the framework for Orvieto's final submission to the Papal State in 1367. The papacy would rule through the city's own institutions and statutes.

Once the Orvietans felt reasonably confident that their autonomy was not threatened, their submission offered a sense of resolution that becomes evident in the arrival of the first-person pronoun in the narrative: "And the legate [Albornoz] promised *us* to observe *our* statutes and ordinances and Carta del Popolo and all of *our* other liberties."[53] The author's use of *us* and *our* marks the fulfillment of the *Discorso*'s quest for a civic identity grounded in a constitutional regime. The journey from "the one party and the other" to *us* was complete. Immediately after the treaty, Albornoz decided to remain in Orvieto for a while. The author comments on the sense of relief that the Orvietans felt during his stay. "Since the legate decided to stay in Orvieto, everyone was very content and was ruled according to reason and justice. And it was no longer a concern among us who was from one party more than the other."[54] The popolani ideal of the commune as a peace community found its guarantor in Albornoz.

Inasmuch as popolani institutions are the flesh of popolani ideals and civic identity, using *us* in reference to Orvietans points to the restoration of popolani institutions. Indeed, Albornoz's success as a state builder in Orvieto was based largely on this restoration. In 1354, he restored the rule of the Seven and established procedures for their election by sortition.[55] These and later electoral reforms broadened the participation of citizens in the Seven and in the General Council.[56] In 1355, the council renewed antimagnate legislation, prescribing harsh punishment against nobles who threatened to break the peace.[57] Albornoz's vicar in 1356, Giovanni Raffacani of Florence, instituted measures to safeguard the city's jurisdiction over its contado. Each time a new vicar came to Orvieto, the chancellor was to read before the General Council a record of the city's rights and jurisdiction over its contado.[58] In 1360, Albornoz even protected the city's jurisdiction to the south in the Val di Lago against the Captain of the Patrimony.[59]

If Albornoz's success depended on his ability to incorporate popolani interests and institutions, what about the nobility? Certainly their interests were too powerful to be excluded. Given the *Discorso*'s popolani perspective, incorporating aristocratic interests into the territorial state does not play a prominent role. Nevertheless, the narrative addresses the problem indirectly. After recounting Orvieto's submission to Albornoz in 1354, the *Discorso* changes significantly. The narrative of 1342–54 was trapped in a cycle of violence and peace, alternately setting aside and reestablishing civic institutions and statutes. As a result, the narrative seemed to run in place as it moved through a series of signori. The city's submission to Albornoz broke the cycle of violence that kept the narrative running in place.

After 1354, Orvieto becomes peripheral to the narrative as the author turns his attention to Albornoz's reconquest of the patrimony. The narrative suddenly possesses a sense of movement, taking the reader on a journey of conquest throughout central Italy. The broadening of the narrative is significant. The ability of Orvietans to look outward demonstrates one of the ways papal state building offered a resolution to the city's internal problems. The ability of Orvietans to participate in a coherent regional policy redirected the complicated and destabilizing forces of civic and regional noble factions toward Albornoz's endeavor of reconquest. The Papal State thus was able to absorb certain powerful families into its political structure, something that the communes found difficult if not impossible.[60] It was in part this ability to redirect the violence of the warrior class that distinguished the territorial state from the long list of outsiders who failed to bring peace.

When Cardinal Albornoz died in 1367, the Orvietans faced an important decision. They had granted lordship in 1354 to Albornoz and Pope Innocent VI for life. Innocent had died in 1362; therefore the death of Albornoz left the city without a signor. During his thirteen-year tenure as signor, Albornoz demonstrated that papal temporal authority and communal autonomy were not mutually exclusive. In 1367, the Orvietans offered lordship over the city in perpetuity to the papacy, not to the pope as a private individual, under the condition that Orvieto remain free from the jurisdiction of the Captain of the Patrimony. Instead, the pope was to exercise direct lordship over the city. Pope Urban V accepted this condition, and the treaty was signed.[61] Thus Orvieto's final submission to the papacy followed the course established by the thirteen-year signoria of Albornoz, who pacified the city by affirming its own institutions and ideals.

Albornoz's intimate involvement in even the smallest details of Orvietan administration led Guillaume Mollat to conclude that the popular government in Orvieto was only a façade for Albornoz's absolute rule.[62] City council minutes indicate that Albornoz and his representatives were indeed actively involved in the affairs of the city. The judgment that popular government was only a façade, however, reflects more an historiographical prejudice than the nature of power in Orvieto. John Najemy has commented on a similar tendency in many studies of late medieval Florence to dismiss institutions as a façade that masked more immediate and personal exercise of power.[63] Such an understanding overlooks the fact that the exercise of power is always negotiated and that institutions are in large part a crystallization of such negotiations.

In more concrete terms, to view Albornoz's rule as absolute underestimates the complexity of regional politics upon which he sought to impose order, and it overestimates Albornoz's own power. Beyond the problems presented by the ever-shifting alliances in the Tuscan Patrimony, Albornoz's own support was grounded in alliances that were little more than quicksand. When the Milanese Archbishop Giovanni Visconti died in 1354, Milanese support not only dried up; Albornoz soon found himself at war with Milan for control of Bologna. To complicate matters further, his military might depended upon mercenary companies whose loyalty went to the highest bidder. When Albornoz moved beyond the Tuscan Patrimony into Romagna, he found that local lords, such as the Malatesta in Rimini, were too deeply entrenched to eliminate. Therefore he grafted them into the administrative apparatus of the Papal State by naming them as papal vicars.[64] Despite Albornoz's attempt to reestablish papal control over central Italy through military conquest, his successes came through negotiation, not military might. Local communities such as Orvieto imposed their interests upon Albornoz as much as he imposed his will on them.

The *Discorso* argues eloquently that although Albornoz could enter into the history of power in Orvieto, he could not erase it. If the territorial state was indeed a web of institutions, it had a long prehistory, reaching back as early as the eleventh and twelfth centuries, when popolani technocrats began spinning the institutional threads that would bind the commune together as a political community. This process of community building was the *sine qua non* of state building in early modern Italy. By the fourteenth century, much of the institutional structure of the territorial states was already in place. The task of state building was to convince smaller communities like Orvieto that larger centers such as the papacy or Florence were the most effective guarantors of local institutions and the ideals that these institutions embodied.

CHAPTER FIFTEEN

Back to the Future

Remaking the Commune in Ducal Modena

Michelle M. Fontaine

In November 1597, the Conservators of Modena wrote two brief but formal letters to their new duke, Cesare I d'Este, who lived in Ferrara. The first expressed their "infinite sorrow" at the death of his predecessor, Alfonso II d'Este. The second letter stated that "all Modena was of great cheer" to learn that Cesare would succeed Alfonso.[1] Little did the Conservators realize then that Alfonso's demise, his choice of successor, and the complicated nature of the Este estate would trigger a series of events that would fundamentally alter Modena's urban character. The Este held Ferrara from the pope, while they received the other areas in their duchy, notably Modena and Reggio Emilia, from the emperor. When Alfonso died "without issue," the pope refused to recognize his chosen heir, Cesare, who was the son of Alfonso's illegitimate uncle. Ferrara devolved to the papacy. As the loss of Ferrara appeared imminent, the Este turned to Emperor Rudolf II, who allowed them to move the seat of their duchy to Modena.[2] In January 1598, the d'Este family left Ferrara and arrived in Modena, where they ruled until the nineteenth century.

The arrival of the d'Este family changed the topography of power in

---

A Faculty Research Grant from the University of Arkansas at Little Rock and a Fellowship from the Institute for Research in the Humanities at the University of Wisconsin allowed me to research and write this chapter. I wish to thank the staff at the Archivio Storico Comunale di Modena, the Banco S. Geminiano e S. Prospero, and the Museo Civico d'Arte Medievale e Moderna for their generous assistance. My thanks for many helpful suggestions also go to my fellow editors and colleagues James A. Levernier, Laurie Taylor-Mitchell, and Laura A. Smoller, and finally to my mentor, William M. Bowsky, who inspired this piece by his own work.

Modena. For three centuries, Modena, like most cities in Italy since the late Middle Ages, had been ruled from afar, incorporated into one of the developing territorial powers, in this case the d'Este Duchy of Ferrara. As long as the seat of ducal power was located in Ferrara rather than Modena, the Commune of Modena, represented by the Conservators, or town councilors, maintained its distinct communal character. But when the Este moved to Modena, they began to transform the little merchant town into their seat of power, the Capital of the new Duchy of Modena. Suddenly, it became difficult to distinguish the Commune of Modena from Modena the Capital.

The sudden transformation of the city from a medieval merchant city into a baroque capital set Modena apart from the normal development of capital cities in early modern Italy. By the sixteenth century, a dozen or so centers of power such as Florence, Milan, and Mantua, the capitals of the territorial states, dominated most of the smaller, less powerful cities throughout the Italian peninsula. Most of these capital cities had become powerful over several centuries through the agency of one or several primary families who built their base in the city for many years, as with the Medici in Florence, the Visconti and Sforza in Milan, the Gonzaga in Mantua, and the d'Este (until 1598) in Ferrara. During the course of the sixteenth and seventeenth centuries, a family might establish a new power base, but it did not relocate the capital to another city (for example, the Spanish seized control of Lombardy, but Milan remained the capital). Or a capital city might subsume a rival capital and its territories into its dominion, as when Florence finally subjugated Siena in 1555. Most power centers, however, became more powerful during the sixteenth and seventeenth centuries. Modena stands alone as having once been a subjugated city but overnight having become a capital.

Other capitals had developed as a center of power over generations, even centuries, but in Modena this development occurred rapidly and thus becomes an interesting case for studying the process in which the commune distinguished itself from the capital. Telescoping events allows the student to observe the process more easily. This chapter highlights the process by examining Modena before and during the two generations following the events of 1598. Its focus is how the Conservators adapted themselves and the commune to the new topography of power that brought the center of the duchy to their town. Initially overshadowed by the display of ducal power in the city, the Conservators reestablished their role as the guardians of the Commune of Modena, represented that role through ritual and art, and thereby differentiated the Commune of Modena from Modena the Capital.

Ducal Power and the Conservators Before 1598

The Este family had governed Modena from 1288 with two brief exceptions. Since they lived in Ferrara, about forty miles away, they ruled through their governor, who lived in the Castello di San Pietro in Modena. During this time, ducal power and authority were intermittently displayed, most usually when the governor apprehended a criminal, collected taxes, or requisitioned troops for the duke's army. Generally, neither the governor nor the duke were vital for daily life in Modena.

The commune, however, was central to Modena and the Modenese. By *commune* I mean the city as an independent or quasi-independent community, distinct from the duchy or the capital of the duchy. The commune included—and incorporated far more than—the municipal government. It meant the city personified, formally called the *Magnifica Comunità* (Magnificent Community). The Modenese owed allegiance and devotion to the commune, their *patria* (fatherland). Represented publicly by the Conservators as its first citizens, the commune was made visible through civic ritual, art, and architecture.[3]

Modena's Communal Palace, one of the oldest buildings in a city founded in the Middle Ages, made the commune visible.[4] The palace bordered the city's main square as did two other important monuments, the Ghirlandina tower and the Romanesque cathedral dedicated to Modena's patron saint, San Geminiano. The main square, with its three major monuments, served as the geographic, civic, spiritual, and symbolic heart of the city before 1598.[5]

The decoration in the Communal Palace also made the commune visible. The Conservators' Hall of State contained the most notable portrayal of the commune. During the fifteenth and sixteenth centuries, their Hall of State was the Sala del Fuoco. Remodeled in a Renaissance classical style, the Sala del Fuoco glorified the city's good government and its founding by Republican Rome in the third century B.C.E. This decoration linked Modena to its communal past. The ceiling of the Sala del Fuoco featured the communal crest, an azure cross on a field of gold.[6] The central position of the crest attested to the primary role of the commune and the Conservators in the life of the Modenese.

The Conservators were the commune's first citizens. These town councilors came mostly from several dozen families of merchant or artisan origin. Every trimester, a dozen of them were elected to office. Serving in important functions for the commune, the Conservators maintained ties to the communal past, promoted civic pride and devotion to the patria, and corporately represented the commune in its many civic religious rituals.

Although they ultimately managed urban affairs through ducal approval,[7] they were the "Conservators" of Modena's welfare. These significant public roles brought honor and dignity to both them and the commune.

The Conservators met several times each week in their Hall of State. From their dozen carved wooden seats, six to each side of the center seat commanded by the podestà (administrative head of the city), the Conservators heard petitions from the citizens of Modena. Guided by their statute book, adorned with striking images of San Geminiano protecting the city, the Conservators discussed regulation of the guilds; provision of staple foods; maintenance of the canals that crisscrossed the city; preservation of social welfare; and, from 1529, supervision of public health.[8] During the occasional moments of chaos that periodically beset Modena, the Conservators, not the duke, worked to preserve civic order, although the duke sometimes assisted financially.[9]

To safeguard Modena, the Conservators frequently sought the aid of its spiritual guardian, San Geminiano, whose remains the city preserved in a crypt in the cathedral, built in 1106. Typical imagery of San Geminiano portrayed him in episcopal robes, holding the city and entrusting it to God in prayer. Devoted to this fourth-century bishop since the early Middle Ages, the Modenese developed several annual feasts to honor their favorite patron and protector. During these celebrations, the Conservators and Modena's religious officials led processions that often drew thousands of devoted Modenese.[10] In times of crisis, the Conservators, on behalf of the commune, invoked the protection of San Geminiano and other saints.[11] Although the ducal governor joined the Conservators in these civic religious rituals, he did not overshadow their role in them.

As long as the duke lived in Ferrara, Modena existed much as it had during its communal phase from the eleventh to the thirteenth centuries. The commune was made visible to the public through its architecture, the Communal Palace, and the cathedral in the main square; through the art decoration on the walls of the Sala del Fuoco and the representations of San Geminiano; and through many civic religious rituals. Like the commune itself, the Conservators were often hidden from public view while they deliberated in the Communal Palace. However, as leaders of Modena's many civic rituals, they appeared frequently in public. In these rituals, the Conservators represented the commune before God, the saints, and the community, a function commonly believed to be crucial to the welfare of the city. More than most other activities of the Conservators, civic religious ritual reinforced their image, dignity, and honor in the eyes of their fellow citizens.

The Este in Modena

The primary role of the commune and the Conservators began to change in 1598, when Cesare I d'Este and his family reluctantly left their grand Castello in Ferrara and came to their new home, the run-down, tiny Castello di San Pietro in Modena. Ducal power now emanated from the Castello throughout the city, no longer evident only through taxation or the control of crime. The Este displayed their power throughout the city in public and private buildings and monuments, urban renewal, and patronage that stripped Modena of its communal character and transformed it into a baroque capital. Although the main square with its cathedral and Communal Palace continued to function as the civic and spiritual core of the city, its primary influence faded before omnipresent ducal magnificence.

The Este changed the city in several ways. Cesare made some immediate, though moderate, physical renovations to the Castello. He brought the ancestral library, the state archives, and much of the Este art collection from Ferrara. As the new political center of Modena and the source of a powerful patronage network, the Castello now drew a steady stream of courtiers, European ambassadors, artists, and literati of wide reputation. Beyond the Castello, the d'Este family also supported extensive urban renewal projects that built or renovated noble palaces and churches, widened streets, renewed porticoes, covered canals, constructed the ducal theater, and (beginning in 1633) rebuilt the little castello into the baroque Ducal Palace.[12]

The Este also extended their authority over the Communal Palace in a process that touched the Conservators directly. Although the duke did not alter their responsibilities in the least, he considerably modified their association with the commune and its representation through imagery. In 1601, Duke Cesare insisted on moving the Conservators from their traditional Hall of State, the Sala del Fuoco, to a new deliberation chamber in the palace. Their council seats were moved to the new deliberation chamber, thus maintaining some of the traditions of old. But the decoration of the ceiling and walls of their new hall of state severed the Conservators and the commune from their traditional roots. The new ceiling incorporated an allegory of shared government between the duke and the commune, but its central image was now the Este eagle. The communal crest, the blue cross on the gold background, which had taken the center spot of the ceiling in the Sala del Fuoco, was now pushed to two corners of the ceiling. In this new arrangement, the Conservators could see only one of them from their seats, the other being behind them. The wall panels immediately underneath the ceiling did depict scenes from the life of San Geminiano, but in stark contrast to the brilliant colors of the ceiling these scenes were painted in grays and neutral tones that seemed to memorialize a distant, faded past.[13] The decoration of the new deliberation chamber attested to the reality of a new Modena that confronted the Conservators whenever they met: like the communal crest, previously located at the center of the ceiling and now placed on its periphery, the Conservators and the commune had been moved to the edges of significance in what was once considered their city.

Several years later, the duke dealt another blow to the image of the commune. For centuries, Modena had been a city of merchants and artisans. In 1612, Duke Cesare altered the constituency of the Conservators by barring merchants and artisans from serving on the council. The duke's actions reflected the general process of aristocratization that had occurred in many other Italian cities previously; in fact, from the mid-sixteenth century several Modenese families attempted to ennoble the office of Conservator, only to be outvoted each time. Earlier attempts to alter the constituency of the town council had failed as the Modenese sought to retain some of the traditions of their past. For the next two hundred years, the Conservators were elected from noble Modenese families.[14] Even though most of the Conservatorial families had already acquired noble status by 1612, this formal reconstitution of the council further severed Modena from its traditional communal character.

Ducal presence also affected civic religious ritual. The Este used ritual piety to enhance and display the honor and influence of their family. Cesare frequently heard Mass before the relics of San Geminiano in the cathedral. More important, the "duke and his court" immediately began to take the place of honor in all the major public processions, particularly those pertaining to San Geminiano. The Conservators, on the other hand, consistently took a secondary or minor role in these rituals, thus losing a significant venue for gaining honor and dignity in the public eye.[15] Equally important, since the Conservators represented the commune, when they took a secondary role in the processions, so too did the commune. The focus of the procession centered on the duke and his court rather than the Conservators, and the Duchy of Modena rather than the commune.

By Cesare's death in 1628, the Conservators had become ambivalent about the presence of the Este and the city's transformation into the capital of the duchy. On the one hand, by the end of Cesare's rule, Este presence had drawn many additional notables to the city. Urban renovation was also turning Modena into a grand city. Modena the Capital had acquired enormous prestige and honor. Now officially noble and brought into the orbit of ducal prestige and patronage, the Conservators also rose in status. These changes were exciting. On the other hand, the presence of the Este seemed to shift Modena's real center to the Castello from the main square. It also relegated the Conservators to a secondary and obscured position of authority, particularly during processions. Their traditional civic symbols found in architecture, art, and ritual, which had gained them honor and dignity in the public eye, were now mixed with or faded out by ducal images. Any status in their position gained by the Conservators came through their association with the duke, not the commune. Even though the Conservators, like town councilors throughout Italy, willingly participated in their own domestication, nonetheless both they and the commune were swallowed by the capital of the Duchy of Modena and had little to distinguish themselves within it.

Reviving the Commune During the Plague of 1630

Against this background of increasing ducal power at the expense of Conservatorial influence and the distinction of the commune, the devastating plague of 1630 came to Modena.[16] This crisis gave the Conservators the opportunity to reassert their traditional influence and authority as the guardians of the commune for the first time since 1598.

By April 1630, ducal, civic, and religious officials took steps to contain the rampant spread of the plague. The *Sanità* (Conservators commissioned as health officers) met daily in the Communal Palace to supervise relief strategies for the city.[17] All leaders in Modena joined forces to seek the aid of the saints. Whereas Modenese officials sought aid from San Geminiano or the universal plague saints (San Rocco and San Sebastiano), the new duke, Francesco I d'Este,[18] sought help from the saints and relics important to other towns in his duchy. In June, for example, he brought the relics of two saints to Modena from Nonantola, a provincial city in his duchy. The bishop of Modena, carrying Modena's own prized relics of the Holy Cross and the arm of San Geminiano, met the duke, his court, and the holy relics from Nonantola. Joined by clergy and confraternities, the bishop carried the relics under a *baldachin* while the Modenese processed solemnly to the cathedral for a special Mass to end the plague.[19] Despite the great piety of the Modenese, neither this nor other strategies worked; the daily mortality rate continued to rise. In July, as measure after measure failed, Duke Francesco and most of his court fled the city to a villa outside Reggio Emilia, where they remained for the duration of the plague. The Conservators stayed in Modena to care for the city by themselves.

During the duke's absence, the influence and authority of the Conser-

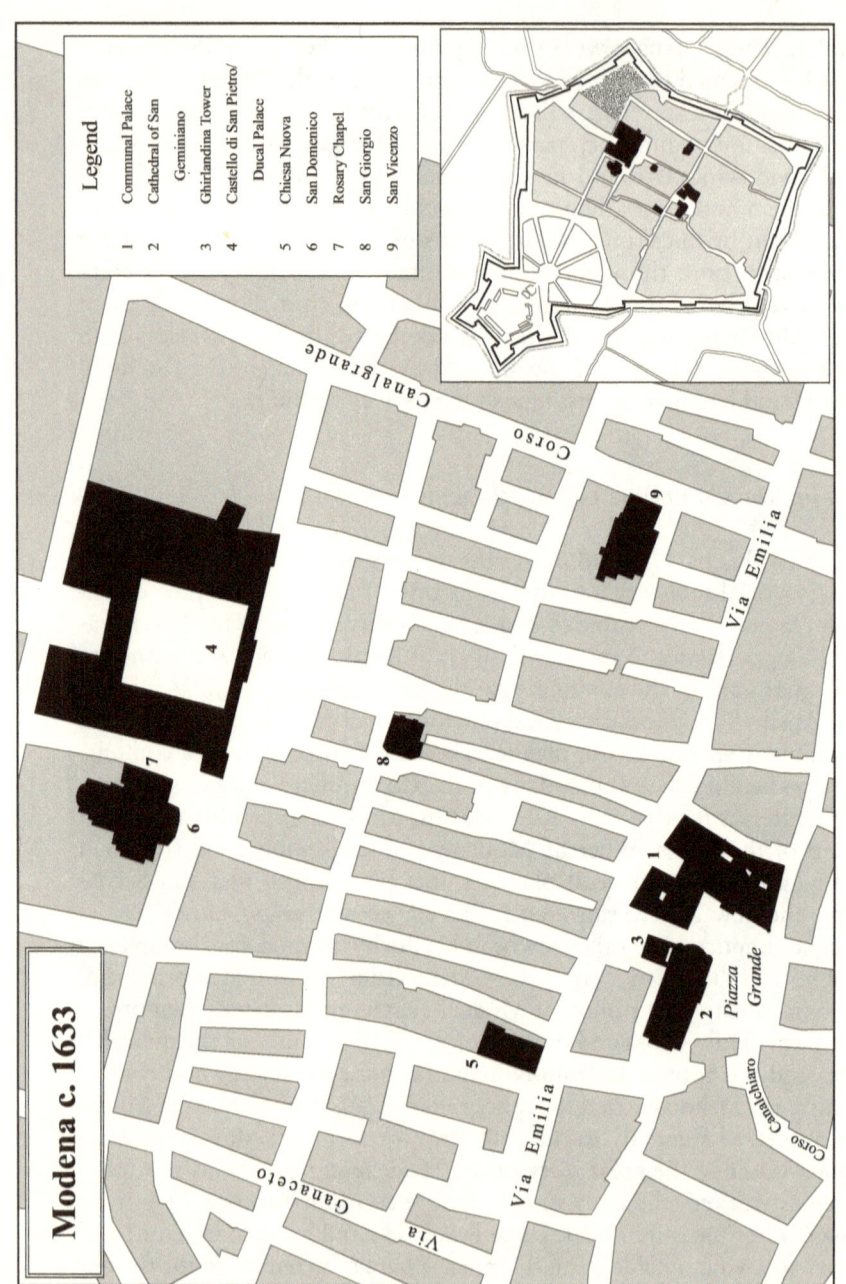

Map 15.1 Modena circa 1633

vators and the commune reverted to their pre-1598 position of centrality in Modena. In September, as the plague claimed more than 150 lives each day, in desperation the Conservators planned a new strategy on the basis of the duke's suggestion that Modena be placed under the protection of the miraculous Madonna of the Ghiara in Reggio, whose cult was famous in his duchy. They decided to make a public vow to build a permanent monument "to memorialize for posterity the grace . . . received from this supreme protectress."[20] On November 1, All Saints Day, while the duke was still outside Reggio, the Conservators, on behalf of the commune, invoked the protection of the Madonna of Reggio during the Offertory of a Mass celebrated in the cathedral by the bishop and vowed to construct a church "from its foundations" at the city's expense.[21]

The Conservators' vow soon proved to be effective. Less than two weeks later, on November 13, no one died in the city for the first time in months. The following day, citizens throughout Modena celebrated by singing the Te Deum Laudamus (a hymn of praise to God) and adoring the Blessed Sacrament. The bishop celebrated an impressive Mass before the relics of San Geminiano, attended by the Conservators and including all the health commissioners.[22] From that day, the plague's force diminished, until it stopped completely in early 1631. Its end was generally credited to the intercession of the Madonna of the Ghiara of Reggio, San Geminiano, and the vow made by the Conservators on behalf of the commune—no thanks to the duke, who remained in isolation outside Reggio.[23] This was the first time since 1598 that the Conservators had come before the public eye *without the duke*, in a crucial role for the preservation of the commune. Acting on behalf of the commune, they had successfully brought the plague to an end by invoking the aid of the saints.

Almost immediately, the Conservators realized that fulfilling their vow to the Madonna of Reggio would not be easy. For three years, Duke Francesco rejected their plans to build a new church, using the excuse that it was too costly, even though the Conservators soon secured funding for it from private donations. He preferred raising a small shrine to the Madonna of Reggio in a church heavily patronized by his family, perhaps San Vicenzo or San Giorgio.[24] The duke's resistance and his own preferences indicate that he wanted control over the foundation of the new shrine—after all, the original idea to seek help from the Madonna of Reggio had been his.

Finally, in December 1633, after three years of disagreement, the duke approved the plans for the new church, commonly known as the *Chiesa Nuova* (New Church; Fig. 15.1). His approval came only after the Conservators had reluctantly agreed that their new church be staffed by the congregation of San Borromeo, a sodality new to Modena and strongly supported by the Este. Not only was the administration of the church linked to the duke rather than the commune but the central image of the Chiesa Nuova was not communal, tied instead to Reggio, another city in the Duchy of Modena. Indeed, San Geminiano, patron of Modena, was originally not included in the iconography of the Chiesa Nuova.[25] By the time the first stone was laid in 1634, the Conservators had lost much of their initial connection to the church, while the duke controlled much of its architecture, art, and administration. Once again, ducal display and influence overshadowed the Conservators and the commune.

New Ritual and Art for the Commune in Ducal Modena

Well before the first stone was laid for the Chiesa Nuova in 1634, the Conservators grew frustrated by the duke's resistance to their attempts to fulfill their vow. Against this background of strained negotiation over the Chiesa Nuova, the Conservators embarked on a new course of action that would soon help them give renewed meaning to their office and to the commune: their creation of a completely new civic religious ritual and image, one completely independent of the duke and the duchy, unlike the establishment of the Chiesa Nuova, which combined civic and ducal symbols. They thereby enacted the commune—that is, they brought it into being and gave it much-needed definition against the capital and duchy.

The communal records state that in March 1633 the Conservators, "with one voice," proclaimed the Madonna of the Rosary as the new coprotectress of Modena with San Geminiano. They vowed to hold a procession annually to the Chapel of the Rosary in San Domenico, hear a Mass, and make an offering to the Virgin.[26] The Conservators also commissioned Ludovico Lana, Modena's most prominent painter (and one rarely employed by the Este), to paint a new communal banner for the procession (Figure 15.2). Painted on silk and adorned with the communal crest, the banner depicted, as commissioned, "Saint Mary Virgin of the Rosary, San Geminiano, and the city of Modena, and she was to bless the city." Lana clearly identified Modena in the banner by the Ghirlandina tower rising above the other buildings in the cityscape. The communal documents further stipulated that the banner permanently remain in the care of the Conservators, kept in their deliberation chamber in the communal palace.[27] No one but the Conservators could use the banner, and then only in the case of a public emergency, should they again need

Remaking the Commune in Ducal Modena 215

Figure 15.1 The Madonna of the Rosary, San Geminiano, and the City of Modena by Ludovico Lana. (Museo d'Arte Medievale e Moderna, Modena.)

to invoke, on behalf of the commune, the aid of the Virgin, San Geminiano, and other saints.

On Sunday the eighth of May (the month dedicated to the Virgin), the Conservators made their procession from the Communal Palace to the Rosary Chapel in the church of San Domenico. Accompanied by a trumpet fanfare, representatives of Modena's religious orders, clergy, confraternities, "good men and women," the entire Confraternity of the Rosary, the bishop, and the Conservators (who carried their communal banner) led the procession to San Domenico.[28] Inside the crowded church, the Conservators carefully placed their banner to the side of the altar in the Rosary Chapel. During the Offertory of the Mass, they rendered their annual offering of candles for the chapel and several bouquets of roses to honor the Virgin. After the Mass, they processed back to the Palazzo Comunale and replaced the banner in their deliberation chamber. This procession then became an annual communal ritual.[29]

The documents do not mention that the duke and his court appeared at this civic event. Certainly, if they were there, their role was minor or nonexistent (since the chronicler who recorded the event always noted ducal presence in other rituals). The absence of the duke; the prominence of the Conservators in the procession and during the Mass; and the care they took to guard their new symbol of authority, the communal banner, all point to the civic nature of this new ritual and image.

The new banner of the Madonna of the Rosary and San Geminiano, and the new ritual procession to San Domenico reestablished the centrality of the commune and the Conservators' traditional role as the guardians of the commune. The banner was undeniably communal, with the Modenese coat of arms and the images of San Geminiano and the city. The Conservators reserved for themselves the sole right to use the banner since it was the fundamental instrument in invoking San Geminiano's protection and that of the Virgin. Because the banner was portable, it was not bound to a particular location. If the duke should again decide to move or abolish their meeting chamber, the Conservators could take their banner with them and not worry about his altering its image, as he had the decoration in their new Hall of State.

The ritual procession communicated many important messages about the Conservators and the commune to those who viewed it. Since the duke and his court were not part of the procession, the presence of the Conservators, Modena's religious organizations, and the Modenese citizens clearly enacted Modena the Commune, not Modena the Capital. In this procession, there were no mixed messages about the importance and honor of the commune, as when the duke participated in the other rituals. As leaders of the procession, the Conservators clearly represented the commune before the sacred, and by invoking the continued protection of the Virgin of the Rosary and San Geminiano they took precautions against *future* emergencies, potentially as malignant as the plague of 1630 had been. This ritual established and proclaimed an exclusive bond among the commune; its temporal guardians, the Conservators; and its spiritual patrons, the Virgin and San Geminiano.

The proximity of the new ritual in San Domenico to the ducal castello—soon to be renovated into the magnificent Ducal Palace—was also significant for redefining the commune. The Este considered San Domenico, located at the immediate west of the Castello, to be their court church and heavily patronized it. The Rosary Chapel was in the east transept of the church and thus at the closest possible point to the

Castello.³⁰ By processing to the Rosary Chapel, the Conservators penetrated ducal space, not as supplicants but as leaders of the commune. Symbolically through this ritual experience, Modena the Commune, represented by the Conservators, now existed side by side with, yet separately from, Modena the Capital.

The Conservators' creation of a purely civic ritual should not be interpreted necessarily as an indication of conflict with the duke. Like their counterparts across the Italian peninsula, the Conservators embraced their new ennobled status and their reinforced role as supplicants to the duke. Yet although noble, they were also concerned about the potential demise of the commune and their traditional place in it, more than about Este power, the construction of Modena the Capital, and the strength of the duchy. They finally made coexistence of the commune and capital possible through ritual and artistic imagery. Since the Conservators knew how to read and interpret ritual and art, they realized that the processions that featured the duchy *and* the commune did not satisfy the need for a civic ritual that presented the Conservators and the commune alone. That the duke did not coopt the procession to the Rosary Chapel may indicate that he, too, recognized that need within his capital. The Conservators successfully mixed the traditional symbols of the communal crest, San Geminiano, and the cityscape of Modena with a contemporary symbol of the Madonna of the Rosary to enact the commune before the Modenese. Dipping back into the past for symbols that conveyed communal meaning, the Conservators preserved the future of the commune within the new capital of the duchy.

The case of Modena highlights for us the process whereby one commune survived in symbolic form alongside the capital in early modern Italy. As we have seen, the Este suddenly transferred their power base to the city and transformed it rapidly into a baroque capital. These changes excited the Modenese—the Este built up the once-quiet and unassuming little Emilian town into the center of the duchy, and an elegant, if modest, European capital. The Modenese were proud of their new city. But these changes did not materialize without considerable cost: the initial overshadowing of traditions and symbols dear to the Modenese.

If Modena was unique in that it suddenly became a capital city in the late sixteenth century, it was not unique in the upheaval it experienced; nor, as some studies have indicated, was it alone in its preservation of the commune.³¹ The rise of ducal power and the growth of the territorial state transformed cities across Italy during the sixteenth and seventeenth centuries. The Medici in ducal and grand-ducal Florence and Siena; the Spanish in Milan; the Doria in Genoa; and the papacy in Rome, Bologna, and finally Ferrara are a few of the regimes that physically and symbolically reconstructed their seat of power and placed the distinct mark of their rule in cities throughout their dominion. Similar to the Este in Modena, these rulers displayed their power and magnificence through architecture, art, and ritual. Perhaps, as in Modena, the encroachment of the territorial state created the need for cities in the many other Italies to define their communes within it. Further research may confirm that civil magistrates throughout Italy resolved the need for communal preservation in a fashion similar to Modena's and may indicate that communal traditions survived well into the early modern period, not just in republics such as Venice. Future studies focusing on the survival of the commune into the seventeenth and eighteenth centuries may also prove that rather than being caught in social and political stagnation and decay, civil magistrates throughout Italy may have been, as in Modena after its period of adjustment, leaders in communal resilience, adaptability, and reform.

CHAPTER SIXTEEN

The Spanish Foundations of Late Renaissance and Baroque Rome

Thomas Dandelet

In 1556, King Philip II of Spain turned to one of Iberia's most accomplished theologians, the Dominican Melchor Cano, for counsel and a philosophical rationale to justify the war he was waging against Pope Paul IV. The Caraffa war (1556–57) held the same threat of disaster for Philip II and Paul IV as the war that led to the infamous sack of 1527 had for Charles V and Pope Clement VII. Subsequently, the Catholic king was anxious to have one of his best theologians' opinions on his rights and risks vis-à-vis the papacy in the war.

In a generally balanced and realistic appraisal of the situation, Cano first pointed out the superior religious authority of the pope and the king's obligation to submit to him on spiritual matters. At the same time, he argued that the king had the right to defend his realms as a temporal ruler. Moreover, Cano pointed out that in economic matters the Spanish monarchy was far more powerful, since the papacy depended upon Spain for its very bread and water.[1]

Cano's strong final claim, a certain level of patriotic rhetoric notwithstanding, was rooted in one of the fundamental, but unrecognized, realities of papal Rome in the late Renaissance and Baroque period: it was the Spanish Empire that provided many of the critical economic foundations for developing the city in its most dynamic period of growth since antiquity. Rather than being the destructive and "barbaric" force in Italy fashioned by many contemporary and modern Italian historians, from Francesco Guicciardini to Benedetto Croce, the history of Rome in the late sixteenth and seventeenth century suggests a far different and more positive picture of the influence of Spain in Rome and Italy in this period. Indeed, this chapter argues there is a substantial amount of archival evidence suggesting that Spanish economic support on a variety of levels was a critical factor that allowed the dramatic urban development of Catholic Reformation Rome. Churches and palaces, cardinals and courtiers, artists and musicians, hospitals and convents; these institutions and individuals and many others benefited from a large flow of Spanish revenue into the city, which played a fundamental role in transforming Rome into what was arguably seventeenth-century Europe's most dramatic and impressive urban stage.

At the same time, the papacy was also a critical economic partner of the Spanish monarchy in its role as the arbiter of ecclesiastical finance and taxation in the realms of the Catholic king. In short, the king relied on the papacy to approve and thereby legitimize a variety of financial concessions and taxes from the Spanish church that were critical for the finances of the Spanish crown. Spanish absolutism and papal absolutism thus went hand in hand and bolstered one another financially to an extent that has typically been overlooked or altogether unrecognized.

This chapter analyzes the developments and characteristics of the economic relationship between the papacy and the Spanish Empire between roughly 1555 and 1645. Typically known as the period of the Spanish preponderance, this century offers a good chronological frame for viewing the economic impact of the Spanish Empire on the papacy in a dynamic period of growth for both powers. Moreover, the argument presented here points to new avenues of interpretation and research for other areas of Italy as well. It is a view that depicts the Spaniards as beneficent, if demanding, patrons who played a critical and positive role in the economy and urban development of Baroque Italy.

Specifically, this chapter analyzes the various ways in which Spanish revenues flowed to the papal court and came to constitute a major segment of the economy. This money and aid came in the form of large ecclesiastical pensions, benefices, and other church offices for cardinals, curia members, and Roman nobles. So too, many smaller church benefices, pensions, and financial concessions from the Spanish church yielded income for a substantial percentage of the Roman population and fueled the urban economy. At the same time, Spanish military support subsidized papal military spending, and grain from Spanish provinces subsidized the Roman food supply.

In short, the king of Spain was one of the most powerful patrons of Rome, and indeed of all of Italy. It is this fact that is virtually invisible in much of the existing literature, but it is an essential one in seriously rethinking Italy in the early modern period. Moreover, the role that the Spanish monarchs played in Rome was a very traditional one that Christian emperors and monarchs had been playing for centuries. It thus brought structural continuity to the medieval period, but also a shift in the international topography of power. The Spanish monarchs became masters at playing Roman patrons, in a role that went back to Constantine, but it was a role that had never been played by Iberian princes before. Instead of French or German princes, it was now the Spanish monarch's turn to dominate much of Italy and Rome. It is important to remember that the Spanish monarch's role as both King of Naples and Duke of Milan shaped Spanish relations with Rome, since the city and Papal State were quite literally in the middle of Spanish-ruled territories. Spanish soldiers, statesmen, and many others moved with great frequency between the two kingdoms via Rome, and the Spanish monarchs increasingly thought of the city and state virtually as a part of their Italian kingdoms.

This was stated most clearly by Charles V in an instructional letter, or political testament, written to his son, Philip II, sometime between 1545 and his death in 1558. Now preserved in Philip II's library in El Escorial, an Italian version of the letter reveals Charles V's bold claim that "the states of the church are in the center of Italy, but [they are] surrounded by ours in such a way that one can say that they form one kingdom."[2]

The idea that the Papal States were a de facto part of the Spanish kingdoms of Italy, where soldiers could be recruited, funding for war raised, and ports freely used for Spanish galleys, was most clearly established and stated by Charles V. It was, quite possibly, the most important contribution of the emperor to future Spanish political policy and mentality toward Rome. Regardless of the continuing sovereignty of the pope as prince of the Papal State, and Spanish official recognition of papal rule, the real political attitude and practice toward Rome and the papacy was one of subjugation and assimilation into the Spanish Italian kingdoms. It was a new stage in the Spanish program toward Rome, a stage of more overt domination.

The Politics of Spanish Financial Support

Not surprisingly, the growth of Spanish economic aid to the papacy in this period was intimately tied to the political relationship between the Spanish monarchy and the papacy. With the defeat of Paul IV in the Caraffa war of 1557, the Spanish empire and Philip II began a long period of domination in Rome that would not be seriously challenged until the papacy of Urban VIII (1623–44). For more than sixty years, then, the Spanish monarchs became the de facto military protector of the city and Papal State and Rome's most powerful foreign financial patron. Rome in that period developed long and deep structural dependence on the Spanish Empire in the realms of military, economic, and material assistance, but it also benefited greatly from Spanish patronage. At the same time, the Spanish monarchy developed ever deeper reliance on ecclesiastical revenues to shore up its shaky finances. Indeed, these were the basic dynamics that shaped political relations between the papacy and Spanish monarchy over most of the next century.

The ritualization of Spanish-papal cooperation was couched in traditional feudal language and embodied in presentation of the annual feudal dues that the Spanish paid to the papacy for the fief of Naples. These dues, paid in some form from the time of the Angevin rulers in the thirteenth century, included the symbolic gift of a white Neapolitan horse, known as the *chinea*, for the papal stable. Indicative of the symbolic importance of the feudal dues was the fact that immediately after the defeat of Paul IV, the Duke of Alba wanted to present the chinea and dues of roughly seven thousand *scudi* to the pope as a sign of Spanish feudal and filial obedience.[3] Paul IV refused the offer, since it actually served to display the Spaniards as the legitimate rulers in Naples; but all of his successors in the next sixty-five years would accept the chinea and the seven thousand scudi.[4]

Far more important than these small feudal dues was the military protection provided by the Spanish or the Papal State in their common fight against the Ottoman Empire. Reports in 1560 warned of preparation in Istanbul of a large Turkish fleet[5]; thus it became an urgent matter to do likewise in Italy. Of the three powers with a long coastline to protect—Venice, Spain, and the Papal State—the Papal State was clearly the weakest power, with no serious fleet to speak of. It was no surprise, then, that the pope turned to Spain as the wealthiest of the Italian powers for help. He was also willing to grant papal favors in return.

Such was the case already in 1560, when Pius IV granted to Philip a renewal of the *subsidio*, a variable tax on ecclesiastical rents, ostensibly to aid in the fight against the Barbary pirates. At the same time came a six-year renewal of the *cruzada*, the tax granted to many previous Spanish monarchs to subsidize the fight against the Moors in Spain. This grant gained new life with the Ottoman threat.[6] In 1567, a third tax on the clergy, the *excusado*, which took in two hundred thousand to four hundred thousand ducats annually, was granted to help pay for the war in Flanders.[7] By 1571, the subsidio was reported to be worth two hundred thousand ducats per year, and the cruzada was worth more than one million ducats during a three-year period.[8] These three taxes, known as the three *gracias*, became a constant and expected part of the king's military budget throughout the period, but they remained the pope's prerogative and his most powerful bargaining chip in negotiations with the monarch.

The pope, for his part, had an interest in the cruzada beyond military concerns. He stipulated in his renewal of the tax that twenty thousand ducats of it would be paid to the papacy every year for building St. Peter's.[9] This was one early example of the financial give-and-take between king and pope that characterized the future pattern of their negotiations. Philip II has often been depicted by pro-papal historians, such as Pastor, as trying to ravage the church of anything he could get against the pope's resistance. But a close look at papal policy clearly shows that the king and pope often acted in collusion to gain access to the rich revenues of the Spanish church.

This was anything but unusual, given the great wealth that various Spanish dioceses, monasteries, and military orders had accumulated over the centuries, and the deep stake the monarchy had in the church, particularly through the *patronato real*.[10] According to a report of 1567 from the papal nuncio in Spain, for instance, total ecclesiastical rents in the kingdoms of Castile and Leon totaled nine million ducats annually.[11] By 1630, the rents had increased to more than twelve million annually.[12] These sums were equal to the king's share of New World treasure over one of the best five-year periods of the late sixteenth century.[13] Subsequently, the constantly indebted Spanish monarchs had come to rely on taxing ecclesiastical revenues to help finance their expensive military ventures, taxes for which they needed papal approval.

The papacy, for its part, made a point of keeping itself well informed about Spanish church revenues.[14] The fact that the money coming into Rome from France, Germany, and England had either completely vanished or was seriously declining by the mid-sixteenth century, largely because of the Reformation, made papal income from the churches under the jurisdiction of the Spanish monarchs doubly important. Indeed, of all the European powers, the Spanish monarchy allowed the papacy the greatest degree of financial concessions and control over the churches in their realms. This was well understood by contemporaries such as the Spanish Cardinal Antonio Zapata (1550–1635). In a secret letter to the king from Rome in 1607, he noted that the civil wars in Spain in the fifteenth century had kept the Spanish monarchs, unlike their French and German counterparts, from getting more control over church finances. Moreover, in the sixteenth century the growing political interests of the monarchs in Italy required smooth relations with the papacy. To avoid conflict, the monarchs subsequently let stand traditional financial privileges that allowed the papacy to collect substantial income from the Spanish church.[15]

Part of this income came from the papal right to collect a share of Spanish ecclesiastical revenue during times of episcopal vacancy,[16] a sum reported to be three hundred thousand *escudo*s in 1560, when Monsignor Francesco Aragonia was sent to Spain as the papal collector.[17] Much of this money was already committed to other individuals, and the collector himself used a substantial quantity for his expenses. Nonetheless, registers for the period from 1589 to 1660 show that the pope's coffers regularly received forty thousand to sixty-five thousand escudos per year from vacancies in the churches of Castile and Aragon, fifteen thousand from the churches of Naples, and five thousand from the churches of Portugal.[18]

Together with this consistent source of Spanish revenue, the pope and his court also received other income from the Spanish church in the form of rich benefices controlled and granted by the king. This was already apparent in 1562, when Philip II gave the pope's nephews and Cardinal Borromeo a combined sum of fifteen thousand ducats from the revenues of the cathedral of Toledo.[19] Moreover, in the same year it was reported in Rome that "many Cardinals and Italian prelates that were found at the court" in Spain were seeking money from the king.[20] Indeed, the Spanish monarch was granting between thirty thousand and seventy-five thousand ducats annually to the Spanish faction of cardinals in Rome between 1560 and 1625.

Warm relations with Rome continued with the election of Pius V in 1565, and he quickly granted another five-year extension of the subsidio, worth four hundred thousand gold ducats, to the king.[21] Clearly, the pope favored the Spanish king and his subjects in the realms of international politics and ecclesiastical affairs, and in the city of Rome itself. There were many good motives for the pope to do so, since he believed from early on in his reign, as had Pius IV, that the stability of the Mediterranean region, including his own realms, depended heavily on Philip II.

Cooperation between the two powers grew throughout the 1560s and 1570s, and in 1571 the pope granted a five-year renewal of the cruzada, worth an estimated 334,000 ducats per year.[22] The pope's desire to form a Holy League against the Turkish threat and his dependence on Spain as the backbone of such an alliance was the immediate rationale for the renewal of the cruzada. When Pius gave preliminary approval to this grant in August 1570, he required that the king use part of the money to make certain contributions to the proposed alliance: four hundred ships of various sizes, ten thousand infantry, five thousand cavalry, and grain for the fleet.[23] Although this did not turn out to be the exact configuration of the Spanish contribution to the league, Philip II did provide the majority of ships, men, and food for the alliance, which was formally announced less than six months after the *cruzada* was renewed.[24]

So began the formal military alliance between the papacy and Spanish monarchy that would continue in one fashion or another for the next fifty years. More than any other single event or agreement, the league solidified the new relationship between Spain and the papacy. It demonstrated to both the people of Rome and the international community the central position of Spain in the "new world order" of the late-sixteenth-century Mediterranean world.

This was doubly true after the famous victory at Lepanto in October of 1571. According to the first dispatch that the Spanish Ambassador Zúñiga sent to the king after the victory, the pope had celebrated a *Te Deum* in St. Peter's immediately upon receiving the news. He later talked to the ambassadors, where he let it be known that "his happiness is great and that he knows that the *republica cristiana* would not have been able to enjoy this [victory] but through the intervention of the king."[25]

The battle at Lepanto not only effectively underlined the naval supremacy of the Spanish fleet—it comprised more than 50 percent of all ships and men of the combined fleet—but also pointed out the relatively small military contribution of the papal forces: the pope was only required to provide twelve ships, three thousand soldiers, and 270 cavalry for the expedition.[26] Although not completely inconsequential, the papal forces were certainly not comparable to the Spanish and Venetian fleets.

This was a basic military reality that was never far in the background when other papal-Spanish matters were negotiated. Philip II sought to neutralize and generally reduce the papacy to a weak and subservient military ally after the war with Paul IV. By 1572, he had succeeded masterfully. Pope Gregory XIII, for his part, was well aware of this dependency, especially after Venice reached a separate treaty with Sultan Selim shortly after Lepanto, which led to formal dissolution of the league. In 1574, for instance, the pope instructed his special envoy to beseech Philip II to renew the league, with these words:

Our Lord God, having preserved Your Majesty with such power together with Christian piety, almost, one can say, as the only sustenance of our holy church and of the Catholic faith; his Holiness has desired to communicate to you his holy thoughts regarding all of the help that your majesty owes to God for the many graces and gifts that he has given you.[27]

With this preface, the pope asked Philip to maintain a large fleet in Italy under the command of Don Juan, with an amount of ships, money, and men equal to that of the previous alliance.

The greatest benefit of Spanish military assistance, and possibly most important for the long-term development and domestic stability of Rome and the papal states in this period, was the financial advantage that the papacy gained from not having to support a large military force. The Spanish king went into repeated bankruptcy trying to defend and expand his empire, but the papacy after the pontificate of Paul IV spent a comparatively small percentage of the budget on its military forces, until Urban VIII's disastrous war of Castro.[28] Papal expenses for the Lepanto expedition, for instance, were 140,000 scudi, or roughly 15 percent of the papal income; generally, from 1560 to 1620 the total military budget never exceeded 20 percent of the total annual budget, which doubled in this period to approximately two million scudi. This was in comparison to the 50–60 percent of the papal budget that commonly went for military expenses in the fourteenth and fifteenth centuries, and the enormous costs of Paul IV's war with Spain, which cost two or three times the annual papal income from 1555 to 1557.[29] In short, Spanish military spending and protection of the Papal State saved the papacy tens of millions of ducats between 1559 and 1630.

Spanish Pensions and Subsidies in the Papal Court

Besides this indirect military subsidy, Rome in the age of Gregory XIII continued to benefit more directly from Spanish money that flowed into the city in a variety of forms for cardinals, courtiers, Spanish agents, and the papal family. The income, or papal share, of the "spoils" from Spanish vacancies, most noticeably, brought into the papal coffers a reported fifty thousand scudi in 1577.[30] This appears to have been the average payment made to Rome by the office of the "collector" during the 1570s and 1580s, a period lacking detailed papal registers. We know more specifically from the papal economic registers starting in 1589 that the Spanish contribution from vacancies was equal or greater in the following decades. In 1589, for example, we find entries that put the contribution from the Spanish realms at these levels: "Dalla Colletoria di Spagna—50,000; Dalla Colletoria di Portugallo—4,000; Da Cleri del Regno di Napoli—15,090; Da Su Maesta Cattolica per il Censo del Regno di Napoli, 8,251."[31] This 77,000 scudi, which included the chinea, comprised roughly 5 percent of recorded papal income of 1,546,279 scudi and was the sixth largest item on the papal register, following taxes from other parts of the papal states.

Besides this direct income from realms of the Catholic king, others in the papal court benefited from the growing patronage of Philip II throughout the 1570s and 1580s. Among the larger pensions granted were those from the revenues of Toledo in 1577: in ducats, Cardinals San Sisto and Madruccio received four thousand; Vastavallano three thousand; Aragona and Orsini twenty-five hundred; and Maffeo, Mont'Albano, Colonna, Delfino, Comillino, Gambara, and Napoli one thousand each.[32] Early in 1578, Cardinal Alessandrino was given a monastery in Sicily with four thousand ducats of pension,[33] and one of the auditors of the Rota was given fourteen thousand ducats from the bishopric of Lerida in 1579.[34]

Large-scale Spanish gifts also contributed substantially to the papal treasury without being recorded in the registers. In 1578, after the pope had sent Pedro Deza his cardinal's hat, the king sent the same Roman envoy who had delivered the hat back to the pope with a gift of seven thousand ducats, together with a necklace worth seven hundred ducats and a jewel worth some thousands.[35] A year later the papal envoy, Giovanni Batta, after delivering another cardinal's hat to Quiroga, the archbishop of Toledo, was given two thousand ducats for himself, a pension of five hundred from a church in Sicily, and a reported fifty thousand ducats' worth of jewels for the pope.[36] Combined with the many pensions and other smaller gifts and commissions from Spain, these larger gifts made it clear that the Catholic king's treasure chest was indeed an important part of the courtly society and economy of Rome in the late sixteenth and early seventeenth century.

In addition to direct financial contributions and military aid, beginning in the 1580s the pope was increasingly dependent upon the realms of the Spanish monarch for another important financial ingredient of internal stability, namely, the grain needed to supplement decreasing production and the increasing frequency of bad harvests in the Papal State.[37] The population of Rome, in particular, which had been growing rapidly over the past two decades, was easily upset by food shortage. Already in 1582, Gregory XIII had imported more than four thousand *rubbi* of grain from Sicily to help feed the city.[38] Late in 1585, Sixtus V again asked the king for increased imports of roughly seven thousand rubbi, and in 1586 almost three thousand rubbi were sent.[39] In fact, over the fifty-year period between 1582 and 1632 the Papal State depended on grain imports from Spanish territories (Sicily, Naples, Sardinia, and Spain itself) with ever greater frequency.

During the reign of Clement VIII (1592–1605), other forms of financial exchange continued between the courts of Rome and Madrid. In 1593, the pope granted Philip II two hundred thousand ducats from vacant benefices of the Order of Santiago.[40] In that same year, he also granted the king the right to new financial concessions annually from the clergy of Catalonia, who were now required to pay the king two fifths of the *decima*.[41] In Rome, various cardinals received substantial pensions from Spanish realms, including five thousand ducats to Cardinal Terranuova from a monastery in Sicily,[42] two thousand to Cardinal Farnese, six thousand to Cardinal Deza,[43] three thousand to Cardinal Sfondrato,[44] and one thousand each to the cardinal nephews of the pope.[45]

Moreover, after the death of Philip II in 1598 and the ascendancy of Philip III, reinvestiture of the fiefs of Naples and Sicily underlined the financial relationship. Clement VIII and a congregation of cardinals had decreed in the summer of 1599 that each new king of Spain was required to be reinvested by the pope with the rights of the *feudo*. Not surprisingly, a payment was also included in the act of investiture; the Duke of Sessa skillfully negotiated the sum of one hundred thousand scudi as the new king's initial feudal dues.[46] With both sides agreeing amicably to these terms, the Duke of Sessa took advantage of the event to stage a large procession from the Piazza Navona to Monte Cavallo, where the congregation of cardinals and pope received him in October. According to Roman reports, he was accompanied by "100 coaches and all of the princes, barons and nobility of Rome" to render formal homage and fidelity in the name of Philip III. Only the French protested.[47]

The procession publicly reaffirmed and presented once again to the city of Rome the close relationship between pope and king and made it clear to everyone present that the Spaniards still dominated the city. Although Philip III came to power owing millions of ducats, his many possessions still produced great wealth; in the case of Naples and Sicily, it was a wealth that benefited Rome in a variety of ways. The viceroys of these kingdoms, of course, sometimes complained that their economy was already hard pressed, but this kept neither pope nor king from using these territories for their own designs.

This was also the case with church lands in the Iberian kingdoms. Specifically, after the last bankruptcy of 1596, Philip II pressured the pope to allow him and his son to take the income from the major offices of the three military orders of Alcantara, Calatrava, and Santiago to pay the large royal debt. By 1602, Philip III could write to the pope with the news that he had paid off the large sum of six million gold ducats of debt with the help of this concession.[48]

Although there was no direct benefit to the papacy from this favor, such was not the case when Clement allowed the bishopric of Zaragoza to be secularized or subsumed into the royal patronato in 1600. This allowed the king the right of appointment for the canons of the church and gave him direct control over its income. To expedite the paperwork for this process, twenty-five thousand ducats were sent to Rome.[49]

The mutually beneficial financial exchange continued during the reign of Paul V (1605–23), who renewed the subsidio, excusado, and cruzada in June 1605.[50] Philip III sent many pensions to Rome, including one for the pope's nephew of four thousand ducats in that same year.[51] The Spanish viceroy in Sicily also shipped more than ten thousand rubbi of grain to Rome, since the Papal State had suffered yet another bad harvest and shortage in 1605.[52] The Sicilian grain was used to good advantage by the Spanish ambassador in Rome, and when the pope ordered his nephew, Cardinal Borghese, to attend to the needs of the poor in Rome in the summer of 1606, the ambassador rode with him for two days throughout the city helping distribute bread.[53] Acknowledging all of this help, the pope wrote the king a warm letter of thanks.[54]

Throughout the pontificate of Paul V, the Spanish-papal military alliance continued; in 1617, the two powers agreed to join their fleets to defend the Italian coasts, and the pope agreed to use the papal share of vacancy revenues collected in Naples, twenty thousand ducats, to build papal galleys that joined the Spanish fleet.[55] After the 1617 agreement, the pope wrote Philip III a letter thanking him for the peace of Italy and "assuring Your Majesty of the paternal affection and care that we bear towards you, and of the desire that we have for your every happiness."[56]

In that same year, the pope gave the king a more tangible sign of his affection in the form of renewal of the three gracias for five years; generally, the pope continued to cooperate with royal requests to secure more revenues from the church in Spain.[57] In 1618, most noticeably, Paul V granted the king the right to raise eighteen million ducats from the *estado ecclesiastico* in the form of increased taxes to help the monarch pay off his debts.[58] This last act was done under pressure from Madrid and reportedly left the pope "displeased" because it upset the Spanish clergy and compelled them to go before the secular courts to contest the ruling. Yet it was another example of the give-and-take between monarch and pope that may have alienated the ruled but aided the rulers. The pope, briefly stated, could not afford a bankrupt Spanish monarchy since his own economy was dependent upon that of Spain. He was subsequently willing to grant ecclesiastical concessions at the cost of the church in Spanish realms.

At the same time, the papal court was itself the continued beneficiary of the traditional Spanish revenues that came to Rome: from the papal collectors in Spanish realms, roughly seventy thousand scudi annually during the pontificate of Paul V[59]; from the many pensions that came to the cardinals, as much as sixty thousand ducats per year[60]; and from the office of the coadjutor in Rome, which reserved the right to distribute many lesser Spanish benefices, at least twenty thousand ducats, which the pope often granted to members of the papal household.[61]

Spanish Ecclesiastical Income and the Local Roman Economy

Besides these regular and direct revenues, moreover, another large flow of Spanish ecclesiastical income came into the Roman economy in the form of smaller ecclesiastical pensions for thousands of Spanish and Italian residents of Rome. These constituted an often-hidden, but critical, part of the Baroque city, and one last major economic piece of the Roman puzzle.

Throughout the sixteenth and early seventeenth centuries, the papacy had claimed and been granted the right to distribute thousands of smaller Spanish benefices and pensions through the curial office of the datary. By the late 1620s, economically hard-pressed Spanish clergy were increasingly indignant when they saw revenues from their depressed lands being spent on an ever more splendid and opulent Rome. This reached a new height in 1633, when Domingo Pimentel, the Bishop of Cordoba, went to Rome as a representative of the Spanish clergy to protest the "offenses committed in that court against the natives of Spain."[62] In a lengthy printed treatise, the Spanish bishop complained that it was reprehensible that bishops in Spain should send their revenues to those of Rome whom he described as "so much richer as they show through their luxury, opulence, palaces, and gardens." How much less, he continued, did the Spanish church owe to the many courtiers, architects, musicians, and many other secular people who were supported by Spanish pensions?[63]

This complaint represented a crescendo of criticism that had been building for decades from Spanish clerics who resided in Iberia. As the economic depression of the early seventeenth century deepened, so too did resentment against Rome. But in a response to this criticism, a Spanish lawyer and cleric living in Rome, Doctor Juan Pablo Frances, wrote to the king to defend the practice. He argued that although it was true roughly eight hundred thousand escudos from Spain came into Rome every year in the form of smaller ecclesiastical pensions and incomes, it was also true that this income supported as many as four thousand Spaniards who were in Rome seeking offices, and another four thousand who were already working in Rome in cardinals' households, churches, monasteries, and various parts of the papal bureaucracy.[64] The implication was that this money clearly was well spent since it supported an important Spanish faction or base in the papal court that represented broader Spanish interests.[65]

Here, then, was one of the most important Spanish financial contributions to the Roman economy, bringing the total annual sum to roughly one million ducats. In 1631, a member of a royal council appointed to evaluate financial issues with Rome estimated that 1.5 million ducats were paid to Rome. Not even taking into account the additional economic benefit of military support, this meant that Spanish economic support equaled roughly one-third to one-half of the entire papal budget, which had grown to about three million escudos by the time of the reign of Urban VIII. Since the papacy paid as much as one-half of the budget to service its debt, the importance of the Spanish contribution was that much greater.

Conclusion

By the 1630s, Melchor Cano could have written that papal Rome depended upon the Spanish for much more than its bread and water. Indeed, Spanish pensions and payments of various kinds underwrote the cardinal's palaces and gardens; the churches and villas; the salaries of thousands of Roman residents; the basic military defenses of Rome; and a substantial part of the papal court.

From the Basilicas of St. Peter's and Santa Maria Maggiore to the churches of San Pietro in Montorio and San Giacomo degli Spagnoli; from the palaces of the Borghese, Colonna, Farnese, Fonseca, and Medici to the Piazza Navona and Piazza di Spagna; all of these centers of worship, social ritual, and cultural display were built up in part with Spanish financial patronage. They and dozens of other churches, convents, and palaces benefited from the Spanish presence in Rome and the general *pax hispanica* in Italy, which allowed one of the longest building booms that Rome has ever known. It exceeds the boundaries of this work to analyze the specific details of Spanish patronage to churches, palaces, and other institutions, but it is certain that their account books contain ample evidence of Spanish patronage.

In exchange, the Spanish monarchy was able to extract revenues from the Spanish church at an ever greater rate to prop up its frail financial system and dig its way out of repeated bankruptcy. At the same time, the monarchy won the political support of the papacy for seventy years. This may not have been as tangible or lasting a gain as that of urban development of Rome, perhaps, but it certainly helps to explain the often-puzzling resiliency of the Spanish monarchy in the early years of decline, and particularly its surprising strength in Italy.

The reign of Urban VIII (1622–45), the first pro-French pope since Paul IV, represented a rupture in this political relationship, as did the protest of the Bishop of Cordoba in 1631. Not surprisingly, the economic exchange also came under pressure, and the Spanish revenues flowing into Rome decreased. Still, Spanish ecclesiastical finances on a smaller scale continued to support the papacy, cardinals, and thousands of other lesser clerics in Rome for the rest of the seventeenth century.

This sheds much light on continuing Spanish influence and power in Rome long after its decline in Europe had begun. So, too, it also hints at how the Spanish monarchs continued to hold onto their Italian possessions, until the death of the last Habsburg king, Carlos II, put an end to the age of the Spanish preponderance in Italy. Spanish imperialism in Rome, at least, was a beneficent imperialism whose economic support allowed Baroque Rome to flourish. Further research may find a similar Spanish role in other parts of Italy as well.

AFTERWORD

Where Is Beyond Florence?

Randolph Starn

Pope Boniface VIII supposedly called the Florentines a "fifth element"—as if they were somehow above or beyond earth, water, air, and fire. Exceptionalism runs deep in the rich vein of panegyrics for, tirades against, and level-headed historical writing about the city. But so does the view of Florence as the Renaissance measure and norm, in Jacob Burckhardt's tribute "the most important workshop of the Italian and indeed of the modern European spirit." At the end of this volume, we might well ask which, if any, Florence we have got "beyond": the exception, or the rule—or something else again. Either way, what might the results and implications be? It is one of the great strengths and rewards of this book and of the work of the scholar it honors that they prompt this line of questioning.

The contributors more or less self-consciously push against and across boundaries of space, time, and topic. They are interested in "other-wheres" to Florence—hinterlands and peripheries; other cities and towns; other regions than Tuscany; other-than-Italian connections. Since they stretch chronology from medieval through early modern, the distinctiveness of the Renaissance as a period is hardly an issue. Over and against litanies of Renaissance individualism, Machiavellianism, and secularism, their Italians were continually negotiating a web of collective identities and obligations, preoccupied with political legitimacy, and no better or worse than conventional Christians. Religion and ritual are the framework and driving force of no fewer than ten chapters; texts and images are read in their own right but also, with prompting from cultural anthropology and sociology, as repositories and instruments of prestige and power. Signature themes of an earlier generation of Florentine Renaissance studies, from the rise of the Medici to the culture of humanism, are conspicuous by their absence.

But Florentine pride of place is not easily outflanked. One revenge of Florentine exceptionalism is to make whatever lies beyond Florence look unexceptional, ordinary, and routine. Another is that Florence will usually win contests of archival oneupmanship since its archival resources are practically unmatched—even Venice plays catch-up in this respect. If the point is to revise or reverse Burckhardt, the best place to look is arguably inside Florence, not beyond it. Despite grumbling to the contrary, Florentine historiography has been predominantly revisionist for more than a generation.

Challenges to many stereotypes and oversimplifications gilding the Florentine lily ran through the benchmark collection of essays, *Florentine Studies*, edited by Nicolai Rubinstein more than thirty years ago. Citing "variety and diversity," Rubinstein's introduction defined the Renaissance broadly as "a period which stretches roughly from the 13th through the 16th centuries."[1] Among the contributors were historians who had written on Pisa, Pistoia, Orvieto, Rimini, Venice, Padua, and Rome. One of the book's main themes was the emergence of Florence as a Tuscan city, deeply rooted in the contado and in many ways closely akin to rival towns (for which Florentine chroniclers reserved their most pungent scorn). Another theme, though not acknowledged as such, was the takeover of Renaissance history by foreign scholars. The language I used long ago in a review of *Florentine Studies* would apply well enough today to *Beyond Florence*: "[i]mpatient with inherited interpretations and external schemes of meaning, close to the sources, susceptible to new methods . . . ; gone are the rigid dichotomies of the heroic age of Renaissance debates—medieval vs. modern; bourgeois vs. feudal; upper guilds vs. lower guilds; town vs. country."[2]

In their opening essays, Gene Brucker and Paula Findlen join forces across generations to map historiographical change as well as continuity. They do so *tra speranza e paura*, hedging their bets "between hope and fear." There are grounds for hope, certainly. Ironically or not, some of the strongest reasons come not so much in spite as because of developments in Florentine history. Brucker offers a succinct survey of recent work proving that rumors of the demise of a dynamic and productive Florentine historiography are greatly exaggerated. The list includes studies that would stand out as pioneering in any field (for example, Michael Rocke's book on homoerotic culture in fifteenth-century Florence or Samuel Cohn's comparative interregional study of the will as an index of shifting patterns of piety). Other entries in Brucker's survey redefine the discourse on key topics for early modern Italian history in general (David Peterson's study of the pre-Reformation Florentine church or Dale Kent's analysis of the multileveled cultural patronage of Cosimo de' Medici). A new wave of monographs on major and minor towns in Tuscany, a Tuscan version of "postcolonial" research, has surged well beyond Florence to give one-time possessions of Florence their own historical identities. *Pace* the competition and the occasional bout of discontent in a mature field of scholarship, Florentine studies are still pace-setting, at least for Anglo-American scholars. Findlen makes the point by taking as her analogy for recent scholarship "studying Italy in all its parts" the "vast collaborative project" of Florentine history.

This polycentrism and the interdisciplinary reach that goes with it are for her the most hopeful signs for the future. As she suggests, the "much broader geography" of Italian history since the 1980s has had a multiplier effect, connecting town, city, country, and region; and raising the historical stakes accordingly. It has also promoted productive exchange between foreign scholars and Italian historians, few of whom have shared ultramontane enthusiasm for Florence or the idea of a Renaissance, tarred as it was by the brush of fascist ideology. Interdisciplinary interests have been a challenge—or occupational hazard—for students of the Renaissance at least since Burckhardt, but the interplay of planes of historical experience and the mix of approaches and methods so well represented here have worked to generate a richly textured, multileveled kind of history. This is history by and large attentive to structures of behavior and identity but also to agency and circumstance; insistent on infusing institutions with human relations of kinship, friendship, and patronage; alert to material circumstances but attuned to their transformation by art and interest.

I want to come back to these qualities, but Brucker and Findlen also hint at worries that should not be passed over. To begin with, there are the liabilities of the virtues. More and more research at the margins may lead to a broader perspective or to tunnel vision, eclecticism to new insight or to distraction and dispersion, microhistorical investigation to the feel of historical experience or to trivia. The calculus of reality and representation in the newer scholarship may look soft and indulgent to the hard-core tradition of research in the Italian archives, not to mention the residual Marxism that still has enough energy to be on the lookout for historians complicitous in the obfuscation of the historical power elite. The chapters answer for themselves on these charges—effectively so, I think. By now, too, a large body of comparable scholarship exists across fields to back them up. The "new" cultural history and the newer areas of research in this collection—religion, ritual, gender, regionalism, and so on—are already mature, if not past their prime.[3] The short life cycle of historiographical innovation these days, from glimmer to glut, might also be worrisome if the contributors were not so busy being resourceful and productive.

Something similar might be said about their nearly complete indifference to the Renaissance as an idea or organizing principle. We may have outgrown old-style European history, with its storybook succession of ages and its "occidentalism," but the fact remains that we owe the flourishing of transatlantic Italian studies to the pivotal place of the Renaissance in the syllabus. In the zigzag career of American detachment and engagement with the world, European history served as the "intermediary between America and world history,"[4] and the Renaissance appealed to an American sense of mission to renew the core values of Western civilization without the inconveniences and mistakes of being European.

This *translatio imperii* called for a cultural alchemy whereby a predominantly WASP culture and a democratic polity found forebears in a Mediterranean, Catholic world of oligarchies and petty despots. An actual translation came with the refugee scholars—Hans Baron, Felix Gilbert, Paul Oskar Kristeller, Erwin Panofsky—who were instrumental in making Italian Renaissance studies one of the most cosmopolitan and professional fields of historical scholarship in this country. This story has been told often in recent years, usually with a critical edge and a parting shot of good riddance.[5] But besides being unseemly, Renaissance bashing by the beneficiaries of the idea of the Renaissance runs the risk of perceived irrelevance and real downsizing. A recent president of the American Historical Association, herself a distinguished European medievalist, has seen fit to pronounce a eulogy over "the last Eurocentric generation" of historians.[6]

There are antidotes for these preoccupations in the book. One is the incentive it offers for just this kind of reflection in an effort to take stock and come to terms with developments in the field. Another is close encounters with received views through highly specific cases and materials. Practically all the chapters after the opening pair bring close focus to large issues in ways that illuminate the particular instance and the general framework within which it can be understood. So, to cite examples almost at random, George Dameron on the shift of historians' views of the relations of the city and countryside from "either symbiotic or exploitative" to "organic and reciprocal," a shift documented by his work on the Tuscan Mugello; or Cynthia J. Polecritti on the turn from the interpretative model of indoctrination to analysis of the interaction and cultural exchange between the clergy and the laity, a point richly demonstrated in the career of the famous preacher San Bernardino of Siena. Michelle Fontaine documents the "resilience, adaptability, and reform" of civic magistrates when the common wisdom would be that transfer of the D'Este court to Modena in 1598 snuffed out the last vestiges of communal autonomy. Against a hoary tradition coupling Spanish domination and Italian decadence, Thomas Dandelet shows how Spanish imperialism actually promoted and subsidized the flowering of Baroque Rome. Most of the chapters turn tables like this on some conventional understanding of the subject at hand.

But do they add up? Under the "early modern" rubric, they do not necessarily need to. Early modernity encompasses a great, not to say indeterminate, stretch of time. It allows early modern people to be alternately early or nonmodern and modern, and their historians to muddle through the mix. It is a doubly slippery notion, however, not just accommodating but also treacherous. In the guise of neutrality, it may actually recycle discredited teleologies of modernization and a priori conceptions of the modern and the traditional. The old binary oppositions and abstracting dichotomies are now regularly treated and traced as a set template of early modernity: *Gemeinschaft* and *Gesellschaft*, status and contract, carnival and lent, enchantment and disenchantment, boorish behavior and civility. Hence a history fixated on the question "How modern is it?" and a historiography that keeps score on this or that figure, trend, institution, or idea. In any case, the label *early modern* does nothing to call an old Whiggish framework of historical progress to account—if anything, it defers any obligation for thinking clearly about directions of change.

Whether it works for Italian history is problematic besides. The best humanist historians of Italy began, as did Burckhardt, with the High Middle Ages, with the rise of the city-states and the Hohenstaufen emperors and the Italian little Caesars who imitated them. In an influential view dating from the nineteenth century and espoused by a curious coalition of aesthetes, Marxists, nationalists, and Catholic ultramontanes, Italy regressed from the modern to turn "medieval" only after the Sack of Rome in 1527, followed by "refeudalization," the Counter-Reformation, and Spanish domination of the peninsula. Judging by the routine criteria of modernity—economic integration, centralization, bureaucratization, secularization, and so forth—the problem of Italian early modernity is, one might say, borrowing a phrase from Bruno Latour, that Italy "has never been modern."[7]

Does this mean that we are left with no more than a scatter of sites or topics, or the fragmentation and loss of direction that some historians like to complain about? I am inclined to think, to the contrary, that there is a kind of emerging consensus, even a paradigm, that is at least as complete and compelling as older ones. It is not simply a matter of new interests, say, in religion or for that matter in whatever is beyond Florence, which, as I've already suggested, are not really so new anyway. Some keywords for the shared working assumptions I have in mind would be terms such as "network," "process," or "hybridity" in contrast with "linearity," "structure," or "consistency" as generic features of history and desiderata of good historical analysis. To put it differently, the chapters of this book show a marked preference—or at least a tolerance—for complex, multivalent materials and ways of reading them. The sources range from archival documents of all sorts to chronicles, legal treatises, festival books, travelers' accounts, and art and architecture. In one context or another, secular and sacred spheres, centrifugal and centripetal political interests, civic and aristocratic values, symbolic and material ambitions not only can mix but usually do so; to follow the grain of such combinations accordingly is the historian's task. The priorities of some level of historical experience or the claims of one kind of history over another hardly figure in these chapters, as they might have even a few years ago when the ideological and explanatory values of patrolling the boundaries seemed more important.

One measure of cumulative change is how hard it is to imagine retreating within the old boundaries and how easy it is to find outside confirmation for the newer directions I have been characterizing. A special issue of the *Journal of Modern History* on state building in Italy 1300–1600 is a convenient point of reference. Like this volume, it grew out of a set of conference papers, in this case mostly by Italian scholars but delivered in Italy and the United States; like this volume, it ranges widely since the contributors are not constrained by strict definitions of the state. For them, the state, as Giorgio Chittolini puts it, is anything but "the semi-imaginary state that historians like to label modern," and its origins do not lie in or necessarily lead to "a history of public structures of governance, tidily planned institutions, hierarchies of power, and actions of magistrates and officials."[8] In the gloss of editor Julius Kirshner, contemporary scholars have come to adopt "the notion of the state as a non-teleological network of multiple interconnected sources of social and political power."[9]

The ramifications run closely parallel to lines of inquiry that are so conspicuous in *Beyond Florence*. Roberto Bizzocchi, for example, citing research that breaks out of the confessional, ecclesiastical, or anticlerical biases of so much writing on the Italian church, offers a formulation that might have been written with several of the chapters of this book in mind:

The foundations of the shared role of the state and the church lie in local events. These events allow us to understand history in a way that a one-sided approach cannot. They also show us that the church's fundamental presence in secular society was not only important but, indeed, fundamental, and consequently that its worldliness was not abnormal. It is very useful to follow the innumerable channels through which the ecclesiastical presence penetrated secular society.[10]

Afterword: Where Is Beyond Florence?

Then again, Chittolini's summary of the effectiveness rather than the failed modernity of the overlap of "private" and "public" in Italy could serve as a kind of epigraph for this book: "institutions appear to be most effective when they are the powerful fairly direct expression of tightly woven private and collective interests."[11] Elena Fasano Guarini, to cite just one more example of affinity, notes the widespread and increasing "interest in the periphery and in the history of single communities," with "the community as 'a sort of ideal unit, open to different approaches and methodologies—from the history of institutions, fiscalism, and justice, to the history of *mentalités*, to social anthropology.'"[12]

To be sure, consensus, if that is what we are seeing here, is not uniformity, let alone conformity. The Italian historians just cited are responding to different scholarly traditions from those of their foreign counterparts—"the regional or territorial state" is itself a peculiarly Italian topos with an intellectual genealogy harking back to the earlier twentieth-century work of Francesco Ercole, Antonio Anzilotti, Gioacchino Volpe, and Federico Chabod. The social science–oriented history of Samuel Cohn's chapter and the vivid refractions of personality and place in Robert Brentano's reading of Franciscan texts are poles apart, and it is usually easy to tell who of the company here would think of themselves as medievalists rather than as early modernists. Nevertheless, the overlapping interests I've pointed to are, after all, about the factoring of differences and the cat's cradle of complex interrelationships in which Italian history is rich to the point of prodigality.

This may be in the end one of the best reasons for optimism about the future. The variety corresponds to the actual state of a community of scholarship that is differentiated and dispersed but arguably more dynamic and interdependent for that. It also draws energy from questions raised by the great transformations of political and social life at the turn of the twentieth century that have prompted rethinking of the narratives of a march toward modernity. As the setting—even a primal scene—for any number of alternatives and the archives to document them, Italian history over the long run represented by this volume calls for an historiographical *aggiornamento* that encompasses and goes beyond Florence.

Reference Matter

Notes

1. BRUCKER

1. Brucker, 1994b, 1–3.
2. Cf. Muir, 1995, 1108–09; Molho, 1998, 271–74.
3. Klapisch-Zuber, 1994, 182.
4. Muir, 1995, 1113.
5. Baron, 1955, 1966.
6. Rubinstein, 1997.
7. Molho, 1996, 100, n. 9.
8. Herlihy and Klapisch-Zuber, 1978; Conti, 1965, 1966.
9. Martines, 1963, 1968.
10. Trexler, 1980.
11. Goldthwaite, 1968, 1980, 1993, 1995.
12. F. W. Kent, 1977; Molho, 1994, Klapisch-Zuber, 1985.
13. Brucker, 1983, 599–616.
14. In this survey, I have counted important collections of articles on Florentine topics.
15. Ciappelli, 1995, 1997; Fabbri; Franceschi; Stella; Zorzi, 1987, 1988, 1989.
16. Used by Mazzi and Raveggi; Franceschi; Mazzi, 1991; Rocke.
17. Starn, 1970, 679.
18. Molho, 1995, 41.
19. Martines, 1988, 300–11.
20. Starn, 1970, 679.
21. Najemy, 1985, 102–59. The five authors were myself, 1977; F. W. Kent, 1977; Goldthwaite, 1980; Trexler, 1980; and Cohn, 1980.
22. Gilbert, 61–66. Gilbert reviewed Trexler, 1980; Cohn, 1980; and Goldthwaite, 1980.
23. Molho, 1979, 9–19.
24. Butters, ix–x.
25. E.g., Molho, 1987; Cohn, 1994.
26. Muir, 1995, 1112.
27. But cf. Molho, 1985, Stella.
28. Brucker, 1994a.
29. Goldthwaite, 1993, 5.
30. Molho, 1994, 347.
31. Cohn, 1992.
32. Cohn, 1999.
33. Verdon and Henderson.
34. Peterson.
35. Dale Kent, 2000.
36. The major collections of essays on Lorenzo; Alison Brown, 1992; Bernard Toscano; Garfagnini, 1992, 1994; Bullard, 1994; Mallett and Mann.
37. *Convegni di studi sulla storia dei ceti dirigenti*; Connell and Zorzi.
38. Kemp.
39. Frigo.
40. Muir, 1995, 1115.

41. E.g., *Storia di Venezia dalle origini*. . . .
42. Starn, 1996, 71.
43. E.g., Fasano Guarini, 1986; Judith Brown, 1982; Benadusi; Connell.
44. Molho, 1990, 63.   45. Brucker, 1998, 7–11.
46. Graham Dixon, 3.   47. Gouwens, 58–63.
48. Welch.   49. Brucker, 1998, 7–22.
50. Steiner, 76–77.

2. FINDLEN

1. Burckhardt, 1960 ed., 40 (quote), 48–56.
2. Herlihy, 1973.
3. The use of manuscript sources can already be found in eighteenth-century historical and antiquarian scholarship, and it played a strong role in the development of local history in the nineteenth and early twentieth centuries. It was also fundamental to the kind of historical scholarship pioneered by Burckhardt's German predecessor, Ranke. Yet I think it safe to say that the professionalization of archival scholarship is a development of the postwar era, when higher education in Europe and America expanded dramatically and the doctorate became an important credential for university teaching and provided the ingredients for embarking on a career of scholarly research and publishing.
4. See Rubinstein, 1966, which cites a great deal of the Italian and German scholarship that preceded his own important work.
5. Many aspects of this scholarship are summarized well in Rubinstein, 1968; Starn, 1970; and Brucker, 1977, 1983a, 1983b, and 1999. This chapter does not pretend to offer a full historiographic treatment of either Florentine studies or historical scholarship on medieval and early modern Italy. I have primarily indicated works that appear in English, on the premise that readers interested in the specialist literature in a variety of other languages will be able to find this material through the notes in many of the books and articles cited in this volume.
6. Baron, 1955. For a recent reassessment of the significance of Baron's work, see Witt et. al., 1996.
7. A great deal of the political history of Florence is surveyed in the works alluded to in note 4; see also Becker, 1967; Martines, 1963 and 1972; Hale, 1977; Kent, 1978; Brown, 1979; Najemy, 1982 and 1985; Bullard, 1980 and 1994; and Fubini, 1994b. The best introduction in English to the economic debates about Italy in this period remains Brown, 1989, which has a full bibliography; see also Goldthwaite, 1993. In a volume devoted primarily to social history, I have chosen not to discuss the rich tradition of intellectual history, embodied especially in the work of such scholars as James Hankins, Arthur Field, and Ronald Witt, that has made Florence an important center for understanding the growth and diversity of humanist thought.
8. Dean and Wickham, 1990, vii.
9. Muir, 1981; see Brucker, 1983b, 614.
10. Burckhardt, 40. The classic synthesis of Venetian history remains Lane, 1973; for the most recent assessment, see Martin and Romano, 1999.

11. Ibid., 45. For further discussion of this subject, see Cohn, 1995, and Klapisch-Zuber, 1996.

12. Herlihy and Klapisch-Zuber, 1978. This tradition of social science history has continued to thrive, most notably in the work of Samuel Cohn; see Cohn, 1980, 1988, 1992, and 1999, among others.

13. Trexler, 1980; Weissman, 1982; Klapisch-Zuber, 1985; and Strocchia, 1992. Weissman, 1985, remains the strongest example of the fascination with social theory among Renaissance historians in the 1980s. For an interesting discussion of the transformation of Florentine social history, see Cohn, 1995.

14. Burke, 1987. Readers should keep in mind the importance of two new historiographic trends, in Italy and France respectively, that greatly influenced Anglo-American scholarship in the 1980s: the development of microhistory by a group of scholars primarily associated with *Quaderni storici*, most notably Carlo Ginzburg; and the renewed interest of the French *Annales* school in history of mentalities, as seen especially in the work of Lucien Febvre, Emmanuel LeRoy Ladurie, and Roger Chartier, and American scholars such as Natalie Zemon Davis and Robert Darnton. Both groups made the medieval and early modern periods the primary testing ground for new methodologies in social history.

15. Molho, 1988.

16. Bouwsma, 1979. Recent reassessments of the situation include Starn, 1994; Muir, 1995; Molho, 1998; and Findlen and Gouwens, 1998.

17. For a recent survey of Renaissance Italy that exemplifies this approach, see Hay and Law, 1989.

18. The following citations are meant to be suggestive rather than comprehensive: Toubert, 1973; Violante, 1981; Rigon, 1988; and Andenna, 1998. For some indication of the Italian work done on the Middle Ages that attends to Tuscany, see Benvenuti Papi, 1986; and Pinto, 1993 and 1996. English works are cited in subsequent footnotes.

19. Cochrane, 1970 and 1973. Molho, 1990, reviews recent work on early modern Tuscany in light of its early modern characteristics, while Sella, 1997, offers a synthetic account of the seventeenth century. Among recent historians of Cochrane's "forgotten centuries," see the work of Dooley, 1999.

20. Excellent examples of this recent trend include Marino, 1988; Nussdorfer, 1992; Davis, 1991 and 1994; and Calabria, 1991. Works such as Sella, 1979, anticipated these developments.

21. American scholarship on the Renaissance has paid much more attention to this work in the past decade. See, e.g., the review essays by John Martin (Martin, 1994, 1995, and 1996).

22. The classic example of this genre is Ginzburg, 1980. For selections of *Quaderni storici* in English and a discussion of microhistory, see Muir and Ruggiero, 1990, 1991, and 1994; and Levi, 1991.

23. The following examples allow readers to delve into this literature: Bizzocchi, 1987; Bornstein, 1993; Bornstein and Rusconi, 1996; Dameron, 1991; Gentilcore, 1992; Miller, 1993; Brentano, 1994; Martin, 1993; and Lansing, 1998. Schutte, 1989; Martin, 1995; and Hudon, 1996, survey recent work on early modern Italian religion.

24. This message is already evident in surveys such as Waley, 1988; and Tabacco, 1989. Dean, 1988; Astarita, 1992; and Muir, 1993, offer recent case studies of the persistence of feudalism in Ferrara, Naples, and the Friuli respectively.

25. Quoted in Hyde, 1973, 5.

26. *Incastellamento* defines the process by which communities form under the jurisdiction and protection of castles and their chatelans. The classic study of this phenomenon remains Toubert, 1973. For a comparative analysis, see Andenna, 1998.

27. See, e.g., Grubb, 1988 and 1996; Romano, 1987; and Kohl, 1998. The best survey of Venetian scholarship remains Grubb, 1986. For an interesting comparative study of Venice and Florence, see Muir and Weissman, 1988.

28. See especially Abulafia, 1977; Bresc, 1986; and Epstein, 1991 and 1992.

29. Villari, 1973; and Galasso, 1997 and 1998. This literature is discussed in Cochrane, 1986; Marino, 1988; Calabria and Marino, 1990; and Astarita, 1992; it is treated comparatively in Elena Fasano Guarini, "Center and Periphery," in Kirshner, 1996, 74–96.

30. See especially Blomquist and Mazzaoui, 1994; and Wickham, 1988. Herlihy, 1967; McArdle, 1978; and Brown, 1982, reflect earlier stages in the discussion of the territorial state, looking at subject cities and towns. The importance of reexamining the relations between city and *contado* is discussed in Dean and Wickham, 1990. Two books have appeared too late for me to assess them in the context of this essay: Cohn, 1999, and Connell and Zorzi, 2000.

31. On Lucca, see Berengo, 1965; Osheim, 1977; Bratchel, 1995; and Wickham, 1998. On Siena, see Bowsky, 1981; Caferro, 1998, and the articles by Mario Ascheri and Duccio Balestracci in Blomquist and Mazzaoui, 1994, all of which cite the growing literature on Siena over the past few decades.

32. Jones, 1997 (Burckhardt is quoted on p. 195); and Molho, "The State and Public Finance: A Hypothesis Based on the History of Late Medieval Florence," in Kirshner, 1996, 133. See also Brucker, 1999, 359.

33. Lansing, 1991, xii. Cf. Kent, 1977; and Kent and Kent, 1982.

34. Trachtenberg, 1997.

35. Cohn, 1992, 4. For a critique of Cohn's methodology, see Bertram, 1995.

36. Muir, 1999, 383.

37. Jones, 1997, 156.

38. Brentano, 1968, 294; and Wickham, 1998, 208ff.

39. See the chapters by Carol Lansing and by Laurie Nussdorfer in this volume.

40. Frugoni, 1991, 54.

41. Botero, 1956, 259.

42. See Andenna, 1998, 33–36.

43. On the city-state, see Martines, 1979; Molho, Raaflaub, and Emlen, 1991; Kirshner, 1996; and Jones, 1997. The "Europa delle Corti" series published by Bulzoni—the primary venue for publications on Italian court culture—continues to grow; examples are Basile, 1984; Fantoni, 1994; Mozzarelli, 1997; and Signorotto and Visceglia, 1998. On the rural commune, see especially Wickham, 1988 and 1998.

44. Cipolla, 1975, 1981, and 1992.

45. On violence, see Martines, 1972; Ruggiero, 1980; Muir, 1993; Davis, 1994; and Dean and Lowe, 1994; on gender, marriage, and sumptuary laws, see Hughes, 1983; Dean and Lowe, 1998; and Brown and Davis, 1998; on sexuality, see Ruggiero, 1985; and Rocke, 1996.

46. Grendler, 1989; see Bentley, 1987, for an interesting example of the geography of fifteenth-century humanism.

47. Recent forays into these subjects include Kent and Simons, 1987; Ago, 1990; Goldthwaite, 1993; and Findlen, 1994 and forthcoming. See the chapter by Robert Davis on tourism and pilgrimage in this volume for a further discussion of travel.

48. Martines, 1979, 8. See the chapter by Carol Lansing in this volume for further bibliography.

49. Trexler, 1980.

50. Klapisch-Zuber, 1985.

51. On Genoa, see Epstein, 1996; and Abulafia, 1977. Spanish Italy has an enormous literature, some of it cited in notes 27 and 28. See also Spagnoletti, 1996; Dandelet, 1997; and the contributions of Thomas Dandelet and Jennifer Selwyn to this volume.

52. See in this volume the section "City and Countryside" and the works cited in notes 29 and 39.

53. Braudel, 1972–73, vol. 1, 161 (quote), 126.

54. For an overview of recent work on Venice, see Martin and Romano, 1999.

55. Starn, 1994.

56. Cantimori, 1992; Prosperi, 1996; and Fragnito, 1997. See also the interesting work of Giovanni Romeo on Naples, e.g., Romeo, 1990.

57. See note 22, and the chapters by Michelle Fontaine, Cynthia Polecritti, and Jennifer Selwyn in this volume.

58. Quoted in Brentano, 1994, 230.

59. Webb, 1996.

60. For an excellent overview of American and Italian approaches to religious history, see Bornstein and Rusconi, 1996. On confraternities, see Black, 1989; Terpstra, 1995; and Eisenbichler, 1997.

61. Muir, 1989.

62. See the chapters by Michelle Fontaine and Maureen Miller in this volume.

63. Miller, 1993; Brentano, 1994; and Lansing, 1998. See also Osheim, 1977.

64. E.g., Ginzburg, 1980; and Gentilcore, 1992.

65. Jones, 1995; for the eighteenth-century flowering of medieval studies from this early work, see Cochrane, 1958.

3. COHN

1. On how Florentine historiography has set the debate for other city-states and the historiography of late-medieval Italy in general, see Cristiani, 829–45; Tabacco, 302–303; and Bowsky, 193. On the "classics" of the city contado liter-

ature (Salvemini, Volpe, Caggese, De Vergottini, Ottokar, Plesner, Fiumi), see Pinto, 1993, 48; and Pini, 1978, 368-70.

2. Caggese.

3. Fiumi, 1956, 18-68; 1957, 385-439; 1958, 443-510; 1959, 427-502, esp. part 3, 440-66; and 1961. Also see Cristiani.

4. Becker, 1967-68; and 1965, 433-66; Molho, 1971; Herlihy, 1964, 385-405; and Herlihy and Klapisch-Zuber, 17-47.

5. Becker, 1966, 32.

6. J. Brown, 1982, 126-76 and 199-202.

7. S. R. Epstein, 1992; 1991, 3-50; 1994, 459-82.

8. Petralia, 639-52.

9. See especially Becker, 1967.

10. Secondarily, the question has considered the politics of grain supply.

11. On this source and changes in Florentine legislation, see Guidi, 1981; and Fubini, 1994a, 41-61.

12. They had risen from ten soldi on the lira for the ordinary tax to one-and-a-half florins (approximately six lire) for the extraordinary tax plus twenty soldi for the ordinary.

13. See Brucker, 1977, 181.

14. Household size declined along with the number of households, reaching its low point of just over three per household in 1412.

15. See, e.g., the population of San Martino a Sesto, which throughout the surviving *estimi* of the latter half of the fourteenth and early fifteenth centuries remained around 130 families.

16. Archivio di Stato, Firenze [hereafter ASF], Provvisioni registri [hereafter Provv.], no. 36, 8v-10v, 1348.ix.12.

17. Minerbetti.

18. Provv., no. 89, 150v-151r, 1400.x.12.

19. E.g., by the lists of dead brothers chronicled in the so-called Necrologies of Santa Maria Novella, the plagues of the early fifteenth century (1413, 1417, and 1424) killed less than a thirtieth of the population killed in 1348. My accumulation of more than thirty-three hundred testaments for Tuscany and Umbria shows a similarly sharp downward trend in the plague's mortality from 1348 to the plague of 1424. I present these results in my book *The Black Death Transformed: Disease and Culture in Early Renaissance Europe* (London, 2002).

20. Sixteen mentioned plague in the first period and thirty-three in the second, or a change from less than one petition mentioning plague every 2.25 years to one a year.

21. On the "penumbra" of preindustrial diseases, see Wills; and Carmichael, 18-35.

22. This seems to have been the case in other regions of Europe as well, on the basis of changing figures of life expectancy; see Daniell, 133-34.

23. Provv., 105, 29r-31r, 1415.iv.26.

24. Provv., 102, 101r-102r, 1413.x.20; no. 108, 107v-108r, 1418.vi.28; no. 111, 152v-53v, 1421.ix.26; no. 112, 116r-17r, 1422.viii.28; no. 112, 176v-77v, 24.x.1422. See also Leverotti, 1988, 122.

25. Sixty-six petitions before 1402, thirty-three afterward.
26. Forty-three and fifteen petitions, respectively.
27. Forty-eight of 433 petitions; earlier these amounted to 23 of 471, or just under 5 percent.
28. Provv., 92, 182v–83v, 1403.xi.27.
29. On the social composition of Monte shareholders, see Herlihy and Klapisch-Zuber, 250–55.
30. Fubini, 1990, 29–62, esp. 51.
31. At the turn of the century, Florence standardized justice in the territory by reorganizing old *podesterie* into new vicariates and by replacing foreign judges (podestà and *capitani*) with Florentine citizens. These changes took place both in the new frontier areas of the Pisano and Aretino as well as within the traditional contado of Florence; see Chittolini, 1979, 299 and 305–306; and Zorzi, 1988, 34 and 45; 1989, 520.
32. Conti, 1981, 213–14; and R. Nenci, ed., 25; and Chittolini, 1990, 69–91.
33. See Cohn, 1999, 98–136. Also, Zorzi, 1988, 55, notes a rise in the percentage of prosecution against crimes of morality with the formation of the new vicariates.
34. ASF, *Statuti della comunità* no. 420 (Mangona), c. 50, 30rv: *Della electione delle guardie segrete*.
35. Zorzi, 1988, 62; 1987, 746–47.   36. See J. Black.
37. Johnson, 2000; and Cohn, 1999, 207.   38. Cohn, 1999, 124–25.
39. On the emergence of this word for the Florentine state by humanists in the early years of the fourteenth century, see A. Brown, 2000; and Machiavelli, 270.

4. DAMERON

1. Jones, 1997; Chittolini, 1996; Chittolini and Willoweit; Tabacco, 1979; Herlihy, 1968, 245–47. I have benefited from the comments and suggestions offered by the editors of this volume and by Samuel Cohn, Jr. This essay is the beginning of a longer study of the Mugello region of Tuscany from the eleventh through early fourteenth centuries.
2. Chittolini, 1992, 594–97; 1996, 419–24; Wickham, 1998, 207–208.
3. For the Lucchesia, see Wickham, 1998, 14, 17; Osheim, 1977, 70–78. For Florence, see Zorzi, 1994; Wickham, 1988, 353–54. For Siena and its contado, see Redon, 91–135; Bowsky, 189–259.
4. G. Cherubini, 78, 90–91, 108–11; Pinto, 1982, 1993; Osheim, 1989a, 317.
5. Zorzi, 1994; Cohn, 1996a, 402–16 (especially 415).
6. The Mugello is one of the principal geographical basins of Tuscany, along with the Garfagnana, the Casentino, the Val Tiberiana, and the Lunigiana. For the purposes of this study, I accept the view of many that the Mugello comprises the basin of the Sieve valley from its source to Dicomano. The lower Val di Sieve (from Dicomano to the Arno) is a separate region (Barbieri, 89, 94–95).
7. In recent years, several local histories have appeared focusing on the eleventh and twelfth centuries (Spicciani and Violante; Wickham, 1988, 1998).

There are few local studies of the thirteenth and early fourteenth. For one of those exceptions, see Osheim, 1989b.

8. For general background on the Mugello, see Barbieri; and Magna, 18n. Principal primary sources include imperial privileges of protection, parchment sheets and rolls, and other documents associated with the cathedral chapter and the bishopric in the Archivio di Stato di Firenze, the Archivio Arcivescovile di Firenze, and the Archivio del Capitolo Fiorentino. There were six notaries working in the Mugello between 1250 and 1330, whose protocols are preserved in the fondo Notarile Antecosimiano [henceforth NA] in the Archivio di Stato di Firenze [hereafter ASF].

9. For roads, see Pinto, 1993, 34; La Roncière, 1976; Szabó, 1992. To estimate the population, I averaged the number of males in three parishes (Borgo San Lorenzo, Ampinana, and Frascole, near Dicomano) to arrive at the number of 20. The males had gathered to elect rectors of their local parish churches (see ASF, NA 7870, fol. 96v; NA 9494, fol. 11r; NA 9502, fol. 25r). Then I used the multiplier of 5 to represent the number of persons per hearth, following David Herlihy's method for calculating the population of Santa Maria Impruneta for the same period (Herlihy, 1968, 249). Arriving at the figure of 100, I then multiplied that number by the number of parishes (145) to arrive at the figure of 14,500. Therefore, out of a total population of 280,000–320,000 in the city and contado around 1338, I estimate about 5 percent lived in the Mugello (Herlihy and Klapisch-Zuber, 1985, 65).

10. M. D. Nenci, 148, 150, 158, 162. More immigrants, however, came from two other regions (sesti) of the hinterland, immediately south and east (including northeast) of the city.

11. In 1307, the members of the commune of Vespignano charged Mercante del fu Cancelliero to apportion the Florentine direct tax in the community ("ad sortiendum extimum nuper datum per communem Florentie inter plebatus et communia et populos comitatus Florentie"; ASF, NA 7870, fol. 9r). In 1309, patrons of a parish within the plebatus of Borgo San Lorenzo gave the rector of San Simone the right to appoint their rector (fol. 96v). For the conveyance of the ten lire to the rector of Vespignano, see ASF, NA 7872, fols. 27v–28r.

12. For money lenders, see ASF, NA 7870, fol. 78v; 8046, fol. 43r. For public works, see Szabó, 1992, 272.

13. For the Ghibelline presence in the Mugello, see G. Villani, 2:641. For Uzzano and Rostolena, see Pirillo, 624–25. For immigration, see M. D. Nenci, 148, 150.

14. Francesco, identified as the son of Giotto the painter of the parish of Santa Maria Novella of Florence (Francischus filius Giotti pictori populi Sancte Marie Novelle de Florentia), served as procurator for his brother, Bondone, also a presbyter. As prior of Vespignano, he also leased mills and lands of the church and worked to complete the bell-tower (ASF, NA 7872, fols. 48v, 49r, 99v, 100r). To my knowledge, no one has yet written about the continued presence of Giotto's family at Vespignano in the early fourteenth century.

15. For settlement patterns, see Barbieri, 299.

16. Wickham, 1996, 343–50.

17. For the Ubaldini and Guidi in the Mugello, see Magna; and Curradi, respectively. For the information on the bishopric and cathedral chapter in the Mugello, see Dameron, 1991, 77–79, 97–107, 159–73; 1996, 1997.

18. Pescaglini Monti, 200 and 204; Wickham, 1988, 391ff; Milo, 207–22; Magna, 15–17, 27.

19. For imperial politics, see Larner, 18–20. For a survey of Ubaldini possessions, as confirmed in 1220, see Magna, 18–20.

20. G. Villani, 1: 341; Davidsohn, 3: 143–45; Magna, 39, 49–51.

21. Magna, 53–55. The Ubaldini paid the estimo in 1288–89, 1296, 1299, and 1300. For interference on the roads, see Davidsohn, 5: 371.

22. G. Villani, 2: 86–87, 109–10, 171–72, 445–46, 490–93, 692.

23. In May 1330, for example, about thirty parishioners of San Michele di Ampinana came together to choose a rector to appear before Florentine officials, including the grain magistrates, the *Sei della Biada* (ASF, NA 9502, fol. 25r). Another indication of more Florentine involvement in the region is Simone della Tosa da Firenze arbitrating in a dispute between two nobles over rights and properties (*iura*) in the Mugello (ASF, NA 9500, fol. 18v).

24. In 1298 at San Godenzo, Count Tegrimo dei Guidi condemned several robbers who had violated the monastery of Vallombrosa by capturing several *conversi* and stealing a hundred cows (ASF, NA 9493, fol. 66r).

25. For example, one count stipulated that his executors draw from his property to restore all illicitly gotten gains and debts ("quamcumque illicitam et in debitam exactionem seu retentionem restituantur vel solvantur de bonis suis"; ASF, NA 9493, fol. 36v); see also NA 9498, fol. 37r.

26. See Piattoli (29–33) for chapter property holding in the tenth century. The chapter held sway over significant properties but did not establish a territorial lordship (*dominatus loci*) there, as had the bishopric. For definition of lordship (signoria), see Wickham, 1996, 346–48.

27. For the texts of imperial, episcopal, and papal privileges to the cathedral chapter, see Piattoli, 47, 54, 56, 64, 109, 102, 141, 385, 111, 146, 182, 197, 231, 372; and Archivio del Capitolo Fiorentino (hereafter ACF), Carte Strozziane 959.

28. In 1058, several sets of sons in the western Mugello, for example, donated six parcels of land in the plebatus of San Gavino Adimari to the cathedral chapter for the remedy of their souls (Piattoli, 160, 169, 191, and 253).

29. ACF, Carte Strozziane 14 and 451.

30. Ibid., Carte Strozziane 80. See Magna, 55–58, for a discussion.

31. Zorzi, 1994, 337–38.

32. For example, see Archivio Arcivescovile di Firenze (hereafter AAF), MAB (Mensa Arcivescovile Bullettoni) 01, fols. 93r–103r.

33. G. Villani, 1: 272. The castello of Lomena was in the possession of the bishopric by 1159 (Dameron, 1991, 77).

34. ASF, Manoscritti 48 (Il Bullettone), 155; AAF, MAB 01, fols. 93r–103r; Dameron, 1991, 98–101; Magna, 37.

35. Dameron, 1991, 103–04.

36. La Roncière, 1976, 3: 837–43, 951–62, 994.

37. Dameron, 1991, 101–03.

38. Tenants had failed to make payments at Montebuiano (plebatus of Pimonte), Valcava, Molezzano, Pagliariccio, and Rabbiacanina in the early fourteenth century; AAF, MAII (Mensa Arcivescovile Serie II) 002 1, fols. 19v, 78r, 82r–83v, 84r; AAF, MAII 001 3, fols. 19r, 26v.

39. Stefani, 62; G. Villani, 1: 547, 1: 576, 1: 579, 2: 221, 2: 285, 2: 670–71. The city and its contado were only able to produce enough grain for five out of twelve months in the early fourteenth century (G. Cherubini, 87, citing the fourteenth-century Florentine Domenico Lenzi).

40. ASF, NA 9500, fol. 35r.; ASF, NA 9569, fol. 9r.

41. The Florentine administrator of the vacant bishopric at the time ordered the men to appear before him in three days or face excommunication ("precepit eisdem quod infra trium dies proximos venturos comporeant coram dicto domino plebano sub pena excommunicationis"). The property under dispute included "fictus dicte ecclesie, omnes fructus et proventus terrarum et rerum et bonorum predicte ecclesie Sancti Martini de Vespignano" (ASF, NA 7871, fol. 97v).

42. For examples from episcopal sources, see AAF, MAII 002 1, fols. 19v, 20r, 39r, and 78r. Several renters eventually made the delinquent payments.

43. For Borgo San Lorenzo (1309 and 1311), see AAF, MAB 04, fol. 42v, 64r. At Valcava (1300), the bishop first charged a single individual with the responsibility of collecting all rents in that district (pieve). See AAF, MAB 03, fol. 16v. A Florentine, Vanni di Albertino dei Malagonelli (parish of Sant'Andrea), leased episcopal income in the plebatus of Botena, Padule, and Corella in the eastern Mugello for four years in 1310 (AAF, MAB 04, fol. 45r).

44. Nelli, 72–75; ASF, NA 7871, fol. 54v; NA 6078, fol. 18r.

45. For a listing of pievi in the Florentine diocese, see Guidi and Giusti, 2: 14–22. The three friaries were located at Borgo San Lorenzo (male), Bosco di Mugello (male), and Vicchio (female) (La Roncière, 1976, 1994, II.49). The monasteries were San Bartolomeo di Buonsolazzo (plebatus of Santa Felicita), Santa Maria di Bovino (plebatus of Viminiccio), San Paolo di Razzuolo (plebatus of San Giovanni Maggiore), Montesenario, and San Pietro di Luco (female, in San Giovanni Maggiore). There were hospitals at Vespignano (San Salvatore), Ronta, and Razzuolo (ASF, NA 8046, fols. 47; NA 15797, fol. 96v–97r; NA 15798, fol. 15r, respectively).

46. La Roncière, 1976, II.103. See also ASF, NA 8046, fol. 43r.

47. Ibid., 9494, fol. 11r; 7871, fols. 56r, 131v.

48. This is one of the central themes of Wickham, 1998, for the immediate hinterland of the city of Lucca in the twelfth century.

49. ASF, NA 9498, fol. 99v. The rent was nominal. The parish of San Michele di Ampinana had leased a parcel to a certain Dano di Ristoro, which was contiguous to his own holdings. The current rector believed the lease was contrary to the episcopal constitutions. Under threat of ecclesiastical sanction, the descendants of the lessee returned the land to the presbyter ("nolentes tenere terram ecclesie pro modico afficctu occupatam timentes deum et sanctum Michele offendere"; fol. 99v).

50. Ibid., 7870, fol. 13.

51. Ibid., 3794, fols. 27v and 40v; 6075, fol. 15r; 6077, fol. 3v.

52. Ibid., 8046, fol. 43r; 7872, fols. 27v–28r.

53. See, e.g., ibid., 8046, fol. 47r–v; 9493, fols. 65v, 103r; 9498, fols. 41r, 42r.

54. Ibid., 6077, fols. 6rff. The fact that they shared a joint confessor may explain why they made legacies to the same parties. Whether they did so out of a sense of guilt (encouraged by the confessor), affection, or both, is irrelevant. One of the testators, Dosa, also gave fifteen soldi to Presbyter Ugolino and ten soldi to Presbyter Benvegnade for masses. They had both appeared as arbitrators in local disputes.

55. Of the four testaments that designated executors, three chose members of the secular clergy (ASF, NA 9494, fol. 88r; 9498, fol. 42r; 9500, fol. 27r) and one chose the abbot of the abbey of Poppi (9501, fol. 3).

56. The burial choices involved the following: Pulicciano (ASF, NA 6075, fol. 56r), Corella (9501, fol. 3r–v); Corniolo (3794, fol. 35v), Botena (3794, fol. 59r, 63v, 70v); Vespignano (8046, fol. 47r); Dicomano (9500, fol. 27r); the abbey of San Godenzo (9493, fol. 36v); two unspecified (8046, fol. 43r; 9495, fol. 131v); the Borgo friary (15797, fols. 31v, 41v, 46v; 15798, fol. 16r; 7872, fols. 27v–28r); and the abbey of Razzuolo (15798, fol. 15r).

57. ASF, NA 9501, fol. 138v. He left enough money for five priests (*sacerdotes*) to celebrate the divine office ("pro offitio divino celebrando") for twenty years.

58. ASF, NA 7871, fol. 113r.

59. Zorzi, 1994, 345; Barbieri, 300.

5. OSHEIM

1. The Italian term *pieve* is used to describe a church that had rights to administer the sacraments in a particular district. The pievano oversaw subaltern churches lacking independent sacramental functions, or *parrocchie* within the district. American English has no clear language to make the distinction. I will refer to parish churches (pievi) and to local churches (parrocchie).

2. Seghieri, 281–83 no. 108 (Feb. 16, 1333): "occasione guerre et abundatione aquarum fluminum ire ad batiçandum parvulos ad plebem Sancti Petri in Campo et propter periculosum iter plures parvuli decesserint sine habendo lavacrum batismatis."

3. The literature on the rural churches is rapidly growing. The best introduction is Violante, 1984. On the reconstruction of the countryside, see Szabó. The best single work on the formation and eventual decline of the rural parish districts is, in fact, a study of the diocese of Lucca; see Nanni.

4. Wickham, 1995, 170–71.

5. On territorial churches, see Bizzocchi, 1987 and 1996.

6. Kirshner, 1996, is a general study of the growth of the state in Italy; see also Cohn, 1999, and the classic studies in Chittolini, 1979.

7. Trexler, 1980, 6; and Bizzocchi, 1987, 1996.

8. On the interests of smaller states, see Bowsky, 160–62 and 182–83; and Bratchel. Both authors make clear that although Siena and Lucca were quite aware of their powerful Florentine neighbor, they altered their policies when necessary but largely maintained their autonomy.

9. Leverotti, 1992, 190–94; Osheim, 1976 and 1989a.
10. On the first attempts to dismember the Lucchese diocese, see Chittolini, 1982.
11. On the problems Lucca faced as it tried to protect these areas against the aggressive, fifteenth-century Florentine state, see Bratchel.
12. The following is based on the information contained in Guidi and Giusti.
13. Górecki, 46–48, where he reports one case where a parish district extended more than one hundred square kilometers. More generally, see Kurze, which offers the best available survey of parish structure in Europe.
14. Archivio Arcivescovile di Lucca [hereafter AAL], *Libro grande dei privilegi*, 52–60; parchments from the Archivio diplomatico of the archiepiscopal archive are cited in Nanni, 178–79. The agreement of 1122 is in Appendix 1 of Nanni, 191–93. Patronage eventually passed to the Clarisses at Gattaiola, but tensions with the bishop and pievano continued.
15. Osheim, 1989b.
16. AAL, Diplomata, ++ O 81, June 27, 1213.
17. Nanni, 194–97, Apr. 22, 1233. Most of the issues between parish rectors and their local churches continued to be mentioned in episcopal documents appointing local priests throughout the thirteenth and fourteenth centuries. See, e.g., AAL, Diplomata, e.g., +A 19 (1357), +G 80 (1357), +G 94 (1362), +K 51 (1278), +M 37 (1360), +P 19 (1266–67), +P 55 (1258), +P 100 (1475), +Q14 (1349). +R (1357); and Libri Antichi, 13, 6r–v, 297v–98v, 311r–12r, 322r–24r355v.
18. On the case, see AAL, Libri Antichi, 9, 36r–v (June 12, 1307), 37r–v (June 22, 1307), 38r–41v, June 22–28, 1307), 42r–43r (June 29, 1307). On Marlia, see Wickham, 1995, 38–55; and Osheim, 1977, 53–54.
19. Leverotti, 1992, 196, and Wickham, 1995, 78, both observe that before 1360 there was an almost exact congruence between rural church and commune.
20. The nunzio reported that he cried loudly and publicly before the church of San Terenzo asking "quicumque vult aliquid dicere vel opponere contra dictam electionem factam de dicto presbytero Bonaiuta ad rectoriam ipsius ecclesie vel contra personam ipsius presbyteri Bonaiute . . . coram ipso vicario luce in episcopali palatio debeat comperere."
21. Bizzocchi, 1987.
22. Osheim, 1977, 39–41.
23. Ibid., 40.
24. AAL, Libri Antichi, 9, 58v–62r (Apr. 3, 1316): "discreto viro Nicholao vocato Telo Amiçi de domo Petri civitatis Pisani . . . cum cura et etiam sine cura non obstante quod ipse non sit in sacris ordinibus constitutus."
25. Ibid., 85v–86v (June 27, 1318): "non obstante quod idem Francischus non sit in sacris ordinibus constitutus aut quod dicatur nescire gramaticum."
26. On the situation at Santa Maria a Monte, see Osheim, 1977, 67–69, 75–78. Meek finds that Pisan fiscal demands were not excessive at a time when they were concerned to maintain control, and Bratchel notes the relative care governments exercised in sensitive border areas.
27. AAL, Diplomata, ++ C 48 (1293). Montopoli was south of the Arno in an area the Pisans threatened but did not control. It did, however, fall under Floren-

tine control in the fourteenth century; see Casini, 3. Other examples of local participation are AAL, Diplomata, + E 86 (1290, 1297), + K 51 (1278), + M 99 (1220), + N 78 (1273), + Q 14 (1349).

28. Guidi and Pellegrinetti, 59–116. Most payments (in wax or pepper) contained in the register were in fact in recognition of jurisdictional rights, for the right to build a new church or hospital (e.g., lines 1703–04); Altopascio (line 1095) did pay three pounds of wax "pro decima de multis locis," but most tithe payments were in money, usually sums of £3 or less.

29. For a number of leases early in the fourteenth century, see e.g., AAL, Libri antichi, 9, 22r–v, 23v–24r, 24v–25v, 35r–v, 72v–73r, 298v–299v, 299v–300v, 352r–v.

30. Guidi and Pellegrinetti, lines 993–94: "Pagò Guccio da Pucci per la chiesa et per lo comune de Aquilea."

31. The conflict is narrated in Nanni, 156–57.

32. The agreement is transcribed in Oneri, 138.

33. This section, unless otherwise noted, is based on Casini, 77–79, 89–90; and Romiti, 38, 50, 51–52, 57–58.

34. The statutes of Mutigliano are in Ferri, esp. 98–103.

35. Archivio di Stato di Lucca [hereafter ASL], Estimo, 11 (1311). As in larger towns, the term (rural) *luminaria* most often referred to the festival in honor of the church's patron saint. The opera was the corporation charged with maintaining the "works" or the fabric of the church itself.

36. AAL, Visite pastorali, 1; and AAL, Diplomata + E 16 (1280), the sentence of a priest who was guilty of concubinage and fraud.

37. The agreements between the rector of Compito and the Monks at the hermitage of Santa Maria (AAL, Diplomata, ++ O 81, June 27, 1213) were witnessed by nine local clerics.

38. Seghieri, 21–22, no. 22.

39. Leverotti, 1992, 190–96.

40. See e.g., AAL, Libri antichi 9, 72v–73r; and Guidi and Pellegrinetti, 59–116.

41. AAL, Diplomata, +A 4 (1248), +A15 (1213), +A 96 (1341), +E 5 (1348), +E 56 (1281), +S 6 (1313), +S 25 (1305), ++F 93 (1238), ++ P 64 (1294).

42. Osheim, 1977, 98–99, 126; Luzzati, 1978 and 1979.

43. ASL, Estimo 7 (compiled 1284–87). The volume lists 503 individuals who paid rents to the bishop, sometimes for land they had sublet from others. In addition to the rent owed to the bishop, the volume records 293 rents paid to other individuals or institutions, 38 of which were owed to the parish or local church.

44. On the Guinigi at Villa Basillica, see Polica.

45. ASL, Curia dei Foretani, 88 141r–v, 1363: a plaintiff claims properties that had been left with the rector of San Giusto di Massa Macinaia; 100, Mar. 13–June 5, 1374, concerns a loan of three florins made by the pievano of Compito.

46. ASL, Cura dei Foretani 57, 147v. For similar suits, see vols. 24, Oct. 30, 1338; and 47 24r, 71r, 1345.

47. ASL, Curia dei Foretani 18 102r, 1337, where the pievano claimed property; 125r, where the rector of Santa Maria a Ripa claimed that the lands in ques-

tion were held from him; and 34 87r (1343) and 57 (May 17, 1356), where churchmen appeared in support of defendants

48. ASL, Capitano del Contado, 2 3v (1346): Andrea Viti had threatened the life of Puccione Meucci of Ruota, saying "se tu fussi più fuore dell uscio che tu non se, tu non torneresi mai om casa." This seems to have been part of a series of problems with a faction in the district.

6. BRENTANO

1. Brooke, 150–51.
2. Baird, 48–49. My citations of Salimbene are to Baird's accessible translation. Although I am accustomed to using the edition of Holder-Egger, thanks to flaws in the electronic catalogue of the University of California, Berkeley, here I use the edition of Scalia. The manuscript is BAV, vat. lat. 7260.
3. Brentano, 1994, 230–31.
4. Brentano, 1991, 258.
5. Baird, 49.
6. Boehmer, 21.
7. Brentano, 1994, 231.
8. Brentano, 1988, 262–66.
9. Brentano, 1994, 231; "intensely local" is from Osheim's description of Guamo; Osheim, 1989b, 100.
10. Brentano, 1994, 268–69; Brentano, 1991, 242–47. See Rusconi, 1984; and Casagrande, 1984, for nuns of central Italy.
11. Pagnani, 1959, 153–77; Pagnani, 1964, cols. 1155–56.
12. Piano de Carpine is easily accessible in Dawson, 1–72.
13. Brentano, 1994, 24–27.
14. Brentano, 1994, 171–72; I chose San Benedetto and Sant'Agostino because of information about the nuns' confessional habits in 1375.
15. Orlandi, xlix, 5.
16. Baird, 302, 18.
17. Carruthers, 122–55.
18. Baird, 8, 11–16, 9.
19. Baird, 60–61.
20. Baird, 160; Scalia, 1: 245–46.
21. Baird, 182, 13.
22. Baird, 544; Scalia, 2: 782.
23. Baird, 18–20; Scalia, 1: 62–63.
24. Baird, 20.
25. Baird, 13–17.
26. Baird, 427.
27. Baird, 47–49, 474–75.
28. William of Rubruck is easily accessible in Dawson, 88–220.
29. Calvino, 86.
30. Baird, 162.
31. Rigon, 1995.
32. Ragusa and Green, 70, plate 59.

7. LANSING

1. The case is edited in Kantorowicz, vol. I, part 2, no. 22: 218–23.
2. English language studies include Brucker, 1986; Cohen and Cohen; and Ruggiero, 1993.
3. Pini, 1969.
4. See Bocchi, 1982.
5. See Pini, 1978.
6. Chabot, 1989, p. 568n.
7. There is a large literature; one starting point is Van Engen.
8. On Bolognese notaries, see Tamba.

9. Klapisch-Zuber, 1985, 213–46; Chojnacki.
10. Chabot, 1989, 570.
11. For Florence, see Cohn, 1996b, 16–38, 172–78.
12. The court's formula was "quod ipsa est publica meretrix et quod publice facit se subponi omnibus hominibus eam volentibus." See, e.g., Archivio di Stato di Bologna [hereafter ASB], Libri Inquisitionum et testium, 14 4r.
13. For recent studies of late medieval Italian marriage, see Dean, 1–21; and Breveglieri.
14. See Karras; M. S. Mazzi.
15. Rinaldi, 109.
16. Frati, book II, rubric 52, p. 310. See Muzzarelli, 136–54.
17. ASB, Curia del Podestà, Corone ed armi 3, 2, 2r.
18. On the limits of reliance on materials of this kind, see Kirshner, 1975; and English.
19. See Vallerani, 1991, and 1993, 306–9.
20. Infamy was a complex legal category. In Roman law, infamy was a sanction derived from a specific legal penalty. *Infamia* meant loss or diminution of legal rights because of a morally blameworthy action. Medieval jurists developed the idea of *infamia ipso iure*, the view that certain crimes because of their notoriety or scandalous consequences conferred immediate infamy, before any legal penalty. This meant that from the perspective of the jurist, social as well as legal norms shaped the category in practice. See Migliorino; and Casagrande, 1996.
21. ASB, Curia del Podestà, Libri Inquisitionum et testium, 46, 2, 41r–47v.
22. See N. Davis, 1987.
23. Bornstein, 1997.
24. Sheedy, 57–59. On legal views of concubinage in medieval towns, see Medici, 146–52; and Brundage.
25. Frati, book IV, rubric 33, p. 197.
26. Mattassoni, 416–19.
27. Mattassoni, 424.
28. Klapisch-Zuber, 1985, 165–77.
29. See Wemple, part I.
30. See Ortalli, tables 2, 4, and 6.
31. See Pini, 1978, 383–89.
32. ASB, Libri Inquisitionum et testium, 2, 6, 28r.
33. See Hughes, 1978.
34. ASB, Accusationes 6a, 12r, 17v, 27r.
35. ASB, Accusationes 5b,15, 12r–v. Floriana's ban is register 19, 6v.
36. ASB, Libri Inquisitionum et testium, 3, 221r–222v.
37. See Duby.
38. ASB, Libri Inquisitionum et testium, 7, 2, 56v.
39. ASB, Libri Inquisitionum et testium, 4, 1, 51r.
40. ASB, Curia del podestà, Accusationes 6a, 17r.
41. See Klapisch-Zuber, 1985, 140–41.
42. ASB, Libri Inquisitionum et testium, 3, 23v–24v.
43. ASB, Libri Inquisitionum 19 (1290), 10, 10r–11v.
44. ASB, Libri Inquisitionum et testium, 10, 5, 1r–4v.
45. See White.
46. ASB, Libri Inquisitionum et testium, 14, 5, 7v.

47. ASB, Accusationes 6a, 1, 46r; their landlord was charged with keeping a brothel: 6a, 4, 9r.
48. ASB, Libri Inquisitionum et testium, 10, 7, 17r–25v.
49. ASB, Libri Inquisitionum et testium, 19, 6, 18r–v.
50. ASB, Libri Inquisitionum et testium, 33 II, 3, 4r–9r.
51. Chabot, 1988 and 1986. Stella, 180–81. See also Farmer.
52. ASB, Libri Inquisitionum et testium, 14, 1, 3v. For six women who stated that half their earnings went to a pimp, Libri Inquisitionum et testium, 23, 5, 54v–56r.
53. ASB, Libri Inquisitionum et testium, 7, 12, 6v.
54. Frati, book IV, rubric 34, later addition, pp. 200–201.
55. ASB, Libri Inquisitionum et testium, 1, 3, 1v.
56. These assumptions shape, for example, the scholarship on marriage strategies. See Dean and Lowe, 1998.
57. See M. S. Mazzi, 326–27.

8. NUSSDORFER

1. Salvioli, 2:439–41; Gualazzini, 13:567–70.
2. Gualazzini, 13:567–68; Salvioli, 2:440; Watson, 9.
3. Giuliani, 37:540–42; Lévy, 160–61.
4. Lévy, 148–60; Salvioli, 2:405–15; Gualazzini, 13:570. Although they originally shared the premier position, notarial writing came to be preferred to oral testimony by witnesses.
5. Del Giudice, 101–2.
6. The publishing history of the *Tractatus universi iuris*, which included hundreds of works, is discussed by Bellingeri, 173, 185.
7. Del Re, 139–41. For his subsequent turbulent career, see 141–64.
8. The first edition of Farinacci's *Praxis et theorica criminalis* came out under various titles from publishers in several Italian cities; for details, see Del Re, 183–86.
9. This bore the title *De falsitate et simulatione* ("On false and fictitious acts"); Del Re, 172–73, 184n. This text appears in vol. 6 of Farinacci's *Operum criminalium*, 8 vols. Nuremberg, 1676–1728.
10. Del Re, 135–61, 171–75. Farinacci also owned a Roman notarial office from which he drew a monthly income.
11. Farinacci, vol. 6, question (Q.) 153, paragraph number (no.) 142. Henceforth all citations to Farinacci will be to question and paragraph number only.
12. Petrucci, 1993; Fortunati. See also the catalogue edited by Petrucci, 1982.
13. Since Farinacci deals with forged writing of all kinds, we often must be attentive to his language to know when he is referring to notaries. In discussing documents in general, Farinacci uses the phrase *scripturae et instrumenta* ("writings and instruments"). When he specifically means notarial writing, he uses the precise legal terms for them: instruments and wills (testamenta) or scripturae publicae ("public writings").
14. Farinacci, Q. 156, no. 146.

15. Ibid., Q. 154, introductory paragraph.

16. Recognizing that usage varied among his readers, Farinacci was careful to define the terms that he employed for the canonical stages in producing a notarial document. English translations of these terms are necessarily clumsy as there is no precise equivalent for these texts or actions in Anglo-American law. The notary's first notes of the agreement between the parties or the intentions of the testator were called the matrix, *originale*, or *abbreviatura* (or *imbreviatura*).

17. Among many examples, see Farinacci, Q. 153, no. 188; Q. 155, nos. 44, 62, 87; Q. 158, nos. 15, 153, 175.

18. Farinacci called the fully elaborated Latin version of the instrument a protocollum. Confusingly, the bound volume in which these full versions were kept on file in the notary's office was also called a protocollum.

19. Farinacci, Q. 157, nos. 19–85.

20. On the notary's need to keep records, see Farinacci's extensive discussion, Q. 154, nos. 28–51.

21. Ibid., Q. 153, nos. 134–35.

22. Ibid., Q. 153, no. 142 ; see also Q. 153, no. 136.

23. Ibid., Q. 153, no. 129.

24. Ibid., Q. 153, no. 145; Q. 154, nos. 30–34.

25. The custom of recording full versions of an instrument in paper booklets later bound and endowed with a table of contents listing clients alphabetically was unknown before the fifteenth century and did not spread until the sixteenth; this discussion is an example of the surfacing of early modern writing practices in Farinacci's text. See Berengo, 1976–77, 165.

26. Farinacci, Q. 158, no. 1.

27. Ibid., Q. 158, no. 28.

28. Ibid., Q. 158, nos. 29–48, are devoted to this debate.

29. Farinacci added, however, that local laws (*statuta*) could give notarial instruments more force, including immunity from contradiction (Q. 158, nos. 49, 50, 51).

30. Ibid., Q. 158, no. 148; for similar views, see also nos. 143, 146, 147, 160.

31. Ibid., Q. 158, nos. 149, 150, 154, 155.

32. Ibid., Q. 158, nos. 138–40. Some jurists specified the evidence (*demonstrationes*) necessary to prove identity; these included surname, birthplace (*patria*), neighborhood or parish, and names of relatives (*parentum*) (no. 140).

33. Ibid., Q. 158, nos. 92–115. Farinacci referred readers repeatedly to the volume of his treatise that dealt with the subject of witnesses. Local laws compensated for the jurists' vagueness by defining precisely the personal qualities necessary for witnesses; they seldom excluded women completely.

34. Ibid., Q. 158, no. 123.

35. Ibid., Q. 158, no. 209.

36. Much of seventeenth-century Romania's first secular law code was taken directly from Farinacci's handbook; Del Re, 177, 183; Del Giudice, 115–16.

37. Pope Paul V's legislation of 1612 to improve judicial procedures in Rome included many provisions on proper handling of documents by notaries; Bullarium.

38. Alessi Palazzolo, 109–12.

9. DAVIS

1. On the British Grand Tour, the most recent works are J. Black; Chaney; Redford; and Pemble.

2. The largest of these foreign colonies were the Germans, Turks, Dalmatians, Greeks, Albanians, Armenians, and Jews, along with resident Italian populations from Lucca, Milan, Bergamo, Friuli, Padua, and so forth; see Costantini; and Fedalto, 499.

3. Newett, 153.

4. On tourist sites and related theories of tourism, see Urry; and MacCannell. On the notion of the pilgrim as tourist and the tourist as pilgrim, see Cohen and Cohen, 90–110; and Graburn, 20–23.

5. On the late medieval pilgrim traffic through Venice (largely in the context of the economics of their transportation, however), see Newett, esp. 23–113; Ashtor; and Tucci, 1980; also Costantini, 886–87.

6. Newett, 124–25. Casola seems to have been referring to both the common talk among travelers of his day and specifically to descriptions of the city that he had read, accounts by earlier pilgrims of their journeys to the Holy Land via Venice, such as that produced by his fellow Milanese, Santo Brasca in 1480; Lepschy, 32–33.

7. For some of these laundry lists of travel items recommended to potential pilgrims, see Wey, 4–7; Letts, 1926, 69–71; and Lepschy, 128–29.

8. Ibid., 48; van Harff, 54–55; Newett, 125; Stewart, 110.

9. Newett, 125–32, 137.

10. Ashtor, 205–12; Letts, 1926, 33 and 47; Newett says that by 1451 the fall galleys had been abandoned completely, largely due to declining demand; Newett, 77–78 and 124.

11. Newett, 337–42; Stewart, 84 and 107.

12. Keep in mind that a skilled Venetian worker earned around forty ducats a year in 1500; Lane, 1934, 177, n. 6; 178–79 and 251–52; Lane, 1973, 46 and 63; Tucci, 1985, 64–65.

13. It is interesting to note how those pilgrims who did go to Florence dispensed with the city (which van Harff called "very pleasant" and Tafur termed "one of the most wonderful in Christendom") in just a few paragraphs, staying only briefly in their apparent eagerness to get to Rome; see van Harff, 12–13; and Letts, 1926, 30 and 227–28.

14. For visitors (and certainly for the Venetians themselves), transferring so many relics from Constantinople to Venice simply replaced one traditional pilgrimage destination with another; see Geary, 98–128; Muir, 1981, 96 and 207; Lane, 1973, 41–2, 104, 106, and 394.

15. Fitz-Simon, quoted in Parks, vol. 1, 579–81; later visitors would add the names of Saints Helena, Massimo, Paul the martyr, Barbara, Giovanni the duke, and Eustachio; see also Guylforde, 8.

16. Newett, 324; also Letts, 1926, 27, for a similar vow.

17. Stewart, 110. Fabri's desire to visit all the Venetian shrines appropriate to travelers took his group all over the city and out to Murano—to San Raffaello, San Michele, San Cristoforo, and finally to Santa Marta.

18. Frescobaldi, 7. Frescobaldi then goes on to list the eleven major saints' relics he visited, along with "a great piece of the Wood of the Cross," and 198 entire bodies of the infants killed by order of Herod.

19. Wey, 89–90; Lepschy, 50–51.

20. Friar Felix also carried the jewels of some of his companions; Stewart, 93–94. Santo Brasca, who was in Venice the same month as Fabri, also stressed that he had "seen and touched" all of the many relics on his list; Lepschy, 50–51; also Geary, 32–35.

21. Evelyn, vol. 1, 200–01. The treasury was also said to contain "the very ring which St. Mark wore on his thumb" (Letts, 1957, 156); plus a painting of the Virgin and the original Gospel of St. Mark, both in the saint's own hand. François Misson claimed to have examined the latter at some length, finding it "so worn, torn, defaced, and rotten with Moisture, and other Injuries of Time . . . [that] it is a hard matter to discern anything in it." In the end, he was unable to tell for sure even if it was written in Latin or in Greek; Misson, vol. 1, 175–76.

22. Tucoo-Chala and Pinzuti, 98; van Harff, 52; Moryson, 80–81; Evelyn, 200–01; *Le Saint Voyage* . . . , 32–34; only Anglure in the *Saint Voyage* mentions the large tooth.

23. Tucoo-Chala and Pinzuti, 98; Newett, 126; van Harff, 52, 54–55.

24. Stewart, 94–95; Letts, 1926, 157–58; Newett, 127.

25. Stewart, 83–84.

26. Muir, 1981, 119–34 and 223–30; Evelyn, 198.

27. Tamizey de Larroque, 18.

28. *Viaggio in Terra Santa* . . . , 17–18; Letts, 1926, 158–59; Stewart, 99; Lepschy, 49.

29. Casola is the first to mention actually marching in the procession, although many earlier pilgrims describe it in great detail; Newett, 146–53; Lepschy, 50; Stewart, 108–09; Tucoo-Chala and Pinzuti, 106–07.

30. Guylforde, 11. Positions of greatest honor were in the center of the procession, as close as possible to its principal figure, whether the doge or the patriarch; Muir, 1981, 189–211.

31. It was hoped that, once back home, they would at least not spread negative stories about the republic, or take reprisals on its merchants; Newett, 49.

32. This was their first mention in the deliberations of the Great Council; ibid., 24–49.

33. Archivio di Stato di Venezia [hereafter ASV], Cattaveri, busta 2, reg. 4, Mar. 22, 1387, and May 20, 1401, Mar. 9, 1429 (cited by Newett). Tucci has noted that the term tolomazi was a Venetian corruption of the German *Dolmetscher*, or guide; Tucci also observes that *messeta*, or agent, was used as well for this profession; see Tucci, 1985, 63 and n. 78. My thanks to Vera Costantini, however, for pointing out the Turkish roots of Dolmetscher and thus of tolomazi, and the fact that the term was used by Venetians more in the sense of "interpreter" than "guide."

34. The tolomazi were permitted around 5 percent for help in booking their clients' passage to the East; ASV, Cattaveri, reg. 4, Mar. 22, 1387, June 28, 1448, and Jan. 14, 1455 (more Veneziano, 1454); cited in Newett, 41 and 73.

35. Costantini has termed the conditions in many osterie pubbliche as "terrifying"; Costantini, 891–92 and note 36; on the dazio, see ibid., 890.

36. Stewart, 79; Zaniboni, 57.

37. Stewart, 80; Fabri goes on to tell the story of St. George's famous "big black dog," who, when Germans came to the inn, "showed how pleased he was by wagging his tail," but who also raged, "barking loudly, leap[ing] furiously upon . . . Italians or Lombards, Gauls, Frenchmen, Slavonians, Greeks, or men of any country except Germany."

38. Newett, 123; *Viaggio in Terra Santa* . . . , 48; van Harff, 50–51; van Harff also had the pleasure of having fellow Germans from the Fondaco as his guides about the city.

39. Stewart, 105–06; Padoan Urban.

40. Venice, Museo Correr, mss. *provinenze diverse*, 396c/II c524: *Forestieri a Venezia nel sec. XVI; osterie e albergatori*, undated but mid-sixteenth century.

41. A 1784 list of all the city's short-term rental facilities names and locates forty licensed osterie, plus nearly two thousand individual albergatori who offered rooms; ASV, Inquisitori di Stato, bu. 760. Interestingly, the albergatori have recently begun to resurface in Venice, in the form of "bed and breakfasts." See "Venezia trasformata in dormitorio." *Nuova Venezia*, Feb. 3, 2000.

42. Newett, 141–42; Crouzet-Pavan, 256, for a partial census of the city in 1509.

43. Fabri's inn of St. George was located just behind the Fondaco dei Tedeschi. Evidently the only churches his group walked to were San Marco, San Bartolomeo (the parish church of the Fondaco), San Salvadore, Santa Maria dei Miracoli, and SS. Giovanni e Paolo; Stewart, 84–110; also Letts, 1926, 167.

44. Coryat, vol. 1, 314. Coryat's estimate of the number of gondolas in Venice is on the low side among the many offered by visitors to the city between the 1400s and the 1700s, ranging from one thousand clear up to eighty thousand.

45. Lassels, 226; Lassels visited Venice several times between 1635 and 1665.

46. Du Mont, 395; Davis, 1991, 28–30.

47. Newett, 111–13. Some activity in this sector apparently continued for many years to come, however; cf. Gailhard, 119, who claimed in the 1660s that the Cattaveri were still available to adjudicate disputes between pilgrims to the Holy Land and the sea captains who carried them.

48. Cf. Coryat, 325–26, 365.

49. Although both Casola and van Harff do discuss at some length (and with some disapproval) the dress and appearance of women who were almost certainly street whores, they never openly named them as such; cf. Newett, 144–45; Letts, 1926; van Harff, 64–65; on the other hand, see Coryat, 407–09.

10. COOPER

1. See, e.g., Bowsky, 260–98, for Siena, and Vauchez, 1993, 153–68, more generally. "Civic religion" lies at the heart of the fine studies of Savonarolan Florence by Weinstein and Polizzotto.

2. Trexler, 1980, 3–6.

3. Ibid., 43; Trexler, 1973, 136.
4. Vauchez, 1993, 162.
5. Guidoni, 123–58.
6. Vita Silvestri [hereafter VS], chap. 1. The Silvestrine vitae are edited in Grégoire, 1983.
7. VS, chap. 2. In point of fact it was not so remote, and Corrado soon discovered Silvestro and his companion, leading them to a rather dismal and not very suitable cave that seeped water continuously. After a short while, Silvestro moved on to a new site along the gorge of the Esino known as Gola della Rossa. Here, at his third refuge at Grottafucile, Silvestro began construction of his first monastery, "S. Maria de Focile in Gricta," as it is called in its earliest extant documents; Archivio del monasterio di S. Silvestro in Montefano [hereafter AMF], fondo Grottafucile n. 17, Feb. 25, 1254).
8. VS, chap. 6: "Cepit deinde homo Dei Silvester loca construere atque in eis homines ad Dei servitium congregare, non secularium hominum conversationem expetens, sed heremitica et vastissima loca pro civitatibus potius eligebat."
9. Ibid.: "Tante vero solitudinis et silvestri loci mons erat iam dictus, ut nullus quavis annositate suffultus ad ipsius montis heremum sine comite se transferret."
10. Ibid., chap. 7: "Non utique hominibus sotiatum, non circumseptum ordine famulorum, non adipe frumenti se reficientem et vini dulcedine, sed duritie ordeacei panis et limpha, corporis inediam expellentem, cum quodam lupo suos prostrato ad pedes, tres predicti ei homines indagarunt."
11. Vita beati Johannis a Baculo confessoris et mirifici heremite [hereafter VJB], in Grégoire, 1983, chap. 2: "Qui propter licterarum et grammaticalium studium pervigilem curam anime non postponens, predicationibus et sermonibus qui fiebant in religiosorum et aliorum ecclesiis cum posse aderat deesse nolebat." Still, we are told that Giovanni performed adequately enough until his academic career was mercifully cut short by the abscess on his leg that gave rise to his appellation dal Bastone, "of the staff," (VJB, chap. 2).
12. Ibid., chap. 10: "Nam vidit in sompnis quoddam solare iubar, a cella viri sancti usque ad locum de Fabriano protensum per devexum montis latus descendere, et super illud habitum et cucullam ordinis gradientem."
13. Ibid., chap. 14. This tribunal, which included a canon of Fabriano's principal collegial church of San Venanzo (representing the Bishop of Camerino), a member of the powerful (Ghibelline) Chiavelli family, and two notaries, was clearly intended to validate evidence for a canonization process.
14. Under the guidance of archivist Ugo Paoli, a project is under way to publish critical editions of most of the documents in the Silvestrine archives at Montefano. Two volumes of this anticipated eight-volume series have been published so far, and a third is in press. The published volumes are *Le Carte dell'Archivio di San Silvestro in Montefano*, I: *Montefano, S. Benedetto, Fabriano*, Fabriano, 1990; and II: *Congregazione*, Fabriano, 1991. These are volumes 14 and 15 in the *Bibliotheca Montisfani* series; documents appearing in these volumes will be cited as (e.g.) BM 14 with appropriate document number.
15. See A. Cherubini for capsule histories of monasteries in the Marches.
16. Castagnari and Lipparoni, particularly tables 14 and 15. Other important

monasteries whose fortunes waned as those of the commune of Fabriano waxed: S. Biagio di Caprile (f. 1035); S. Croce di Tripezzo, near Sassoferrato (f. 12th c.); and S. Angelo infra Ostia (f. 10th c.).

17. Avarucci and Paoli.

18. Thus in 1090 Abbot Morico I granted to Ugo, Alberto, and Suppo, sons of Albrico nobilissimus comes, the castello of Genga, "and to their sons and grandsons"; Sassi, 1962, doc. 71.

19. Sassi, 1930.

20. Sassi, 1950, 117–29. For S. Maria d'Apennino, a papal bull of 1156 placing S. Maria d'Apennino in direct dependence upon the Holy See mentions thirty-two churches dependent upon the monastery. See Sassi, 1929, doc. 11.

21. Sassi, 1962, doc. 40 (1041).

22. Fiecconi; also Zonghi, doc. 34 (1202): "in castello novo de fabriano"; doc. 60 (1213): "actum in burgo veteri castri fabriani"; Mittarelli and Costadoni, 3: app. 328 (ca. 1160): "per stradam infra ambo castra Fabriani."

23. Luzzatto.

24. Zonghi, doc. 8 (1165): "ego Albertus, et Raynaldus Comes Filii de Rodulpho Comite, et pro Nepote nostro Offredusio, et pro heredibus nostris perpetualiter promittimus vobis Consulibus Brunello, et Ugolino, vestrisque successoribus, et aliis hominibus Fabriani majoribus atque minoribus." For discussion of the early commune, see Quagliarini.

25. Castagnari.

26. Zonghi, doc. 56 (1212); Avarucci and Paoli, 269.

27. Zonghi, doc. 86 (1224).

28. Sassi, 1962, docs. 143 (1218) and 170 (1232).

29. Ibid., docs. 210–13. An indication of the continued lure of S. Vittore delle Chiuse's power and influence is the fact that during election of a new abbot, in 1308 Crescenzio Chiavelli, who at that time was a member of the Silvestrine order, put together a group of family members and retainers and secured his own election as abbot of S. Vittore by bribing five monks and holding the other ten incommunicado until the "election" was over. Despite howls of protest, Crescenzio retained the post of abbot until his death in 1348, weathering at least three substantial periods of excommunication. His story is recounted in Sassi, 1926a, 219–39.

30. See, e.g., Da Campagnola; also, P. Jansen; and Grégoire, 1986.

31. Pagnani, 1962b, 4–5.

32. Golubovich.

33. Pagnani, 1962a; Sassi, 1926a, 5–12. In Fabriano, although tradition holds that St. Francis first preached in the central piazza in 1209, the first permanent Franciscan convent was established well outside of town in 1234 (Archivio Storico Comunale di Fabriano [ASCF], busta II, pergamena 104, 1234: "ad faciendum locum pro fratribus Minoribus"). See also Sassi, 1948. They next moved to a site just outside the city walls, in 1266 (Pagnani, 1959). It was not until 1282 that the Franciscans acquired their magnificent site across from the Palazzo del Podestà (ASCF, busta IV, pergamena 191, 1282).

34. Rano. The Hermits of Montefavale ultimately rejected Augustinian Rule in favor of the Rule of St. Benedict.

35. Roth, 2: 121–22.

36. Ibid., 149; Bellini, 170–71. The Giamboniti were followers of Giovanni Bono.

37. See Giorgi for a discussion of Benedictine hermits in the southern Marches.

38. Sassi, 1957, for Fabriano and, in general, Casagrande, 1988.

39. BM 14 doc. 63 (1276): Suor Benentesa di Morico di Gentile, living in carcere, offers herself and her property, and her cell. Also, BM 14 doc. 40 (1278).

40. Lambert, 160.

41. Roth, 2: 138.

42. Ibid., 2: 240–44.

43. The earliest Silvestrine hagiographic work is the *Hystoria de Vita Sancti Bonfilij Episcopi et Confessoris*, attributed to Silvestro himself and probably written ca. 1250. It recounts the life and miracles of a monk, bishop, and crusader turned hermit of the previous century, whose relics were incorporated into the Silvestrine church and monastery in Cingoli. Among Silvestrines the vita is read essentially as an autobiography by their founder. Although it is important for its evocation of eremitic values and contains a convincing denunciation of lawyers and professors seduced by worldly vanity, it reveals nothing of the early history of the order. Composition of the *Vita Silvestri* can be dated by internal evidence between 1274 and 1282 and is fairly securely attributed to Andrea di Giacoma. The *Vita Johannes a Bacaluo* can be dated by internal evidence and accompanying dedication to 1299–1315, more likely toward the latter date, and quite definitely attributed to Andrea. The *Vita Ugonis* probably dates to the mid-fourteenth century.

44. The earliest constitutions date from the first decade of the fourteenth century. Neither of the two surviving manuscripts makes any reference to mendicancy. See Weissenberger; and Serpelli.

45. Canon 13 (Tanner, I: 242).

46. VS, chap. 4.

47. Canon 23 (Tanner, 326–27).

48. VS, chap. 19: "Nam die quadam ad querendas elemosynas ad predictam Roccam Contradam Symon vir Dei accedens."

49. *Vita vel poius miracula beati Ugonis monachi silvestrini* [hereafter VU], chap. 3. Réginald Grégoire attributes the *Vita Ugonis* to Prior Andrea, following a Silvestrine tradition.

His opinion should not be lightly discarded, for Dom Réginald's work in preparing critical editions of the Silvestrine hagiographic texts has attuned him to Prior Andrea's authorial idiosyncrasies. Still, another venerable Silvestrine tradition can be found as early as the eighteenth century doubting Andrea's authorial role. In the prologue, for example, the author of the VU asserts "ideoque prisci temporis senes ferme ultra nonagenariam etatem agentes, crebro de vita, moribusque viri sancti solerter inquirendum curavimus." Interrogating the nonagenarians among the brothers would have been an eccentric way to conduct research about Ugo, who was, after all, a near contemporary of Andrea's.

50. BM, 15, docs. 10–29 (Oct. 13, 1268–Apr. 18, 1272); AMF, fondo San Bartolo di Serra San Quirico, doc. 16 (Mar. 15, 1269–June 17, 1269). Many of Bishop Guido's actual orders are no longer extant, but the Silvestrine appeals reference specific language in their counterarguments.

51. BM, 15, doc. 17 (Mar. 28, 1269): "non debeat elemosinas petere nec recipere asserendo eos proprium habere et possesiones suas colere."

52. AMF, fondo San Bartolo di Serra San Quirico, doc. 16 pergamena 4 (Mar. 28, 1269):"sine aliorum sufragio et elimosinis non possent vivere nec Deo servire."

53. See Dal Pino, 108–9.

54. VJB, chap. 2: "Si remaneret, dampna puritatis et casum anime fortius formidabat." The festering abscess on his leg that forced the end of his studies is presented here as divine deliverance.

55. True of Christian ascetics since the time of the Desert Fathers; see Goehring.

56. E.g., notes 3 and 4 to this chapter; and see Fattorini.

57. VS, chap. 14. See Constable, 47–130, on the practice and meaning of beards.

58. S. Maria Nuova in Perugia (1296); S. Marco in Florence (1300); S. Benedetto in Fabriano (1323).

59. Guidoni, 123–58.

60. As suggested by Saracco Previdi, 217–29.

61. VS, chap. 7.

62. BM, 14, docs. 1 and 2 (June 1, 1231), 4 (Mar. 7, 1234). In November 1234—three years after the first Montefano acquisitions—the canons of San Venanzo were midwifing entry of another order new to Fabriano. A distinguished cast of notables, including the bishop of Camerino, the abbot of San Vittore delle Chiuse, and "fratre Silvestro," witnessed the donation of a parcel of land in Cantiro, somewhat farther from town than Montefano, for construction of the first Franciscan convent in Fabriano. See note 31.

63. BM, 14, docs. 5 and 6 (July 25, 1235), 7, 8, and 9 (July 26, 1235), 10 (Aug. 10, 1235), 11 (Aug. 14, 1235).

64. Ibid., doc. 12 (July 30, 1235). Avarucci and Paoli put this document in 1236, resolving the conflict between the year and indiction given by the notary in favor of the indiction.

65. Ibid., doc. 13 (Jan. 7, 1237).

66. Ibid., doc. 131 (July 10, 1244).

67. Ibid., doc. 24 (Aug. 5, 1270): "vocatis ad examinandum rationem fratris Iacopi et fratris Benemcase, fratrum de Montefano, super administratione pecunie comunis predicti per eos facta in opere et occasione operis murorum comunis."

68. BM, 15, doc. 5 (Jan. 5, 1268).

69. Battisti, 1988–90.

70. VS, chap. 44.

71. BM, 14 doc. 237 (June 10, 1275); Zonghi, doc. 216 (1275).

72. BM, 14 doc. 29 (June 13, 1275).

73. Ibid., doc. 237.

74. Ibid., doc. 239 (Dec. 5, 1278).

75. Ibid.

76. Ibid., doc. 41 (Dec. 6, 1278).

77. For example, BM 14, docs. 147 (Aug. 29, 1312): asks burial in S. Benedetto and construction of altar to Blessed Virgin Mary; 148 (Aug. 29, 1312): asks burial in S. Benedetto; 149 (Sept. 7, 1314): leaves large bequest to Montefano, but asks burial in S. Benedetto. First mention of a Silvestrine church (ecclesia), in addition to the house (domus) in the Borgo Nuovo district, is in 1280; ibid., doc 47 (May 22, 1280).

78. Moronti.

79. BM 14, doc. 50 (Jan. 4, 1282).

80. Ibid., doc. 138 (Mar. 18, 1286).

81. BM, 14, doc. 141 (Aug. 16, 1290): Prior general Bartolo and seventeen brothers, meeting as a conventual chapter of Montefano, actually meet in the church in Fabriano: "Congregato capitulo heremi Montisfani in trasanda ... ecclesie Sancti Benedicti de Fabriano." BM, 14, doc. 143 (Oct. 6, 1290) records a similar meeting.

82. BM, 15, docs. 53, 55, 56 (Sept. 8, 1298).

83. AMF, fondo Cumulo Comune, quaderno 30 contains letters to each monastery announcing the general chapter to be held at Montefano in September 1298, to elect a new prior general. The letters record the monks present at the conventual chapters of each monastery receiving the letters, and those monks who will not be able to attend the general chapter. According to these convocation letters, there were 144 monks in attendance to receive the message, including two monks who were presented the letter at a location apart from their monastery. From these letters, it appears that there were seventy-one monks at the five monasteries of Montefano (nineteen), Perugia (seventeen), Rome (sixteen), Viterbo (eleven), and Orvieto (eight); seventy-three monks were distributed among the other fourteen monasteries.

84. Paoli, 1983, 18.

85. BM, 14, doc. 239.

86. BM, 15, doc. 5 (Jan. 4, 1268).

87. Zonghi, doc. 219 (Sept. 3, 1277).

88. AMF, fondo S. Marco di Firenze, doc. 1 rogito 2 (May 12, 1299).

89. BM, 15, doc. 77 (Apr. 21, 1303) lists seventeen monks.

90. Vauchez, 1997, 329–30.

91. Trapè.

92. P. Jansen, 56–64, map, p. 78.

93. Castagnari and Lipparoni, table 16.

94. *Licet Ecclesie Catholice*: "et ex pluribus cuneis acies una consurgent fortior ad hostiles spiritualis nequitie impetus conterendos."

95. Jordan of Saxony, 100.

96. Ibid., 101.

11. POLECRITTI

1. Bernardino, 1934, I, 282. For the reader's convenience, individual sermons are cited by year and location preached. Four major groups of vernacular sermon were recorded by Bernardino's listeners: Florence 1424 and 1425, along with Siena 1425, are in the Cannarozzi edition, while the best-known sermon cycle,

Siena 1427, is in the Delcorno edition. The most important contemporary lives of Bernardino are by Barnabò da Siena, Benvoglienti, and the Anonymous Friar. The best modern biography is by Origo; also see Mormando and Polecritti for recent studies of Bernardino's preaching against witches, Jews, and homosexuals, and on his peacemaking.

2. According to the merchant Sandro di Marco dei Marcovaldi; see Livi, 461.

3. See N. Z. Davis, 1982, 323–24; and K. L. Jansen, 6. Luria offers an excellent discussion of the inadequacies of "popular religion" as a category; 1–16. For model studies of lay piety in the later middle ages, see Vauchez; and Bornstein, 1993.

4. The thirteenth-century Dominican Humbert de Romans also saw the preacher as a man of multiple roles: doctor, singer, hunter, craftsman, and peddler; see the Tugwell edition, 198–99. An early thirteenth-century Cistercian implied that the preacher was a tender hen and that "the hearer ought to make a nest for the Word of God, a place to put the chicks and keep them safe"; see Kienzle, 97.

5. Bernardino, 1934, I, 327–28.

6. Bernardino, 1980, I, 147: "O tu che non udisti mai predica, secci venuto?"—"Sì."

7. Ibid., II, 89.

8. Ibid., I, 165. Similar complaints are common throughout the late middle ages. The same nonchalance continued even after the Protestant Reformation was well under way. A Lutheran reformer in Nassau-Wiesbaden in 1594 observed that "the moment the sermon ends, everybody runs out. No one stays for a hymn, prayer, and blessing. They behave as if they were at a dance, not a divine service"; cited by Strauss, 284.

9. Bernardino, 1934, II, 226.

10. Ibid., I, 283.

11. Ibid., I, 279. The Augustinian Girolamo da Siena (d. 1420) also had an ideal church-going audience in mind when he warned women to conduct themselves modestly, not sociably: "Nella chiesa entrate, non come quelle vane femmine che tutti i mercati e vicinati e parentadi e amicizie ritruovano nella chiesa di Dio; ma state sole, e divote, e con perpetuo silenzio." Cited by Rusconi, 1981, 177.

12. Bernardino, 1980, I, 561.

13. Ibid., II, 842–43: "Non dico che sieno donne quelle tali, no; ma più tosto ribalde; ché so' di quelle tante ardite e sfacciate, che co giovani vi ponete a vagheggiare eziandio dentro ne le chiese." The blasphemous sodomite "va in Vescovado, nel luogo dove si celebra a Dio, e ponsi ine a vegheggiare il garzone e la garzona a dispetto di Dio e de' santi"; ibid., II, 1161.

14. Ibid., I, 621: "Doh! diciamo che per istamane basti." A few seconds before ending the sermon, Bernardino accused anyone who engaged in such behavior of being beasts, without feeling, who "non si curano nulla."

15. Bernardino, 1934, II, 461–64.

16. Bernardino, 1980, II, 744.

17. Even in this case, Bernardino favored a moderate asceticism and casti-

gated the spiritually ambitious: "Sono molti, che come lo' viene uno pensiero, si vogliono fare romiti, e poi subito vorrebbe diventare papa collo desiderio"; Bernardino, 1934, II, 135.

18. There is an extensive, and still-growing, literature on Italian confraternities. Three recent overviews are by Black, 1989; Eisenbichler; and Donnelly and Maher. For similarities between the lay piety cultivated within this milieu and the Observant movement, see Henderson, 230–49.

19. Bernardino, 1980, I, 144.   20. Bernardino, 1934, II, 226.
21. Bernardino, 1980, II, 746. 22. Ibid., I, 263.
23. Bernardino, 1934, II, 240. 24. Ibid., I, 89.

25. Weissman argues that external devotions are not necessarily opposed to an "interior" religion; see his discussion of the relationship between humanist lay preachers and the wider world of the Florentine confraternities; 1990, 251–71.

26. Bernardino, 1980, I, 322.
27. Ibid., I, 149.
28. Ibid., I, 174.
29. Ibid., I, 130: "Io vi voglio fare tutti predicatori, e voi, donne, predicatrici." And the next day: "O donne, domane vi voglio fare tutte predicatrici"; 142.
30. Ibid., II, 1367.
31. Ibid., I, 160. But another fifteenth-century Observant, Cherubino da Spoleto, put the responsibility on the male head of household, who was supposed to set a good example, by either sending those under his care to the sermon or afterwards teaching them what was said ("debbigli mandare alle predicazioni . . . o vero ci va' tu, e poi in casa racconta o fa raccontare la predicare, accioché quegli che non ci sono stati venghino a imparare alcuna cosa; se non tutto, parte"); Rusconi, 1981, 191. Although Bernardino had more faith in his female listeners, he agreed that the head of household was supposed to see that the family received communion; Bernardino (Florence 1424), II, 264.
32. Bernardino, 1980, I, 149.
33. Ibid., II, 894.
34. Bernardino, 1934, I, 32–33. For a typical example of morning and evening self-reminders, see the popular late-fifteenth-century catechism by the German Observant Dietrich Kolde; Janz, 84–85, 98–100, 104–5.
35. Bernardino, 1934, II, 248.
36. Ibid., I, 7–8.
37. Ibid., I, 45.
38. Ibid., I, 67: lit., "Adunque ti conviene isforzare al modo del navicatore, quando à il vento a contrario, che si sforza co' remi in luogo salvo. E così, sforzandosi, va di bene in meglio. Così fa colui che vuole far bene, che dice: 'Che feci già uno anno? Feci el tale bene, e ora voglio agiognare el tale, e sarà cotanto meglio.' E in questo modo sempre va allo 'nnanzi e none adrieto.'"
39. Ibid., II, 233.
40. Bernardino, 1980, I, 619: lit., "Io ho udite cose tanto sterminate, che per l'anima mia io non le direi né in predica né in ragionamento."
41. Bernardino, 1934, II, 98.
42. See the Anonymous Friar, 316–17.

43. Boccaccio, Sixth Day, Tenth Tale, 505–14.
44. Bernardino, 1980, I, 143.
45. See Polecritti for a comprehensive discussion of audience response during sermon rituals.
46. Bernardino, 1934, I, 291. Several excited children are prominently depicted in the foreground of Agostino di Duccio's relief of Bernardino preaching before a bonfire (Capella di San Bernardino, Perugia).
47. Ibid., II, 12–13. Some of Bernardino's critics argued that he should sell the evil goods and donate the money to charity.
48. Ibid., I, 202. For the YHS controversy, see the critique by Bernardino's most prominent critic, the learned Augustinian Andrea Biglia. Also see Arasse.
49. Bernardino, 1934, I, 57.
50. Ibid., I, 1–3.
51. Ibid., I, 6. K. L. Jansen, 336, notes that "the laity of the later Middle Ages were nothing if not creative consumers in the rich symbolic economy of the medieval world."
52. Bernardino, 1934, I, 3. Bernardino associated witchcraft with heresy, unlike many less fanatic Tuscan preachers. See the discussions by Paton; and Mormando, 52–108 and 235–37.

12. SELWYN

1. For a valuable discussion of the importance of peacemaking to the Jesuits' broader missionary agenda, see O'Malley, esp. 168–71. O'Malley's study of the first twenty-five years of Jesuit activity and institutional formation is a remarkable introduction to the complex and controversial history (and historiography of the Society of Jesus.
2. See Selwyn, chap. 3, "Reverberations from the New World," 133, for D'Orta's letter to his *paesani*.
3. Santagata 4:202–03 (All translations are mine unless otherwise noted.) Santagata's two-volume *Istoria*, though an independent work, is the continuation, and hence always referred to as volumes 3 and 4, of the history of the Jesuits in Naples begun in Schinosi's two-volume *Istoria*.
4. Ibid.
5. Ibid.
6. Villari. On rising social tensions from the late sixteenth-century, and the impact of banditry, see esp. 29–55.
7. Giovanni Della Porta, for example, refers to the "vulgar man" (*Il volgo*) as "an untamed animal," lacking in sound judgment, and driven by "his violent inclination[s]" (*genio furioso*). For Della Porta's comments, and other views of the Neapolitan Plebe in the late-sixteenth and seventeenth centuries, see Mozzillo, 148–67, esp. 153. For a fascinating study of Naples' vibrant late medieval cultural milieu, see Bentley; an excellent recent study of the cultural context for intellectual production in seventeenth- and eighteenth-century Naples is Stone.
8. For consideration of the historiographical debates surrounding the Revolt of Naples, its relationship to other mid-seventeenth-century popular revolts, and

the interest in popular accounts of the "Revolt of Masaniello," see Villari, 153–88. For an excellent comparable study of violence, vendetta, and social revolt in another so-called backward region of Italy, the Friuli, see Muir, 1993.

9. Biblioteca Apostolica Vaticana [hereafter BAV], mss. Chigiani G. VII, 210, "Delle Rivolutioni di Napoli," vol. I, "Succinto Relatione della sollevatione di Napoli occorse nel presente anno 1647 à 7 di Luglio giorno di Domenica sino alla mort'di Tomm'Aniello," 63–102, esp. 79–80. Bandini, "Breve Lettera," as cited in Mozzillo, 85, 87.

10. Reports of J. Van Sonnevelt, Dutch consul in Venice, to the States General, July–Dec. 1647 (specific date not given), as cited in Villari, 171–88, esp. 184–85.

11. One desperate Jesuit missive suggests as much. See Archivio Storico Societatis Iesu [hereafter ARSI], Neap. 74, "Rumori di Napoli," Dec. 2, 1647, fols. 370r–371v.

12. For use of the expression "angels of peace," see Paolucci, 126–28.

13. On the theological basis for reconciliation, see Osborne. On the complex relationship between social reconciliation and the public mass, see Bossy.

14. On peacemaking efforts in medieval Italian towns, see Jones, 1997.

15. On a different set of medieval peacemakers, see Webb, 1979.

16. For a good discussion of the Capuchins' place in the wider context of sixteenth-century religious oratory and reform efforts, see D'Ascoli, esp. 50–79.

17. Osborne, 157–59. See also Tentler.

18. For a thorough discussion of these deliberations during the Council of Trent, including complex doctrinal debate among Catholic clergy, see Osborne, 157–97, esp. 159–84.

19. Prosperi, 642–49, esp. 643. Prosperi's wider study asserts that to understand the complex relationship between power and piety in early modern Italy, one must examine the interconnected roles of inquisitorial power, the confessor, and active missionary orders such as the Jesuits. For him, the Church pursued its disciplinary functions through a mixture "of persuasion and of repression, of rewards and of punishments" ("di persuasione e di repressione, di premi e di punizioni"); xii.

20. The *Formula of the Institute of the Society of Jesus*, in Loyola, 67.

21. Ibid., 282.

22. See, e.g., ARSI, Fondo Gesuitico [hereafter FG] 720A/I/1/1 (1590), unfoliated.

23. This is a question that deserves further investigation. At this point, I offer only tentative suggestions, but my hunch is that the truth probably lies somewhere among these three hypotheses.

24. On Mastrilli's intervention, see Selwyn, 65.

25. Schinosi, 89.

26. For Orfini's observations of clerical misconduct throughout the viceroyalty and the need for reconciliation, see Selwyn, 59–63, esp. 63.

27. Orfini, as cited in P. Villani, 47, 41, 51–52.

28. Mozzillo, 333–45.

29. Paolucci, 152–53.

30. For an overview of the postrevolt period, see, e.g., Ghirelli, 64–78. On the extent of the devastation wrought by the plague, Ghirelli estimates that nearly

half the population of Naples was decimated; 73. For a more detailed assessment of the demographic impact of the plague, see also Petraccone, 108.

31. ARSI, Neap. 74. "Relatione d'una Missione fatta in Capua" (1649), fols. 260r–284v, esp. 264r–267v.
32. Ibid., fols. 265r–265v.
33. ARSI, Neap. 76, doc. IV (Anonymous, 1666), fols. 23r–28v, esp. 25r–v.
34. Di Girolamo, 142–44, esp. 143.
35. Ibid., 143–44.
36. For an interesting discussion of this phenomenon, see Muir, 1989.
37. Di Girolamo, 147–49.   38. Ibid., 152–53.
39. Ibid., 68.   40. Ibid., 68–69.
41. De Geronimo as cited in D'Aria, 347–49.
42. Ibid., 349.
43. Di Girolamo, 73–76, esp. 74–75.
44. Ibid.

13. MILLER

1. Davidsohn, 7: 513–14, 519–22; Cardini, 179–89; Paul, 207–25; Rubinstein, 1995, 5–24; Rodolico and Marchini, 155–57; Trachtenberg, 27–85, 87–147; Fei, G. Sica, and P. Sica, 43–45.
2. Rubinstein, 1995, 6–10; Russell, 201–2, 239–41; Bocchi, 1993, 38–40.
3. Trachtenberg, 32.
4. The cities are Ascoli Piceno, Asti, Bergamo, Bologna, Brescia, Como, Cremona, Fabriano, Faenza, Florence, Genoa, Gubbio, Lucca, Mantua, Milan, Modena, Novara, Orvieto, Padua, Parma, Pavia, Perugia, Piacenza, Pisa, Pistoia, Ravenna, Reggio-Emilia, Siena, Spoleto, Treviso, Verona, Vicenza, and Viterbo.
5. Golinelli, 1993; Tabacco, esp. 166–76; Mor and Schmidinger; Dameron, 1991; Miller, 1993, 143–74; Brentano, 1968.
6. Miller, 2000, 163–69, 253–56.
7. Miller, 1999, 3–12; Trovabene and Serrazanetti; Sandonnini; Golinelli, 1990.
8. Andenna, 1987, 52; A. Mazzi; Cassinelli, Pagnoni, and Colmuto Zanella, 16–17; Miller, 1996, 27–41; Voltini and Guazzoni, 9, 60–61; Miller, 1995; Frigerio and Baserga; Frigerio, 301–2; Nironi, 23–35, esp. table 4; Golfieri; Bullough, 101–2; Panazza, 195–203; Gurrieri, 28–30, 129–56; Langeli and Silvestrelli; and Bruno Toscano.
9. Bocchi, 1993, and city plan at 252–53.
10. Miller, 1991–92, 161 n. 55, 165ff; Montanari, 28–29.
11. Ravaldini; *Storia di Ravenna*, 3: 422.
12. *Monumenta Germaniae historica, Diplomatum* 2, no. 250; Nasalli Rocca; Racine, 1980, 1: 53–70.
13. Archivio di Stato di Piacenza, Archivio Diplomatico degli Ospizi Civili di Piacenza, Atti Privati, cartella 4, perg. 6 (Dec. 9, 1171) was redacted "in palacio veteri episcopi" and perg. 35 (Sept. 6, 1179) "in palatio novo domini episcopi."
14. Falconi and Peveri, nos. 30, 43–45, 72–73, 95, 98–99, 102–03, 105, 115, 118, 121–22, 126–27, 129, 135, 165, 176, 178–79, 182, 187, 190, 198, 202,

205, 212–13, 231–32, 234, 242, 246, 251, 258, 264, and 267–68. We know that this "old palace" was the bishop's because nos. 95 (veteris palatii Placentini episcopi) and 242 (veteri Placentino palatio domini episcopi) specifically identify it in this fashion.

15. Paul, 179–80.
16. Ibid.; Racine, 1980, 317–20, 1246ff.
17. *Storia di Ravenna*, 3: 214ff; the quote is on 221–22.
18. *Storia di Ravenna*, 3: 559–69; for the "guayta" of San Michele, see the diagram on 409 in the same volume.
19. Rauty, 1988, 273–74, 327–31; Vasina, 103–4.
20. McLaughlin, 13–50, 100–08.
21. Schumann, 132–40, 231–39.
22. Guidoni, 75–76.
23. Mumford, 273; Racine, 1981, 138–39.
24. Racine, 1980, 316. 25. Bordone, 180, 198 (map).
26. Rubinstein, 1995, 8. 27. Ibid., 7.
28. For example, writing of the Palazzo della Ragione in Padua, Carlo Guido Mor explained "Perchè sorgesse un edificio monumentale come il nostro Palazzo della Ragione, occorreva che il Comune padovano avesse fatto le ossa, cioè si fosse ben rassodato nella sua organizzazione amministrativa, in modo da sentire la necessità di un edificio esclusivamente addetto al disbrigo degli affari giudiziari. . . . È chiaro che un palazzo apposito per i tribunali non potè sorgere se non quando il Comune padovano avesse sicuramente riassunto in sè tutti i poteri già del conte."; Mor, 1.
29. Brühl.
30. Miller, 2000, chaps. 3 and 4.
31. Miller, 1995, 178; Racine, 1981, 135; Archivio Arcivescovile di Lucca, Diplomatico, ++ N 99; Blomquist and Osheim.
32. Ronzani.
33. Nicolini, 35–37.
34. San Francesco was begun in 1278; it involved the Friars Minor in a substantial controversy with the bishop that resulted in their excommunication. The controversy involved the rights of the secular clergy and the cathedral chapter, both strongly threatened by the movement of the Franciscans into the very heart of the city. Racine, 1980, 316, 331.
35. The Romanesque cathedral was consecrated in 1184 by Pope Lucius III; San Pietro was not rebuilt until the early seventeenth century. Fasoli, 337; Bergonzoni; Ronzani, 499–504.
36. See, e.g., Heers; and Szabó.

14. FOOTE

1. Kirshner, 1996, 1–10.
2. Braudel, 1:20–21.
3. For a good introduction to the vast literature on state building and the trend toward analysis of local communities, see Ertman; and Given.

4. For an introduction to the types of questions these studies examine, see Chittolini, 1979, vii–lx.

5. For an introduction to this literature, see Brown, xvii–xxv.

6. De Benedictis, 9–17; Chittolini, 1995, 34–39.

7. Howard Kaminsky and James Van Horn Melton present an excellent discussion of Brunner's reconception of the state in their introduction to the English translation of Brunner's *Land und Herrschaft*; Brunner, xiii–lxi.

8. Chittolini, 1995, 53; Fasano Guarini, 1996, 95.

9. Carpentier, 1962, 200; Waley, 1952, 138. For the history of Orvieto during the late thirteenth and early fourteenth centuries, see also Carpentier, 1986.

10. *Codice Diplomatico*, 26; Waley, 1952, 2–3.

11. For development of papal administration in the patrimony, see Waley, 1961. For the various conflicts between Orvieto and the papacy during these years, see Waley, 1952, 12–14, 28–29, 32–34, 44–45, 56, 61–69, 76.

12. Buccolini, 50–52.

13. *Codice Diplomatico*, 449; Antonelli, 1902, 374–85.

14. Buccolini, 56ff.

15. See Jones, 1997, 537–44.

16. For the weakness of the Orvietan popolo, see Waley, 1952, 112–20. The story of a popolo dominated by the nobility was typical for most Italian cities. See Jones, 1997, 575, 585–601.

17. *Discorso Historico*. The extant portion of the chronicle is a fragment of a larger work. The narrative begins abruptly in 1342 and breaks in the middle of a sentence in 1368.

18. *Discorso Historico*, 68.	19. Carpentier, 1962, 15.
20. *Ephemerides Urbevetani*, ix.	21. See Pini, 1972, 1:107.
22. Waley, 1952, 133–38.	23. Ibid., 3.
24. Ibid., 5.	25. Ibid., 8.
26. Ibid., 16–17.	27. Ibid., 36–37.
28. Ibid., 39, 40, 42.	29. Ibid., 48–50.

30. The captain of the patrimony, which plays such an important role in the Orvietan sources, is the rector of the Tuscan patrimony, one of the provinces of the papal territories. It was located to the northwest of Rome and included Viterbo, Montefiascone, Orvieto, and Perugia. The rector, or captain, was the principal official of a province, charged with exercising and defending the economic and juridic claims of the papacy. Among his duties were to receive the oath of subjects in the province, call parliament, collect taxes and revenues, and exercise justice; see Waley, 1961, 83–84, 95ff. The captain of the popolo was the supreme executive official of the popolo. The captain of the popolo was usually a foreigner appointed to serve a tenure of six months or a year. The actual power of the captain of the popolo fluctuated according to circumstances. At times the office was equivalent to that of the podestà, the city's supreme executive official, and even fused with it, as is the case here. See Waley, 1988, 134–35.

31. *Codice Diplomatico*, 506–7. The Carta del Popolo was the constitution of the popolo as an institutionally organized political body. The carta consisted of legislation regulating the popolo and their relation to the commune. Beyond its

legal function, it seems to have served as a patriotic symbol for the popolo as well. The fortunes of the carta as a part of communal law fluctuated with the political fortunes of the popolo.

32. *Discorso Historico*, 5.
33. *Codice Diplomatico*, 510-11.
34. The council minutes of August 30 called for the return of money, vestments, records, and other possessions within eight days; *Ephemerides Urbevetani*, 8, n. 3.
35. The Seven was an executive council of the popolo, exercising authority in conjunction with the captain of the popolo. The popolo instituted the Seven in 1292 as a Council of the Seven Guild Consuls. Its composition changed during the early fourteenth century. Nevertheless it remained a popolani institution and symbol of their authority. See Waley, 1952, 80-81.
36. *Discorso Historico*, 8.
37. *Codice Diplomatico*, 512-13.
38. *Discorso Historico*, 13.
39. *Ephemerides Urbevetani*, 13-14, n. 1.
40. Ibid.
41. *Discorso Historico*, 14-22. For the suspension of city statutes and Carta del Popolo, see *Codice Diplomatico*, 521-22.
42. During the middle decades of the fourteenth century, Perugia extended its realm of influence throughout the Duchy of Spoleto and as far south as Orvieto; Fop, 1:611-12.
43. For the actual legislation, see *Codice Diplomatico*, 525-26.
44. *Discorso Historico*, 26.
45. *Ephemerides Urbevetani*, 27-28, n. 2.
46. *Discorso Historico*, 30.
47. Ibid.
48. *Ephemerides Urbevetani*, 38-39, n. 1.
49. *Discorso Historico*, 46.
50. Partner, 1972, 338-54; Antonelli, 1903, 313-36.
51. *Codice Diplomatico*, 535-37.   52. *Discorso Historico*, 68.
53. Ibid., 68.   54. Ibid., 69.
55. *Correspondance des Légats*, 396.
56. *Ephemerides Urbevetani*, 74, n. 1.
57. Ibid., 70-72, n. 1.
58. Ibid., 74, n. 1.
59. *Correspondance des Légats*, 201.
60. Another Orvietan chronicle, the *Cronaca del Conte Francesco di Montemarte*, written within several decades of the *Discorso Historico*, offers an interesting comparison to the latter's popolani perspective, illustrating how Albornoz incorporated the interests and sense of identity of powerful aristocratic families into the territorial state by assigning them to important military and administrative posts throughout the patrimony.
61. *Codice Diplomatico*, 546-48.   62. Mollat, 396.
63. Najemy, 1991, 282-83.   64. See Jones, 1974, 42-101.

15. FONTAINE

1. Archivio di Stato di Modena [hereafter ASM], Rettori dello Stato di Modena [hereafter Rettori], busta 98, two letters dated Nov. 16, 1597, from the conservators to the duke.
2. Southorn, 3–5; Amorth, 7–12; Rombaldi, 1989, 7–24.
3. For ritual making the state visible, see Muir, 1997, 230.
4. The traditional date for the founding of the palace is 1046. For an argument that sets that date in the late twelfth century, see Miller, 1999, 9.
5. For Modena's main square, see Baracchi. For the expression of power in civic monuments and their squares, see Trachtenberg, 245–74. For other unified city plans, see Chapter 13, by Maureen Miller, in this volume.
6. For the Sala del Fuoco, see Guandalini, 101–34. For representation of civic power through decoration of a civic hall of state, see Starn and Partridge, 5, 12–13, 58.
7. Cattini, 1997b, 16–17.
8. Melloni, 27–32.
9. Often, the duke did not help financially; see ASM, Rettori, cartella 62, letter of July 9, 1550, from the governor requesting aid from the duke; and the ducal response in a letter of July 13 stating he could not assist because of "these bad times."
10. Pistoni, 1983, 167–84, 445–58; Golinelli, 1990, 9–33; and Biondi, 1997.
11. See, e.g., Di Bianchi, 9:10 and 10:340; Biondi, 1997, 42–43; and Trexler, 1980, on rituals of celebration and crisis, 213–33, 256–62, and 331–64.
12. For Cesare, see Rombaldi, 1989, 7–24. For renovation of the palace and the city, see Southorn, 13; and Amorth, 13–15, 95. For renovation of churches, see Solì, 1:125, 374–81; 3:346–50.
13. Archivio Storico Comunale di Modena [hereafter ASCM], *Riformagioni, Consilii, e Provvigioni della Comunità di Modena* [hereafter *Vacchette*], 1601: 13r–v; 1602: 263r–v; and 1604: 154r, 159v, 181r. See also Guandalini, 135–64, for decoration in the new chamber.
14. Biondi, 1990, 548, 559; Melloni, 32–34.
15. For the Este and San Geminiano, see Biondi, 1997, 45; and ASCM, *Camera Segreta, Mss. Cronaca Spaccini* [hereafter *Cronaca Spaccini*], 1633: 362r–v; and 1634: 12r.
16. In three years the plague would claim 20–80 percent of many cities in northern and central Italy; see Cochrane, 1988, 280. Modena lost about 25 percent; see Serra, 255.
17. See Di Pietro, 1985, 11; ASCM, Magistrato di Sanità, busta 11.
18. Francesco I became the new duke when his father, Alfonso III, renounced that title and joined the Cappucins in 1629. See ASM, Rettori, busta 98, duke to the conservators, July 31, 1629, and their response, Aug. 13; and Rombaldi, 1992, 9–11, 133–34.
19. ASCM, *Vacchette*, 1630: 155r–v, 158r, 181r; Solì, 2:307; ASCM, *Cronaca Spaccini*, 1630: 210r–211r.
20. ASCM, *Vacchette*, 1630: 239r, 244v–246v. For the cult of the Madonna

of Reggio, see Balletti, 394–468; ASCM, *Cronaca Spaccini*, 1630: 186v, 193rv; Serra, 41–45; Di Pietro, 1990, 581. The Este family promoted this cult; see Biondi, 1990, 553. For other responses to the plague in Italy, see Muir, 1981, 214–16; Calvi, 199–212; and Nussdorfer, 1992, 153–55. For the functions vows played in the local religious cult, see Christian, 23–69.

21. ASCM, *Vacchette*, 1630: 265r–265v, promiserunt ac obtulerunt aedificare ac a fundamentis construere Ecclesiam in honorem eiusdem Beatissimae Virginis Mariae expensis civitas.

22. ASCM, *Cronaca Spaccini*, 1630: 247v–248r; *Vacchette*, 1630: 272r–v.

23. For a similar situation where a vow imparted special authority to the invokers, see Smoller, 451–53.

24. ASCM, *Cronaca Spaccini*, 1630: 249r, 254r; Ex Actis, 1630: ducal letter of Dec. 12 [misfiled under Nov. 12], 1r–2r; ASCM, *Vacchette*, 1630: 297r.

25. In 1636, the Conservators commissioned a painting that featured San Geminiano with the Madonna of Reggio for the Chapel of the Commune in the Chiesa Nuova; see Silingardi, 74.

26. Devotion to the Virgin of the Rosary had proliferated in Europe, especially in Italy, since 1571, when the pope attributed the defeat of the Turks at the Battle of Lepanto to the Virgin's intercession. The Confraternity of the Rosary had been active in Modena since the mid-1500s. See Black, 1999, 9–11, and ASM, Soppressione Napoleoniche, Congregazione, 1706, for the earliest documents of the rosary confraternity in Modena.

27. ASCM, *Vacchette*, 1633: 47r, 51v–53v; ASCM, Ex Actis, May 9, 1633, for receipt of the banner. See also ASCM, *Cronaca Spaccini*, 1633: 348v–349v. For Lana, see Silingardi, 74–75.

28. ASCM, *Vacchette*, 1633: 356v–357r. The conservators continued this ritual into the eighteenth century. The banner is now framed and hangs above their council seats. See also ASCM, *Cronaca Spaccini*, 356v.

29. The following year, the procession was recorded in full detail; see ASCM, *Vacchette*, 1634: 51v–52r. For the significance of candles and the Madonna of the Rosary, see ASM, Soppressione Napoleoniche, Congregazione, busta 1705, fasc. 6, "Rinovazione dele Antico Rito de Benedire le Candele del Rosario."

30. Solì, 1: 373–81.

31. E.g., see Nussdorfer, 1992.

16. DANDELET

1. Hispanic Society of America [hereafter HAS], Ms. HC 380/170, f. 10r. *Repuesta de Fray Melchor Cano a una consulta de Phelipe Segundo sobre hacer guerra al Papa*. In Cano's words, the king had leverage "por que no dependiendo en lo temporal de la providencia de Roma, Roma dependeria de la nuestra, y les podriamos dar el pan y agua"; f. 10r.

2. Biblioteca El Escorial, Ms I.III.30–31. The document is entitled *Raggionamento di Carlo V Imperatore al Re Filippo suo Figliuolo nella consignatione del governo de suoi stati e regni dove si contiene come debba governare in tempo della pace e della guerra*, ff. 24–112r. The specific reference to the Papal State

reads: "Li Stati della chiesa sono posti nel centro d'Italia ma cinti dalli vostri di sorte che si puo dire che gli faccino Corona"; f. 108r.

3. Biblioteca Apostolica Vaticana [hereafter BAV], Ms. Urb. Lat. 1038, f. 266r.

4. The three primary monetary units that were central to the financial transactions between the Spanish Empire and the Papal State between 1555 and 1625 were the Spanish ducat, Spanish escudo, and Roman scudo. In the late sixteenth century, the value of the Spanish ducat declined slightly in relation to the escudo, but by 1600 the ducat was a stable unit of account worth 375 *maravedis*, while the gold escudo coin stabilized at 440 maravedis after 1609. See Lynch, appendix 1. Exchange rates between Rome and Spain fluctuated little during this period, with the Spanish ducat worth roughly 1.3 Roman gold scudi. See Calabria, xiii, for exchange rates between Spain and Naples and Naples and Rome in this period. For the complex details of the broader implications of Spanish monetary policy in Italy, including questions of inflation and exchange fluctuation, see esp. Braudel, 1: 418–542.

5. BAV, Urb. Lat. 1039, f. 136r.

6. For a good history of ecclesiastical taxes, including the subsidio, cruzada, and decima in the late fifteenth and early sixteenth century see Azcona, 3-1: 190–91.

7. See Elliott, 201 and 286. Elliott notes that the excusado consisted of the tithes paid on the wealthiest piece of property in each parish.

8. BAV, Vat. Lat. 13411, *Memoria di quel che fruttano al Re di Spagna un anno per altro le Bolle della Crucciata, et altre Bolle di Chiese, et Monasterii: et Giubilei che chiamano di Cura, et sussidio Ecc.o*, ff. 167v–202v. The cruzada was reported to bring in 1,080,000 ducats, of which the king received 864,000 over three years.

9. BAV, Urb. Lat. 1039, f. 138v.

10. For the most thorough treatment of the patronato real in both Iberia and the New World, see Shields.

11. Serrano, 2: xlviii, note 5, cited by López Martínez, 238.

12. For the later figures, see Quintín, 23.

13. The royal share of New World treasure first reached 9,060,725 ducats in the period 1581–85. From 1561 to 1565, the total was 2,183,440. For a complete account for the period 1503 to 1660, see Elliott, 184.

14. Archivio di Stato di Roma [hereafter ASR], Camerale II, *Spogli*, buste 1. The last pages contain a list entitled "Nota delli'Arcivescovati et Vescovati di Spagna e delle entrate loro," which listed the estimated incomes in 1561 for the seven archbishoprics and forty-one bishoprics of Spain.

15. Biblioteca Nacional Madrid [hereafter BNM], Ms. 13013, ff. 202-206, *Memorial del Cardenal A. Zapata Sobre Abusos de la dataria*, 1607.

16. For the medieval origins of the office of collector, see Lunt, 36–38.

17. BAV, Urb. Lat. 1039, f. 137v. The office of the collector was often contentious, and although there were occasional calls for abolishment, it continued throughout the sixteenth and seventeenth centuries.

18. ASR, Camerale II, *Conti delle Entrate e dell'Uscita*, buste 1, f. 6r, f. 21r.

By 1589, papal income from the Spanish vacancies are listed as follows: "Dalla Colletoria di Spagna—50,000"; "Dalla Colletoria di Portugallo—4,000"; "Da Cleri del Regno di Napoli—15,090." The revenue from Spanish lands was the fifth or sixth largest item on the papal register, coming after taxes from other parts of the papal states and, together with the payment of 8,000 escudos for the feudal dues from Naples, comprising roughly 5 percent of the 1,546,279 escudos in total papal income for 1589.

19. BAV, Urb. Lat. 1039, f. 344r.   20. BAV, Urb. Lat. 1039, f. 375r.
21. Pastor, 18:8.   22. BAV, Urb. Lat. 1042, f. 34v.
23. BAV, Urb. Lat. 1041, f. 323r.

24. See Beeching, 192. He puts the number of Spanish galleys at roughly ninety and the number of men paid for by Philip II at twenty thousand. See also Parker for a more detailed account of the Spanish contribution, estimated at 1.2 million escudos out of an estimated total cost of 2 million escudos.

25. Serrano, 2:498.
26. García-Villoslada, 60.
27. Archivo General Simancas [hereafter AGS], Estado, Roma, leg. 924, unfoliated. The text reads: "havendo N.S.r Dio preservata la M.ta V.ra con tanta potentia congionta con pietà Christiana, quasi si puo dire per unico sostentamento della sua santa Chiesa et della fede catholica, Sua B.ne ha voluto comunicar con lei i suoi santi pensieri aspettando tutto quello aiuto, che la M.ta V.ra deve à Dio per la tante gratie et doni che le ha concesso."

28. For a succinct analysis of papal finances in this period, see Partner, 1980, 52; he notes that "from the time of the signature of the treaty of Cateau-Cambresis in 1559 the Habsburgs were in effect bearing a large part of the true defense of the Papal State."

29. Ibid., 50–52.
30. BAV, Urb. Lat. 1045, f. 444r. "Le vacanti di Spagna ascendonoa 330,000 scudi d'entrato computatori l'Arcivescovo di Toledo, havendo questa settimana la cancelleria guadagnatti 50,000 scudi."

31. ASR, Camerale II, *Conti delle Entrate e dell'Uscita*, buste 1, f. 21r.
32. BAV, Urb. Lat. 1045, f. 440r.   33. BAV, Urb. Lat. 1046, f. 21r.
34. BAV, Urb. Lat. 1047, f. 26r.   35. BAV, Urb. Lat. 1046, f. 377r.
36. BAV, Urb. Lat. 1047, f. 372r.

37. For the definitive study of the grain supply in early modern Rome and the Papal State, see Reinhardt.

38. For the best description of the complicated system of Italian weights and measures, see Zupko.

39. Reinhardt, 131.   40. BAV, Urb. Lat. 1061, f. 71v.
41. Ibid., f. 609r.   42. BAV, Urb. Lat. 1060, f. 174r.
43. Ibid., f. 305v.   44. Ibid., f. 388r.
45. Ibid., f. 307r.

46. BAV, Urb. Lat. 1067, f. 558r. The text reads: "se assicurá la paga di 100M scudi che si doveva far per d.a Investitura come e obligato ogni nuovo Re."

47. BAV, Urb. Lat. 1067, f. 579v.
48. AGS, Estado, Roma, leg. 1856, unfoliated.

49. Ibid.
50. AGS, Estado, Roma, leg. 1858, unfoliated.
51. BAV, Urb. Lat. 1073, f. 542r.
52. See BAV, Urb. Lat. 1073, where it is reported that the pope sent his nephew to Palermo to seek grain (f. 480r) and that he was successful in his negotiations (f. 606r).
53. BAV, Urb. Lat. 1074, f. 37r. The reports noted that the Cardinal "in mezzo delli SS.ri Amb.re di Spagna, et D. Virginio Orsino cavaliar per la città a far le provisioni per mandarle a gli assediati et di pane, carne, vino, et del resto."
54. Ibid., f. 394r.
55. ASR, Camerale II, "Conti delle entrate e dell'uscita," buste 4, f. 92v.
56. AGS, Estado, Roma, leg. 1865, unfoliated. The text reads: "assicurando V.M.ta della paterna affett.ne et volunta', che le portiamo, et del desiderio che habbiamo d'ogni sua felicita."
57. Ibid.
58. AGS, Estado, Roma, leg. 1865, unfoliated.
59. ASR, Camerale II, buste 1. The main register from the *depositeria generale* records the income from the papal collectors in Spanish realms in 1609 as 67,000 scudi. Total revenues were 1,790,521 in that year.
60. AGS, Estado, Roma, leg. 1860, unfoliated. A report from the Spanish ambassador in 1608 giving detailed notes of cardinals' revenues calculated that close to sixty thousand ducats from churches in Spanish realms were being given to twenty-three cardinals.
61. AGS, Estado, Roma, leg. 1868, unfoliated. In 1620, the Council of State in Spain complained about the many benefices that were distributed to *non-naturali*, which were said to total twenty-two thousand ducats.
62. BNM, MS. 5801, Don Juan Chumacero y Carillo and Don Fr. Domingo Pimentel, *Memorial sobre los excessos, que se cometen en Roma, contra los Naturales de estos Reynos de Espana*, 1633, 1–96.
63. Ibid., 39. The text reads: "Que deben (Padre Santo) los Padres, Curatos, ò Prabendas de Espana, para que quedando con toda la carga de su ministerio, contribuyan à los Eclesiasticos de esta Provinicia, tanto mas ricos, quanto muestran su lucimiento, opulencia, Palacios, y Jardines? Y quanto menos deben à muchos Palafreneros, Barberos, Ayudas de Camara, de gente Secular, Architectos, Musicos, Fontarolos, y otras personas mas inferiores, que el dia de oy gozan mucha parte de estas pensiones."
64. BNM, MSS. 1323, *Informe y consulta a V. Magestad, en razon de los memoriales dados en nombre de los Reynos y diversas Iglesias, acerca de algunos despachos, y negocios de Roma*, 1629, f. 101r. The text reads in part: "Pudiera tanto dezir, y informar à V. Magestad, respeto de lo contenido en los memoriales, sobre los despachos destos Reynos en la Corte Romana, pretendiendo, y assegurando en ellos por relacion de hombres practicos, que los despachos de gracia, coadjutorias, resignaciones, permutas, uniones, pensiones, dispensas con los pleitos, y negocios de justicia, y otros importen cada ano ochocientos mil ducados por lo menos, entendiendose sin las Bulas de provisiones de Obispados, y demas prebendas y vacantes forçosas à despacharse en Roma, y las pensiones Re-

gias por merced de V.M. de la cantidad no podrè atestiguar; y quando sea verdadera, repare V.M. que no son todos en beneficio de la Camara Apostolica, ni de sus ministros, porque con ellos se sustentan quatro mil pretendientes Espanoles en Roma, y otros tantos, ò pocos menos Curiales y Notarios, agentes de tales despachos en estos Reynos."

65. For a detailed discussion of the Spanish nation in Rome, see Dandelet.

AFTERWORD. STARN

1. Rubinstein, 1968, 6.
2. Starn, 1970, 682.
3. See, e.g., Bonnell and Hunt.
4. Gillis, 1996b; Krieger, 236.
5. See, e.g., Bouwsma (reprinted in Starn, 1990, 348–65); Starn, 1994; Muir, 1995; Molho, 1998; and Findlen and Gouwens.
6. Bynum.
7. Latour; cf., on the fortunes of the notion of Italian "decadence," Fasano Guarini, 1996, 83–84; and on the "Italian Paradigm" of an Italy that, "thanks to its relative backwardness and its premodern vestiges, is better able to absorb each future shock," the pungent remarks of Enzensberger, 80.
8. Chittolini, 1996, 42.
9. Kirshner, 1996, 9.
10. Bizzocchi, 1996, 156.
11. Chittolini, 1996, 50.
12. Fasano Guarini, 1996, 90.

Bibliography

Abulafia, David. *The Two Italies: Economic Relations Between the Norman Kingdom of Sicily and the Northern Communes.* Cambridge, 1977.
Ago, Renata. *Carriere e clientele nella Roma barocca.* Rome and Bari, 1990.
Aldea, Quintín. "La economía en las iglesias locales." *Hispania Sacra* 26 (1973): 27–68.
Alessi Palazzolo, Giorgia. *Prova legale e pena: la crisi del sistema tra evo medio e moderno.* Naples, 1979.
Amorth, Luigi. *Modena capitale. Storia di Modena e di suoi duchi dal 1598–1860.* Milan, 1967.
Andenna, Giancarlo. "Honor et ornamentum civitatis. Trasformazioni urbane a Novara tra XIII e XVI secolo." In *Museo novarese. Documenti studi e progetti per una nuova immagine delle collezioni civiche*, ed. Maria Laura Tomea Gavazzoli, 50–73. Novara, 1987.
———. *Storia della Lombardia medioevale.* Turin, 1998.
Anonymous Friar. "Vie inédite de S. Bernardino de Sienne par un frère mineur, son contemporain." Ed. Ferdinand Delorme. *Analecta Bollandiana* 25 (1906): 304–38.
Antonelli, M. "Vicende della dominazione pontificia nel Patrimonio di S. Pietro in Tuscia dalla traslazione della sede alla restaurazione dell'Albornoz." *Archivio della società romana di storia patria* 25 (1902): 355–96; 26 (1903): 249–341; 27 (1904): 109–46, 313–50.
Arasse, Daniel. "André Biglia contre Saint Bernardin de Sienne: L'Humanisme et la fonction de l'image religieuse." In *Acta Conventus Neo-Latini Turonensis, Troisième Congrès International D'Etudes Neo-Latines, Tours*, ed. Jean-Claude Margolin, vol. 1, 417–37. Paris, 1980.
Ashtor, Eliyahu. "Venezia e il pellegrinaggio in Terrasanta nel basso medioevo." *Archivio storico italiano* 143 (1985): 197–223.
Astarita, Tommaso. *The Continuity of Feudal Power: The Caracciolo di Brienza in Spanish Naples.* Cambridge, 1992.
Avarucci, Giuseppe, and Ugo Paoli. "The Monastery of San Vittore delle Chiuse: Preliminary Notes for a History." *Princeton University Library Chronicle* 55 (1994): 262–76.
Azcona, Tarsicio de. "Aspectos económicos referentes al episcopado y al clero." In *Historia de la Iglesia en España*, ed. Ricardo García-Villoslada, vol. 3-1. Madrid, 1980.
Baird, Joseph L. *The Chronicle of Salimbene de Adam.* Trans. Giuseppe Baglivi and John Robert Kane. Binghamton, N.Y., 1986.
Balletti, Andrea. *Storia di Reggio nell'Emilia.* Rome, 1968.

Baracchi, Orianna. *Modena: Piazza Grande*. Modena, 1981.
Barbieri, Giuseppe. "Il Mugello. Studio di geografia umana." *Rivista Geografica Italiana* 60 (June 1953): 89–133, 296–378.
Barnabò da Siena. "Vita sancti Bernardini senensis." In *Acta Sanctorum*. Maii, Tomus V, die vigesima. Paris and Rome, 1866.
Baron, Hans. *The Crisis of the Early Italian Renaissance*. 2 vols. Princeton, 1955; 2nd ed. in one volume, Princeton, 1966.
Basile, Bruno, ed. *Bentivolorum magnificentia: principe e cultura a Bologna nel Rinascimento*. Rome, 1984.
Battisti, Maria Cristina. "Fra Bevignate nei documenti e nelle fonti." *Inter Fratres* 38 (1988): 133–45; 39 (1989): 109–35; 40 (1990): 87–130.
Becker, Marvin. "Problemi della finanza pubblica fiorentina della seconda metà del Trecento e dei primi anni del Quattrocento." *Archivo Storico Italiano* 123 (1965): 433–66.
———. "Economic Change and the Emerging Florentine Territorial State." *Studies in the Renaissance* 13 (1966): 7–39.
———. *Florence in Transition*. 2 vols. Baltimore, 1967–68.
Beeching, Jack. *The Galleys at Lepanto*. London, 1982.
Bellingeri, Luca. "Editoria e mercato: la produzione giuridica." In *Il libro italiano del Cinquecento: produzione e commercio*, 155–85. Rome, 1989.
Bellini, Pietro. "Il movimento augustiniano nelle Marche nel secolo XIII." In *San Nicola, Tolentino, le Marche: contributi e ricerche sul processo (a. 1325) per la canonizzazione di San Nicola da Tolentino*, 161–80. Tolentino, 1986.
Benadusi, Giovanna. *A Provincial Elite in Early Modern Tuscany*. Baltimore and London, 1996.
Bentley, Jerry. *Politics and Culture in Renaissance Naples*. Princeton, 1987.
Benvenuti Papi, Anna. *Uomini, terra e città nel Medioevo*. Milan, 1986.
Benvoglienti, Leonardo. "Vie de Saint Bernardin par Léonard Benvoglienti." Ed. François van Ortroy. *Analecta Bollandiana* 21 (1902): 53–80.
Berengo, Marino. *Nobili e mercanti nella Lucca del '500*. Turin, 1965.
———. "Lo studio degli atti notarili dal XIV al XVI secolo." *In Fonti medioevali e problematica storiografica*. Atti del Congresso Internazionale tenuto in occasione del 90 anniversario dell'Istituto Storico Italiano, 2 vols., 1:149–72. Rome, 1976–77.
Bergonzoni, Franco. "La chiesa cattedrale di S. Pietro: un'ipotesi storico-urbanistica." *Strenna storica bolognese* 38 (1988): 61–65.
Bernardino da Siena. *Le Prediche volgari*. (Florence 1424 and 1425; Siena 1425). Ed. Ciro Cannarozzi. 7 vols. Pistoia, 1934, and Florence, 1940 and 1958.
———. *Prediche volgari sul Campo di Siena 1427*. Ed. Carlo Delcorno. 2 vols. Milan, 1980.
Bertelli, Sergio, Nicolai Rubinstein, and Craig Hugh Smyth, eds. *Florence and Venice: Comparisons and Relations*. 2 vols. Florence, 1979.
———, Nicolai Rubinstein, and Craig Hugh Smyth, eds. *Florence and Milan: Comparisons and Relations*. 2 vols. Florence, 1989.
Bertram, Martin. "'Renaissance Mentality' in Italian Testaments?" *Journal of Modern History* 67 (1995): 358–69.

Biglia, Andrea. "Le mémoire d'André Biglia sur la prédication de S. Bernardin de Sienne." Ed. Baudouin de Gaiffier. *Analecta Bollandiana* 53 (1935): 308–58.
Biondi, Albano. "Modena fin di secolo: da comune borghese a città di corte." In *Storia illustrata di Modena*, eds. Paolo Golinelli and Giuliano Muzzioli, 2:541–60. Modena, 1990.
———. "La Comunità e il Santo nel Cinquecento." In *'Civitas Geminiana': La città e il suo Patrono*, ed. Francesca Piccinini, 35–46. Modena, 1997.
Bizzocchi, Roberto. *Chiesa e potere nella Toscana del Quattrocento*. Bologna, 1987.
———. "Church, Religion and the State in the Early Modern Period." In Kirshner, 1996.
Black, Christopher F. *Italian Confraternities in the Sixteenth Century*. Cambridge, 1989.
———. "Confraternities and the Parish in the Context of Italian Catholic Reform." In *Confraternities and Catholic Reform in Italy, France, and Spain*, eds. John Patrick Donnelly, S.J., and Michael W. Maher, S.J., 1–26. Sixteenth Century Essays and Studies, 44. Kirksville, Mo., 1999.
Black, Jane. "Constitutional Ambitions, Legal Realities and the Florentine State." In Connell and Zorzi, 2000, 48–64.
Black, Jeremy. *The British Abroad: The Grand Tour in the Eighteenth Century*. New York, 1992.
Blomquist, Thomas W., and Duane J. Osheim. "The First Consuls at Lucca: 10 July 1119." *Actum Luce* 7 (1978): 37–39.
———, and Maureen F. Mazzaoui, eds. *The "Other Tuscany": Essays in the History of Lucca, Pisa, and Siena during the Thirteenth, Fourteenth, and Fifteenth Centuries*. Kalamazoo, 1994.
Boccaccio, Giovanni. *The Decameron*. Trans. G. H. McWilliam. New York, 1972.
Bocchi, Francesca. "I debiti dei contadini (1235). Nota sulla piccola proprietà terriera bolognese nella crisi di feudalesimo." In *Studi in memoria di Luigi del Pane*, 169–209. Bologna, 1982.
———. "Il Broletto." In *Milano e la Lombardia in età comunale secoli XI–XIII*, 38–42. Milan, 1993.
———, ed. *Atlante storico di Bologna*. Vol. 2 *Il Duecento*. Bologna, 1995.
Boehmer, H., ed. *Chronica fratris Jordani*. Paris, 1908.
Bonnell, Victoria E., and Lynn Hunt, eds. *Beyond the Cultural Turn: New Directions in the Study of Society and Culture*. Berkeley, 1999.
Bordone, Renato. *Città e territorio nell'alto medioevo: La società astigiana dal dominio dei franchi all'affermazione comunale*. Turin, 1980.
Bornstein, Daniel E. *The Bianchi of 1399: Popular Devotion in Late Medieval Italy*. Ithaca, 1993.
———. "Priests and Villagers in the Diocese of Cortona." *Ricerche storiche* 27 (1997): 93–106.
———, and Roberto Rusconi, eds. *Women and Religion in Medieval and Renaissance Italy*. Trans. Margery J. Schneider. Chicago, 1996.

Borsari, Aldo, and Laura Anna Strozzi, eds. *Magistrato di Santità. Inventario.* Atti ed inventari del Archivio Storico II. Modena, 1985.

Bossy, John. "The Mass as a Social Institution, 1200–1700." *Past and Present* 100 (1983): 29–61.

Botero, Giovanni. *The Reason of State and the Greatness of Cities.* Eds. and trans. P. J. Waley and D. P. Waley. London, 1956.

Bouwsma, William J. "The Renaissance and the Drama of Western History." *American Historical Review* 84 (1979): 1–15.

———. *A Usable Past: Essays in European Cultural History.* Berkeley and Los Angeles, 1990.

Bowsky, William. M. *A Medieval Italian Commune: Siena Under the Nine, 1287–1355.* Berkeley, 1981.

Bratchel, Michael E. *Lucca 1430–1494: The Reconstruction of an Italian City-Republic.* Oxford, 1995.

Braudel, Fernand. *The Mediterranean and the Mediterranean World in the Age of Philip II.* 2 vols. Trans. Siân Reynolds. New York, 1972–73.

Brentano, Robert. *Two Churches: England and Italy in the Thirteenth Century.* Princeton, 1968; 2nd ed. Berkeley, 1988.

———. *Rome Before Avignon.* Berkeley and Los Angeles, 1991.

———. *A New World in a Small Place: Church and Religion in the Diocese of Rieti, 1188–1378.* Berkeley, 1994.

Bresc, Henri. *Un monde méditerranéen: Économie et société en Sicile, 1300–1450.* 2 vols. Rome and Palermo, 1986.

Breveglieri, Bruno. "Predestinazioni matrimoniali di ragazzi nella Bologna del Trecento (1309–1322)." *Deputazione di Storia patria per le provincie di Romagna, Atti e Memorie* n.s. 46 (1995): 199–221.

Brooke, Rosalind B., ed. *Scripta Leonis, Rufini et Angeli. Sociorum S. Francisci: The Writings of Leo, Rufino and Angelo. Companions of St. Francis.* Oxford, 1970.

Brown, Alison. *Bartolomeo Scala, 1430–1497, Chancellor of Florence: The Humanist as Bureaucrat.* Princeton, 1979.

———. *The Medici in Florence. The Exercise and Language of Power.* Florence and Perth, 1992.

———. *The Renaissance.* 2nd ed. London and New York, 1999.

———. "The Language of Empire." In Connell and Zorzi, 2000, 32–47.

Brown, Judith C. *In the Shadow of Florence: Provincial Society in Renaissance Pescia.* Oxford, 1982.

———. "Prosperity or Hard Times in Renaissance Italy?" *Renaissance Quarterly* 42 (1989): 761–80.

———, and Robert C. Davis, eds. *Gender and Society in Renaissance Italy.* London, 1998.

Brucker, Gene. *The Civic World of Early Renaissance Florence.* Princeton, 1977.

———. *Renaissance Florence.* 2nd ed. Berkeley, 1983a.

———. "Tales of Two Cities: Florence and Venice in the Renaissance." *American Historical Review* 88 (1983b): 599–616.

———. *Giovanni and Lusanna: Love and Marriage in Renaissance Florence.* Berkeley and Los Angeles, 1986.

———, ed. *Two Memoirs of Renaissance Florence: The Diaries of Buonacorso Pitti and Gregorio Datti.* Trans. Julia Martines. Prospect Heights, Ill., 1991.

———. "The Economic Foundations of Laurentian Florence." In *Lorenzo de' Medici e il suo mondo,* ed. Gian Carlo Garfagnini, 3–15. Florence, 1994a.

———. "Researching the Renaissance: An American in Florence, 1952." *Renaissance News and Notes* 7 (1994b): 1–3.

———. *Florence: The Golden Age, 1183–1737.* Berkeley and Los Angeles, 1998.

———. "Civic Traditions in Premodern Italy." *Journal of Interdisciplinary History* 29 (1999): 357–77.

Brühl, Carlrichard. "'Palatium' e 'Civitas' in Italia dall'epoca tardo-antica fino al-l'epoca degli Svevi." In *I problemi della civiltà comunale,* Atti del Congresso Storico Internazionale per l'VIIIo Centenario della prima Lega Lombarda (Bergamo, 4–8 sett. 1967), ed. Cosmo Damiano Fonseca, 157–65. Milan, 1971.

Brundage, James. "Concubinage and Marriage in Medieval Canon Law." *Journal of Medieval History* 1 (1975): 1–17.

Brunner, Otto. *Land and Lordship: Structures of Governance in Medieval Austria.* Trans. Howard Kaminsky and James Van Horn Melton. Philadelphia, 1992.

Buccolini, Geralberto. "Serie critica dei Vescovi di Bolsena e di Orvieto." *Bollettino della (regia) Deputazione di Storia patria per l'Umbria* 33 (1941): 5–130.

Bullard, Melissa Meriam. *Filippo Strozzi and the Medici: Favor and Finance in Sixteenth-Century Florence and Rome.* Cambridge, 1980.

———. *Lorenzo il Magnifico: Image and Anxiety, Politics and Finance.* Florence, 1994.

Bullarium diplomatum et privilegiorum sanctorum romanorum pontificum. 25 vols., 12:58–163. Turin, 1857–72.

Bullough, Donald A. "Urban Change in Early Medieval Italy: The Example of Pavia." *Papers of the British School at Rome* 34 [n.s. 21] (1966): 82–130.

Burckhardt, Jacob. *The Civilization of the Renaissance in Italy.* Trans. S.G.C. Middlemore. 6th ed. Garden City, N.Y., 1960.

Burke, Peter. "The Virgin of the Carmine and the Revolt of Masaniello." *Past and Present* 99 (1983): 3–22.

———. *The Historical Anthropology of Early Modern Italy.* Cambridge, 1987.

Butters, Humfrey. *Governors and Government in Early Sixteenth Century Florence 1502–1519.* Oxford, 1985.

Bynum, Caroline Walker. "The Last European Generation." *Perspectives,* American Historical Association newsletter (Feb. 1996).

Caferro, William. *Mercenary Companies and the Decline of Siena.* Baltimore, 1998.

Caggese, Romolo. *Classi e comuni rurali nel Medio Evo italiano.* 2 vols. Florence, 1908.

Calabria, Antonio. *The Cost of Empire: The Finances of the Kingdom of Naples in the Time of Spanish Rule.* Cambridge, 1991.

———, and John A. Marino, eds. *Good Government in Spanish Naples*. New York, 1990.
Calvi, Giulia. *Histories of a Plague Year: The Social and the Imaginary in Baroque Florence*. Trans. Dario Biocca and Bryant T. Ragan, Jr., foreword Randolph Starn. Berkeley, 1989.
Calvino, Italo. *Invisible Cities*. Trans. William Weaver. San Diego, New York, and London, 1978.
Cantimori, Delio. *Eretici italiani del Cinquecento e altri scritti*. Ed. Adriano Prosperi. Turin, 1992.
Cardini, Domenico, ed. *Il Bel San Giovanni e Santa Maria del Fiore: Il Centro religioso di Firenze dal Tardo Antico al Rinascimento*. Florence, 1996.
Carmichael, Ann. *Plague and the Poor in Renaissance Florence*. Cambridge, 1986.
Carpentier, Elisabeth. *Une ville devant la peste. Orvieto et la peste noire de 1348*. Paris, 1962.
———. *Orvieto à la fin du XIIIe siècle: ville et campagne dans le cadastre de 1292*. Paris, 1986.
Carruthers, Mary J. *The Book of Memory*. Cambridge, 1990.
Le Carte dell'Archivio di San Silvestro in Montefano. I: Montefano, S. Benedetto, Fabriano. Eds. Giuseppe Avarucci and Ugo Paoli. Bibliotheca Montisfani 14. Fabriano, 1990. (= BM 14).
Le Carte dell'Archivio di San Silvestro in Montefano. II: Congregazione. Eds. Giuseppe Avarucci and Ugo Paoli. Bibliotheca Montisfani 15. Fabriano, 1991.
Casagrande, Giovanna. "I francescani a Perugia." In *Francesco d'Assisi. Documenti e Archivi*, eds. A. Bartoli Langeli and C. Cutini, 9–10. Milan, 1982.
———. "Forme di vita religiosa femminile nell'area di Città di Castello nel sec. XIII." In *Il Movimento religioso femminile in Umbria nei secoli XIII–XIV*, ed. Roberto Rusconi, 125–57. Perugia, 1984.
———. "Il fenomeno della reclusione volontaria nei secoli dal basso Medioevo." *Benedictina* 35 (1988): 475–507.
———. *Religiosità penitenziale e città al tempo dei comuni*. Rome, 1995.
———. "Fama e diffamazione nella letteratura teologica e pastorale del sec. XIII." *Ricerche storiche* 26 (1996): 7–24.
Casini, Bruno, ed. *Statuto del Comune di Montopoli (1360)*. Fonti sui Comuni Rurali Toscani, 5. Florence, 1968.
Cassinelli, Bruno, Luigi Pagnoni, and Graziella Colmuto Zanella. *Il Duomo di Bergamo*. Bergamo, 1991.
Castagnari, Giancarlo. "Il Monastero di S. Vittore delle Chiuse: Ricerche su un feudo comitale." In *Aspetti e problemi del monachesimo nelle Marche: Atti del Convegno di Studi tenuto a Fabriano, Monastero S. Silvestro Abate, 4–7 giugno 1981*, 61–72. 2 vols. Fabriano, 1982.
———, and Nora Lipparoni. "La rete viaria nell'area fabrianese dal Medioevo al XV secolo." In *Le strade nelle Marche: Il problema nel tempo*, 637–67. Extracts from Atti e Memorie del Deputazione di Storia Patria per le Marche 89–91 (1984–86). Ancona, 1987.
Cattini, Marco, ed. *Al Governo del Comune: Tremilacinquecento modenesi per*

la comunità locale dal XV secolo ad oggi. 2 vols. Quaderni dell'Archivio Storico, 5. Modena, 1997a.

———. "Tremilacinquecento Modenesi al Governo del Comune." In *Al Governo del Comune: Tremilacinquecento modenesi per la comunità locale dal XV secolo ad oggi,* ed. Marco Cattini, 1:9–23. 2 vols. Quaderni dell'Archivio Storico, 5. Modena, 1997b.

Cavallo, Sandra. *Charity and Power in Early Modern Italy: Benefactors and Their Motives in Turin, 1541–1789.* Cambridge, 1995.

Chabod, Federico. *Il ducato di Milano e l'impero di Carlo V.* 3 vols. Turin, 1971–85.

Chabot, Isabelle. "'Sola, dona, non gir' mai Le solitudini femminili nel Tre-Quattrocento." *Rivista di storia delle donne* 18 (1986): 7–24.

———. "Widowhood and poverty in late medieval Florence." *Continuity and Change* 3 (1988): 291–311.

———. "La reconnaissance du travail des femmes dans la Florence du bas Moyen Age: contexte idéologique et réalité." In *La Donna nell'economia secc. XIII–XVIII,* ed. S. Cavaciocchi, 563–76. Atti della 'Ventunesima Settimana di Studi' 10–15 apr. 1989, Istituto internazionale di storia economia F. Datini. Florence, 1989.

Chaney, Edward. *The Evolution of the Tour: Anglo-Italian Cultural Relations Since the Renaissance.* London, 1998.

Cherubini, Alvise. "Territorio e abbazie nelle Marche." In *Le abbazie delle Marche: Storia e arte,* 249–362. Atti del Convegno Internazionale, Macerata, 3–5 apr. 1990. Rome, 1992.

Cherubini, Giovanni. "Qualche considerazione sulle campagne dell'Italia centro-settentrionale tra l'XI e il XV secolo." In G. Cherubini, *Signori, contadini, e borghesi: ricerche sulla società italiana del basso medioevo,* 51–119. Florence, 1974.

Chittolini, Giorgio. *La formazione dello stato regionale e le istituzioni del contado, secoli XIV e XV.* Turin, 1979.

———. "Progetti di riordinamento ecclesiastico della Toscana agli inizi del Quattrocento." In *Forme e tecniche del potere nella città (secoli XIV–XVII),* 275–96. Perugia, 1982.

———. "Cities, 'city-states,' and regional states in north-central Italy." *Theory and Society* 18 (1989): 689–706.

———. "Civic Religion and the Countryside in Late Medieval Italy." In *City and Countryside in Late Medieval and Renaissance Italy: Essays Presented to Philip Jones,* eds. Trevor Dean and Chris Wickham, 69–91. London, 1990.

———. "The Italian City-State and Its Territory." *Journal of Interdisciplinary History* 23 (1992): 589–601.

———. "The 'Private,' the 'Public,' the State." In Kirshner, 1995, 34–61.

———. "A Geography of the 'Contadi' in Communal Italy." In *Portraits of Medieval and Renaissance Living: Essays in Honor of David Herlihy,* eds. Samuel K. Cohn, Jr., and Steven A. Epstein, 417–38. Ann Arbor, 1996.

———, and Dietmar Willoweit, eds. *L'organizzazione del territorio in Italia e Germania: secoli XIII–XIV.* Bologna, 1994.

Chojnacki, Stanley. "Dowries and Kinsmen in Early Renaissance Venice." *Journal of Interdisciplinary History* 5 (1975): 571–600.
Christian, William. *Local Religion in Sixteenth-Century Spain.* Princeton, 1981.
Ciappelli, Giovanni. *Una famiglia e le sue ricordanze: i Castellani a Firenze nel Tre-Quattrocento.* Florence, 1995.
———. *Carnevale e Quaresima: comportamenti sociale e cultura a Firenze nel Rinascimento.* Rome, 1997.
Cipolla, Carlo. *Public Health and the Medical Profession in the Renaissance.* Cambridge, 1975.
———. *Fighting the Plague in Seventeenth Century Italy.* Madison, Wis., 1981.
———. *Miasmas and Disease: Public Health and the Environment in the Pre-Industrial Age.* New Haven, 1992.
Cochrane, Eric. "The Settecento Medievalists." *Journal of the History of Ideas*, 19 (1958): 35–61.
———, ed. *The Late Italian Renaissance.* London, 1970.
———. *Florence in the Forgotten Centuries 1527–1800.* Chicago and London, 1973.
———. "Southern Italy in the Age of the Spanish Viceroys: Some Recent Titles." *Journal of Modern History*, 58 (1986): 194–217.
———. *Italy: 1530–1630.* Ed. Julius Kirshner. New York, 1988.
Codice diplomatico della città d'Orvieto: Documenti e regesti dal secolo XI al XV e la carta del popolo. Ed. Luigi Fumi. Documenti di Storia Italiana. Florence, 1884.
Cohen, Elizabeth, and Thomas Cohen. *Words and Deeds in Renaissance Rome: Trials Before the Papal Magistrates.* Toronto, 1993.
Cohn, Samuel K., Jr. *The Laboring Classes of Renaissance Florence.* New York, 1980.
———. "La 'nuova storia sociale' di Firenze." *Studi storici* 26 (1985): 353–71.
———. *Death and Property in Siena, 1200–1800: Strategies for the Afterlife.* Baltimore, 1988.
———. *The Cult of Remembrance and the Black Death: Six Renaissance Cities in Central Italy.* Baltimore and London, 1992.
———. "David Herlihy—il ricordo di uno studente." *Archivio storico italiano* 152 (1994): 192–201.
———. "Burckhardt Revised from Social History." In *Language and Images in Renaissance Italy*, ed. Alison Brown, 217–34. Oxford, 1995.
———. "Inventing Braudel's Mountains: The Florentine Alps After the Black Death." In *Portraits of Medieval and Renaissance Living: Essays in Honor of David Herlihy*, eds. Samuel K. Cohn, Jr., and Steven A. Epstein, 383–416. Ann Arbor, 1996a.
———. *Women in the Streets.* Baltimore, 1996b.
———. *Creating the Florentine State: Peasants and Rebellion, 1348–1434.* Cambridge, 1999.
———. *The Black Death Transformed: Disease and Culture in Early Renaissance Europe.* London, 2002.
Connell, William. *La città dei cruci.* Campo Bisenzio, Italy, 1999.

———, and Andrea Zorzi, eds. *Florentine Tuscany: Structures and Practices of Power.* Cambridge, 2000.
Constable, Giles. "Introduction." In *Apologiae Duae: Gozechini Epistola ad Walcherum; Burchardi, ut Videtur, Abbatis Bellevallis Apologia de Barbis,* 47-130. Corpus Christianorum Continuatio Mediaevalis 62. Brepols, 1985.
Conti, Elio. *La formazione della struttura agraria moderna nel contado fiorentino.* 2 vols. Rome, 1965.
———. *I catasti agrari della repubblica fiorentina e il catasto particellare toscano (secoli XIV–XIX).* Rome, 1966.
———, ed. *Le "Consulte" e "Pratiche" della repubblica fiorentina nel Quattrocento 1. (1401) (Cancellierato di Coluccio Salutati).* Pisa, 1981.
———. *L'imposta diretta a Firenze nel Quattrocento (1427–1494).* Rome, 1984.
Convegni di studi sulla storia dei ceti dirigenti dal Medioevo alla fine del Granducato. 4 vols. Pisa and Impruneta, 1981–83.
Correspondance des Légats et Vicaires-Généraux: Gil Albornoz et Androin de la Roche (1353–1367). Eds. Jean Glénisson et Guillaume Mollat. Paris, 1964.
Coryat, Thomas. *Coryat's Crudities Hastily Gobled up in Five Moneths Travells in France, Savoy, Italy, Rhetia Commonly Called the Grisons Country, Helvetia Alias Switzerland, Some Parts of Germany, and the Netherlands.* 2 vols. Glasgow, 1905.
Costantini, Massimo. "Le strutture dell'ospitalità." In *Storia di Venezia, dalle origini alla caduta della Serenissima,* 18 vols., 5:881–911. Rome, 1996.
Cristiani, Emilio. "Città e campagna nell'età comunale in alcune pubblicazioni dell'ultimo decennio." *Rivista storica italiana* 75 (1963): 829–45.
Crouzet-Pavan, Elisabeth. "Police des mœurs, société et politique à Venise à la fin du Moyen Âge." *Revue Historique* 264 (1980): 241–88.
Curradi, Currado. "I conti Guidi nel secolo X." *Studi romagnoli* 28 (1977): 17–64.
Da Campagnola, Stanislao. "Correnti religiose nel duecento marchigiano." In *Atti del III Convegno del Centro di Studi Avellaniti: Fonte Avellana nella società dei secoli XIII e XIV,* 27–52. Urbino, 1980.
Dal Pino, Franco. "Scelte di povertà all'origine dei nuovi ordini religiosi dei secoli XII–XIV." In *La conversione alla povertà nell'Italia dei secoli XII–XIV: Atti di XXVII Convegno storico internazionale, Todi 14–17 ott. 1990,* 53–125. Centro di Studi sulla Spiritualità Medievale dell'Università degli Studi di Perugia. Spoleto, 1991.
Dameron, George. *Episcopal Power and Florentine Society 1000–1320.* Cambridge, Mass., 1991.
———. "Patrimony and Clientage in the Florentine Countryside: The Formation of the Estate of the Cathedral Chapter, 950–1200." In Cohn, 1996: 259–82.
———. "Società e devozione nella Firenze medievale: il caso del capitolo della cattedrale (1250–1340)." *Ricerche Storiche* 27 (1997): 39–52.
Dandelet, Thomas. "Spanish Conquest and Colonization at the Center of the Old World: The Spanish Nation in Rome, 1555–1625." *Journal of Modern History* 69 (1997): 479–511.

Daniell, Christopher. *Death and Burial in Medieval England 1066–1550*. London, 1997.
D'Aria, F. M. *Un restauratore sociale. Storia critica della vita di San Francesco de Geronimo da documenti inediti. Saggio sui suoi autografi. Le sue lettere inedite*. Rome, 1943.
D'Ascoli, Arsenio. *La predicazione dei Cappuccini nel Cinquecento Italia*. Loreto, 1956.
Davidsohn, Robert. *Storia di Firenze*. 8 vols. Florence, 1960–78.
Davis, Natalie Zemon. "From 'Popular Religion' to Religious Cultures." In *Reformation Europe: A Guide to Research*, ed. Steven Ozment, 321–41. St. Louis, Mo., 1982.

———. *Fiction in the Archives: Pardon Tales and Their Tellers in Sixteenth-Century France*. Stanford, 1987.

Davis, Robert C. *Shipbuilders of the Venetian Arsenal: Workers and Workplace in the Preindustrial City*. Baltimore, 1991.

———. *The War of the Fists: Popular Culture and Public Violence in Late Renaissance Venice*. Oxford, 1994.

Dawson, Christopher. *Mission to Asia*. Toronto, Buffalo, and London, 1980.
Dean, Trevor. *Land and Power in Late Medieval Ferrara: The Rule of the Este, 1350–1450*. Cambridge, 1988.

———, and K.J.P. Lowe, eds. *Crime, Society, and the Law in Renaissance Italy*. Cambridge, 1994.

———, and K.J.P. Lowe, eds. *Marriage in Italy, 1300–1650*. Cambridge, 1998.

———, and Chris Wickham. *City and Countryside in Late Medieval and Renaissance Italy*. London, 1990.

De Benedictis, Angela. *Repubblica per contratto. Bologna: Una città europea nello Stato della Chiesa*. Bologna, 1995.
De Giorgio, Michela, Christiane Klapisch-Zuber, and Marina Beer, eds. *Storia del matrimonio*. Bari, 1996.
Del Giudice, Pasquale. *Fonti: Legislazione e scienza giuridica dal secolo decimosesto ai giorni nostri*. Vol. 2 of *Storia del diritto italiano*, ed. Pasquale Del Giudice. Milan, 1923. Reprint Milan, 1969.
Del Re, Niccolò. "Prospero Farinacci giureconsulto romano (1544–1618)." *Archivio della società romana di storia patria* 98 (1975): 135–220.
Di Bianchi, Tommasino. *Cronaca modenese*. Monumenta di storia patria delle provincie modenese. Serie delle cronache. 12 vols. Parma, 1862–84.
Di Girolamo, Francesco. *S. Francesco di Girolamo e le sue missioni. Dentro e fuori di Napoli*. Ed. Giuseppe Boero. Florence, 1882.
Di Monte, Giuseppina, and Isabella Scaramuzzi, eds. *Una provincia ospitale. Itinerari di ricerca sul sistema turistico veneziano*. Bologna, 1996.
Di Pietro, Pericle. "Cenni storici di Pericle Di Pietro." *Magistrato di Santità. Inventario*, eds. Aldo Borsari and Anna Laura Strozzi, 11–16. Atti ed inventari dell Archivio Storico II. Modena, 1985.

———. "Medicina e igiene." In *Storia di Modena illustrata*, eds. Paolo Golinelli and Giuliano Muzzioli, 3 vols., 2:551–600. Modena, 1990.

"Discorso historico con molti accidenti occorsi in Orvieto et in altri parti." In *Ephemerides urbevetani*, 1903, 2–93.

Donnelly, John Patrick, S.J., and Michael W. Maher, S.J., eds. *Confraternities and Catholic Reform in Italy, France, and Spain*. Sixteenth Century Essays and Studies, 44. Kirksville, Mo., 1999.

Dooley, Brendan M. *The Social History of Skepticism: Experience and Doubt in Early Modern Culture*. Baltimore, 1999.

Duby, Georges. *The Knight, the Lady and the Priest*. Trans. B. Bray. New York, 1983.

Du Mont, Jean, Baron de Carlscroon. *A New Voyage to the Levant*. 2nd ed. London, 1696.

Eisenbichler, Konrad, ed. *Crossing the Boundaries: Christian Piety and the Arts in Italian Medieval and Renaissance Confraternities*. Kalamazoo, Mich., 1991.

———. "Italian Scholarship on Pre-Modern Confraternities in Italy." *Renaissance Quarterly* 50 (1997): 567–80.

Elliott, John H. *Imperial Spain 1469–1716*. London, 1988.

English, Edward. "Prassi testimentaria delle famiglie nobili a Siena e a Toscana del Quattrocento." In *I ceti dirigenti nella Toscana del Quattrocento*, ed. Ricardo Fubini, 463–72. Florence, 1986.

Enzensberger, Hans Magnus. "Italian Extravagances [1983]." In *Europe, Europe*, trans. Martin Chalmers. New York, 1989, 36–86.

Ephemerides urbevetani. Ed. Luigi Fumi. Rerum Italicarum Scriptores, 15.5. Città di Castello, 1903.

Epstein, Stephan R. "Cities, Regions and the Late Medieval Crisis: Sicily and Tuscany Compared." *Past and Present* 130 (1991): 3–50.

———. *An Island for Itself: Economic Development and Social Change in Late Medieval Sicily*. Cambridge, 1992.

———. "Regional Fairs, Institutional Innovation and Economic Growth in Late Medieval Europe." *Economic History Review*, 2nd ser., 47 (1994): 459–82.

Epstein, Steven A. *Genoa and the Genoese, 958–1528*. Chapel Hill, 1996.

Ertman, Thomas. *The Birth of Leviathan: Building States and Regimes in Medieval and Early Modern Europe*. Cambridge, Mass., 1997.

Evelyn, John. *Diary and Correspondence*. 4 vols. London, 1854.

Fabbri, Lorenzo. *Alleanza matrimoniale e patriziato nella Firenze del '400*. Florence, 1991.

Falconi, Ettore, and Roberta Peveri. *Il Registrum Magnum del Comune di Piacenza*. 4 vols. Milan, 1984.

Fantoni, Marcello. *La corte del Granduca: forma e simboli del potere fra Cinque e Seicento*. Rome, 1994.

Farinacci, Prospero. *Operum criminalium*. 8 vols. Nuremberg, 1676–1728.

Farmer, Sharon. "Down and Out and Female in Thirteenth-Century Paris." *American Historical Review* 103 (1998): 344–72.

Fasano Guarini, Elena, ed. *Prato: storia di una città*. 2 vols. Florence, 1986.

———. "Center and Periphery." In Kirshner, 1996, 74–96.

Fasoli, Gina. "Momenti di storia urbanistica bolognese nell'alto Medio Evo."

Atti e Memorie della Deputazione di Storia Patria per le province di Romagna, n.s. 12 (1960–63): 313–43.

Fattorini, Vincenzo. "L'eremitismo nell'agiografia silvestrina." In *Atti del Convegno di studi storici VIII centenario nascita S. Silvestro 1177–1977*, 161–89. Studi Picena 44 (1977).

Fedalto, Giorgio. "Stranieri a Venezia e a Padova." In *Storia della cultura veneta*, vol. 3, part 1. Vicenza, 1980.

Fei, Silvano, Grazia Gobbi Sica, and Paolo Sica. *Firenze: profilo di storia urbana*. Florence, 1995.

Ferri, Claudio, ed. "Statui del secolo XIV: Mutigliano, Lugliano, Spulizano di Coreglia (S. Romano di Borgo a Mozzano)." *Actum Luce* 16 (1987): 95–116.

Fiecconi, Anna. "Luoghi fortificati e strutture edilizie del fabrianese nei secoli XI–XIII." *Nuova Rivista Storica* 49 (1975): 7.

Findlen, Paula. *Possessing Nature: Museums, Collecting, and Scientific Culture in Early Modern Italy*. Berkeley, 1994.

———. *A Fragmentary Past: The Making of Museums and the Making of the Renaissance*, forthcoming.

———, and Kenneth Gouwens. "The Renaissance at the Turn of the Millennium." *American Historical Review* 103 (1998): 51–114.

Fiumi, Enrico. "Sui rapporti economici tra città e contado nell'eta comunale." *Archivio Storico Italiano* 114 (1956): 18–68.

———. "Fioritura e decadenza dell'economia fiorentina, *Archivio Storico Italiano* 1957–59, 115: 385–439; 116: 443–510; 117: 427–502.

———. *Storia economica e sociale di San Gimignano*. Florence, 1961.

Fontaine, Michelle. "Urban Religious Culture and the Good Bishop in Sixteenth-Century Italy." Ph.D. dissertation, University of California, Berkeley, 1990.

Fop, Maria Pecugi. "Lineamenti di una storia dei rapporti tra il cardinal Egidio Albornoz ed il comune di Perugia attraverso i documenti perugini." In *El Cardenal Albornoz y el colegio de España*, 6 vols., 1:609–33. Bologna, 1972.

Fortunati, Maura. *Scrittura e prova: i libri di commercio nel diritto medievale e moderno*. Rome, 1996.

Fragnito, Gigliola. *La Bibbia al rogo: la censura ecclesiastica e i volgarizzamenti della Scrittura, 1471–1605*. Bologna, 1997.

Franceschi, Franco. *Oltre il 'Tumulto': i lavoratori fiorentini dell'Arte della Lana fra Tre e Quattrocento*. Florence, 1993.

Frati, Luigi, ed. *Statuti di Bologna dall'anno 1245 all'anno 1267*. Monumenti istorici pertinenti alle province della Romagna, ser. 1, 3 vols. Bologna, 1869–1884.

Frescobaldi, Lionardo. *Viaggio in Terrasanta*. Novara, 1961.

Frigerio, Federico. *Il Duomo di Como e il Broletto*. Como, 1950.

———, and Giovanni Baserga. "Il palazzo vescovile di Como." *Rivista archeologica dell'antica provincia e diocesi di Como*, 125–26 (1944): 9–102.

Frigo, Daniela, ed. *Politics and Diplomacy in Early Modern Italy. The Structure of Diplomatic Practice*. Cambridge, 1999.

Frugoni, Chiara. *A Distant City: Images of Urban Experience in the Medieval World*. Trans. William McCuaig. Princeton, 1991.

Fubini, Riccardo. "La rivendicazione di Firenze della sovranità e il contributo delle Historiae di Leonardo Bruni." In *Leonardo Bruni cancelliere della repubblica di Firenze (Convegno di studi [Firenze, 27–29 ott. 1987])*, ed. Paolo Viti, 29–62. Florence, 1990.

———. "Dalla rappresentanza sociale alla rappresentanza politica. Sviluppi politico-costituzionali in Firenze dal Tre al Cinquecento." In *Italia Quattrocentesca: Politica e diplomazia nell'età di Lorenzo il Magnifico*, 41–61. Milan, 1994a.

———. *Italia quattrocentesca: politica e diplomazia nell'età di Lorenzo il Magnifico*. Milan, 1994b.

Gailhard, J. *The Present State of the Republic of Venice*. London, 1669.

Galasso, Giuseppe. *L'altra Europa: per un'antropologia storica del Mezzogiorno d'Italia*. Rev. ed. Lecce, 1997.

———. *Napoli capitale: identità politica e identità cittadina: studi e ricerche (1266–1860)*. Naples, 1998.

García-Villoslada, R. "Felipe II y la contrarreforma católica." In *Historia de la Iglesia de España*, vol. 3, part 2, 3–106. Madrid, 1980.

Garfagnini, Gian Carlo, ed. *Lorenzo de' Medici e il suo tempo*. Florence, 1992.

———, ed. *Lorenzo de' Medici e il suo mondo*. Florence, 1994.

Geary, Patrick J. *Furta Sacra: Thefts of Relics in the Central Middle Ages*. Rev. ed. Princeton, 1990.

Gentilcore, David. *From Bishop to Witch: The System of the Sacred in Early Modern Terra d'Otranto*. Manchester, UK, 1992.

Ghirelli, Antonio. *Storia di Napoli*. Turin, 1973.

Gilbert, Felix. "The Medici Megalopolis." *New York Review of Books* (Jan. 21, 1982): 61–66.

Gilfoyle, Timothy. "Prostitutes in History: From Parables of Pornography to Metaphors of Modernity." *American Historical Review* 104 (1999): 117–41.

Gillis, John R. "Conflicting Paths: Growing Up in America." *Journal of Interdisciplinary History* 27 (1996a): 344–46.

———. "The Future of European History." *Perspectives, American Historical Association Newsletter* (Apr. 1996b).

Ginzburg, Carlo. *The Cheese and the Worms: The Cosmos of a Sixteenth-Century Miller*. Trans. John and Anne Tedeschi. Baltimore, 1980.

Giorgi, Raniero. *La grotta di S. Angelo e l'ordine eremitico di S. Benedetto*. Ascoli Piceno, 1963.

Giraffi, Alessandro. *An Exact History of the Revolutions of Naples; And Their Monstrouse Successes, Not to Be Parallel'd by Any Antient or Modern History*. Trans. James Howell. London, 1650.

Giuliani, Alessandro. s.v. "Prova." *Enciclopedia del Diritto*. Milan, 1958–95.

Given, James. *State and Society in Medieval Europe: Gwynedd and Languedoc Under Outside Rule*. Ithaca and London, 1990.

Goehring, James E. "The Encroaching Desert: Literary Production and Ascetic Space in Early Christian Egypt." *Journal of Early Christian Studies* 1 (1993): 281–96.

Goldthwaite, Richard. *Private Wealth in Renaissance Florence*. Princeton, 1968.

———. *The Building of Renaissance Florence*. Baltimore, 1980.
———. *Wealth and the Demand for Art in Italy 1300–1600*. Baltimore, 1993.
———. *Banks, Palaces and Entrepreneurs in Renaissance Florence*. Brookfield, Vt., 1995.
Golfieri, Ennio. "Topografia medioevale delle aree intorno al duomo di Faenza." *Ravennatensia* 6 (1977): 25–42.
Golinelli, Paolo. "La città prima e dopo il Mille." In *Storia Illustrata di Modena*, eds. Paolo Golinelli and Giuliano Muzzioli, 3 vols., 1:181–200. Milan, 1990.
———. "Strutture organizzative e vita religiosa nell'età del particolarismo." In *Storia dell'Italia religiosa, 1. L'antichità e il medioevo*, ed. André Vauchez, 155–72. Bari, 1993.
———. "San Geminiano e Modena. Un Santo, il suo tempo, il suo culto nel Medioevo." In *'Civitas geminiana': La città e il suo patrono*, ed. Francesca Piccinini, 9–33. Modena, 1997.
———, and Giuliano Muzzioli, eds. *Storia illustrata di Modena*. 3 vols. Milan, 1990.
Golubovich, Hieron. "Series provinciarum Ordinis Fratrum Minorum saec. XIII e XIV." *Archivum Franciscanum Historicum* 1 (1908): 20.
Górecki, Piotr. *Parishes, Tithes, and Society in Earlier Medieval Poland, c. 1100–c. 1250*. Philadelphia, 1993.
Gouwens, Kenneth. "Perceiving the Past: Renaissance Humanism After the 'Cognitive Turn.'" *American Historical Review* 103 (1998): 55–82.
Graburn, Nelson H. H. "Tourism: The Sacred Journey." In *Hosts and Guests: The Anthropology of Tourism*, ed. Valerie Smith, 20–35. Philadelphia, 1989.
Graham Dixon, Andrew. *Renaissance*. London, 2000.
Grégoire, Réginald, ed. *Agiografia silvestrina medievale*. Fabriano, 1983.
———. "Movimenti spirituali nelle Marche nei secoli XIII–XIV." In *San Nicola, Tolentino, le Marche: contributi e ricerche sul processo (a. 1325) per la canonizzazione di San Nicola da Tolentino*, 81–94. Tolentino, 1986.
Grendler, Paul F. *Schooling in Renaissance Italy: Literacy and Learning, 1300–1600*. Baltimore, 1989.
Grubb, James S. "When Myths Lose Power: Four Decades of Venetian Historiography." *Journal of Modern History* 58 (1986): 43–94.
———. *Firstborn of Venice: Vicenza in the Early Renaissance State*. Baltimore, 1988.
———. *Provincial Families of the Renaissance: Private and Public Life in the Veneto*. Baltimore, 1996.
Gualazzini, Ugo. s.v. "Documento e documentazione, diritto intermedio." *Enciclopedia del Diritto*. Milan, 1958–95.
Guandalini, Gabriella, ed. *Il Palazzo Comunale di Modena: le sedi, la città, il contado*. Modena, 1985.
Guidi, Guidubaldo. *Il Governo della città-repubblica di Firenze del primo Quattrocento*. 2 vols. Florence, 1981.
Guidi, Pietro, and E. Pellegrinetti, eds. *Inventari del vescovato, della cattedrale e di altre chiese di Lucca*. Roma, 1921.

Guidi, Pietro, and Martino Giusti, eds. *Tuscia. Rationes decimarum Italiae.* 2 vols. Vatican City, 1932–42.
Guidoni, Enrico. *La città dal Medioevo al Rinascimento.* Rome and Bari, 1981.
Gurrieri, Francesco. *La Piazza del Duomo a Pistoia.* Bergamo, 1995.
Guylforde, Richard. *This Is the Begynnynge, and Contynuaunce of the Pylgrymage of Sir Richard Guylforde Knygth, & Controuler unto Our Late Soueraygne Lorde Kynge Henry the vii.* London, 1511.
Hale, John R. *Florence and the Medici: The Pattern of Control.* London, 1977.
Hay, Dennis, and John Law. *Italy in the Age of the Renaissance 1380–1530.* New York, 1989.
Heers, Jacques. "Les villes d'Italie centrale et l'urbanisme: origines et affirmation d'une politique (environ 1200–1350)." *Mélanges de l'École française de Rome—Moyen Age* 101 (1989): 67–93.
Henderson, John. *Piety and Charity in Late Medieval Florence.* Oxford, 1994.
Herlihy, David. "Direct and Indirect Taxation in Tuscan Urban Finances, ca. 1200–1400." In *Finances et comptabilité urbaines du XIIIe au XIVe siècle*, 385–485. Brussels, 1964.
———. *Medieval and Renaissance Pistoia: The Social History of an Italian Town, 1200–1430.* New Haven, 1967.
———. "Santa Maria Impruneta: A Rural Commune in the Late Middle Ages." In *Florentine Studies: Politics and Society in Renaissance Florence*, ed. Nicolai Rubinstein, 242–76. Evanston, 1968.
———. "The Population of Verona in the First Century of Venetian Rule." In *Renaissance Venice*, ed. John R. Hale, 91–120. Totowa, N.J., 1973.
———, and Christiane Klapisch-Zuber. *Les Toscans et leurs familles.* Paris, 1978. Eng. trans. New Haven and London, 1985.
Holder-Egger, O., ed. *Chronica Fratris Salimbene de Adam.* Hanover and Leipzig, 1905–13.
Hudon, William V. "Religion and Society in Early Modern Italy: Old Questions, New Insights." *American Historical Review* 101 (1996): 783–804.
Hughes, Diane. "From Brideprice to Dowry in Mediterranean Europe." *Journal of Family History* 3 (1978): 262–96.
———. "Controlling Consumption in Renaissance Italy." In *Disputes and Settlements: Law and Human Relations in the West*, ed. John Bossy, 69–99. Cambridge, 1983.
Humbert de Romans. "Treatise on the Formation of Preachers." In *Early Dominicans: Selected Writings*, ed. Simon Tugwell, 184–370. Ramsey, N.J., 1982.
Hyde, John K. *Society and Politics in Medieval Italy: The Evolution of the Civil Life, 1000–1350.* London, 1973.
Jansen, Katherine Ludwig. *The Making of the Magdalen: Preaching and Popular Devotion in the Later Middle Ages.* Princeton, 2000.
Jansen, Philippe. "La santità nelle Marche nei secoli XIII e XIV e la sua spontanea affermazione." In *San Nicola, Tolentino, le Marche: contributi e ricerche sul processo (a. 1325) per la canonizzazione di San Nicola da Tolentino*, 55–80. Tolentino, 1986.

Janz, Denis, ed. *Three Catechisms: Catholic, Anabaptist, and Lutheran*. New York, 1982.
Johnson, G. "Lion on the Piazza: Patrician Politics and Public Statuary in Central Florence." In *Secular Sculpture, 1350–1550*, eds. T. Frangenberg and P. Lindley. Stamford, UK, 2000.
Jones, Pamela. *Federico Borromeo and the Ambrosiana: Art Patronage and Reform in Seventeenth-Century Milan*. Cambridge, UK, 1995.
Jones, Philip J. *The Malatesta of Rimini and the Papal State: A Political History*. London and New York, 1974.
———. *The Italian City-State: From Commune to Signoria*. Oxford, 1997.
Jordan of Saxony. *The Life of the Brethren: Liber Vitas Fratrum*. Trans. Gerard Deigham. Villanova, Pa., 1993.
Kantorowicz, Hermann. *Albertus Gandinus und der Strafrecht der Scholastik*. 2 vols. Berlin, 1907.
Karras, Ruth. *Common Women: Prostitution and Sexuality in Medieval England*. New York, 1996.
Kemp, Martin. "Not So Eccentric." Review in *Times Literary Supplement*, Nov. 11, 1994, 12.
Kent, Dale. *The Rise of the Medici: Faction in Florence, 1426–1434*. Oxford, 1978.
———. *Cosimo de' Medici and the Florentine Renaissance*. New Haven and London, 2000.
Kent, F. W. *Household and Lineage in Renaissance Florence: The Family Life of the Capponi, Ginori, and Rucellai*. Princeton, 1977.
———, and Dale Kent. *Neighbours and Neighbourhoods in Renaissance Florence*. Locust Valley, N.J., 1982.
———, and Patricia Simons, eds. *Patronage, Art and Society in Renaissance Italy*. Oxford, 1987.
Kienzle, Beverly Mayne. "Maternal Imagery in the Sermons of Hélinant of Froidmont." In *De Ore Domini: Preacher and the Word in the Middle Ages*, eds. Thomas L. Amos, Eugene A. Green, and Beverly Mayne Kienzle, 93–103. Kalamazoo, Mich., 1989.
Kirshner, Julius. "Some Problems in the Interpretation of Legal Texts *Re* the Italian City States." *Archiv für Begriffsgeschichte* 19 (1975): 16–27.
———, ed. *The Origins of the State in Italy, 1300–1600*. Chicago, 1996. (First appeared as supplement to *Journal of Modern History*, Dec. 1995)
———. "The State Is 'Back In.'" In Kirshner, 1996, 1–10.
Klapisch-Zuber, Christiane. *Women, Family and Ritual in Renaissance Italy*. Trans. Lydia Cochrane. Chicago and London, 1985.
———. "Ripensando al catasto." *Archivio storico italiano* 152 (1994): 182–92.
———. "David Herlihy and the Florentine Catasto." In *Portraits in Medieval and Renaissance Living*, eds. Samuel K. Cohn and Steven A. Epstein, 29–36. Ann Arbor, 1996.
Kohl, Benjamin. *Padua under the Carrara, 1318–1405*. Baltimore, 1998.
Krieger, Leonard. "European History in America." In *History*, eds. John Higham with Leonard Krieger and Felix Gilbert. Englewood Cliffs, N.J., 1965.

Kurze, Dietrich. *Pfarrerwahlen im Mittelalter. Ein Beitrag zur Geschichte der Gemeinde und des Niederkirchenwesens.* Cologne and Graz, 1966.
Lambert, M. D. *Franciscan Poverty: The Doctrine of the Absolute Poverty of Christ and the Apostles in the Franciscan Order 1210–1323.* London, 1961.
Lane, Frederic C. *Venetian Ships and Shipbuilders of the Renaissance.* Baltimore, 1934.
———. *Venice: A Maritime Republic.* Baltimore, 1973.
Langeli, Attilio Bartoli, and Maria Rita Silvestrelli. "Il comune duecentesco e i suoi palazzi." In *Il Palazzo dei Priori di Perugia*, ed. Francesco Federico Mancini, 3–12. Perugia, 1997.
Lansing, Carol. *The Florentine Magnates: Lineage and Faction in a Medieval Commune.* Princeton, 1991.
———. *Power and Purity: Cathar Heresy in Medieval Italy.* Oxford, 1998.
Larner, John. *Italy in the Age of Dante and Petrarch, 1216–1380.* London and New York, 1980.
La Roncière, Charles M. de. *Florence: Centre économique régional au XIVe siècle*, 5 vols. Aix-en-Provence, 1976.
———. *Réligion paysanne et réligion urbaine en Toscane (c. 1250–1450).* Aldershot, UK, and Brookfield, Vt., 1994.
Lassels, Richard. *An Italian Voyage, or a Compleat Journey Through Italy.* 2nd ed. London, 1698.
Latour, Bruno. *We Have Never Been Modern.* Cambridge, Mass., 1991.
Lepschy, Anna Laura Momigliano, ed. *Viaggio in Terrasanta di Santo Brasca, 1480, con l'itinerario di Gabriele Capodilista, 1458.* Milan, 1966.
Letts, Malcolm, ed. and trans. *Pero Tafur, Travels and Adventures, 1435–1439.* New York, 1926.
———. *The Pilgrimage of Arnold van Harff, Knight.* Hakluyt Society, ser. 2, vol. 94. London, 1946.
———. *The Travels of Leo of Rozmital through Germany, Flanders, England, France, Spain, Portugal and Italy, 1465–1467.* Hakluyt Society, ser. 2, vol. 108. Cambridge, 1957.
Leverotti, Franca. "La crisi demografica nella Toscana del trecento: l'esempio delle Sei Miglia lucchesi." In *La Toscana nel secolo XIV. Caratteri di una civiltà regionale.* Pisa, 1988.
———. *Popolazione, famiglie, insediamento: le Sei Miglia lucchesi nel XIV e XV secolo.* Pisa, 1992.
Levi, Carlo. "On Microhistory." In *New Perspectives on Historical Writing*, ed. Peter Burke, 93–113. Cambridge, 1991.
Lévy, Jean-Philippe. "Le problème de la preuve dans les droits savants du moyen âge." *Recueils de la Société Jean Bodin* 17, part 2 (1965): 137–67.
Licet Ecclesie Catholice. Critical edition in "Bulla Alexandri Papae IV qua Plures Eremitarum congregationes Ordini Eremitarum S. Augustini an. 1256 fuerunt Unitae." *Analecta Augustinia* 5 (1913): 1–4.
Livi, Ridolfo, ed. "San Bernardino e le sue prediche secondo un suo ascoltatore pratese del 1424." *Bollettino Senese di Storia Patria* 20 (1913): 458–69.

López Martínez, Nicolás. "La desamortización de bienes eclesiásticos en 1574." *Hispania* 86 (1962): 230–50.
Loyola, Ignatius. *The Constitutions of the Society of Jesus.* Ed. and trans. George E. Ganss. St. Louis, 1970.
Lubkin, Gregory. *A Renaissance Court: Milan under Galeazzo Maria Sforza.* Berkeley, 1994.
Lunt, William E. *Papal Revenues in the Middle Ages.* New York, 1965.
Luria, Keith. *Territories of Grace: Cultural Change in the Seventeenth-Century Diocese of Grenoble.* Berkeley, 1991.
Luzzati, Michele. "Contratti agrari e rapporti di produzione nelle campagne pisane dal XIII al XVI secolo." In *Studi in memoria di Federigo Melis*, 5 vols., 1:569–85. Naples, 1978.
———. "Toscana senza mezzadria: il caso pisano alla fine del medioevo." In *Contadini et proprietari nella Toscana moderna: Atti del Convegno di studi in onere di Giorgio Giorgetti*, 279–343. Florence, 1979.
Luzzatto, Gino. *Rustici e signori a Fabriano alla fine del XII secolo.* Milan, 1909. Now in Luzzatto, Gino. *Dai servi della glebe agli albori dal capitalismo: saggi di storia economica*, 230–43. Bari, 1966.
Lynch, John. *The Hispanic World in Crisis and Change.* Cambridge, 1992.
MacCannell, Dean. *The Tourist: A New Theory of the Leisure Class.* New York, 1989.
Machiavelli, Niccolò. *Istorie fiorentine*, ed. F. Gaeta. Milan, 1962.
Magna, L. "Gli Ubaldini del Mugello." *I ceti dirigenti dell'età comunale nei secoli XII e XIII*, 13–65. Pisa, 1982.
Mallett, Michael, and Nicholas Mann, eds. *Lorenzo the Magnificent: Culture and Politics.* London, 1996.
Marino, John. *Pastoral Economics in the Kingdom of Naples.* Baltimore, 1988.
Martin, John. *Venice's Hidden Enemies: Italian Heretics in a Renaissance City.* Berkeley, 1993.
———. "Recent Italian Works on the Renaissance: Perspectives on Intellectual, Political, and Social History." *Renaissance Quarterly* 47 (1994): 623–38.
———. "Recent Italian Scholarship on the Renaissance: Aspects of Christianity in Late Medieval and Early Modern Italy." *Renaissance Quarterly* 48 (1995): 593–610.
———. "Knowledge, Politics, and Memory in Early Modern Italy: Recent Italian Scholarship." *Renaissance Quarterly* 49 (1996): 598–616.
———, and Dennis Romano, eds. *Venice Reconsidered: Venetian History and Civilization, 1297–1797.* Baltimore, 1999.
Martines, Lauro. *The Social World of the Florentine Humanists 1390–1460.* Princeton, 1963.
———. *Lawyers and Statecraft in Renaissance Florence.* Princeton, 1968.
———, ed. *Violence and Civil Disorder in Italian Cities 1200–1500.* Berkeley, 1972.
———. *Power and Imagination: City-States in Renaissance Italy.* New York, 1979.

———. "Forced Loans: Political and Social Strain in Quattrocento Florence." *Journal of Modern History* 60 (1988): 300–11.
Mattasoni, Iole. "'Piangere Miseria.' Le motivazioni dei Bolognesi per impietosire gli ufficiali addetti all'estime del 1329." *Atti e memorie della Deputazione di Storia patria per le province di Romagna*, n.s. 46 (1996): 413–27.
Mazzi, Angelo. "Appunti sulle notizie riguardanti il restabilimento degli antichi palazzi comunali di Bergamo." *Bollettino della Civica Biblioteca di Bergamo* 14 (1920): 1–28.
Mazzi, Maria Serena. *Prostitute e lenoni nella Firenze del Quattrocento*. Milan, 1991.
———, and Sergio Raveggi. *Gli uomini e le cose nelle campagne fiorentine del Quattrocento*. Florence, 1983.
McArdle, Frank. *Altopascio: A Study in Tuscan Rural Society, 1587–1784*. Cambridge, 1978.
McLaughlin, Richard Gabriel. "The Church and Commune in Medieval Asti: Political, Social and Economic Change in the Astigiana 9–13 Centuries." Ph.D. dissertation, University of Wisconsin. Madison, 1972.
Medici, Maria Teresa Guerra. *L'Aria di città*. Naples, 1996.
Meek, Christine. *The Commune of Lucca under Pisan Rule, 1342–1369*. Cambridge, Mass., 1980.
Melloni, Claudia. "Il ceto dirigente modenese dal XV al XVIII secolo: Composizione e dinamiche sociali." In *Al governo del comune: Tremilacinquecento modenesi per la comunità locale dal XV secolo ad oggi*, ed. Marco Cattini, 2 vols., 1:25–42. Quaderni dell'Archivio Storico, 5. Modena, 1997.
Migliorino, Francesco. *Fama e infamia. Problemi della società medievale nel pensiero giuridico nei secoli XII e XIII*. Catania, 1985.
Miller, Maureen C. "The Development of the Archiepiscopal Residence in Ravenna, 300–1300." *Felix Ravenna* 141–4 (1991–92): 145–73.
———. *The Formation of a Medieval Church: Ecclesiastical Change in Verona, 950–1150*. Ithaca, 1993.
———. "From Episcopal to Communal Palaces: Places and Power in Northern Italy (1000–1250)." *Journal of the Society of Architectural Historians* 54 (1995): 175–85.
———. "Vescovi, palazzi e lo sviluppo dei centri civici nelle città dell'Italia settentrionale, 1000–1250." In *Albertano da Brescia: Alle origini del Razionalismo economico, dell'Umanesimo civile, della Grande Europa*, ed. Franco Spinelli, 27–41. Brescia, 1996.
———. "Il 'Palazzo della Città di Modena': Di chi era questo 'palazzo'?" In *Atti e memorie della R. Deputazione di storia patria per le provincie modenesi* ser. 11, 21 (1999): 3–12.
———. *The Bishop's Palace: Architecture and Authority in Medieval Italy*. Ithaca, 2000.
Milo, Yoram. "Political Opportunism in Guidi Tuscan Policy." In *I Ceti dirigenti in Toscana nell'età precomunale*, 207–23. Pisa, 1981.
Minerbetti, Piero di Giovanni. *Cronica volgare di Anonimo Fiorentino dall'anno*

1385 al 1409 già attribuita a Piero di Giovanni Minerbetti. Ed. Elina Bellondi. Rerum Italicarum Scriptores, 27, part 2. Città di Castello, 1915-18.

Misson, François. *A New Voyage to Italy with Curious Observations on Several Other Countries*. 2 vols. London, 1699.

Mittarelli, J. B., and A. Costadoni. *Annales Camaldulenses Ordinis Sancti Benedicti*. vol. 3. Venice, 1758.

Molho, Anthony. *Florentine Public Finances in the Early Renaissance, 1400-1433*. Cambridge, Mass., 1971.

———. "Cosimo de' Medici: Pater Patriae or Padrino?" *Stanford Italian Review* 1 (1979): 5-33.

———. "Il padronato a Firenze nella storiografia anglofona." *Richerche storiche* 15 (1985): 5-16.

———. Review of *Giovanni and Lusanna. Love and Marriage in Renaissance Florence* by Gene Brucker. *Renaissance Quarterly* 40 (1987): 96-100.

———. "The Closing of the Florentine Archives." *Journal of Modern History* 60 (1988): 290-9.

———. "Recent Works on the History of Tuscany: Fifteenth to Eighteenth Centuries." *Journal of Modern History* 62 (1990): 57-77.

———. *Marriage Alliance in Late Medieval Florence*. Cambridge, Mass., 1994.

———. "Società e fisco nell'interpretazione di Elio Conti." *Nuovi studi storici* 29 (1995): 41-60.

———. "The State in Public Finance." In Kirshner, 1996, 97-135.

———. "The Italian Renaissance, Made in the USA." In *Imagined Histories: American Historians Interpret the Past*, eds. Anthony Molho and Gordon Wood, 263-94. Princeton, 1998.

———, Kurt Raaflaub, and Julia Emlen, eds. *City States in Classical Antiquity and Medieval Italy*. Ann Arbor, 1991.

Mollat, Guillaume. "L'administration d'Orvieto durant la légation d'Albornoz (1354-1367)." *Mélanges d'archéologie et d'histoire* 70 (1958): 395-406.

Montanari, G. Bermond. "Ravenna—1980—Lo scavo della Banca Popolare. Relazione preliminare." *Felix Ravenna* 127-30 (1984-85): 21-36.

Monumenta Germaniae historica, Diplomatum regum et imperatorum Germaniae. Berlin, 1879-.

Mor, Carlo Guido. "Il Palazzo della Ragione nella vita di Padova." In *Il Palazzo della Ragione di Padova*, 1-25. Padua, 1964.

———, and Heinrich Schmidinger, eds. *I poteri temporali dei vescovi in Italia e in Germania nel medioevo*. Annali dell'Istituto storico italo-germanico, Quaderno 3. Bologna, 1979.

Mormando, Franco. *The Preacher's Demons: Bernardino of Siena and the Social Underworld of Early Renaissance Italy*. Chicago, 1999.

Moronti, Stefano. *Reportorio de le scritture de tutt'i luoghi del la Congregazione Silvestrina, ordinatamente registrate secondo l'ordine de lo Archivio di San Benedetto di Fabriano*. Archivio del Monastero di S. Silvestro in Montefano, ms. of 1581.

Moryson, Fynes. *Itinerary Written by Fynes Moryson, Gent*. London, 1617.

Mozzarelli, Cesare. *La corte di Mantova nell'età di Andrea Mantegna, 1450–1550*. Rome, 1997.
Mozzillo, Atanasio. *Passaggio a Mezzogiorno: Napoli e il Sud nell'immaginario barocco e illuminista europeo*. Milan, 1993.
Muir, Edward. *Civic Ritual in Renaissance Venice*. Princeton, 1981.
———. "The Virgin on the Street Corner: The Place of the Sacred in Italian Cities." In *Religion and Culture in the Renaissance and Reformation*, 25–40. Kirksville, Mo., 1989.
———. *Mad Blood Stirring: Vendetta and Factions in Friuli During the Renaissance*. Baltimore, 1993.
———. "The Italian Renaissance in America." *American Historical Review* 100 (1995): 1095–1118.
———. *Ritual in Early Modern Europe*. Cambridge, 1997.
———. "The Sources of Civil Society in Italy." *Journal of Interdisciplinary History* 29 (1999): 379–406.
———, and Guido Ruggiero, eds. *Sex and Gender in Historical Perspective*. Trans. Margaret A. Gallucci, with Mary M. Gallucci and Carole C. Gallucci. Baltimore, 1990.
———, and Guido Ruggiero, eds. *Microhistory and the Lost Peoples of Europe*. Trans. Eren Branch. Baltimore, 1991.
———, and Guido Ruggiero, eds. *History from Crime*. Trans. Corrada Biazzo, Margaret A. Gallucci, and Mary M. Gallucci. Baltimore, 1994.
———, and Ronald Weissman. "Social and Symbolic Places in Renaissance Venice and Florence." In *The Power of Place: Bringing Together Geographical and Sociological Imaginations*, eds. John. A. Agnew and James S. Dunca, 89–103. Boston, 1988.
Mumford, Lewis. *The City in History*. New York, 1961.
Muzzarelli, Maria Giuseppina. *Gli inganni delle apparenze: Disciplina di vesti e ornamenti alla fine del medioevo*. Turin, 1996.
Najemy, John. *Corporatism and Consensus in Florentine Electoral Politics, 1280–1400*. Ithaca, 1982.
———. "Linguaggi storiografici sulla Firenze rinascimentale." *Rivista storica italiana* 97 (1985): 102–59.
———. "The Dialogue of Power in Florentine Politics." In *City States in Classical Antiquity and Medieval Italy*, eds. Anthony Molho, Kurt Raaflaub, and Julia Emlen, 269–87. Ann Arbor, 1991.
Nanni, Luigi. *La parrocchia studiata nei documenti lucchesi dei secoli VIII–XIII*. Rome, 1948.
Nasalli Rocca, Emilio. "Sui poteri comitali del vescovo di Piacenza." *Rivista Storica Italiana* 49 (1932): 1–20.
Nelli, Renzo. *Signoria ecclesiastica e proprietà cittadina: Monte di Croce tra XIII e XIV secolo*. Pontassieve, 1985.
Nenci, Maria Daniela. "Ricerche sull'immigrazione dal contado alla città di Firenze nella seconda metà del XIII secolo." In *Ricerche Storiche* 1 (1981): 139–77.

Nenci, R. *Le Consulte e pratiche della repubblica fiorentina (1404)*. Fonti per la storia d'Italia. Rome, 1991.
Newett, Margaret, ed. *Canon Pietro Casola's Pilgrimage to Jerusalem, in the Year 1494*. Manchester, 1907.
Nicolini, Gianna Suitner. "Il monastero benedettino di Sant'Andrea in Mantova: L'evoluzione del organismo ed il suo ruolo nella formazione della città medievale." In *Il Sant'Andrea di Mantova e Leon Battista Alberti*, 35–50. Mantua, 1974.
Nironi, Vittorio. "I palazzi reggiani del Comune e del Capitano del Popolo dal secolo XII agli inizi del XIV." *Bollettino Storico Reggiano* 47 (1980): 23–35.
Norman, Corrie. "The Franciscan Preaching Tradition and Its Sixteenth-Century Legacy: The Case of Cornelio Musso." *Catholic Historical Review* 75 (1999): 208–32.
Nussdorfer, Laurie. *Civic Politics in the Rome of Urban VIII*. Princeton, 1992.
———. "Writing and the Power of Speech: Notaries and Artisans in Baroque Rome." In *Culture and Identity in Early Modern Europe (1500–1800)*, eds. Barbara Diefendorf and Carla Hesse, 103–15. Ann Arbor, 1993.
O'Malley, John W. *The First Jesuits*. Cambridge, Mass., 1993.
Oneri, Alberto Maria. *L'Abbazia di San Salvatore a Sesto e il Lago di Bientina*. Florence, 1984.
Origo, Iris. *The World of San Bernardino*. New York, 1962.
Orlandi, Stefano, ed. *"Necrologio" di S. Maria Novella*, I. Florence, 1955.
Ortalli, Gherardo. "La famiglia tra la realtà dei gruppi inferiori e la mentalità dei gruppi dominanti a Bologna nel XIII secolo." In *Famille e parenté dans l'Occident médiéval*, eds. Georges Duby and Jacques LeGoff. Collection de l'École Française de Rome 30, 1977.
Osborne, Kenan. *Reconciliation and Justification: The Sacrament and Its Theology*. New York, 1990.
Osheim, Duane J. "Rural Population and the Tuscan Economy in the late Middle Ages." *Viator* 7 (1976): 329–46.
———. *An Italian Lordship: The Bishopric of Lucca in the Late Middle Ages*. Berkeley, 1977.
———. "Countrymen and the Law in Late Medieval Tuscany." *Speculum* 64 (1989a): 317–37.
———. *A Tuscan Monastery and Its Social World, San Michele of Guamo (1156–1348)*. Rome, 1989b.
Pagnani, Giacinto. "Frammenti della cronaca del B. Francesco Venimbeni da Fabriano." *Archivum Franciscanum Historicum* 52 (1959): 153–77.
———. *San Liberato e il suo convento*. Falconara (Ancona), 1962a.
———. *I Viaggi di S. Francesco d'Assisi nelle Marche*. Milan, 1962b.
———. "Francesco da Fabriano (F. Venimbeni) beato." In *Bibliotheca Sanctorum* 5 (1964), cols. 1155–56.
Panazza, Gaetano. "Appunti per la storia dei Palazzi Comunali di Brescia e Pavia." *Archivio Storico Lombardo* ser. 9, 4 (1964–65): 181–203.

Paoli, Ugo. "Cronotassi dei Superiori Generali della Congregazione Silvestrina." *Inter Fratres* 33 (1983): 9–74.
———. "Sylvester Guzzolini and His Congregation." *Inter Fratres* 36:2 (1986).
Paolucci, Scipione. *Missioni de Padri della Compagnia di Gesù nel Regno di Napoli*. Naples, 1651.
Parker, Geoffrey. "Lepanto (1571): The Costs of Victory." In *Spain and the Netherlands, 1559–1659*, 122–33. London, 1979.
Parks, George B. *The English Traveler to Italy*. 2 vols. Stanford, 1954.
Partner, Peter. *The Lands of St. Peter: The Papal State in the Middle Ages and the Early Renaissance*. Berkeley, 1972.
———. "Papal Financial Policy in the Renaissance and Counter-Reformation." *Past and Present* 88 (1980): 17–62.
Pastor, Ludwig. *History of the Popes*, ed. Ralph Francis Kerr, vol. 18. St. Louis, 1918.
Paton, Bernadette. "'To the Fire! Let Us Burn a Little Incense to God': Bernardino, Preaching Friars, and Maleficio in Late Medieval Siena." In *No Gods Except Me: Orthodoxy and Religious Practice in Europe, 1200–1600*, ed. Charles Zika, 7–36. Melbourne, 1991.
Paul, Jürgen. *Die mittelalterlichen Kommunalpaläste in Italien*. Cologne, 1963.
Pedenzini, Cristiana, and Isabella Scaramuzzi, eds. *Commercio e città. Un laboratorio per il piano commerciale di Venezia*. Bologna, 1997.
Pemble, John. *Venice Rediscovered*. Oxford, 1995.
Penco, Gregorio. *Storia de monachesimo in Italia: Dalle origini alla fine del Medioevo*. 3rd ed. Milan, 1995.
Pescaglini Monti, R. "I conti Cadolingi." In *I ceti dirigenti in Toscana nell'età precomunale*, 191–205. Pisa, 1981.
Peterson, David. *From the 'Eight Saints' to Saint Antoninus: the Church in Florence, 1375–1460*. 2 vols. Baltimore and London (forthcoming).
Petraccone, Claudia. *Napoli dal '500 all' '800: problemi di storia demografia e sociale*. Naples, 1974.
Petralia, G. "L'imposizione diretta e dominio territoriale nella repubblica fiorentina del Quattrocento." *Società, istituzioni, spiritualità: Studi in onore di Cinzio Violante*, 2 (1994): 639–52.
Petrucci, Armando, ed. *Notari: Documenti per la storia del notariato italiano*. Milan, 1958.
———, ed. *Scrittura e popolo nella Roma barocca 1585–1721*. Rome, 1982.
———. "Introduzione alle pratiche di scrittura." *Annali della Scuola Normale Superiore di Pisa*, 3rd ser., 23 (1993): 549–62.
———. *Readers and Writers in Medieval Italy*. Trans. Charles M. Radding. New Haven, 1995.
Piattoli, Renato. *Regesta Chartarum Italiae: le carte della canonica della cattedrale di Firenze (723–1149)*, vol. 23. Rome, 1938.
Piccinini, Francesca, ed. *"Civitas geminiana": La città e il suo patrono*. Modena, 1997.
Pini, Antonio Ivan. "Problemi demografici bolognesi del Duecento." In *Atti e*

Memorie della Deputazione di storia patria per le provincie di Romagna, n.s. 16–17, 1969.

———. "Il cardinale Albornoz nelle cronache bolognesi." In *El Cardenal Albornoz y el colegio de España*, 6 vols., 1:99–140. Bologna, 1972.

———. "Un aspetto dei rapporti tra città e territorio nel Medioevo: la politica demografica 'ad elastico' di Bologna fra il XII e il XIV secolo." In *Studi in memoria di Federigo Melis*, 5 vols., 1:365–408. Naples, 1978.

Pinto, Giuliano. "Ordinamento delle colture e proprietà fondiaria cittadina." *La Toscana nel tardo medio evo: ambiente, economia rurale, società*, ed. G. Pinto, 157–204. Florence, 1982.

———. *Toscana medievale: paesaggi e realtà sociali*. Florence, 1993.

———. *Città e spazi economici nell'Italia commune*. Bologna, 1996.

Pirillo, Paolo. "I beni comuni nelle campagne fiorentine basso medievali: evidenze documentarie ed ipotesi di ricerca." In *Mélanges de l'École française de Rome. Moyen Âge–Temps Modernes* 99 (1987: 2), 621–47.

Pistoni, Giuseppe. *Il Palazzo Arcivescovile di Modena*. Modena, 1976.

———. *San Geminiano: Vescovo e protettore di Modena nella vita nel culto nell'arte*. Modena, 1983.

Polecritti, Cynthia. *Preaching Peace in Renaissance Italy: Bernardino of Siena and His Audience*. Washington, D.C., 2000.

Polica, Sante. "An Attempted 'Reconversion' of Wealth in XVth Century Lucca: the Lands of Michele di Giovanni Guinigi." *Journal of European Economic History* 9 (1980): 655–707.

Polizzotto, Lorenzo. *The Elect Nation: The Savonarolan Movement in Florence, 1494–1545*. Oxford, 1994.

Prescott, H.F.M. *Jerusalem Journey: Pilgrimage to the Holy Land in the Fifteenth Century*. London, 1954.

Prosperi, Adriano. *Tribunali della coscienza: inquisitori, confessori, missionari*. Turin, 1996.

Quagliarini, Ivo. "I primi statuti ed ordinamenti comunali." In *La città della carta: Ambiente società cultura nella storia di Fabriano*, ed. Giancarlo Castagnari, 2nd ed., 263–327. Fabriano, 1986.

Racine, Pierre. *Plaisance du Xème a la fin du XIIIème siècle*. 3 vols. Paris, 1980.

———. "Les Palais publics dans les communes italiennes (XII–XIIIe siècles)." In *Le Paysage urbaine au Moyen-Age*, 133–53. Lyon, 1981.

Ragusa, Ida, and Rosalie B. Green, eds. and trans. *Meditations on the Life of Christ*. Princeton, 1977.

Rano, B. "Eremiti di Brettino." *Dizionario degli Istituti di Perfezione*, 1: 1566–69. Rome, 1976.

Rauty, Natale. *L'antico palazzo dei vescovi a Pistoia*. 2 vols. in 3. Florence, 1981.

———. *Storia di Pistoia, I: Dall'alto medioevo all'età precomunale, 406–1105*. Florence, 1988.

Ravaldini, Gaetano. *Il Palazzo Comunale di Ravenna*. Ravenna, 1975.

Redford, Bruce. *Venice and the Grand Tour*. New Haven, 1996.

Redon, Odile. *L'Espace d'une cité: Sienne et le pays siennois (XIIIe–XIVe siècles)*. Rome, 1994.

Reinhardt, Volker. *Überleben in der frühneuzeitlichen Stadt: Annona und Getreideversorgung in Rom 1563–1797*. Tübingen, 1991.
Rigon, Antonio. *Clero e città. "Fratalea cappellanorum," parrocci, cura d'anime in Padova dal XII al XV secolo*. Padua, 1988.
———. "S. Antonio da 'Pater Padue' a 'Patronus Civitatis.'" In *Religion civique à l'époque medievale et moderne*, ed. Andre Vauchez, 65–76. Rome, 1995.
Rinaldi, Rosella. "'Mulieres publicae.' Testimonianze e note sulla prostituzione tra pieno e tardo Medioevo." In *Donna e lavoro nell'Italia medievale*, eds. Maria Giuseppina Muzzarelli, Paola Galetti, and Bruno Andreoli. Turin, 1991.
Rocke, Michael. *Forbidden Friendships: Homosexuality and Male Culture in Renaissance Florence*. Oxford, 1996.
Rodolico, Niccolò, and Giuseppe Marchini. *I Palazzi del Popolo nei comuni toscani nel medio evo*. Milan, 1962.
Romano, Dennis. *Patricians and Popolani: The Social Foundations of the Venetian State*. Baltimore and London, 1987.
Rombaldi, Odoardo. *Cesare d'Este. Al governo dei ducati Estensi (1598–1628)*. Modena, 1989.
———. *Il Duca Francesco I d'Este (1629–1658)*. Modena, 1992.
Romeo, Giovanni. *Inquisitori, esorcisti e streghe nell'Italia della Controriforma*. Florence, 1990.
Romiti, Antonio. *Anchiano nel quattrocento, aspetti di vita quotidiana*. Lucca, 1977.
Ronzani, Mauro. "La 'chiesa del Comune' nelle città dell'Italia centro-settentrionale (secoli XII–XIV)." *Società e storia* 21 (1983): 499–534.
Roth, Francis. "Cardinal Richard Annibaldi: First Protector of the Augustinian Order." *Augustinia* 2 (1952): 26–60, 108–49, 230–47; 3 (1953): 21–34, 283–313; 4 (1954): 5–24.
Rubinstein, Nicolai, ed. *Florentine Studies: Politics and Society in Renaissance Florence*. Evanston, 1968.
———. *The Palazzo Vecchio 1298–1532: Government, Architecture, and Imagery in the Civic Palace of the Florentine Republic*. Oxford, 1995.
———. *The Government of Florence Under the Medici 1434–1494*. Oxford, 1966; 2nd ed. 1997.
Ruggiero, Guido. *Violence in Early Renaissance Venice*. New Brunswick, N.J., 1980.
———. *The Boundaries of Eros: Sex Crime and Sexuality in Renaissance Venice*. Oxford, 1985.
———. *Binding Passions: Tales of Magic, Marriage and Power at the End of the Renaissance*. Oxford, 1993.
Rusconi, Roberto. *Predicazione e vita religiosa nella società italiana*. Turin, 1981.
———, ed. *Il movimento religioso femminile in Umbria nei secoli XII–XIV*. Perugia, 1984.
Russell, Robert Douglass. "Vox Civitatis: Aspects of Thirteenth-Century Communal Architecture in Lombardy." Ph.D. dissertation, Princeton University. Princeton, 1988.

Le Saint Voyage de Jérusalem par le Baron d'Anglure, 1395. Paris, 1858.

Salvioli, Giuseppe. *Storia della procedura civile e criminale.* Vol. 3, parts 1 and 2 of *Storia del diritto italiano*, ed. Pasquale Del Giudice. Milan, 1927. Reprint, Milan, 1969.

Sandonnini, T. "Del Palazzo Comunale di Modena." *Atti e memorie della R. Deputazione di storia patria per le provincie modenesi* ser. 4, 8–9 (1897–99): 93–132.

Santagata, Saverio. *Istoria della compagnia di Gesu appartenente al regno di Napoli.* 2 vols. Naples, 1756–57.

Saracco Previdi, Emilia. "Scelte insediative dell'ordine monastico di S. Silvestro tra XIII e XIV secolo." In *Il monachesimo silvestrino nell'ambiente marchigiano del duecento: Atti del Convegno di Studi tenuto a Fabriano Monastero S. Silvestro Abate 30 magg.–2 giugno 1990*, 217–29. Fabriano, 1993.

Sassi, Romualdo. "Un abbate guerriero simoniaco e mondano ai tempi di Dante." *Atti e Memorie di R. Deputazione di Storia Patria per le Marche* 4 (1926a): 219–39.

———. "Tradizioni e santuari francescani nella Provincia d'Ancona." *Rassegno Marchigiana* 4 (1926b): 5–12.

———. "Le carte di S. Maria d'Apennino." *Studia Picena* 5 (1929): 89–91.

———. "Due documenti capitali su le origini del monastero di S. Vittore della Chiuse." *Rassegna Marchigiana* 8 (1930): 13–14.

———. "Orme poco note di S. Silvestro abate nella vita fabrianese contemporanea." *Benedictina* 2 (1948): 42–43.

———. "Chiese dependenti da monasteri benedettini nel contado fabrianese." *Benedictina* 4 (1950): 87–131.

———. "Incarcerati, reclusi, cellari, murati et eremiti." *Studia Picena* 25 (1957): 67–85.

———. *Le carte del monastero di S. Vittore delle Chiuse sul Sentino: Regesto con introduzione e note.* Deputazione di Storia Patria per le Marche, Studi e Testi, 1. Milan, 1962.

Scalia, Giuseppe, ed. *Cronica di Salimbene de Adam.* 2 vols. Bari, 1966.

Schinosi, Francesco. *Istoria della Compagnia di Gesu Appartenente al Regno di Napoli.* 2 vols. Naples, 1706–11.

Schumann, Reinhold. *Authority and the Commune, Parma 833–1133.* Parma, 1973.

Schutte, Anne Jacobson. "Periodization of Sixteenth-Century Italian Religious History: The Post-Cantimori Paradigm Shift." *Journal of Modern History* 61 (1989): 269–84.

Seghieri, Mario, ed. *Le pergamene di Vivinaia, Montechiari, San Petro in Campo (secc. XI–XIV).* Lucca, 1995.

Sella, Domenico. *Crisis and Continuity: The Economy of Spanish Lombardy in the Seventeenth Century.* Cambridge, Mass., 1979.

———. *Italy in the Seventeenth Century.* New York, 1997.

———, and Carlo Capra. *Il ducato di Milano dal 1535 al 1796.* Turin, 1984.

Selwyn, Jennifer. "Planting Many Virtues There: Jesuit Popular Missions in the

Viceroyalty of Naples, 1550–1700." Ph.D. dissertation, University of California, Davis, 1997.
Serpelli, Bonifacio. "Le più antiche costituzioni silvestrini." *Benedictina* 10 (1956): 211–58.
Serra, Giovanni. *La Peste dell'anno 1630 nel ducato di Modena*. Modena, 1959.
Serrano, Luciano, ed. *Correspondencia diplomática entre España y la Santa Sede*. 2 vols. Madrid, 1914.
Sheedy, Anna. *Bartolus on Social Conditions in the Fourteenth Century*. New York, 1942.
Shields, Eugene. *King and Church: The Rise and Fall of the Patronato Real*. Chicago, 1961.
Signorotto, Gianvittorio, and Maria Antonietta Visceglia. *La corte di Roma tra Cinque e Seicento: teatro della political europea*. Rome, 1998.
Silingardi, Giancarlo. *La Chiesa della Madonna del Voto nella storia e nell'arte*. Modena, 1991.
Smoller, Laura A. "Miracle, Memory, and Meaning in the Canonization of Vincent Ferrer, 1453–1454." *Speculum* 73 (1998): 429–54.
Solì, Gusmano. *Le Chiese di Modena*, ed. Giordano Bertuzzi. 3 vols. Reprint, Modena, 1974.
Southorn, Janet. *Power and Display in the Seventeenth Century: The Arts and Their Patrons in Modena and Ferrara*. Cambridge, 1988.
Spagnoletti, Angelantonio. *Principi italiani e Spagna nell'età barocca*. Milan, 1996.
Spicciani, Amleto, and Cinzio Violante, eds. *Alluccio da Pescia (1070 c. a.–1134): religione e società nei territori di Lucca e della Valdinievole*. Pisa, 1991.
Starn, Randolph. "Florentine Renaissance Studies." *Bibliothèque d'humanisme et Renaissance* 32 (1970): 677–84.
———. "Who's Afraid of the Renaissance?" In *The Past and Future of Medieval Studies*, ed. John van Engen, 129–47. Notre Dame, 1994.
———. Review of *Art and Authority in Renaissance Milan* by Evelyn Welch. *Apollo* 144 (1996): 71.
———, and Loren Partridge. *Arts of Power: Three Halls of State in Italy, 1300–1600*. Berkeley, Los Angeles, and Oxford, 1992.
Stefani, Marchionne di Coppo. *Cronaca fiorentina*, ed. Niccolò Rodolico. Città di Castello, 1903.
Steiner, George. "Stones of Light: How Florence Created Civilization Amid Catastrophe." *New Yorker* (Jan. 13, 1997): 76–77.
Stella, Alessandro. *La Révolte des Ciompi*. Paris, 1993.
Stewart, Aubrey, ed. and trans. *The Wanderings of Felix Fabri (part 1)*. The Library of the Palestine Pilgrims' Text Society, vol. 7. London, 1887–97.
Stone, Harold. *Vico's Cultural History. The Production and Transmission of Ideas in Naples, 1685–1750*. Leiden and New York, 1997.
Storia di Ravenna. 5 vols. Ravenna, 1992–93.
Storia di Venezia dalle origini alla caduta della Serenissima. 8 vols. Rome, 1992–98.

Strauss, Gerald. *Luther's House of Learning: Indoctrination of the Young in the German Reformation.* Baltimore, 1978.
Strocchia, Sharon. *Death and Ritual in Renaissance Florence.* Baltimore, 1992.
Szabó, Thomas. "Pievi, parrocchie e lavori pubblici nella Toscana dei secoli XII–XIV." In *Pievi e parrocchie in Italia nel basso medioevo (sec. XIII–XV).* Atti del Convegno di Storia della Chiesa in Italia (Firenze, 21–25 Sett. 1981), 2 vols., 2:793–809. Rome, 1984.
———. *Comuni e politica stradale in Toscana e in Italia nel Medioevo.* Bologna, 1992.
Tabacco, Giovanni. *Egemonie sociali e strutture del potere nel medioevo italiano.* Turin, 1979; trans. Rosalind Brown Jensen. Cambridge, 1989.
Tamassia, Nino. *La famiglia italiana nei secoli decimoquinto e decimosesto.* Rome, 1971.
Tamba, Giorgio. *La società dei notai di Bologna.* Rome, 1988.
Tamizey de Larroque, ed. *Voyage à Jérusalem de Philippe de Voisins, Seigneur de Montaut.* Paris, 1883.
Tanner, Norman P., ed. *Decrees of the Ecumenical Councils.* 2 vols. London and Washington, D.C., 1990.
Tentler, Thomas. *Sin and Confession on the Eve of the Reformation.* Princeton, 1977.
Terpstra, Nicholas. *Lay Confraternities and Civic Religion in Renaissance Bologna.* Cambridge, 1995.
Theseider, Eugenio Dupré. "Come Orvieto venne sotto il Cardinale Albornoz." *Bollettino dell'istituto storico artistico orvietano* 16 (1960): 3–20.
Toscano, Bernard, ed. *Lorenzo de' Medici. New Perspectives.* New York, 1993.
Toscano, Bruno. "Cattedrale e città: Studio di un esempio." In *Topografia urbana e vita cittadina nell'alto medioevo in occidente.* 2 vols., 2:711–47. Spoleto, 1975.
Toubert, Pierre. *Les structures du Latium médiéval. Le Latium méridional et la Sabine du IXe à la fin du XIIe siècle.* 2 vols. Rome, 1973.
Trachtenberg, Marvin. *Dominion of the Eye: Urbanism, Art, and Power in Early Modern Florence.* Cambridge, 1997.
Trapè, Agostino. "La figura e la santità di S. Nicola come emergono nel Processo." In *San Nicola, Tolentino, le Marche: contributi e ricerche sul processo (a. 1325) per la canonizzazione di San Nicola da Tolentino,* 183–93. Tolentino, 1986.
Trexler, Richard C. "Ritual Behavior in Renaissance Florence: The Setting." *Medievalia et Humanistica* n.s. 4 (1973): 125–44.
———. *Public Life in Renaissance Florence.* Ithaca and London, 1980.
Trovabene, Giordana, and Gloria Serrazanetti. "Il Duomo nel tessuto urbanistico." In *Lanfranco e Wiligelmo. Il Duomo di Modena,* 265–74. Modena, 1984.
Tucci, Ugo. "Mercanti, viaggiatori, pellegrini nel Quattrocento." In *Storia della cultura veneta: Vol. 3, pt. 2: Dal Primo '400 al Concilio di Trento,* 348–53. Vicenza, 1980.

———. "I Servizzi marittimi veneziani per il pellegrinaggio in Terrasanta nel Medioevo." *Studi veneziani* 9 (1985): 43–66.
Tucoo-Chala, Pierre, and Noël Pinzuti, eds. "Le Voyage de Pierre Barbatre à Jérusalem en 1480." *Annuaire-Bulletin de la Société de l'Histoire de France* (1972–73): 73–174.
Urban, Lina Padoan. *Locande a Venezia, dal XIII al XIX secolo.* Venice, 1989.
Urry, John. *The Tourist Gaze: Leisure and Travel in Contemporary Societies.* London, 1990.
Vallerani, Massimo. *Il sistema giudiziario del comune di Perugia. Conflitti, reati e processi nella seconda metà del XIII secolo.* Perugia, 1991.
———. "L'amministrazione della giustizia a Bologna in età podestarile." *Atti e memorie delle Deputazione di storia patria per le provincie di Romagna,* n.s. 43 (1993).
Van Engen, John. "The Christian Middle Ages as an Historiographical Problem." *American Historical Review* 91 (1986): 519–52.
Vasina, Augusto. "Società ed economia a Faenza dopo il mille." In *Parliamo della nostra città. Atti del Convegno, Faenza 21-23-28-30 ott. 1976,* 101–9. Faenza, 1977.
Vauchez, André. *The Laity in the Middle Ages: Religious Beliefs and Devotional Practices,* ed. Daniel E. Bornstein, trans. Marjery J. Schneider. Notre Dame, Ind., 1993.
———. *Sainthood in the Later Middle Ages.* Trans. J. Birrell. Cambridge, 1997.
Verdon, Timothy, and John Henderson, eds. *Christianity and the Renaissance.* Syracuse, N.Y., 1990.
Viaggio in Terra Santa fatto e descritto per Roberto da Sanseverino. Bologna, 1888.
Villani, Giovanni. *Nuova cronica,* ed. Giuseppe Porta. 3 vols. Parma, 1990–91.
Villani, Pasquale, ed. *La visita apostolica di Tommaso Orfini nel regno di Napoli (1566–1568): documenti per la storia dell'applicazione del Concilio di Trento.* Rome, 1962.
Villari, Rosario. *La rivolta antispagnola a Napoli. Le origini (1585–1657).* Bari, 1973; trans. James Newell. Cambridge, 1993.
Violante, Cinzio. *La società milanese nell'età precomunale.* 2nd ed. Rome and Bari, 1981.
———. "Sistemi organizzativi della cura d'anime in Italia tra medioevao e rinascimento. Discorso introdottivo." In *Pievi e parrocchie in Italia nel basso medioevo (sec. XIII–XV).* Atti del Convegno di Storia della Chiesa in Italia (Firenze, 21–25 sett. 1981), 2 vols., 1:3–42. Rome, 1984.
Voltini, Franco, and Valerio Guazzoni. *Cremona, La Cattedrale.* Milan, 1989.
Waley, Daniel. *Mediaeval Orvieto: The Political History of an Italian City-State, 1157–1334.* Cambridge, 1952.
———. *The Papal State in the Thirteenth Century.* London, 1961.
———. *The Italian City-Republics.* 3d ed. London, 1988.
Watson, Alan. *The Making of the Civil Law.* Cambridge, Mass., 1981.
Webb, Diana. "Penitence and Peace-making in City and Contado: The Bianchi of

1399." In *Studies in Church History: The Church in Town and Countryside*, ed. Derek Baker, 243–56. Oxford, 1979.

———. *Patrons and Defenders: The Saints in the Italian City States*. London, 1996.

Weinstein, Donald. *Savonarola and Florence: Prophecy and Patriotism in the Renaissance*. Princeton, 1970.

Weissenberger, Paulus. "Die ältesten Statuta Monastica der Silvestriner." *Römische Quartalschrift für christliche Altertumskunde und für Kirchengeschichte* 47 (1939): 31–109.

Weissman, Ronald F. E. *Ritual Brotherhood in Renaissance Florence*. New York, 1982.

———. "Reconstructing Renaissance Sociology: The 'Chicago School' and the Study of Renaissance Society." In *Persons in Groups: Social Behavior as Identity Formation in Medieval and Renaissance Europe*, ed. Richard Trexler, 39–46. Binghamton, N.Y., 1985.

———. "Sacred Eloquence: Humanist Preaching and Lay Piety in Renaissance Florence." In *Christianity and the Renaissance: Image and Religious Imagination in the Quattrocento*, ed. Timothy Verdon and John Henderson, 250–71. Syracuse, 1990.

Welch, Evelyn. *Art and Society in Italy, 1350–1500*. Oxford, 1997.

Wemple, Suzanne. *Women in Frankish Society: Marriage and the Cloister, 500–900*. Philadelphia, 1981.

Wey, William. *The Itineraries of William Wey, Fellow of Eton College. To Jerusalem, A.D. 1458 and A.D. 1462; and to Saint James of Compostella, A.D. 1456*. London, 1857.

White, Luise. *The Comforts of Home: Prostitution in Colonial Nairobi*. Chicago, 1990.

Wickham, Chris. *Early Medieval Italy: Central Power and Local Society, 400–1600*. Ann Arbor, 1981.

———. *The Mountains and the City: The Tuscan Apennines in the Early Middle Ages*. Oxford, 1988.

———. *Comunità e clientèle nella Toscana del XII secolo. Le origini del comune rurale nella Piana di Lucca*. Rome, 1995; English ed., Oxford, 1998.

———. "La signoria rurale in Toscana." In *Strutture e trasformazioni della signoria rurale nei secoli X–XIII*, eds. Gerhard Dilcher and Cinzio Violante, 343–409. Bologna, 1996.

Wills, C. *Plagues: Their Origin, History and Future*. London, 1996.

Witt, Ronald G., et. al. "Hans Baron's Renaissance Humanism." *American Historical Review* 101 (1996): 107–29.

Zaniboni, E. *Alberghi italiani e viaggiatori stranieri (sec. XIII–XVIII)*. Naples, 1921.

Zonghi, Aurelio. *Carte diplomatiche fabrianesi*. Ancona, 1872.

Zorzi, Andrea. "I fiorentini e gli uffici pubblici nel primo Quattrocento: concorenza, abusi, illegalità." *Studi storici* 66 (1987): 746–47.

———. *L'amministrazione della giustizia penale nella Repubblica fiorentina: aspetti e problemi*. Florence, 1988.

———. "Giusdicenti e operatori di giustizia nello stato territoriale fiorentino del XV secolo." *Ricerche storiche* 19 (1989): 517–52.
———. "La formazione del territorio in area fiorentina tra XIII e XIV secolo." In *L'organizzazione del territorio in Italia e in Germania: secoli XIII–XIV*, eds. G. Chittolini and D. Willoweit, 279–349. Bologna, 1994.
Zupko, Ronald E. *Italian Weights and Measures from the Middle Ages to the Nineteenth Century*. Philadelphia, 1981.

Index

Abbondanza, Roberto, 5
Abulafia, David, 18–19
Ady, Cecelia, 6
Albertus Gandinus, 85
Albornoz, Gil, Cardinal, 192–93, 195, 196, 197, 200–204, 275n60
Alexander IV, 137, 138, 145–46
Alleluia, the, 79
Alpi Fiorentine, 38–39
amaxias/amaxios, 91–92, 96–98, 99
Ampinana, 51, 53
Anciano, 67–68
Andrea di Giacomo, 140, 141, 142–43, 144–45, 146, 265n43
Angelo of Clareno, 138
Anghiari, 43
Anzilotti, Antonio, 239
Aquilea, 67
Aragonia, Francesco, 224
architecture. *See* urban development
Archivio storico italiano, 5, 18
Arezzo, 45; historiography of, 11
art, 12, 22
Asti, 186, 187, 188
Augustinians, 73, 75, 80, 137, 138, 145–46
Aversa, 161–62, 164–65
Azo, 102

Baldus Ubaldi, 102, 104, 108
Barbadoro, Bernardino, 5
Bari, 168
Barnabites, 166
Baron, Hans, 5, 14–15, 236; *Crisis of the Early Italian Renaissance*, 6
Baronio, Cesare, 27
Bartolus of Sassoferrato, 102, 104
Batta, Giovanni, 227
Becker, Marvin, 5, 6, 33, 34
Benedetto di Bonconte, 196–200, 201
Benedictines, 74, 133–46
Bergamo, 157, 183, 185
Bernardino of Siena, 115–16, 147–59, 165, 236, 267n1, 269n31, 270n52

Bernardo del Lago, 197–98, 199, 200, 201
Bevignate of Cingoli, 142
Bizzocchi, Roberto, 60, 65, 238
Black Death, 19, 36, 38–40, 46, 192, 211–12, 248nn14,19
Bologna, 35, 85–100, 203, 218; *amaxias/amaxios* in, 91–92, 96–98, 99; church of San Petronio in, 188–89; church of San Pietro in, 188–89; concubinage and informal marriage in, 85, 86, 87, 91–96, 97, 98; elites compared to the poor in, 81, 86, 88–89, 91, 99; immigration to, 23, 87–88; legal marriage in, 81, 85, 91, 92, 93–96; legal status of prostitutes in, 81, 86, 91; the poor in, 81, 85, 86–91, 97–100; population of, 87; prostitution in, 81, 86, 89, 90, 91, 96–100; relations with countryside, 87–88; relations with Florence, 50–51; trial documents for, 81, 89–91; urban development in, 186, 188–89
Bonagrazia di Bartolo, 143
Bonaiuto del fu Guglielmo, 65
Bonconte faction, 196–201
Boniface VIII, 233
Bonvesin de la Riva, 21
Borghese, Scipione, Cardinal, 229
Borgia, Gaspar, Cardinal, 161
Borgo San Lorenzo, 48, 50, 52–53, 54, 57
Borgo San Pietro, 74
Bornstein, Daniel, 91
Borromeo, Carlo, Cardinal, 27, 224
Borromeo, Federico, Cardinal, 27
Botena, 52, 53, 54
Botero, Giovanni, 21, 27
Bottone, Angelino, 198–99
Bowsky, William, 19, 25
Brasca, Santo, 121, 124, 127, 129, 261n20
Braudel, Fernand, 24

Brentano, Robert, 20
Bresc, Henri, 18–19
Brescia, 183, 185
Brown, Judith, 33
Brucker, Gene, 15
Brühl, Carlrichard, 187
Bruni, Leonardo, 12, 26, 44
Brunner, Otto, 191, 197
Burckhardt, Jacob: on cities, 26, 189, 237; on Florence, 11–12, 13, 15, 18, 233, 234; on Italian history, 13–14, 28; and Ranke, 244n3; on the Renaissance, 9, 11–12, 13–14, 25
burial rights, 62, 67
Burke, Peter, 16
Butters, Humfrey, 9

Cadalus of Parma, 186
Cadolingi family, 185
Caggese, Romolo, 5, 33
Calvino, Italo, 79
Camaiore, 61
Campiano, 49, 52
Cano, Melchor, 219, 231
Canon 23, 139
Cantimori, Delio, 5
Caponsacchi family, 54
Capua, 169–70
Capuchins, 166
Caraffa war, 219, 221
Carlos II (King of Spain), 232
Carpaccio, Vittore, 130
Carpentier, Elisabeth, 192, 195
carroccio wars, 79
Carruthers, Mary, 76
Casentino, 39, 47, 49, 51
Casola, Pietro, 121, 122, 123, 124, 127, 129, 130, 261n29, 262n49
Casole, 53
Casollo, 171
Castel di Pagnano, 36–37
Castellina, 38
Castracane, Castruccio, 51
Ceccho di Ranuccio, 196
Chabod, Federico, 239
Chabot, Isabelle, 92
Charles of Anjou, 184
Charles V (Holy Roman Emperor), 219, 221
Chartier, Roger, 245n14
Cherubino da Spoleto, 269n31
Chianti, 40

Chittolini, Giorgio, 191, 238, 239
Chojnacki, Stanley, 88
Ciecchino di Birretto, 47
Ciompi revolt, 36
Cipolla, Carlo, 22
Cistercians, 74
city and countryside, relations between: Bologna, 87–88; Fabriano, 141; Florence, 8, 9, 10, 19, 29, 33–44, 45–58, 60, 65, 191, 234, 236, 249n31, 251n23, 252n39; Lucca, 29–30, 45, 59–61, 65–66, 69–71; in March of Ancona, 135, 141; Orvieto, 192; Parma, 186
Claro, Giulio, 102
Clement VI, Pope, 200
Clement VII, Pope, 193, 219
Clement VIII, Pope, 227–28
Cochrane, Eric, 17
Cohn, Samuel K., Jr., 10, 20, 46, 234
Colle, 46
communes, 25, 133–34, 135; decline of, 190–91, 192; definition, 207; relations with bishops, 182–83, 184–86, 187–89; rural communes, 19, 20, 21, 26, 59–60, 66–68; urban development in, 177–78, 181–89. *See also* Fabriano; Modena; Orvieto
Como, 183, 187–88
Compito, pieve of, 62, 63–64, 68, 70
concubinage and informal marriage, 85, 86, 87, 91–96; Church attitudes toward, 91–92; vs. *amaxias/amaxios*, 91–92
confession, 88, 99, 155–56, 159, 165, 166, 172
confraternities, 26, 67, 152
Connell, William, 10
Conti, Elio, 5, 6, 8
Cordoba, Bishop of, 230, 231
Corella, 54
Corrado di Rovellone, 134, 135, 146, 263n7
Cortona, 91
Coryat, Thomas, 131, 132, 262n44
Cosimo de' Medici and the Florentine Renaissance, 10
Costantini, Vera, 261n33
Creating the Florentine State, 10
Cremona, 183, 185
Crisis of the Early Italian Renaissance, 6, 14–15

Croce, Benedetto, 25, 219
The Cult of Remembrance and the Black Death, 20

Dante Alighieri, 12
Da Polenta family, 185
D'Aria, F. M., 172–73
Darnton, Robert, 245n14
Dati, Gregorio, 95
Davidsohn, Robert, 5, 7, 14, 50
Davis, Natalie Zemon, 148, 245n14
Davis, Robert, 24
Deakin, William, 6
Dean, Trevor, 18
Decius, Philip, 102
De Geronimo, Francesco, 170–74, 175
De Roover, Raymond, 5, 6
diplomacy, 11
Discorso historico con molti accidenti occorsi in Orvieto et in altri parti, 194–204
Dixon, Graham, 11
Dominicans, 73, 75, 80, 144, 219
Doren, Alfred, 6
Doria family, 218
D'Orta, Carlo, 161
dowries, 85, 88, 92, 93, 95, 99

Egidio di Giovanni di Gentile, 143
Elici, 64, 68
Empoli, 41
Epstein, Stephan, 18–19
Ercole, Francesco, 239
Este family, 13, 205–12, 214, 216, 217–18, 236; Duke Alfonso II d'Este, 205; Duke Cesare I d'Este, 205, 209–10; Duke Franco I d'Este, 211–12

Fabri, Felix, 121, 122, 124–25, 126, 127, 129, 130–31, 132, 260n17, 261n20, 262nn37,43
Fabriano: Borgo Nuovo quarter, 141, 142, 143; church of San Biagio in, 136–37; church of San Venanzo in, 141, 142, 146; Franciscans in, 264n33, 266n62; monastery/church of San Benedetto in, 134–35, 141, 143, 145; relations between elites and Silvestrines in, 140–41, 146; relationship with San Vittore delle Chiuse, 136–37; San Francesco at, 74; Silvestrines in, 115, 134–35, 141–46
Faenza, 76, 79, 183, 185
Faltona, 50
Fano, 78
Farfa, 74
Farinacci, Prospero, 82, 102–14, 258n13, 259nn16,18,33
Fasano Guarini, Elena, 191, 239
Febvre, Lucien, 245n14
Ferrara, 13, 18, 205, 206, 207, 209, 218
Fiastra, Cistercian house of, 74
Field, Arthur, 244n7
Figline, 38
Filomarino, Ascanio, Cardinal, 163
Firenzuola, 36–37, 38
Fitz-Simon, Simon, 123
Fiumi, Enrico, 33, 34, 35
Flagellants, 79
Florence: Archivio di Stato, 5, 6, 14, 15, 16, 250n8; art in, 12, 123; associations in, 9, 10; Biblioteca Nazionale, 5; the *castato*, 6, 7–8, 15, 34, 35; Ciompi revolt, 36; as commune, 9, 16, 20, 29, 133, 181; culture in, 8, 9–10, 11–12, 15–16; Dominicans in, 75; during Middle Ages, 7, 19–20; ecclesiastical institutions in, 29; economic conditions, 6, 8, 9, 11, 12, 15, 18, 19; elites in, 9, 10, 12, 29, 40, 44, 47, 54, 60, 65, 87, 88, 91, 95, 181, 206, 218, 233, 234; evolution of territorial state, 6, 10, 13, 18, 19, 29, 34, 43–44, 56–58, 60, 62, 191, 192, 204, 206, 234, 249n31, 251n23, 254n27; funded debt (*Monte*), 34, 42, 43; Guelfs and Ghibellines, 48, 49, 50–51, 52, 58; homoeroticism in, 10, 234; humanism in, 6, 12; immigration to, 19, 23, 47, 48–49, 57, 87; insignia of the lion (Marzocco), 44; lawyers in, 6; marriage/family in, 15, 19, 88; the Medici in, 10, 17, 206, 218, 233, 234; middling class in, 9; modernity of, 9–10; money lenders in, 48; patron-client relations in, 9, 10, 16; peasant revolts against, 36–37, 40, 43, 44, 46; pilgrim-tourists in, 260n13; political conditions, 8, 9, 10, 11, 12, 15, 16, 18, 19, 34, 50–51, 203; the poor in, 9, 87; the *provvisioni*, 34, 36, 37, 40;

relations with Bologna, 50–51; relations with Lucca, 19, 30, 60–61, 66, 253n8; relations with Milan, 34, 35, 36; relations with Siena, 206, 218, 253n8; relations with subject cities, 19, 206; relations with surrounding countryside, 8, 9, 10, 19, 29, 33–44, 45–58, 60, 65, 191, 234, 236, 249n31, 251n23, 252n39; religion in, 10, 11, 18, 140, 148, 149, 152, 154, 155, 189, 234; and the Renaissance, 9, 11–12, 13–15, 17, 233–35; as republic, 9, 12, 13, 16, 18; Salimbene on, 76; Santa Maria Novella in, 75; social conditions, 8, 9, 11, 15–16, 235; tax policies, 33–44, 46, 54; urban development in, 181–82, 184, 185, 187; vs. Venice, 11, 18, 24, 123, 234; wills in, 10; women in, 88, 95
Florentine historiography, 5–12, 13–28, 181, 189, 191, 203, 250n8; Biblioteca Nazionale in, 5; the *castato* in, 6, 7–8; growth of, 1, 5–6; the Middle Ages in, 7; and notarial registers, 20–21; the Renaissance in, 1–2, 13–15, 17, 233–35; role of Archivio di Stato in, 5, 6, 14, 15, 16; role of documents in, 6, 7–8, 14, 20–21, 244n3; vs. Venetian historiography, 11
Foiano, 42
Fonte Vembrici, 141
Fossatelli, 143
Foucault, Michel, 100
Frances, Juan Pablo, 230
Francesco di Girolamo. See De Geronimo, Francesco
Francis, St., 30, 74, 76, 77, 137, 154, 264n33; at Perugia, 26, 72, 75, 80
Franciscans, 76, 77–79, 188, 239, 266n62, 273n34; in March of Ancona, 137, 138, 146; Spirituals, 138; and urban identity, 30, 72–73, 74–75, 80. See also Bernardino of Siena; Francis, St.
Frederick I Barbarossa, Emperor, 182, 186, 187
Frederick II, Emperor, 13, 49–50, 52, 184
Frescobaldi, Lionardo, 124, 261n18
Frigo, Daniela, 11
Friuli, 18, 27
Fucecchio, 62
Fumi, Luigi, 195

Galasso, Giuseppe, 19
Galliano, 50
Galigai de'Macci, Pietro, 75
Garin, Eugenio, 5
Genoa, 13, 16, 17, 23, 77, 218
Ghibellines, 48, 49, 50–51, 52, 76–77, 196
Giacomo di Bonora, 142
Giamboniti, the, 137
Gilbert, Felix, 5, 8–9, 236
Ginzburg, Carlo, 245n14
Giordano of Giano, 73
Giotto di Bondone, 47, 49, 250n14
Giovanni dal Bastone, 134–35, 140, 145, 146, 263n11
Giovanni dei Velletri, Bishop, 53
Giovanni di Vico, 196, 200–201
Giovenazzo, 168
Goldthwaite, Richard, 6, 9
Gonzaga family, 13, 206
Grand Tour, 22, 119, 132
Great Union of 1256, 137, 138, 145
Greccio, Franciscan hermitage of, 74, 76
Grégoire, Réginald, 265n49
Gregory IX, 137, 138
Gregory XIII, 225, 226, 227
Grendler, Paul, 22
Grubb, James, 24
Guelfs, 49, 50–51, 52, 58, 185
Guicciardini, Francesco, 13, 219
Guidi, family, 48, 49, 50, 51, 57
Guido, Bishop of Orvieto, 193
Guido di Simone, 196, 199
Guidoni, Enrico, 140–41, 186
Guido of Camarino, Bishop, 139, 266n50
Guido of Sovana, 196, 199
Guiducci, Pierino, 54
Guzzolini, Silvestro, 134–5, 139, 140, 146, 263n7
Guylforde, Richard, 127

Hankins, James, 244n7
Herlihy, David, 5, 6, 7, 8, 14, 15, 25, 33, 250n9
Hermits of Brettino, 137, 138, 139, 145
Hermits of S. Angelo, 137–38
Holmes, George, 5
Hospital of San Jacopo of Altopascio, 66–67
humanism, 6, 12, 17, 22, 27, 102, 244n7

Index

Humbert de Romans, 268n4

Iacobus Tebelii, 143
Ignatius Loyola, 167
immigration, 19, 22–23, 47, 48–49, 57, 59, 70–71, 87–88
individualism, 9, 13, 233
Innocent III, Pope, 110
Innocent VI, Pope, 192, 200–201, 203
Isle of Giglio, 42
Italy: Baroque era in, 25; *castelli* in, 18, 49, 50, 51, 52, 53, 135–36, 246n26; Christianization in, 88, 99–100, 149–54; city-states in, 21, 23, 60, 177–78, 181–89, 190–91; confraternities in, 26; culture of, 22, 81; elites in, 177, 193–94, 235; evolution of territorial states in, 45–46, 190–92, 194–95, 197, 202–4, 206, 217–18, 238–39; family in, 22; fascism in, 235; foreign relations, 24; heresy in, 27; historiography of, 13–14, 17–18, 20–25, 27–28, 148, 190–91, 234–39, 245n14; immigration in, 22–23, 59, 87–88; marriage and family in, 88–89; medieval pilgrimages in, 22; notaries in, 82, 88, 90, 101–14; patronage in, 22; the *podestà* in, 23; political conditions in, 21, 23, 25, 26; public health boards in, 22; Reformation in, 25–27; relations between neighbors in, 23; religion in, 25–28; Renaissance schools in, 22; social conditions in, 20–23, 26, 81–82, 87–89, 97–98, 190–91; Spanish influence in, 23, 206, 219–32, 236–37; urban development in, 177–78, 181–89, 272n4; urban identity in, 30, 72–80, 115–16. *See also* Bologna; city and countryside, relations between; communes; Fabriano; Florence; Lucca; Modena; Mugello, the; Naples; Orvieto; Pisa; Rome; Venice

Jansen, Katherine Ludwig, 148
Jesi, 79
Jesuits: in Naples, 115–16, 160–75; relations with elites, 163–64, 167
Joachim of Flora, Abbot, 79, 125
John of Parma, 74
John of Piano de Carpine, 73
John XXII, Pope, 193
Jones, Philip, 5, 6, 20

Jordan of Saxony, 145–46

Kent, Dale, 10, 19, 234
Kent, F. W., 6, 10, 19
Kirshner, Julius, 238
Klapisch-Zuber, Christine, 6, 8, 15, 16, 33, 88
Kristeller, Paul Oskar, 5, 236

Ladurie, Emmanuel LeRoy, 6, 245n14
Lana, Ludovico, 214–15
Lane, Frederic, 24, 123
Lansing, Carol, 19
La Roncière, Charles M. de, 55
Lateran Council, Fourth, 88, 139
Latino, Malabranca, Cardinal, 52
Latium, historiography of, 17
Latour, Bruno, 237
law: *fama*/infamy in, 90, 94, 99, 100, 111, 257n20; and Farinacci's manual, 82, 102–14, 258n13, 259nn16,18,33; hierarchy of proof in, 102, 114, 258n4; legal treatises, 81–82, 101–14; Lombard law, 23, 81; relating to marriage, 81, 85, 86, 91, 92, 93–94, 98; relating to prostitution, 81, 89, 90, 97, 98, 99; relationship to Christianization, 99–100; relationship to society, 81–82; role of notaries in, 82, 88, 90, 101–14; Roman law, 23, 81, 88, 99, 101–2, 109, 257n20; trial documents, 81, 89–91
Leonardo di Simone, 196–97
Lepanto, battle of, 224–25, 226, 277n26, 279n24
Leverotti, Franca, 69
Levey, Michel, 12
Lewis of Bavaria, Holy Roman Emperor, 48
Liber Paradisus, 92
Lombardy, 18, 23, 206; historiography of, 17, 20
Lomena, 52, 53
Lopez, Robert, 18
Lucca, 187–88; bishop of, 30; country parishes at, 59–71, 253n1; Curia dei Foretani, 70; historiography of, 11, 17, 19; Martilogio of 1364, 66–67; relations with Florence, 19, 30, 60–61, 66, 253n8; relations with Pisa, 29–30, 60–61, 65–66, 77; relations with surrounding countryside, 29–30, 45, 59–61, 65–66, 69–71

Luco, 50
Luther, Martin, 166
Lyon, Second Council of, 138, 139, 142

Machiavelli, Niccolò, 13, 178, 233
Malatesta, family, 203-4
Mangona, 35, 36, 38
Mantua, 186, 188, 206
March of Ancona, 115, 134-35; Franciscans in, 137, 138, 146; religious movements in, 137-41, 145-46. *See also* Fabriano
Mareri, Santa Filippa, 74
Marks, Louis, 5
Marlia, 65, 68, 69
marriage: and adultery, 93; dowries, 85, 88, 92, 93, 95, 99; in Florence, 15, 19, 88; law relating to, 81, 85, 86, 91, 92, 93-94, 98; and parental consent, 94
Marsilius of Padua, 178
Martin, John, 24
Martines, Lauro, 5, 6, 177
Marxism, 235
Mastrilli, Carlo, 167
Matilda of Canossa, Countess, 60
Mazzi, Maria Serena, 100
Medici family, 10, 17, 206, 218, 233, 234
Medici, Cosimo de', 10, 234
Medici, Lorenzo de', 10
Melis, Federico, 6
mendicant orders, 133, 134, 137-38, 139, 140-41
Mezzogiorno, 19, 116, 164, 174. *See also* Naples
microhistory, 18, 245n14
Middle Ages: bishops during, 26-27; Florence during, 7, 19-20; historiography of, 25-28; pilgrimages in, 22; population growth during, 59, 87; relationship to the Reformation, 25-26; relationship to the Renaissance, 25-28. *See also* communes; religion
Milan, 11, 13, 16, 27, 148, 203; evolution as territorial state, 192, 206; relations with Florence, 34, 35, 36; Spanish influence in, 21, 217, 221; urban development in, 181, 183
Misson, François, 261n21
Modena, 79, 205-18; art in, 177; bishop's place in, 183; Castello di San Pietro in, 207, 209; cathedral of San Geminiano in, 183, 210; Chiesa Nuova in, 213, 214; church of San Domenico in, 214-17; communal palace in, 183; Conservators of, 206, 207-12, 214-17; Este family in, 13, 205-12, 214, 216, 217-18, 236; Madonna of the Rosary in, 214-17, 277n26; plague of 1630 in, 211-12; religious ritual in, 177, 210, 214-17; Sala del Fuoco in, 207, 208, 209; and San Geminiano, 207, 208, 210, 211, 213, 214-15, 216; urban development in, 183, 185
Molezzano, 52, 53
Molho, Anthony, 6, 9-10, 19, 33
Mollat, Guillaume, 203
Mommsen, Theodor, 5-6
Monaldeschi, Ermanno, 192, 196
Monaldo di Ermanno, 197, 199-200
Montaccianico, 50, 51
Montaigne, Michel, 132
Montecarelli, 36
Montecarlo, fortress of, 59
Montefano, monastery of, 134, 140, 141, 143-44, 263n14
Montefavale, 137, 138
Montefiascone, 274n30
Monte Morello, 40
Montepoli, 50
Monte Senario, 50
Montopoli, 66, 68, 254n27
Morandini, Francesca, 5
Moriano, 67, 69
Moronti, Stefano, Abbot, 143
Moryson, Fynes, 132
Muffati faction, 196-201
Mugello, the: *castelli* in, 49, 50, 51, 52, 53; Florentine bishopric in, 47, 48, 49, 51-55, 250n8, 251n26; Florentine cathedral chapter in, 47, 49, 51-52, 54, 250n8, 251n26; Florentine money lenders in, 48; Ghibellines in, 48, 49, 50, 51, 52; grain production in, 47, 53, 252n39; Guelfs in, 48, 49, 50, 51, 52, 58; the Guidi in, 48, 49, 50, 51, 57; historiography of, 250n8; immigration to Florence from, 47-48, 57; local secular clergy in, 55-57; location of, 249n6; population of, 47, 250n9; relations with Florence, 29, 35-36, 38-39, 46-58, 236, 250n8, 251n23, 252n39; the Ubaldini in, 48, 49-51, 52, 57
Muir, Edward, 11, 15, 20, 24

Mumford, Lewis, 186–87
Mutigliano, 68

Najemy, John, 8, 9, 203
Naples, 23, 161–68, 221, 222, 227, 228; historiography of, 2, 13, 16, 17, 19, 27; Jesuits in, 115–16, 160–75; prostitution in, 172, 173–74; Revolt of Naples (1585), 167; Revolt of Naples (1647–48), 161, 163, 164, 169, 174
Nicola da Tolentino, 145
Nonantola, 211
notaries, 20, 82, 88, 90, 101–14, 194, 250n8, 258nn4,13, 259nn16,18; physical appearance of notarial instruments, 105–9; private writing vs. notarial instruments, 110, 113; witnesses to notarial instruments, 105, 109–13, 259n33
Novara, 183

Orentano, 67
Orfini, Tommaso, 168
Orsini, Matteo, 196–98
Orsini, Nicola, 196
Orvieto, 142, 274n31, 275n35; and Archbishop of Milan, 196, 197, 201; bishops in, 193, 194; Black Death in, 192; elites in, 193–94, 202–3; factional violence in, 195–201; historiography of, 27, 234; relations with countryside, 192; relations with Papal State, 177, 192–93, 194–95, 196, 197, 198, 200–204, 274n30, 275n60; relations with Perugia, 196, 199, 201; urban identity in, 194–95
Ostuni, 168
Otranto, 24
Otto III, 184
Ottokar, Nicola, 7
Ottoman Empire, 24, 131, 222, 224–25, 277n26

Padua, 17, 80, 186, 234
Padule, 4, 52, 53, 66
Pagliariccio, 52, 53
Pallavicino, Oberto, 184
Pampaloni, Guido, 5
Panofsky, Erwin, 236
Paoli, Ugo, 263n14
Paolucci, Scipione, 169
papacy, 183, 205; Alexander IV, 137, 138, 145–46; Clement VI, 200; Clement VII, 193, 219; Clement VIII, 227–28; Gregory IX, 137, 138; Gregory XIII, 225, 226, 227; Innocent III, 110; Innocent VI, 192, 200–201, 203; John XXII, 193; Paul IV, 219, 221, 222, 225–26, 231; Paul V, 103, 228–29; Pius IV, 222, 224; Pius V, 224; Sixtus V, 227; Urban V, 203; Urban VIII, 221, 226, 231, 231–32
Papal State, 17, 218; and Ottoman Empire, 222, 224–25, 277n26; relations with Orvieto, 177, 192–93, 194–95, 196, 197, 198, 200–204, 274n30, 275n60; relations with Spain, 178, 220–32, 278n4
Parma, 76, 77–78, 79–80, 186
Partner, Peter, 5
Pastor, Ludwig, 223
Paul IV, Pope, 219, 221, 222, 225–26, 231
Paul V, Pope, 103, 228–29
Pavia, 183
Pazzi family, 54
peacemaking, 115–16, 160–76, 268n1
penance, 166
Perugia, 140, 142, 183, 196, 199, 201, 274n30, 275n42; St. Francis at, 26, 72, 75, 80
Pescia, 60–61, 62; historiography of, 11, 33
Peterson, David, 10, 234
Petrarch, 27
Philip II, King, 219, 221, 222–23, 224, 225–27, 228, 279n24
Philip III, King, 228–29
Piacenza, 181, 184, 187, 188, 273n34
Piedmont, 18
Pieve San Paulo, 62
Pila, 50
Pimentel, Domingo, 230, 231
Pini, Antonio, 87
Pisa, 43, 186, 234, 254n27; historiography of, 7, 11, 17, 25; relations with Genoa, 77; relations with Lucca, 29–30, 60–61, 65–66, 77; Salimbene on, 76–78, 79
Pisano, Nicola and Giovanni, 142
Pistoia, 51, 61, 62, 183, 185, 234; historiography of, 7, 11
Pistoiese, the, 47
Pius IV, Pope, 222, 224
Pius V, Pope, 224

plague, 19, 36, 38–40, 46, 192, 211–12, 248nn14,19
Podere Fiorentino, 38–39
Polcanto, 50
Ponzio of Orvieto, Bishop, 193
Poppi, historiography of, 11
Po Valley, 45
Prato, 38, 148; historiography of, 11
printing, 105
Prosperi, Adriano, 166–67, 271n19
prostitution: in Bologna, 81, 86, 89, 90, 91, 96–100; law relating to, 81, 89, 90, 97, 98, 99; in Naples, 172, 173–74; in Venice, 132, 262n49
pseudo-Minerbetti, 40
public health boards, 22
Pulicciano, 51, 52, 56

Quaderni storici, 18, 245n14

Rabbiacanina, 53
Raffacani, Giovanni, 202
Ranke, Leopold von, 14, 244n3
Ravenna, 76, 80, 183–85
Reformation, 2, 25–27, 166, 223, 268n8
Reggio Emilia, 79, 183, 185, 205, 211–12, 214
religion: Christianization, 88, 99–100, 149–54; confession, 88, 99, 155–56, 159, 165, 166, 172; elite vs. popular, 148, 150, 158–59; in Florence, 10, 11, 18, 140, 148, 149, 152, 154, 155, 189, 234; historiography of, 18, 148; Lenten season, 149, 155; mendicant orders, 133, 134, 137–38, 139, 140–41; and peacemaking, 115–16, 160–76; penance, 166; relationship to urban identity, 26–27, 72–80, 115–16, 133–46; religious movements, 137–41, 145–46, 166; sacralization of urban space, 133, 135, 146–47, 172; sermons and preachers, 26, 88, 99, 115–16, 147–59, 165–66, 169–70, 236, 267nn1,4, 268n8, 269n31, 270n52; in Siena, 140, 149–50, 151, 152, 153, 154, 156–57; tithes, 62, 66–67; among women, 74, 148, 152–53, 154, 158, 269n31. *See also* Augustinians; Benedictines; Dominicans; Franciscans
Renaissance: Burckhardt on the, 9, 11–12, 13–14, 25; historiography of the, 1–2, 13–14, 17, 20–25, 233–36; relationship to Middle Ages, 25–28; relationship to Reformation, 25
Rieti, 27, 73, 74, 75
Rimini, 204, 234
Rivista storica italiana, 18
Rocke, Michael, 10, 234
Rodolico, Niccolò, 5
Romagna, 47, 48, 50, 203–4
Romagna Fiorentina, 39, 40
Roman Catholic Church. *See* papacy; Papal State; religion
Romano, Dennis, 24
Rome, 27, 73; 1527 sack of, 237; historiography of, 11, 15, 16, 17, 234; Spanish influence in, 178, 219–32, 236–37; tourism in, 123, 131. *See also* papacy; Papal State
Ronta, 52
Ronzani, Mauro, 188
Rostolena, 48
Rubinstein, Nicolai, 5, 6, 7, 14, 234
Rudolf II, Emperor, 205
Ruggerius, 102
Ruggiero, Guido, 24

Sabina, 73–74
Salimbene of Parma, 73, 76–80
Saltarelli family, 54
Salvemini, Gaetano, 5, 7, 8, 14
San Bartolo, monastery of, 139
San Bartolomeo de Corbinaria, 40, 43
San Benedetto in Fabriano, monastery/church of, 134–35, 141, 143–44, 145
San Gavino Adimari, 53–54
San Giovanni di Compito, parish church of, 63–64
San Giovanni Valdarno, 41
San Jacobo di Frascole, 55
San Martino di Vespignano, 55
San Michele of Guamo, monastery of, 6, 63–64
San Miniato al Tedesco, 46
San Pastore, Cistercian house of, 74
San Paulo a Castiglione, 36
San Pietro in Campo, 59, 68–69
San Salvatore di Valle, 136
Sanseverino, Roberto da, 126–27
San Silvestro in Capite, 74
Santagata, Saverio, 161
Santa Lucia Ognissanti, 34–35
Santa Maria a Monte, 61, 66

Santa Maria d'Appennino, 135, 136, 264n20
Santa Maria di Fontanelle/di Valle Eremita, 63–64
Santa Maria Novella, 75
San Terenzo, 65
Santi Giovanni e Martino di Tripallo, 66
San Venanzo, church of, 141, 142, 146, 266n62
San Vittore delle Chiuse, 135–37, 146, 264n29
Sapori, Armando, 5, 6
Sardinia, 227
Sassi, Romualdo, 138
Scarperia, 38, 51
Schinosi, Francesco, 167–68
Scotti, Alberto, 184
Ser Jacobo del fu Ser Aldobrandino, 56
Sestan, Ernesto, 5
Sesto, 40
Sesto, Abbey of, 67
Settimo, 41
sexuality, 151, 157
Sforza, Francesco, 126
Sforza family, 13, 126, 206
Sicily, 23, 49–50, 227, 228; historiography of, 17, 18–19
Siena: historiography of, 11, 17, 19, 25; relations with Florence, 206, 218, 253n8; religion in, 140, 149–50, 151, 152, 153, 154, 156–57; urban development in, 181
Signa, 41
Silvestrines, 115, 134–35, 138–46, 263nn11,14, 264n29, 265n43, 266n50
Sixtus V, 227
Spain: influence in Milan, 218; influence in Rome, 178, 219–32, 236–37; and Ottoman Empire, 222, 224, 225; Philip II, 219, 221, 222–23, 224, 225–27, 279n24; Philip III, 228–29; relations with Papal State, 178, 220–32, 278n4
Spirituals, the, 138
Spoleto, 183
Starn, Randolph, 8
state, the: Chittolini on, 238, 239; relationship to society, 190–92
Stefani, Marchionne di Coppo, 38, 40
Stefano de Broy, 54
Steiner, George, 12

Strozzi, Lapo, 48
Studi storici, 18

Tafur, Pero, 122, 127, 260n13
Tancredus, 102
Theatines, 166
Tintoretto, 132
tithes, 62, 66–67
Titian, 132
Tommaso da Spello, 142
Trachtenberg, Marvin, 20
Trent, Council of, 26, 27, 166
Trentino, 23
Treviso, 186
Trexler, Richard, 6, 15–16, 60, 133, 146
Tucci, Ugo, 123, 261n33
Tuscany: city and countryside in, 45; economic conditions, 46; historiography of, 17, 19, 20; religion in, 46; social conditions, 46

Ubaldini, the, 48, 49–51, 52, 57
Ugo of Parma, Bishop, 186
urban development, 177–78; economic explanations of, 186–87, 189; functional explanations of, 186, 189; placement of communal palaces, 177, 181–89, 207, 208; political and religious centers in, 181–89; as visual expression of power, 177, 181–89
urban identity, 30, 72–80, 115–16, 133–46, 194–95, 201–4
Urban V, Pope, 203
Urban VIII, Pope, 221, 226, 231, 231–32
Urbino, 13
Uzzano, 48

Valcava, 48, 53, 54
Valdarno Superiore, 43
van Harff, Arnold, 121, 125, 129, 260n13, 262n38
Vasari, Giorgio, 12
Vauchez, André, 145
Veneto, 20
Venice, 13, 23, 27, 218; art in, 130, 132; day of the Ascension in, 126–27, 128; economic conditions, 119, 120, 122, 123; elites in, 88; evolution of territorial state, 192; feast of Corpus Christi in, 126, 127–28; vs. Florence, 11, 18, 24, 123, 234; gondolas in, 130–31, 262n44; and Grand Tour,

119, 132; guides (*tolomazi*) in, 128–29, 261nn33,34; historiography of, 2, 11, 15, 16, 17, 18, 24–25, 234; holy relics in, 123–25, 261n18, 261n21; holy sites in, 121, 123; Jaffa galleys in, 122, 126, 127, 131; lodging in, 129–30; and Ottoman Empire, 222, 225; pilgrim-tourism in, 115, 119–32, 260n17, 261nn18,20,21, 29,33,34, 262nn37,38,43,44,45; prostitution in, 132, 262n49; San Marco in, 125–26, 127–28, 188; social conditions, 119; St. Mark's day in, 126, 128; women in, 88–89, 132, 262n49
Venimbene di Guido, 143
Verona, 14, 17, 27, 186, 187–88
Veronese, 132
Vespignano, 48, 49, 53, 54, 55, 56–57
Vico/Vicchio, 51
Villani, Giovanni, 50
Villani, Matteo, 38, 40
Villari, Rosario, 19, 162, 164
Violante, Cinzio, 7
Virgin Mary, 153; Madonna of the Rosary, 214–17, 277n26
Visconti, Giovanni, 200, 203
Visconti family, 13, 18, 206

Viterbo, 274n30
Vivinaia, 59, 68–69
Voisons, Philippe de, 126
Volpe, Gioacchino, 7, 239
Volterino, 137–38

Waley, Daniel, 192
Walter of Brienne, 6
Weissman, Ronald, 15–16, 269n25
Wey, William, 124, 132
White, Luise, 96
Wickham, Chris, 20, 59–60, 70–71
Williamite Hermits, 137, 138, 139
William of Rubruck, 79
Witt, Ronald, 244n7
women: as *amaxias*, 91–92, 96–98, 99; in Bologna, 85–87, 89–100; as concubines, 85, 86, 87, 91–96, 97, 98; the *fama* of, 90, 94, 99, 100; in Florence, 88, 95; married status of, 81, 85, 88–89, 91, 92, 93–96; prostitution among, 81, 86, 89, 90, 91, 96–100, 132, 172, 173–74, 262n49; religion among, 74, 148, 152–53, 154, 158, 269n31; in Venice, 88–89, 132, 262n49

Zapata, Antonio, Cardinal, 233
Zorzi, Andrea, 10

The authorized representative in the EU for product safety and compliance is:
Mare Nostrum Group
B.V Doelen 72
4831 GR Breda
The Netherlands

www.ingramcontent.com/pod-product-compliance
Lightning Source LLC
Chambersburg PA
CBHW030606230426
43661CB00053B/1858